Study Guide to Accompany

AN INTRODUCTION TO
Management Scien

Quantitative Approaches
to Decision Making

Seventh Edition

David R. Anderson
University of Cincinnati

Dennis J. Sweeney
University of Cincinnati

Thomas A. Williams
Rochester Institute of Technology

Prepared by

John Loucks
St. Edward's University

John Lawrence
California State University–Fullerton

Barry Pasternack
California State University–Fullerton

West Publishing Company
Minneapolis/St. Paul   New York   Los Angeles   San Francisco

 PRINTED ON 10% POST CONSUMER RECYCLED PAPER

COPYRIGHT © 1994 by WEST PUBLISHING CO.
        610 Opperman Drive
        P.O. Box 64526
        St. Paul, MN 55164–0526

ISBN 0–314–03368–8

Table of Contents

Preface

The Study Guide to Accompany Introduction to Management Science, 7th ed. has been written with several goals in mind. Its objectives are:

1. To provide an outline of the material in the parent text via an opening key concepts page from which the student may design a course of study of the individual techniques and concepts of each chapter.

2. To organize and summarize the material in the parent text in a structured review section.

3. To illustrate the basic concepts of the parent text in detail through the presentation of 114 illustrated problems.

4. To reinforce the basic concepts by providing 182 additional problems and 285 true/false questions whose answers are in the back of the book.

5. To challenge the student by giving several problems requiring more than simple, straightforward application of the techniques of the chapter.

6. To expand the coverage of certain areas beyond the parent text by offering additional insights and algorithms to assist in the solution strategy.

7. To illustrate business applications areas in the management sciences to which the quantitative techniques may be applied.

To accomplish these goals, each chapter has been divided into five basic parts:

1. <u>Key</u> <u>Concepts</u> Cover Page:
   This page notes the main topic areas of each chapter and denotes
   which problems illustrate the concept, and which answered
   problems require the use of the concept in its solution.
      Every major concept of the text is illustrated in at least one
   problem worked out in detail and in at least one answered
   problem with its answer provided in the back of the book.

2. <u>Review</u> <u>Section</u>:
   This section summarizes point by point the theoretical
   foundations, the definitions, and the approaches of every topic
   area of the chapter. This provides an excellent check-list for
   understanding the essential points of the chapters.
      A categorical list of important <u>formulas</u> is included in this
   section when applicable.
      Major <u>algorithms</u> are described in sentence form and with <u>flow</u>
   <u>charts</u> at the end of this section when applicable.

3. <u>Illustrated</u> <u>Problems</u>:
   These are problems worked out in full, giving the cumbersome
   step-by-step details as the problem is worked through to
   fruition.

4. <u>Answered</u> <u>Problems</u>:
   These problems are for the student to do on his/her own with the
   answers provided in the back of the book. This enables the
   student to test him/herself on the individual concepts with
   brief answers to validate his results.

5. <u>True/False</u> <u>Questions</u>:
   Each chapter contains fifteen questions designed to reinforce
   the theoretical concepts of the chapter. The answers are
   provided in the back of the book.

In addition, <u>note</u> <u>boxes</u> appear throughout the study guide
mentioning students' common errors and misconceptions and providing
helpful tips and reminders.

Again, every major concept of the text is covered in at least one
illustrated problem and at least one answered problem. Through the
use of the <u>Key</u> <u>Concepts</u> page, the student may select the topic area
he wishes to study and see the concept demonstrated in an
illustrated problem, and/or he may test himself on the concept by
solving a corresponding answered problem.

We hope you find this study guide instructive and a useful
supplement in your study of management science.

                                        John S. Loucks

CHAPTER

1

Introduction

KEY CONCEPTS

CONCEPT	ILLUSTRATED PROBLEMS	ANSWERED PROBLEMS
Management Science Approach	1,2	5,6
Mathematical Models Development	3,4	7,8,9,10,11

REVIEW

1. <u>Management</u> <u>science</u> is a <u>quantitative</u> <u>approach</u> to decision making based on the <u>scientific</u> <u>method</u> of problem solving. A synonymous term is <u>operations</u> <u>research</u>. It had its early roots in World War II and is flourishing in business and industry with the aid of computers in general and the microcomputer in particular.

2. <u>Problem</u> <u>solving</u> is a process designed to better a current state of affairs, It consists of two phases: (1) decision making; and (2) implementation and evaluation.

3. The <u>decision</u> <u>making</u> <u>process</u> involves: (1) structuring the problem; and (2) analyzing the problem.

4. <u>Structuring</u> <u>the</u> <u>problem</u> includes: (1) defining the problem; (2) identifying the alternatives; and (3) choosing the criteria (single or multiple) to be used to evaluate the alternatives.

5. <u>Analyzing</u> <u>the</u> <u>problem</u> consists of: (1) qualitatively and quantitatively evaluating the alternatives; and (2) making a decision recommendation (choosing an alternative).

6. Evaluating alternatives is often accomplished by experimenting with a <u>model</u>. A model is a representation of a real object or situation. Generally, experimenting with a model is <u>less</u> <u>costly</u>, requires <u>less</u> <u>time</u>, and involves <u>less</u> <u>risk</u>.

7. Three forms of models are iconic, analog, and mathematical. <u>Iconic</u> <u>models</u> are physical replicas (scalar representations) of real objects. <u>Analog</u> <u>models</u> are physical in form, but do not physically resemble the object being modeled.

8. <u>Mathematical</u> <u>models</u> (also called symbolic models), represent real world problems through a system of mathematical formulas and expressions. They are idealizations of real-life problems based on key assumptions, estimates, "guesstimates", and/or statistical analyses.

9. After the problem has been structured, the steps in the <u>quantitative</u> <u>analysis</u> are: (1) mathematical modeling; (2) data preparation; (3) model solution (and refinement); and (4) report generation.

10. Mathematical models relate <u>decision</u> <u>variables</u> (or <u>controllable</u> <u>inputs</u>) with fixed or variable parameters (or <u>uncontrollable</u> <u>inputs</u>). Frequently mathematical models seek to maximize or minimize some <u>objective</u> <u>function</u> subject to <u>constraints</u>.

11. If any of the uncontrollable inputs is subject to variation the model is said to be <u>stochastic</u>. Otherwise the model is said to be <u>deterministic</u>. Generally, stochastic models are more difficult to analyze.

12. The values of the decision variables that provide the mathematically-best output are referred to as the <u>optimal solution</u> for the model.

13. <u>Cost/benefit considerations</u> must be made in selecting an appropriate mathematical model. Frequently a less complicated (and perhaps less precise) model is more appropriate than a more complex and accurate one due to cost and ease of solution considerations.

14. Quantitative analysis should be used as <u>one of many input factors</u> for managerial decision making. It is not a replacement for human decision making.

15. Primary reasons for the use of quantitative analysis are: (1) the <u>problem is complex</u>; (2) the <u>problem is important</u> and/or the decision must be thoroughly justified (to stockholders, etc.); (3) the <u>problem is new</u> and there is little or no previous experience to help guide the decision maker; (4) the <u>problem is repetitive</u> (with varying values for the uncontrollable inputs) <u>and time-consuming</u>; and (5) <u>what-if questions</u> need to be answered in an efficient manner.

16. <u>Break-even analysis</u> uses a basic mathematical model of the relationship between a volume variable and cost, revenue, or profit. The <u>break-even point</u> is the volume that results in total revenue equaling total cost (no loss or gain).

17. Some of the <u>primary applications areas</u> of management science are forecasting, production scheduling, inventory control, capital budgeting, and transportation.

18. Statistical analysis, simulation, linear programming, PERT/CPM, and queueing theory are among the <u>most frequently used quantitative techniques</u> in business.

ILLUSTRATED PROBLEMS

> **NOTE:** Certainty about almost any uncontrollable
> input is rare. Unfortunately, stochastic models are
> generally more difficult to analyze than are
> deterministic models.
>   So, models are often simplified out of necessity.
> The challenge lies in simplifying a model without
> significantly reducing its effectiveness in helping
> to solve a real problem.

PROBLEM 1

Consider a construction company building a 250-unit apartment
complex. The project consists of hundreds of activities
involving excavating, framing, wiring, plastering, painting,
landscaping, and more. Some of the activities must be done
sequentially and others can be done simultaneously. Also, some
of the activities can be completed faster than normal by
purchasing additional resources (workers, equipment, etc.).

a) How could management science be used to solve this problem?

b) What would be the uncontrollable inputs?

c) What would be the decision variables of the mathematical
   model? The objective function? The constraints?

d) Is the model deterministic or stochastic?

e) Suggest assumptions that could be made to simplify the model.

SOLUTION 1

a) Management science can provide a structured, quantitative
   approach for determining the minimum project completion time
   based on the activities' normal times and then based on the
   activities' expedited (reduced) times.

b) Normal and expedited activity completion times; activity
   expediting costs; funds available for expediting; precedence
   relationships of the activities.

c) Decision variables--which activities to expedite and by how
   much, and when to start each activity; objective function--
   minimize project completion time; constraints--do not violate
   any activity precedence relationships and do not expedite in
   excess of the funds available.

d) Stochastic--activity completion times, both normal and expedited, are uncertain and subject to variation; activity expediting costs are uncertain; the number of activities and their precedence relationships might change before the project is completed due to a project design change.

e) Make the model deterministic by assuming normal and expedited activity times are known with certainty and are constant. The same assumption might be made about the other stochastic, uncontrollable inputs.

PROBLEM 2

Consider a department store that must make weekly shipments of a certain product from two different warehouses to four different stores.

a) How could management science be used to solve this problem?

b) What would be the uncontrollable inputs for which data must be gathered?

c) What would be the decision variables of the mathematical model? The objective function? The constraints?

d) Is the model deterministic or stochastic?

e) Suggest assumptions that could be made to simplify the model.

SOLUTION 2

a) Management science can provide a systematic, quantitative approach for determining a minimum shipping cost from the warehouses to the stores.

b) Fixed costs and variable shipping costs; the demand each week at each store; the supplies each week at each warehouse.

c) Decision variables--how much to ship from each warehouse to each store; objective function--minimize total shipping costs; constraints--meet the demand at the stores without exceeding the supplies at the warehouses.

d) Stochastic--weekly demands fluctuate as do weekly supplies; transportation costs could vary depending upon the amount shipped, other goods sent with a shipment, etc.

e) Make the model deterministic by assuming fixed shipping costs per item, that demand is constant at each store each week, and that the weekly supplies in the warehouses are also constant.

PROBLEM 3

An auctioneer has developed a simple mathematical model for
deciding the starting bid he will require when auctioning a used
automobile. Essentially, he sets the starting bid at seventy
percent of what he predicts the final winning bid will (or
should) be. He predicts the winning bid by starting with the
car's original selling price and making two deductions, one
based on the car's age and the other based on the car's mileage.
The age deduction is $800 per year and the mileage deduction is
$.025 per mile.

a) Develop the mathematical model that will give the starting
   bid (B) for a car in terms of the car's original price (P),
   current age (A) and mileage (M).

b) Suppose a four-year old car with 60,000 miles on the odometer
   is up for auction. If its original price was $12,500, what
   starting bid should the auctioneer require?

c) The model is based on what assumptions?

SOLUTION 3

a) The expected winning bid can be expressed as:
          $P - 800(A) - .025(M)$

   The entire model is:
          $B = .7$(expected winning bid)   or
          $B = .7(P - 800(A) - .025(M))$ or
          $B = .7(P) - 560(A) - .0175(M)$

b) $B = .7(12,500) - 560(4) - .0175(60,000) = \$5460$.

c) The model assumes that the only factors influencing the value
   of a used car are the original price, age, and mileage (not
   condition, rarity, or other factors). Also, it is assumed
   that age and mileage devalue a car in a linear manner and
   without limit. (Note, the starting bid for a very old car
   might be negative!)

PROBLEM 4

A firm manufactures two products made from steel and just received this month's allocation of b pounds of steel. It takes a_1 pounds of steel to make a unit of product 1 and it takes a_2 pounds of steel to make a unit of product 2. Let x_1 and x_2 denote this month's production level of product 1 and product 2 respectively.

Denote by p_1 and p_2 the unit profits for products 1 and 2, respectively. The manufacturer has a contract calling for at least m units of product 1 this month. The firm's facilities are such that at most u units of product 2 may be produced monthly.

a) Write a mathematical model for this problem.

b) Suppose b = 2000, a_1 = 2, a_2 = 3, m = 60, u = 720, p_1 = 100, p_2 = 200. Rewrite the model with these specific values for the uncontrollable inputs.

c) The optimal solution to (b) is x_1 = 60 and x_2 = 626 2/3. If the product were engines, explain why this is not a true optimal solution for the "real-life" problem.

SOLUTION 4

a) The total monthly profit = (profit per unit of product 1)x (monthly production of product 1) + (profit per unit of product 2) x (monthly production of product 2) = $p_1 x_1$ + $p_2 x_2$.

The total amount of steel used during monthly production = (steel required per unit of product 1)x(monthly production of product 1) + (steel required per unit of product 2)x(monthly production of product 2) = $a_1 x_1$ + $a_2 x_2$.

This quantity must be less than or equal to the allocation of b pounds of steel: $a_1 x_1$ + $a_2 x_2 \leq$ b.

The monthly production level of product 1 must be greater than or equal to m: $x_1 \geq$ m.

The monthly production level of product 2 must be less than or equal to u: $x_2 \leq$ u.

However, the production level for product 2 cannot be negative: $x_2 \geq$ 0.

Thus, the model is:

$$\text{MAXIMIZE} \quad p_1 x_1 + p_2 x_2$$

$$\begin{aligned}
\text{S.T.} \quad a_1 x_1 + a_2 x_2 &\leq b \\
x_1 &\geq m \\
x_2 &\leq u \\
x_2 &\geq 0
\end{aligned}$$

b) Substituting, the model is:

$$\text{MAXIMIZE} \quad 100 x_1 + 200 x_2$$

$$\begin{aligned}
\text{S.T.} \quad 2 x_1 + 3 x_2 &\leq 2000 \\
x_1 &\geq 60 \\
x_2 &\leq 720 \\
x_2 &\geq 0
\end{aligned}$$

c) One cannot produce and sell 2/3 of an engine. Thus the problem is further restricted by the fact that both x_1 and x_2 must be integers. They could remain fractions if it is assumed these fractions are work in progress to be completed the next month.

ANSWERED PROBLEMS

PROBLEM 5

Zipco Printing operates a shop that has five printing machines.
The machines differ in their capacities to perform various
printing operations due to differences in the machines' designs
and operator skill levels.

At the start of the workday there are five printing jobs to
schedule. The manager must decide what the job-machine
assignments should be.

a) How could management science be used to solve this problem?

b) What would be the uncontrollable inputs for which data must
   be collected?

c) Define the decision variables, objective function, and
   constraints to appear in the mathematical model.

d) Is the model deterministic or stochastic?

e) Suggest some simplifying assumptions for this problem.

PROBLEM 6

Zizzle Company is a new small local company that is about to
manufacture Zizzle briefcases in three styles. The company
wants to determine how to use its resources most efficiently to
get the product mix that will maximize its profits.

One manager has advocated hiring an outside consulting firm to
analyze sales potentials and customer preferences. He suggests
doing a complete time and motion study of the production process
and analyzing the potential for acquiring additional manpower
and material resources. In short, he is advocating an extremely
accurate but complex study.

A second manager suggests a simplified model using "best
guess", rough approximations and simplifying assumptions as a
starting point. The data for this model can be obtained in a
short period of time, and the model can be solved in-house at a
fraction of the cost of the more complex model.

a) Which manager's advice would you follow? Explain.

b) Would your answer change if Zizzle Company were a large
   national conglomerate which plans to market tens of thousands
   of briefcases?

PROBLEM 7

A client of an investment firm has $10,000 available for
investment. He has instructed that his money be invested in
three stocks so that no more than $5,000 is invested in any one
stock but at least $1,000 is invested in each stock. He has
further instructed the firm to use its current data and invest
in a manner that maximizes his expected overall gain during a
one-year period. The stocks, the current price per share, and
the firm's projected stock price a year from now are summarized
in the following table.

Stock	Current Price	Projected Price 1 Year Hence
James Industries	$25	$35
QM Inc.	$50	$60
Delicious Candy Co.	$100	$125

a) Let s_j = the number of shares of stock j purchased for
   j = 1 (James), 2(QM), 3(Delicious). Formulate a mathematical
   model for this problem using these decision variables.

b) Let x_j = the number of dollars invested in stock j.
   Reformulate this mathematical model in terms of these
   decision variables instead of those used in part (a).

c) If both models were solved using management science
   techniques, how would you expect the results of the models to
   compare?

PROBLEM 8

Bank Guard Company provides security service for banks and
savings and loan companies during business hours. The number of
guards supplied is a function of the average number of people in
the facility. One guard is provided for an average of 25
customers. Let L = the average number of customers in the
facility, C_g = the hourly cost per guard, N = the number of
guards required, and C = the daily cost for guard service (based
on an 8-hour day).

a) Develop a mathematical model for N in terms of L. Then
   develop a mathematical model for C in terms of N and C_g.
   Finally, express C in terms of L and C_g.

b) If night guard service costs a flat $$C_n$, develop a
   mathematical model for 24 hour guard service. Discuss the
   results with C_g = $10 per hour, C_n = $100 per night and
   L = 50. Discuss the results with L = 65.

PROBLEM 9

Comfort Plus Inc. (CPI) manufactures a standard dining chair
used in restaurants. The demand forecasts for quarter 1
(January- March) and quarter 2 (April-June) are 3700 chairs and
4200 chairs, respectively. CPI has a policy of satisfying all
demand in the quarter in which it occurs.

  The chair contains an upholstered seat that can be produced by
CPI or a subcontractor. The subcontractor currently
charges $12.50 per seat, but has announced a new price of $13.75
effective April 1. CPI can produce the seat at a cost of
$10.25.

  Seats that are produced or purchased in quarter 1 and used to
satisfy demand in quarter 2 cost CPI $1.50 each to hold in
inventory.

a) What are the controllable inputs?

b) Develop a mathematical model for the total cost (objective)
   function.

PROBLEM 10

Continuing with problem 9, consider the following additional
information. CPI's seat-producing capacity is 3800 seats per
quarter. CPI cannot hold more than 300 seats in inventory from
quarter to quarter.

a) Complete the mathematical model started in problem 9 by
   modeling the constraints in the problem.

b) Is the model stochastic or deterministic?

c) How would adding a third quarter to the problem change the
   model?

PROBLEM 11

A retail furniture store has set aside 800 square feet to display its new 18th Century Collection of sofas and chairs. Considering aisle space, it is estimated that each sofa utilizes 50 sq. ft. and each chair utilizes 30 sq. ft. At least five sofas and at least five chairs are to be displayed.

a) Write a mathematical model representing the store's constraints.

b) Suppose the profit on sofas is $200 and on chairs is $100. On a given day, the probability that a displayed sofa will be sold is .03 and that a displayed chair will be sold is .05. Mathematically model each of the following objectives:

1) Maximize the total pieces of furniture displayed.

2) Maximize the total expected number of daily sales.

3) Maximize the total expected daily profit.

TRUE/FALSE

12. The optimal solution to a mathematical model is always the policy that should be implemented by the company.

13. A problem to decide monthly shipping patterns is dependent on the amount of product available at the factory. This amount can be modeled by a normal distribution. Thus, this is a stochastic mathematical model.

14. Microcomputers have made most management science techniques more accessible to even moderate size firms.

15. The three most commonly used management science techniques are statistical analyses, simulation, and linear programming.

16. A company seeks to maximize profit subject to limited availability of man-hours. Man-hours is a controllable input.

17. Past data may frequently be used to test the validity of a mathematical model.

18. A toy train layout designed to represent an actual railyard is an example of an analog model.

19. A feasible solution is one that satisfies at least one of the constraints in the problem.

20. The terms stochastic and deterministic have the same meaning in management science.

21. If you are deciding whether to buy machine A, B, or C with the objective of minimizing the sum of three costs (labor, material and utilities), you are dealing with a multicriteria decision.

22. If your decision alternatives for dealing with increased product inventory are: (1) build another warehouse, (2) reduce the production rate, and (3) increase the sales rate, you are dealing with a multicriteria decision.

23. Model development should be left to management scientists; the model user's involvement should begin at the implementation stage.

24. The volume that results in marginal revenue equaling marginal cost is called the break-even point.

25. In quantitative analysis, the optimal solution is the mathematically-best solution.

26. Problem solving is narrower in scope than decision making.

CHAPTER

2

Linear Programming: The Graphical Method

KEY CONCEPTS

CONCEPT	ILLUSTRATED PROBLEMS	ANSWERED PROBLEMS
Formulation	7,8	15,16,18,19,20
Minimization	2,5	9,10,15,19
Standard Form	1	14
Slack/Surplus Variables	1	16
Equal-to Constraints	3,5	14
Redundant Constraints	5,7	12,13
Extreme Points	2,5	11,16
Alternate Optimal Solutions	7	10,11,15
Infeasibility	4	14
Unboundedness	4	11
Objective Function Changes	6,8	17-20
Righthand Side Changes	6,8	17-20

REVIEW

1. A <u>mathematical</u> <u>programming</u> problem is one that seeks to maximize an objective function subject to constraints. If both the objective function and the constraints are linear, the problem is referred to as a <u>linear</u> <u>programming</u> problem.

2. <u>Linear</u> <u>functions</u> are functions in which each variable appears in a separate term raised to the first power and is multiplied by a constant (which could be 0).

3. <u>Linear</u> <u>constraints</u> are linear functions that are restricted to be "less than or equal to", "equal to", or "greater than or equal to" a constant.

4. The properties of linear programming models are:
     (1) <u>proportionality</u> -- the profit contribution and the amount of the resources used by a decision variable is directly proportional to its value;
     (2) <u>additivity</u> -- the value of the objective function and the amount of the resources used can be calculated by summing the individual contributions of the decision variables;
     (3) <u>divisibility</u> -- fractional values of the decision variables are permitted.

5. The <u>maximization</u> or <u>minimization</u> of some quantity is the objective in all linear programming problems.

6. A <u>feasible</u> <u>solution</u> satisfies all the problem's constraints.

7. A linear program which is overconstrained so that no point satisfies all the constraints is said to be <u>infeasible</u>. Changes to the objective function coefficients do not affect the feasibility of the problem.

8. An <u>optimal</u> <u>solution</u> is a feasible solution that results in the largest possible objective function value, Z, when maximizing or smallest possible Z when minimizing.

9. A <u>graphical</u> <u>solution</u> <u>method</u> can be used to solve a linear program with two variables.

10. If a linear program possesses an optimal solution, then an <u>extreme</u> <u>point</u> will be optimal.

11. If a constraint can be removed without affecting the shape of the feasible region, the constraint is said to be <u>redundant</u>. If changes are anticipated to the linear programming model, constraints which were redundant in the original formulation may not be redundant in the revised formulation.

12. In the graphical method, if the objective function line is parallel to a boundary constraint in the direction of optimization, there are <u>alternate</u> <u>optimal</u> <u>solutions</u>, with all points on this line segment being optimal.

13. A feasible region may be <u>unbounded</u> and yet there may be optimal solutions. This is common in minimization problems and is possible in maximization problems.

14. The <u>feasible</u> <u>region</u> for a two-variable linear programming problem can be: a) nonexistent, b) a single point, c) a line, d) a polygon, or e) an unbounded area.

15. <u>Any</u> <u>linear</u> <u>program</u> either (a) is infeasible, (b) has a unique optimal solution or alternate optimal solutions, or (c) has an objective function that can be increased without bound.

16. A linear program in which all the variables are non-negative and all the constraints are equalities is said to be in <u>standard</u> <u>form</u>. Standard form is attained by adding <u>slack</u> <u>variables</u> to "less than or equal to" constraints, and by subtracting <u>surplus</u> <u>variables</u> from "greater than or equal to" constraints. They represent the difference between the left and right sides of the constraints.

17. <u>Slack</u> and <u>surplus</u> <u>variables</u> have objective function coefficients equal to 0. If, however, extra resources could be sold at a a profit, or if there were a penalty for surplus resources, the objective function coefficients would not be 0 and these variables would, in effect, become new decision variables.

18. <u>Sensitivity</u> <u>analysis</u> is used to determine effects on the optimal solution within specified ranges for the objective function coefficients, constraint coefficients, and right hand side values. This provides answers to certain <u>what-if</u> <u>questions</u>.

19. A <u>range</u> <u>of</u> <u>optimality</u> of an objective function coefficient is found by determining an interval for the objective function coefficient in which the <u>original</u> <u>optimal</u> <u>solution</u> remains optimal while keeping all other data of the problem constant. The value of the objective function may change in this range.

20. Graphically, the limits of a <u>range</u> <u>of</u> <u>optimality</u> are found by changing the slope of the objective function line within the limits of the slopes of the binding constraint lines. This would also apply to simultaneous changes in the objective coefficients. The slope of an objective function line, MAX $c_1x_1 + c_2x_2$, is $-c_1/c_2$, and the slope of a constraint i, $a_{i1}x_1 + a_{i2}x_2 = b_i$, is $-a_{i1}/a_{i2}$.

21. A <u>shadow</u> <u>price</u> for a right hand side value (or resource limit) is the amount the objective function will <u>change</u> per unit increase in the right hand side value of a constraint.

22. Graphically, a <u>shadow</u> <u>price</u> is determined by adding +1 to the right hand side value in question and then resolving for the optimal solution in terms of the same two binding constraints. The shadow price is equal to the difference in the values of the objective functions between the new and original problems.

23. A <u>dual</u> <u>price</u> for a right hand side value (or resource limit) is the amount the objective function will <u>improve</u> per unit increase in the right hand side value of a constraint. Thus, for maximization problems dual prices and shadow prices are the same, whereas for minimization problems, shadow prices are the negative of dual prices.

24. A <u>nonbinding</u> <u>constraint</u> is one in which there is <u>positive</u> <u>slack</u> or <u>surplus</u> when evaluated at the optimal solution. The shadow price for a nonbinding constraint is 0.

25. The <u>range</u> <u>of</u> <u>feasibility</u> for a change in the right hand side value is the range of values for this coefficient in which the original <u>shadow</u> <u>price</u> remains constant.

26. Graphically, the <u>range</u> <u>of</u> <u>feasibility</u> is determined by finding the values of a right hand side coefficient such that the same two lines that determined the original optimal solution continue to determine the optimal solution for the problem.

GRAPHICAL SOLUTION PROCEDURE

1. Graph the constraints and shade in the feasible region, considering the feasible side of each constraint line.

2. Set the objective function equal to any arbitrary constant and graph it. If the line does not lie in the feasible region, move it (maintaining its slope) into the feasible region.

3. Move the objective function line parallel to itself in the direction that increases its value when maximizing (decreases its value when minimizing) until it touches the last point(s) of the feasible region.

4. If the optimal extreme point falls on an axis (say, X_2 axis), use the binding constraint equation to solve for the unknown X* (in this case X_2^*, since X_1^* is zero). Otherwise, solve the two equations (binding constraints) in two unknowns (X_1^* and X_2^*) that determine the optimal extreme point.

5. Find Z by substituting X_{1*} and X_{2*} in the objective function.

GRAPHICAL SOLUTION PROCEDURE
FLOW CHART

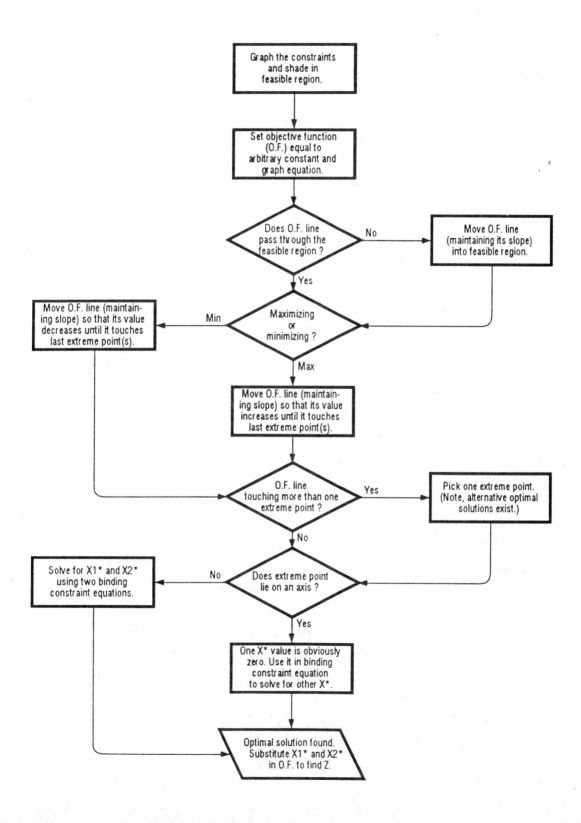

ILLUSTRATED PROBLEMS

> **NOTE:** Plotting an initial objective function line
> involves little more than reversing the objective
> coefficients for X_1 and X_2. Consider Problem 1 below
> The objective line will cross the X_1 axis at 4 (X_2's
> coefficient) and the X_2 axis at 3 (X_1's coefficient).
> If the coefficients are too large (or small) for
> convenient graphing, scale them down (or up) in a
> consistent manner by dividing (or multiplying) both
> by, say, 10.

PROBLEM 1

Given the following linear program:

$$\text{MAX} \quad Z = 3X_1 + 4X_2$$

$$\text{S.T.} \quad 2X_1 + 3X_2 \leq 24$$

$$3X_1 + X_2 \leq 21$$

$$X_1 + X_2 \leq 9$$

$$X_1, X_2 \geq 0$$

a) Solve the problem graphically.

b) Write the problem in standard form.

c) Given your answer to (a), what are the optimal values of the
slack variables.

SOLUTION 1

a) (1) <u>Graph the constraints</u>. (See graph on next page.)
Constraint 1: When $X_1 = 0$, then $X_2 = 8$; when $X_2 = 0$,
then $X_1 = 12$. Connect (12,0) and (0,8). The "<" side
is below the line.
Constraint 2: When $X_1 = 0$, then $X_2 = 21$; when $X_2 = 0$,
then $X_1 = 7$. Connect (7,0) and (0,21). The "<" side
is below the line.
Constraint 3: When $X_1 = 0$, then $X_2 = 9$; when $X_2 = 0$,
then $X_1 = 9$. Connect (9,0) and (0,9). The "<" side
is below the line.
<u>Shade in the feasible region</u>.

(2) <u>Graph</u> <u>the</u> <u>objective</u> <u>function</u> by setting the objective function equal to any arbitrary value (say 12) and graphing it. For $3X_1 + 4X_2 = 12$, when $X_2 = 0$, $X_1 = 4$; when $X_1 = 0$, $X_2 = 3$. Connect (4,0) and (0,3), the thick line on the graph.

(3) <u>Move</u> <u>the</u> <u>objective</u> <u>function</u> <u>line</u> <u>parallel</u> <u>to</u> <u>itself</u> in the direction that increases its value (upward) until it touches the last point of the feasible region. It is at the intersection of the first and third constraint lines.

(4) <u>Solve</u> <u>these</u> <u>two</u> <u>equations</u> <u>in</u> <u>two</u> <u>unknowns</u>:

$$2X_1 + 3X_2 = 24 \quad ======> \quad 2X_1 + 3X_2 = 24$$
$$X_1 + X_2 = 9 \quad ======> \quad 2X_1 + 2X_2 = 18$$
$$\overline{ \quad X_2 = 6}$$

Substituting into $X_1 + X_2 = 9$, then $X_1 = 3$.

(5) <u>Solve</u> <u>for</u> <u>Z</u>: $Z = 3X_1 + 4X_2 = 3(3) + 4(6) = 33$. Thus the optimal solution is $X_1 = 3$, $X_2 = 6$, $Z = 33$.

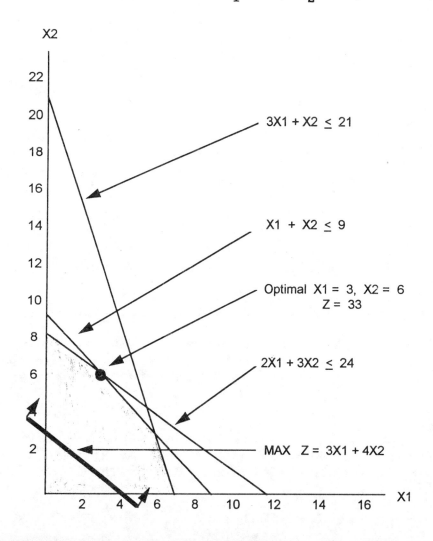

b) To write the problem in standard form, since each constraint
   is a "$\leq$" constraint, add a slack variable to each constraint.

$$\text{MAX} \quad Z = 3X_1 + 4X_2 + 0S_1 + 0S_2 + 0S_3$$

$$\text{S.T.} \quad 2X_1 + 3X_2 + S_1 \qquad\qquad = 24$$

$$3X_1 + X_2 \qquad + S_2 \qquad = 21$$

$$X_1 + X_2 \qquad\qquad + S_3 = 9$$

$$X_j \geq 0 \qquad j = 1,2$$

$$S_j \geq 0 \qquad j = 1,2,3$$

c) Since the optimal solution was $X_1 = 3$, $X_2 = 6$, then
   substituting these values into the above equations gives:

$$S_1 = 24 - 2(3) - 3(6) = 0$$

$$S_2 = 21 - 3(3) - 1(6) = 6$$

$$S_3 = 9 - 1(3) - 1(6) = 0$$

PROBLEM 2

Given the following linear program:

$$\text{MIN} \quad Z = 5X_1 + 2X_2$$

$$\text{S.T.} \quad 2X_1 + 5X_2 \geq 10$$

$$4X_1 - X_2 \geq 12$$

$$X_1 + X_2 \geq 4$$

$$X_1, X_2 \geq 0$$

a) Solve graphically for the optimal solution.

b) How does one know that although $X_1 = 5$, $X_2 = 3$ is a feasible
   solution for the constraints, it will never be the optimal
   solution no matter what objective function is imposed?

SOLUTION 2

a) (1) Graph the constraints. (See graph next page.)
   Constraint 1: When $X_1 = 0$, then $X_2 = 2$; when $X_2 = 0$, then
   $X_1 = 5$. Connect (5,0) and (0,2). The ">" side is above
   this line.

Constraint 2: When $X_2 = 0$, then $X_1 = 3$. But setting X_1 to 0
will yield $X_2 = -12$, which is not on the graph. Thus, to
get a second point on this line, set X_1 to any number
larger than 3 and solve for X_2: when $X_1 = 5$, then $X_2 = 8$.
Connect $(3,0)$ and $(5,8)$. The ">" side is to the right.
Constraint 3: When $X_1 = 0$, then $X_2 = 4$; when $X_2 = 0$, then
$X_1 = 4$. Connect $(4,0)$ and $(0,4)$. The ">" side is above
this line.
Shade in the feasible region.

(2) Graph the objective function by setting the objective
function equal to an arbitrary constant (say 20) and graphing
it. For $5X_1 + 2X_2 = 20$, when $X_1 = 0$, then $X_2 = 10$; when
$X_2 = 0$, then $X_1 = 4$. Connect $(4,0)$ and $(0,10)$.

(3) Move the objective function line in the direction which
lowers its value (down) until it touches the last point of
the feasible region. It is determined by the last two
constraints.

(4) Solve these two equations in two unknowns.

$$4X_1 - X_2 = 12$$
$$X_1 + X_2 = 4$$

Adding these two equations gives: $5X_1 = 16$ or $X_1 = 16/5$.
Substituting this into $X_1 + X_2 = 4$ gives: $X_2 = 4/5$.

(5) Solve for $Z = 5X_1 + 2X_2 = 5(16/5) + 2(4/5) = 88/5$.
Thus the optimal solution is $X_1 = 16/5$; $X_2 = 4/5$; $Z = 88/5$.

b) Although $(5,3)$ lies in the feasible region, it is not an
extreme point (or on the boundary). Hence it can never be
the last point touched by moving the objective function line,
and thus, can never be optimal.

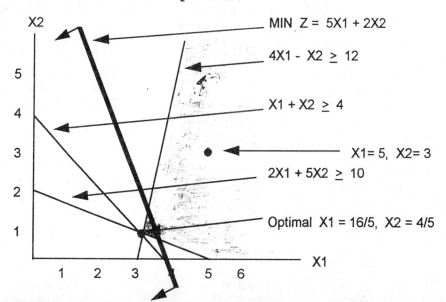

PROBLEM 3

Given the following linear program:

$$\text{MAX} \quad Z = 4X_1 + 5X_2$$

$$\text{S.T.} \qquad X_1 + 3X_2 \leq 22$$

$$-X_1 + X_2 \leq 4$$

$$X_2 \leq 6$$

$$2X_1 - 5X_2 \leq 0$$

$$X_1, X_2 \geq 0$$

a) Solve the problem by the graphical method.

b) What would be the optimal solution if the second constraint were $-X_1 + X_2 = 4$?

c) What would be the optimal solution if the first constraint were $X_1 + 3X_2 \geq 22$?

SOLUTION 3

a) (1) <u>Graph the constraints</u>. (See graph next page.)
Constraint 1: When $X_1 = 0$, $X_2 = 22/3$; when $X_2 = 0$, then $X_1 = 22$. Connect $(22,0)$ and $(0,22/3)$. The "<" side is below this line.
Constraint 2: When $X_1 = 0$, then $X_2 = 4$. Setting X_2 to 0 would give $X_1 = -4$, which is outside the graph. Set X_2 to a number greater than 4 and solve for X_1. When $X_2 = 6$, then $X_1 = 2$. Connect $(0,4)$ and $(2,6)$. $(0,0)$ is on the "<" side.
Constraint 3: This is a horizontal line through $X_2 = 6$.
Constraint 4: When $X_2 = 0$, then $X_1 = 0$; Set X_1 to any positive constant and solve for X_2. When $X_1 = 5$, then $X_2 = 2$. Connect the points $(0,0)$ and $(5,2)$. To determine the "<" side select any arbitrary point on one side of the line and substitute into the inequality. Arbitrarily choosing $(0,5)$, this gives $2(0) - 5(5) = -25$. Thus the side containing $(0,5)$ is the "<" side.
<u>Shade in the feasible region</u>.

(2) <u>Graph the objective function</u> by setting it to an arbitrary value, say 20. For $4X_1 + 5X_2 = 20$, when $X_1 = 0$, then $X_2 = 4$; when $X_2 = 0$, then $X_1 = 5$. Connect with a broker line the points $(5,0)$ and $(0,4)$.

(3) Move the objective function line parallel to itself in
the direction which increases its value until it touches the
last point of the feasible region. This is at the
intersection of the first and fourth constraints.

(4) Solve these two equations in two unknowns:

$$X_1 + 3X_2 = 22 \quad ========> \quad 2X_1 + 6X_2 = 44$$
$$2X_1 - 5X_2 = 0 \quad ========> \quad 2X_1 - 5X_2 = 0$$

Subtracting the second equation from the first yields:
$11X_2 = 44$ or $X_2 = 4$. Substituting $X_2 = 4$ into the first
equation gives $X_1 = 10$.

(5) Substitute for $Z = 4X_1 + 5X_2 = 4(10) + 5(4) = 60$.
Thus the optimal solution is $X_1 = 10$; $X_2 = 4$; $Z = 60$.

b) The feasible region is now the line segment of $-X_1 + X_2 = 4$
between $(0,4)$ and $(2,6)$. $(2,6)$ now gives the optimal
solution.

c) The feasible region is now the triangular section between
$(4,6)$, $(15,6)$, and $(10,4)$. $(15,6)$ is now the optimal
solution.

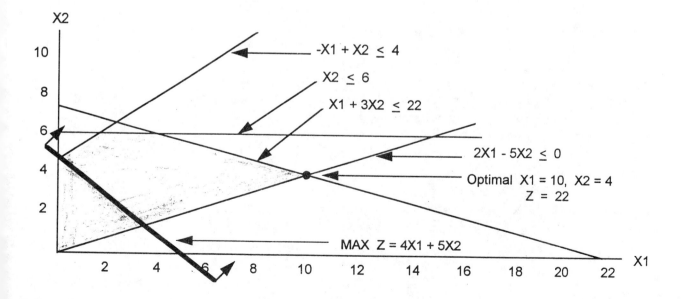

PROBLEM 4

Show graphically why the following two linear programs do not have optimal solutions and explain the difference between the two.

(a) MAX Z = $2X_1 + 6X_2$

    S.T. $4X_1 + 3X_2 \leq 12$

             $2X_1 + X_2 \geq 8$

                  $X_1, X_2 \geq 0$

(b) MAX Z = $3X_1 + 4X_2$

    S.T. $X_1 + X_2 \geq 5$

             $3X_1 + X_2 \geq 8$

                 $X_1, X_2 \geq 0$

SOLUTION 4

Refer to the graphs below. Note that (a) has no points that satisfy both constraints, hence has no feasible region, and no optimal solution. (a) is infeasible.

Note that in (b) the feasible region is unbounded and the objective function line can be moved parallel to itself without bound so that Z can be increased infinitely. (b) is unbounded.

(a)

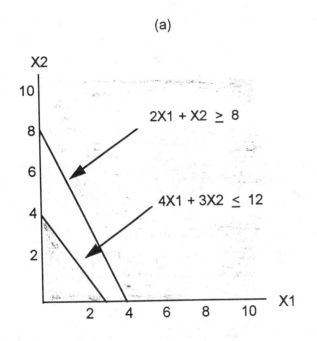

(b)

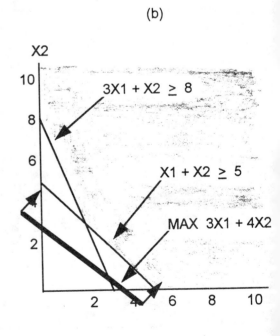

PROBLEM 5

Given the following linear program:

$$\text{MIN } Z = 150X_1 + 210X_2$$

$$\text{S.T.} \quad 3.8X_1 + 1.2X_2 \geq 22.8$$

$$X_2 \geq 6$$

$$X_2 \leq 15$$

$$45X_1 + 30X_2 = 630$$

$$X_1, X_2 \geq 0$$

a) Solve the problem graphically. How many extreme points exist for this problem?

b) What would be the optimal solution if the "=" in the fourth constraint was changed to "$\leq$"?

c) If the "=" in the fourth constraint was changed to "$\geq$", how would the problem be affected?

SOLUTION 5

a) (1) <u>Graph</u> <u>the</u> <u>constraints</u>.
   Constraint 1: When $X_1 = 0$, $X_2 = 19$; when $X_2 = 0$, then
   $X_1 = 6$. Connect (6,0) and (0,9). The ">" side is
   to the right of this line.
   Constraint 2: This is a horizontal line through $X_2 = 6$.
   The ">" side is above this line.
   Constraint 3: This is a horizontal line through $X_2 = 15$.
   The "<" side is above this line.
   Constraint 4: When $X_1 = 0$, $X_2 = 21$; when $X_2 = 0$, then
   $X_1 = 14$. Connect (14,0) and (0,21).
   <u>Shade</u> <u>in</u> <u>the</u> <u>feasible</u> <u>region</u>.

> **NOTE:** The feasible region in this problem is limited
> to a segment of the line representing the "equal to"
> constraint. Only two extreme points exist.

(2) <u>Graph</u> <u>the</u> <u>objective</u> <u>function</u> by setting the objective
function equal to an arbitrary constant as previously
demonstrated or by using the following approach. Scale
down the objective coefficients c_1 and c_2 (say, by dividing
both by 10 to get 8 and 13, respectively). Now, use X_1's
coefficient as a value to plot on the X_2 axis and use X_2's
coefficient as a value to plot on the X_1 axis. Connect

points (0,15) and (21,0).

(3) <u>Move</u> <u>the</u> <u>objective</u> <u>function</u> <u>line</u> in the direction that lowers its value until it touches the last point of the feasible region. The point is determined by the second and fourth constraints.

(4) <u>Solve</u> <u>for</u> <u>the</u> <u>unknown</u> <u>X</u> by substituting $X_2 = 6$ into $45X_1 + 30X_2 = 630$, yielding $X_1 = 10$.

(5) <u>Solve</u> <u>for</u> <u>Z</u> = $150X_1 + 210X_2 = 150(10) + 210(6) = 2760$. Thus the optimal solution is $X_1 = 10$, $X_2 = 6$, and $Z = 2760$.

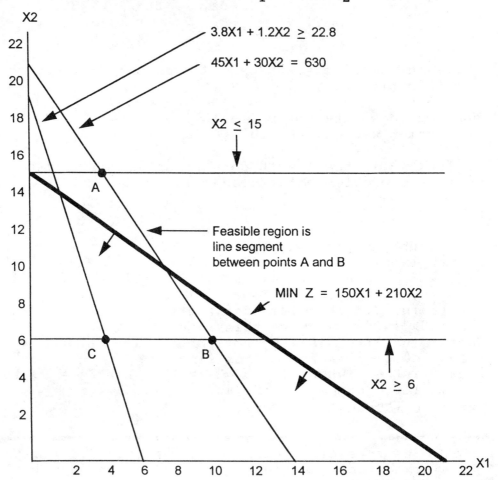

b) The feasible region is now shaped by all four constraints. The optimal extreme point is determined by the first and second constraints. Solving these two equations in two unknowns, the optimal solution is (4.105,6), point C on the graph.

c) The optimal solution is now (10,6), point B on the graph, and the first constraint is now redundant.

PROBLEM 6

Given the following linear program:

$$\text{MAX } Z = 5X_1 + 7X_2$$

$$\text{S.T.} \quad X_1 \qquad\qquad \leq \quad 6$$

$$2X_1 + 3X_2 \leq 19$$

$$X_1 + X_2 \leq 8$$

$$X_1, X_2 \geq 0$$

a) Solve the problem graphically.

b) Calculate the range of optimality for each objective function coefficient.

c) Calculate the shadow prices for each resource.

SOLUTION 6

a) From the graph below we see that the optimal solution occurs at $X_1 = 5$, $X_2 = 3$, $Z = 46$.

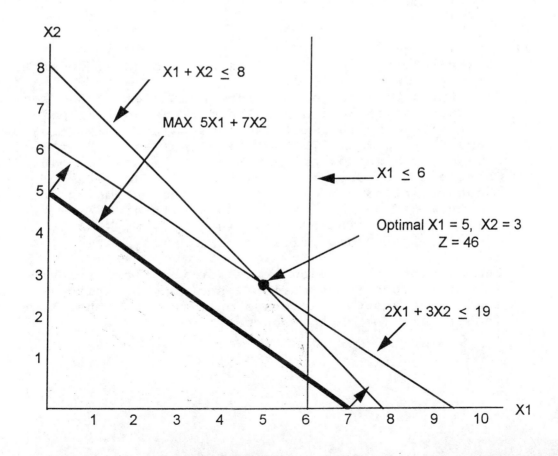

b) The slope of the objective function line is $-C_1/C_2$. The slope of the first binding constraint, $X_1 + X_2 = 8$, is -1 and the slope of the second binding constraint, $2X_1 + 3X_2 = 19$ is $-2/3$.

Range of optimality for C_1:
Find the range of values for C_1 (with C_2 staying 7) such that the objective function line slope lies between that of the two binding constraints:
$$-1 \leq -C_1/7 \leq -2/3.$$

Multiplying through by -7 (and reversing the inequalities):

$$14/3 \leq C_1 \leq 7.$$

Range of optimality for C_2:
Find the range of values for C_2 (with C_1 staying 5) such that the objective function line slope lies between that of the two binding constraints:
$$-1 \leq -5/C_2 \leq -2/3.$$

Multiplying by -1:
$$1 \geq 5/C_2 \geq 2/3.$$

Inverting, $1 \leq C_2/5 \leq 3/2.$

Multiplying by 5: $5 \leq C_2 \leq 15/2.$

c) Shadow prices:
Constraint 1: Since $X_1 \leq 6$ is not a binding constraint, its shadow price is 0.
Constraint 2: Change the right hand side of the second constraint to 20 and resolve for the optimal point determined by the last two constraints: $2X_1 + 3X_2 = 20$ and $X_1 + X_2 = 8$. The solution is $X_1 = 4$, $X_2 = 4$, $Z = 48$. Hence, the shadow price = $Z_{new} - Z_{old} = 48 - 46 = 2$.
Constraint 3: Change the right hand side value of the third constraint to 9 and resolve for the optimal point determined by the last two constraints: $2X_1 + 3X_2 = 19$ and $X_1 + X_2 = 9$. The solution is: $X_1 = 8$, $X_2 = 1$, $Z = 47$. Hence, the shadow price is $Z_{new} - Z_{old} = 47 - 46 = 1$.

Summarizing, the shadow price for the first resource is 0, for the second resource is 2, and for the third is 1. Note that these shadow prices are only valid in the range of feasibility for each resource.

PROBLEM 7

A manager of a small fabrication plant must decide on a
production schedule of two new products for the automobile
industry. The profit on product 1 is $1(thousand) and on
product 2 is $3(thousand).
  The manufacture of these products depends largely on the
availability of certain subassemblies the plant receives daily
from a local distributor. It takes three of these subassemblies
for each unit of product 1 and two for each unit of product 2.
Twelve such subassemblies are delivered daily.
  Further, it takes two hours to make a unit of product 1 and
six hours to make a unit of product 2. The plant has assigned
only three workers working 8-hour shifts for these new products.
  Due to limited demand, the manager does not want more than
seven units of product 2 produced daily.

a) Formulate this problem as a linear program.

b) Solve graphically for the optimal solution. Describe the set
   of all optimal solutions. Identify any redundant
   constraints.

c) Give an optimal daily production schedule that manufactures
   exactly one unit of product 1.

d) Discuss the applicability of linear programming for this
   problem.

SOLUTION 7

a) (1) Define variables: X_1 and X_2 = the amount of product 1
   and product 2 produced daily.

   (2) Define objective:
       Maximize total daily profits:
       MAX $1X_1 + 3X_2$ (in thousands of dollars).

   (3) Define constraints:
       Subassemblies: Number used daily $\leq$ number available
       $3X_1 + 2X_2 \leq 12$

       Labor: Number of hours used daily $\leq$ (3 men)x(8 hrs./day)
       $2X_1 + 6X_2 \leq 24$

       Product 2: Quantity produced daily $\leq$ specified limit
       $X_2 \leq 7$

       Non-negativity of variables:
       $X_1, X_2 \geq 0$

Summarizing,

$$\text{MAX} \quad Z = 1X_1 + 3X_2$$

$$\text{S.T.} \qquad 3X_1 + 2X_2 \leq 12$$

$$2X_1 + 6X_2 \leq 24$$

$$X_2 \leq 7$$

$$X_1, \; X_2 \geq 0$$

b) Graphically,

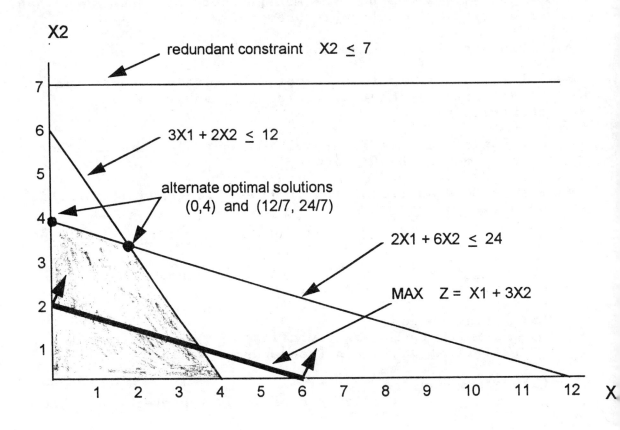

The optimal solution occurs at $X_1 = 0$, $X_2 = 4$ and at $X_1 = 12/7$, $X_2 = 24/7$, and at all points in between on the line $2X_1 + 6X_2 = 24$. At any point on this line, $Z = 12$ (thousand). The $X_2 \leq 7$ constraint does not help shape the feasible region and thus is redundant.

c) On the optimal solution line, $2X_1 + 6X_2 = 24$, when $X_1 = 1$, then $X_2 = 11/3$. Still, $Z = 1(1) + 3(11/3) = 12$ (thousand).

d) One must consider whether these variables can be allowed to assume values which are not integers. For continuous production, frequently a fractional value can be considered as "work in progress"; products not finished on one day are simply completed the next day. Thus, linear programming appears to be appropriate for this problem.

PROBLEM 8

A small company will be introducing a new line of lightweight bicycle frames to be made from special aluminum and steel alloys. The frames will be produced in two models, deluxe and professional. The anticipated unit profits are currently $10 for a deluxe frame and $15 for a professional frame. The number of pounds of each alloy needed per frame is summarized in the table below. A supplier delivers 100 pounds of the aluminum alloy and 80 pounds of the steel alloy weekly.

	Aluminum Alloy	Steel Alloy
Deluxe	2	3
Professional	4	2

a) What is the optimal weekly production schedule?

b) Within what limits must the unit profits lie for each of the frames for this solution to remain optimal?

c) Suppose the unit profits assumed all aluminum purchased would be used and hence the profit figures did not include a unit cost for the aluminum. Now extra aluminum can be purchased at $2.50 per pound. Should the company purchase additional pounds of aluminum at that price?

SOLUTION 8

a) Let,

X_1 = number of deluxe frames produced weekly
X_2 = number of professional frames produced weekly

$$\text{MAX } Z = 10X_1 + 15X_2$$

$$\text{S.T.} \quad 2X_1 + 4X_2 \leq 100$$

$$3X_1 + 2X_2 \leq 80$$

$$X_1, X_2 \geq 0$$

Solving graphically (on the next page), observe that the
optimal production schedule is to produce X_1 = 15 deluxe
frames weekly and X_2 = 17.5 professional frames weekly for
an optimal weekly profit of $412.50.

b) Note that the binding constraints are the aluminum and the
steel constraints, with slopes -1/2 and -3/2 respectively.

Range of optimality for deluxe profits (C_1):
    $-3/2 \le -C_1/15 \le -1/2$ OR $15/2 \le C_1 \le 45/2$.

Range of optimality for professional profits (C_2):
    $-3/2 \le -10/C_2 \le -1/2$ OR $20/3 \le C_2 \le 20$.

c) The aluminum costs are then considered <u>sunk</u> costs and the
shadow price for aluminum would yield the maximum worth for
additional aluminum. Resolve the two equations and two
unknown with the right hand side of the aluminum constraint
changed to 101. This results in X_1 = 59/4, X_2 = 143/8,
Z = $415.625. Hence the shadow price for aluminum is
$415.625 - $412.50 = $3.125. Since this is greater than the
selling price of $2.50 per pound of aluminum, additional
aluminum should be purchased at this price.

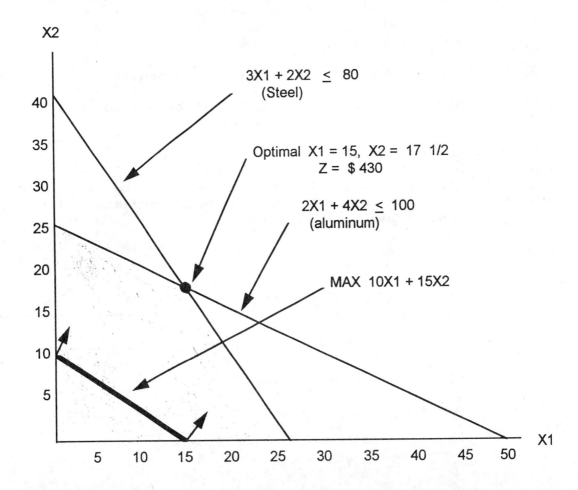

ANSWERED PROBLEMS

PROBLEM 9

Solve graphically for the optimal solution to the following linear program:

$$\text{MIN} \quad Z = 16X_1 + 12X_2$$

$$\begin{array}{llrll}
\text{S.T.} & 8X_1 + & 4X_2 & \leq & 36 \\
& X_1 + & X_2 & \leq & 7 \\
& 3X_1 + & 12X_2 & \geq & 24 \\
& 4X_1 + & 5X_2 & \geq & 20 \\
& & X_1, X_2 & \geq & 0
\end{array}$$

PROBLEM 10

Given the following linear program:

$$\text{MAX} \quad Z = 4X_1 + 2X_2$$

$$\begin{array}{llrll}
\text{S.T.} & X_1 & & \leq & 4 \\
& 3X_1 + & 8X_2 & \leq & 24 \\
& 2X_1 + & X_2 & \geq & 6 \\
& & X_1, X_2 & \geq & 0
\end{array}$$

a) Solve the problem graphically.

b) What would be the optimal solution(s) if the objective function were a minimization rather than a maximization objective?

PROBLEM 11

Consider a linear programming problem with the following constraint set:

$$\begin{array}{rrll}
2X_1 + & X_2 & \geq & 4 \\
X_1 + & 2X_2 & \geq & 5 \\
X_1 - & 2X_2 & \leq & 1 \\
& X_1, X_2 & \geq & 0
\end{array}$$

a) Graph the feasible region and note it is unbounded.

> **NOTE:** One might think an unbounded maximization problem would always have an unbounded objective function value. This problem proves the contrary.

b) Identify all extreme points.

c) Solve the problem with each of the three following possible objective functions. Discuss the implications of the results.

$$(1) \quad \text{MAX } Z = 2X_1 - 5X_2$$
$$(2) \quad \text{MAX } Z = 2X_1 - 4X_2$$
$$(3) \quad \text{MAX } Z = 2X_1 - 3X_2$$

PROBLEM 12

Given the following linear programming problem:

$$\text{MAX} \quad Z = 3X_1 + 5X_2$$

$$\text{S.T.} \quad 4X_1 + 3X_2 \geq 24$$

$$2X_1 + 3X_2 \leq 18$$

$$X_2 \geq 3$$

$$X_1, X_2 \geq 0$$

a) Solve the problem graphically.

> **NOTE:** The feasible region in this problem is limited to a single point. A common error is to mistake this situation for infeasibility.

b) Suppose the objective function were changed to:
$\text{MAX } Z = 5X_1 + 4X_2$. What effect would this have on the model?

PROBLEM 13

Given the following linear programming problem:

$$MAX\ Z = 8X_1 + 10X_2$$

$$S.T. \quad X_1 + X_2 \leq 35$$

$$3X_1 + 2X_2 \leq 60$$

$$X_2 \leq 15$$

$$X_1,\ X_2 \geq 0$$

a) Solve for the optimal solution.

b) State why the first constraint is redundant.

c) Suppose the second constraint's right hand side is changed from 60 to 100. Solve for the new optimal solution and show that the first constraint is now binding and NOT redundant.

PROBLEM 14

Consider the following linear program:

$$MAX\ Z = 60X_1 + 43X_2$$

$$S.T. \quad X_1 + 3X_2 \geq 9$$

$$6X_1 - 2X_2 = 12$$

$$X_1 + 2X_2 \leq 10$$

$$X_1,\ X_2 \geq 0$$

a) Write the problem in standard form.

b) What is the feasible region for the problem?

c) Show that regardless of the values of the actual objective function coefficients, the optimal solution will occur at one of two points. Solve for these points and then determine which one maximizes the current objective function.

PROBLEM 15

A businessman is considering opening a small specialized trucking firm. To make the firm profitable, it is estimated that it must have a daily trucking capacity of at least 84,000 cu. ft. Two types of trucks are appropriate for the specialized operation. Their characteristics and costs are summarized in the table below. Note that truck 2 requires 3 drivers for long haul trips. There are 41 potential drivers available and there are facilities for at most 40 trucks.
  The businessman's objective is to minimize the total cost outlay for trucks.

Truck	Cost	Capacity (Cu. ft.)	Drivers Needed
X_1	$18,000	2,400	1
X_2	$45,000	6,000	3

Solve the problem graphically and note there are alternate optimal solutions. Which optimal solution

a) uses only one type of truck?

b) utilizes the minimum total number of trucks?

c) uses the same number of truck X_1 as truck X_2?

PROBLEM 16

A baseball glove manufacturer has 1200 linear feet of cowhide and 800 linear feet of synthetic material. It makes two styles of baseball gloves: child's and adult's. Requirements and profit PER DOZEN are summarized below:

	COWHIDE	SYNTHETIC	PROFIT
CHILDS	4	4	$60
ADULTS	12	6	$95

a) Solve for the optimal number of dozen of each model to manufacture. What are the values of the slack variables?

b) Suppose the company could make $1 on each unused linear foot of cowhide and $.25 on each unused linear foot of synthetic material. Reformulate the linear programming model. By the methods of Chapter 5, the new optimal solution is to make 200 dozen child models and no adult models and sell 400 linear feet of cowhide. Locate this new point on your graph and show it is not the optimal extreme point of part (a).

PROBLEM 17

Given the following linear program:

$$\text{MAX} \quad Z = 6X_1 + 5X_2$$

$$\text{S. T.} \quad X_1 + X_2 \leq 6$$

$$2X_1 + X_2 \leq 8$$

$$X_1 \leq 3$$

$$X_1, X_2 \geq 0$$

a) Solve graphically for the optimal solution.

b) Calculate the range of optimality for both C_1 and C_2.

c) What is the new optimal point when C_2 slightly exceeds the upper limit determined in (a)?

d) Determine the shadow price for iron, the resource of the second constraint. Interpret.

e) For what values of zinc, the third resource, will its shadow price be 0?

PROBLEM 18

The Asia Import Company (AIC) has 600 cu. ft. of excess cargo space on its ships and has decided to import two new items: jade figurines and linen placemats. Each container of jade figurines is 4 cu. ft. and will net a profit of $80 per container. Each box of linen placemats is 2 cu. ft. and will realize a profit of $60 per container. AIC expects no more than 140 containers of jade figurines available on any trip.
Additionally, AIC wishes to use no more than 480 man-hours for loading, storing, and processing the items through customs. The normal estimate is that a container requires 2 man-hours. However, because of special agricultural restrictions, an extra 2 man-hours can be expected for the linen products.

a) Using the graphical method, determine the number of containers of each item that should be shipped.

b) What is the range of profit on jade containers for which the solution in (a) remains optimal?

c) Determine the value of: (1) an extra man-hour; (2) an extra cubic foot of cargo space; and, (3) the availability of an extra jade container.

PROBLEM 19

Tom manages Leisure Time Motors, a dealership selling minivans and large travel trailers. He is trying to decide how to allocate 90,000 square feet of outside display space to his two products. The products differ in terms of required display space, monthly upkeep, and generated monthly profit as summarized below on a per-unit basis:

	Space Requirement	Monthly Upkeep	Monthly Profit
Minivan	300 sq. ft.	2.0 man-hours	$3200.
Trailer	500	3.2	4500.

Leisure Motors has three yard men, each working a 150-hour month, keeping the minivans and trailers clean. Tom feels he needs a minimum of 50 minivans on display. The manufacturer of his trailers requires that he display at least 75 trailers.

a) Graphically solve for the numbers of minivans and trailers on display that will maximize Leisure Time's profit.

b) Calculate the range of optimality for both C_1 and C_2.

c) Determine the shadow price for yard men, the resource of the second constraint. Interpret.

PROBLEM 20

Harvey owns a Harley (motorcycle) and a Hauler (pickup truck). The Harley gets an average of 45 miles per gallon (mpg) using 93 octane gasoline that sells for $1.35 per gallon. The Hauler averages 26 mpg using 89 octane that sells for $1.17 per gallon.
   The Harley requires 15 hours of maintenance work per 5000 miles ridden. The Hauler requires 10 hours of maintenance per 5000 miles. Harvey does his own maintenance work, but he cannot devote more than 100 hours annually to the task.
   Harvey predicts he will have to transport himself 45,000 miles in the upcoming year. He would like to ride his Harley a minimum of 5,000 miles annually in order to stay in practice.

a) How should Harvey divide his mileage among his Harley and Hauler so that his annual fuel expense is minimized.

b) What is the value of an additional hour of Harvey's time per year for maintenance?

c) By how much will Harvey's annual fuel expense increase for each mile that he travels in excess of 45,000?

TRUE/FALSE

21. A problem formulation that includes a term that is the product of two variables would not be a linear program.

22. A nonbinding constraint, like a binding constraint, helps form the shape (boundaries) of the feasible region.

23. If a linear program has an optimal solution, then an extreme point must be optimal.

24. All optimal solutions are extreme points.

25. A redundant constraint lies entirely within the feasible region.

26. It is possible to have exactly two optimal solutions to a linear programming problem.

27. A linear programming problem can be both unbounded and infeasible.

28. If a problem has a constraint which is parallel to the objective function, then there must be alternate optimal solutions.

29. An infeasible problem is one in which the objective function can be increased to infinity.

30. A slack variable is a variable that represents the difference between the amount of a resource that was available and the actual amount used by the solution.

31. In a feasible problem, an equal-to constraint cannot be redundant.

32. A variable in a linear programming problem must be allowed to assume fractional values.

33. Any change to an objective function coefficient of a variable that is positive in the optimal solution will change the optimal solution.

34. An unbounded feasible region might not result in an unbounded solution for a minimization or maximization problem.

35. Increasing the right-hand side of a nonbinding constraint will not cause a change in the optimal solution.

CHAPTER

3

Linear Programming: Formulation, Computer Solution, and Interpretation

KEY CONCEPTS

CONCEPT	ILLUSTRATED PROBLEMS	ANSWERED PROBLEMS
Changes to Objective Function Coefficients		
Reduced Costs	4	
Range of Optimality	1-4	5-9
Changes to Right Hand Side Values		
Shadow/Dual Prices	1-4	6-9
Range of Feasibility	1-3	6-9
Sunk/Relevant Costs	3	6
100% Rule	1-4	6-9

REVIEW

1. <u>Sensitivity</u> <u>analysis</u> is used to determine how the optimal solution is affected by changes, within specified ranges, in the objective function coefficients, the right-hand side (RHS) values, and the constraint coefficients.

2. <u>Sensitivity</u> <u>analysis</u> is important to the manager who must operate in a dynamic environment with imprecise estimates of the coefficients. Sensitivity analysis allows him to ask certain <u>what-if</u> <u>questions</u> about the problem.

3. A <u>reduced</u> <u>cost</u> for a decision variable whose value is 0 in the optimal solution is the amount the variable's objective coefficient would have to improve (increase for maximization problems, decrease for minimization problems) before this variable could assume a positive value. Thus, the reduced cost for a decision variable with a positive value is 0.

4. A <u>range</u> <u>of</u> <u>optimality</u> of an <u>objective</u> <u>function</u> <u>coefficient</u> is found by determining an interval for the objective function coefficient in which the original solution remains optimal while keeping all other data of the problem constant. The value of Z might change in this range.

5. The <u>100%</u> <u>rule</u> states that <u>simultaneous</u> <u>changes</u> <u>in</u> <u>objective</u> <u>function</u> <u>coefficients</u> will not change the optimal solution as long as the sum of the percentages of the change divided by the corresponding maximum allowable change in the range of optimality for each coefficient does not exceed 100%.

6. A <u>shadow</u> <u>price</u> for a right-hand side value (or resource limit) is the amount the objective function value Z will change per unit increase in the right-hand side value of a constraint.

7. A <u>Shadow</u> <u>price</u> reflects the value of an additional unit of the resource if the <u>resource</u> <u>cost</u> is <u>sunk</u>. It represents the extra value over the normal cost of the resource when the resource cost is <u>relevant</u>.

8. A <u>resource</u> <u>cost</u> is <u>relevant</u> if the amount paid for it is dependent upon the amount of the resource used by the decision variables. Relevant costs are reflected in the objective function coefficients.

9. A <u>resource</u> <u>cost</u> is <u>sunk</u> if it must be paid regardless of the amount of the resource actually used by the decision variables. Sunk resource costs are not reflected in the objective function coefficients.

10. A <u>dual</u> <u>price</u> for a <u>right-hand</u> <u>side</u> (or resource limit) is the amount the objective function will improve per unit increase in the right-hand side value of a constraint. Thus, for maximization problems dual prices and shadow prices are the same, whereas for minimization problems, shadow prices are the negative of dual prices.

11. A <u>nonbinding</u> <u>constraint</u> is one in which there is <u>positive</u> <u>slack</u> <u>or</u> <u>surplus</u> when evaluated at the optimal solution. The shadow price for a nonbinding constraint is 0.

12. The <u>range</u> <u>of</u> <u>feasibility</u> for a change in a right-hand side value is the range of values for this parameter in which the original <u>shadow</u> <u>price</u> remains constant.

13. The <u>100%</u> <u>rule</u> also states that <u>simultaneous</u> <u>changes</u> <u>in</u> <u>right-hand</u> <u>sides</u> will not change the shadow prices as long as the sum of the percentages of the changes divided by the corresponding maximum allowable change in the range of feasibility for each right-hand side does not exceed 100%.

14. <u>Computer</u> <u>software</u> <u>packages</u> (such as <u>The</u> <u>Management</u> <u>Scientist</u> or <u>LINDO/PC</u>) that solve linear programming problems all give five sections of relevant information about the optimal solution:

    1. The optimal value of the objective function;

    2. Information about the decision variables:
       (a) their values, (b) their reduced costs;

    3. Information about the constraints:
       (a) the amount of slack or surplus, (b) the dual prices;

    4. Objective function coefficient ranges (ranges of optimality):
       (a) lower limit, (b) upper limit; and

    5. Right-hand side ranges (ranges of feasibility):
       (a) lower limit, (b) upper limit.

ILLUSTRATED PROBLEMS

PROBLEM 1

Consider the following linear program:

$$\text{MAX } Z = 3X_1 + 4X_2 \quad (\$ \text{ Profit})$$

$$\text{S.T.} \quad X_1 + 3X_2 \leq 12$$

$$2X_1 + X_2 \leq 8$$

$$X_1 \quad\quad \leq 3$$

$$X_1, X_2 \geq 0$$

This problem was solved by The Management Scientist giving the following output:

```
==================================================================
OBJECTIVE FUNCTION VALUE =    20.000
```

VARIABLE	VALUE	REDUCED COST
X1	2.400	0.000
X2	3.200	0.000

CONSTRAINT	SLACK/SURPLUS	DUAL PRICES
1	0.000	1.000
2	0.000	1.000
3	0.600	0.000

OBJECTIVE COEFFICIENT RANGES

VARIABLE	LOWER LIMIT	CURRENT VALUE	UPPER LIMIT
X1	1.333	3.000	8.000
X2	1.500	4.000	9.000

RIGHTHAND SIDE RANGES

CONSTRAINT	LOWER LIMIT	CURRENT VALUE	UPPER LIMIT
1	9.000	12.000	24.000
2	4.000	8.000	9.000
3	2.400	3.000	NO UPPER LIMIT

```
==================================================================
```

a) What is the optimal solution including the optimal value of the objective function?

b) Suppose the profit on X1 is increased to $7. Is the above solution still optimal? What is the value of the objective function when this unit profit is increased to $7?

c) If the unit profit on X2 was $10 instead of $4, would the optimal solution change?

d) If simultaneously the profit on X1 was raised to $5.5 and the profit on X2 was reduced to $3, would the current solution still remain optimal?

SOLUTION 1

a) According to the output X1 = 2.4 and X2 = 3.2, and the objective function value = $20.00.

b) The output states that the solution remains optimal as long as the objective function coefficient of X1 is between 1.333 and 8.0. Since 7 is within this range, the optimal solution will not change. However, the optimal profit will be affected: Z = 7X1 + 4X2 = 7(2.4) + 4(3.2) = $29.60.

c) The output states that the solution remains optimal as long as the objective function coefficient of X2 is between 1.5 and 9.0. Since 10 is outside this range, the optimal solution would change.

d) Use the 100% rule for simultaneous changes. If C1 = 5.5, the amount C1 changed is 5.5 - 3 = 2.5. The maximum allowable increase is 8 - 3 = 5, so this is a 2.5/5 = a 50% change. If C2 = 3, the amount that C2 changed is 4 - 3 = 1. The maximum allowable decrease is 4 - 1.5 = 2.5, so this is a 1/2.5 = a 40% change. The sum of the change percentages is 50% + 40% = 90%. Since this does not exceed 100% the optimal solution would not change.

> **NOTE:** For the 100% rule, a reduction does not offset (or negate, cancel-out) an increase. For example, increasing C1 by 70% of its allowed maximum increase and <u>decreasing</u> C2 by 50% of its allowed maximum decrease does <u>not</u> result in a combined change of 20%. The combined change is 120%, which means the problem should be solved again because the simultaneous changes to C1 and C2 might have (probably) changed the optimal solution (X1 and X2's values).

PROBLEM 2

Consider the following linear program:

$$\text{MIN } Z = 6X_1 + 9X_2 \quad (\$ \text{ cost})$$

$$\text{S.T.} \quad X_1 + 2X_2 \leq 8$$

$$10X_1 + 7.5X_2 \geq 30$$

$$X_2 \geq 2$$

$$X_1, X_2 \geq 0$$

This problem was solved by The Management Scientist giving the following output:

```
================================================================
OBJECTIVE FUNCTION VALUE =    27.000
```

VARIABLE	VALUE	REDUCED COST
X1	1.500	0.000
X2	2.000	0.000

CONSTRAINT	SLACK/SURPLUS	DUAL PRICES
1	2.500	0.000
2	0.000	-0.600
3	0.000	-4.500

OBJECTIVE COEFFICIENT RANGES

VARIABLE	LOWER LIMIT	CURRENT VALUE	UPPER LIMIT
X1	0.000	6.000	12.000
X2	4.500	9.000	NO UPPER LIMIT

RIGHTHAND SIDE RANGES

CONSTRAINT	LOWER LIMIT	CURRENT VALUE	UPPER LIMIT
1	5.500	8.000	NO UPPER LIMIT
2	15.000	30.000	55.000
3	0.000	2.000	4.000

```
================================================================
```

a) What is the optimal solution including the optimal value of the objective function?

b) Suppose the unit cost of X1 is decreased to $4. Is the above solution still optimal? What is the value of the objective function when this unit cost is decreased to $4?

c) How much can the unit cost of X2 be decreased without concern for the optimal solution changing?

d) If simultaneously the cost of X1 was raised to $7.5 and the cost of X2 was reduced to $6, would the current solution still remain optimal?

e) If the right-hand side of constraint 3 is increased by 1, what will be the effect on the optimal solution?

SOLUTION 2

a) According to the output X1 = 1.5 and X2 = 2.0, and the objective function value = 27.00.

b) The output states that the solution remains optimal as long as the objective function coefficient of X1 is between 0 and 12. Since 4 is within this range, the optimal solution will not change. However, the optimal total cost will be affected: Z = 6X1 + 9X2 = 4(1.5) + 9(2.0) = $24.00.

c) The output states that the solution remains optimal as long as the objective function coefficient of X2 does not fall below 4.5.

d) Use the 100% rule for simultaneous changes. If C1 = 7.5, the amount C1 changed is 7.5 - 6 = 1.5. The maximum allowable increase is 12 - 6 = 6, so this is a 1.5/6 = 25% change. If C2 = 6, the amount that C2 changed is 9 - 6 = 3. The maximum allowable decrease is 9 - 4.5 = 4.5, so this is a 3/4.5 = 66.7% change. The sum of the change percentages is 25% + 66.7% = 91.7%. Since this does not exceed 100% the optimal solution would not change.

e) A dual price represents the improvement in the objective function value per unit increase in the right-hand side. A negative dual price indicates a deterioration (negative improvement) in the objective, which in this problem means an increase in total cost because we're minimizing. Since the right-hand side remains within the range of feasibility, there is no change in the optimal solution. However, the objective function value increases by $4.50.

PROBLEM 3

A small company will be introducing a new line of lightweight
bicycle frames to be made from special aluminum and steel
alloys. The frames will be produced in two models, deluxe and
professional. The anticipated unit profits are currently $10
for a deluxe frame and $15 for a professional frame.

The number of pounds of each alloy needed per frame is
summarized in the table below. A supplier delivers 100 pounds
of the aluminum alloy and 80 pounds of the steel alloy weekly.

	Aluminum Alloy	Steel Alloy
Deluxe	2	3
Professional	4	2

This problem was solved by The Management Scientist giving the
following output:

```
================================================================
Objective Function Value = 412.500
```

VARIABLE	VALUE	REDUCED COST
X1	15.000	0.000
X2	17.500	0.000

CONSTRAINT	SLACK/SURPLUS	DUAL PRICES
1	0.000	3.125
2	0.000	1.250

OBJECTIVE FUNCTION RANGES

VARIABLE	LOWER LIMIT	CURRENT VALUE	UPPER LIMIT
X1	7.500	10.000	22.500
X2	6.667	15.000	20.000

RIGHTHAND SIDE RANGES

CONSTRAINT	LOWER LIMIT	CURRENT VALUE	UPPER LIMIT
1	53.333	100.000	160.000
2	50.000	80.000	150.000

```
================================================================
```

a) What is the optimal solution including the optimal value of the objective function?

b) Suppose the profit on deluxe frames is increased to $20. Is the above solution still optimal? What is the value of the objective function when this unit profit is increased to $20?

c) If the unit profit on deluxe frames were $6 instead of $10 would the optimal solution change?

d) If simultaneously the profit on deluxe frames were raised to $16 and the profit on professional frames were raised to $17, would the current solution still remain optimal?

e) Given that aluminum is a sunk cost, what is the maximum amount the company should pay for 50 extra pounds of aluminum? (Constraint 1 pertains to aluminum availability.)

f) How would your answer to (e) change if aluminum were a relevant cost?

SOLUTION 3

a) According to the output X1 (deluxe frames) = 15, and X2 (professional frames) = 17.5, and the objective function value = $412.50.

b) The output states that the solution remains optimal as long as the objective function coefficient of X1 is between 7.5 and 22.5. Since 20 is within this range, the optimal solution will not change. However the optimal profit will be affected: Z = 20X1 + 15X2 = 20(15) + 15(17.5) = $562.50.

c) The output states that the solution remains optimal as long as the objective function coefficient of X1 is between 7.5 and 22.5. Since 6 is outside this range, the optimal solution would change.

d) Use the 100% rule for simultaneous changes. If C1 = 16, the amount C1 changed is 16 - 10 = 6 . The maximum allowable increase is 22.5 - 10 = 12.5, so this is a 6/12.5 = a 48% change. If C2 = 17, the amount that C2 changed is 17 - 15 = 2. The maximum allowable increase is 20 - 15 = 5 so this is a 2/5 = 40% change. The sum of the change percentages is 48% + 40% = 88%. Since this is less than 100% the optimal solution would not change.

e) Since the cost for aluminum is a sunk cost, the shadow price provides the value of extra aluminum. The shadow price for aluminum is the same as its dual price (for a maximization problem). The shadow price for aluminum is $3.125 per pound. Thus, the value of 50 additional pounds is = $156.25.

This analysis is valid only if the change is within the range of feasibility for aluminum. From the output we can see that the maximum allowable increase for aluminum is 60. Since 50 is in this range, then the $156.25 is valid.

f) If aluminum were a relevant cost, the shadow price would be the amount above the normal price of aluminum the company would be willing to pay. Thus if initially aluminum cost $4 per pound, then additional units in the range of feasibility would be worth $4 + $3.125 = $7.125 per pound.

PROBLEM 4

Comfort Plus Inc. (CPI) manufactures a standard dining chair used in restaurants. The demand forecasts for quarter 1 (January-March) and quarter 2 (April-June) are 3700 chairs and 4200 chairs, respectively. CPI has a policy of satisfying all demand in the quarter in which it occurs.

The chair contains an upholstered seat that can be produced by CPI or purchased from DAP, a subcontractor. DAP currently charges $12.50 per seat, but has announced a new price of $13.75 effective April 1. CPI can produce the seat at a cost of $10.25.

Seats that are produced or purchased in quarter 1 and used to satisfy demand in quarter 2 cost CPI $1.50 each to hold in inventory, but maximum inventory cannot exceed 300 seats.

The problem was formulated as follows:

$X1$ = number of seats produced by CPI in quarter 1,
$X2$ = number of seats purchased from DAP in quarter 1,
$X3$ = number of seats carried in inventory from quarters 1 to 2,
$X4$ = number of seats produced by CPI in quarter 2, and
$X5$ = number of seats purchased from DAP in quarter 2.

$$\text{MIN } Z = 10.25X_1 + 12.5X_2 + 1.5X_3 + 10.25X_4 + 13.75X_5 \quad \text{(costs)}$$

$$\text{S.T.} \quad X_1 + X_2 - X_3 \geq 3700 \quad \text{(quarter 1 demand)}$$

$$X_3 + X_4 + X_5 \geq 4200 \quad \text{(quarter 2 demand)}$$

$$X_1 \leq 3800 \quad \text{(CPI's production}$$
$$\text{capacity in}$$
$$X_4 \leq 3800 \quad \text{quarters 1 and 2)}$$

$$X_3 \leq 300 \quad \text{(inventory capacity)}$$

$$X_1, X_2, X_3, X_4, X_5 \geq 0$$

This problem was solved by The Management Scientist giving the following output:

```
==============================================================
OBJECTIVE FUNCTION VALUE =  82175.000
```

VARIABLE	VALUE	REDUCED COST
X1	3800.000	0.000
X2	0.000	0.250
X3	100.000	0.000
X4	3800.000	0.000
X5	300.000	0.000

CONSTRAINT	SLACK/SURPLUS	DUAL PRICES
1	0.000	-12.250
2	0.000	-13.750
3	0.000	2.000
4	0.000	3.500
5	200.000	0.000

OBJECTIVE COEFFICIENT RANGES

VARIABLE	LOWER LIMIT	CURRENT VALUE	UPPER LIMIT
X1	NO LOWER LIMIT	10.250	12.250
X2	12.250	12.500	NO UPPER LIMIT
X3	1.250	1.500	3.500
X4	NO LOWER LIMIT	10.250	13.750
X5	11.750	13.750	14.000

RIGHTHAND SIDE RANGES

CONSTRAINT	LOWER LIMIT	CURRENT VALUE	UPPER LIMIT
1	3500.000	3700.000	3800.000
2	3900.000	4200.000	NO UPPER LIMIT
3	3700.000	3800.000	4000.000
4	0.000	3800.000	4100.000
5	100.000	300.000	NO UPPER LIMIT

```
==============================================================
```

a) What is the optimal solution including the optimal value of the objective function?

b) If the per-unit inventory cost increased from $1.50 to $2.50, would the optimal solution change? Would the optimal value of the objective function change?

c) If in quarter 2 CPI's per-seat production cost increased by $1.25 and DAP changed its mind about the announced price increase (thus leaving it at $12.50 per seat), would the optimal solution change?

d) If DAP reduced its per-seat selling price in quarter 1 from $12.50 to $12.25, should CPI purchase any seats in quarter 1?

e) How much is it worth to CPI to increase its inventory capacity from 300 seats to 400?

f) If CPI increased its production capacity by 100 seats in both quarters 1 and 2, what would be the savings for CPI (ignoring the capacity-expansion expense)?

SOLUTION 4

a) CPI will produce 3800 seats in quarter 1 and another 3800 in quarter 2. 100 seats will be carried in inventory from quarter 1 to quarter 2. 300 seats will be purchased from DAP in quarter 2. Total cost for this plan is $82,175.

b) The optimal solution will not change as a result of a change in the per-unit inventory cost as long as the cost remains in the range of $1.25 to $3.50. The objective function value _will_ change; it will increase by $100 to $82,275.

c) Use the 100% rule for simultaneous changes. The amount C4 changed is 1.25. The maximum allowable increase is 13.75 – 10.25 = 3.50, so this is a 1.25/3.50 = 35.7% change. If C5 = 12.50, the amount that C5 changed is 13.75 – 12.50 = 1.25. The maximum allowable decrease is 13.75 – 11.75 = 2.00, so this is a 1.25/2.00 = 62.5% change. The sum of the change percentages is 98.2%. Since this is less than 100% the optimal solution would not change.

d) X2 is the number of seats purchased from DAP in quarter 1 and its current value is 0. Its reduced cost value is 0.25, indicating that if C2 improved (decreased in this case) by 0.25 or more, X2 would have a positive value in the new optimal solution. C2 = $12.25 represents an improvement of exactly 0.25, so the answer is yes.

e) Increasing the inventory capacity (without other changes) will not benefit CPI. Actually, a _decrease_ as great as 200 seats will not change the optimal solution. This is indicated by the slack value of 200 for constraint 5.

f) Based on the dual prices for constraints 3 and 4, the objective function value (total cost) will decrease (remember, we're minimizing) by $5.50 (2.00 + 3.50) for each unit increase in CPI's production capacity in quarters 1 and 2. We can conclude that a 100-unit capacity increase will reduce the total cost by $550 _if_ the 100% rule has not been violated. It has not. (For constraint 3 the percent of allowed increase is 50% (100/200) and for constraint 4 the percent of allowed increase is 33%, for a total of 83%.)

ANSWERED PROBLEMS

PROBLEM 5

Regal Investments has just received instructions from a client
to invest in two stocks, one an airline stock, the other an
insurance stock. The total maximum appreciation in stock value
over the next year is to be maximized subject to the following
restrictions:
(1) The total investment shall not exceed $100,000.
(2) At most $40,000 is to be invested in the insurance stock.
(3) Quarterly dividends must total at least $2,600.
The airline stock is currently selling for $40 per share and
its quarterly dividend is $1 per share. The insurance stock is
currently selling for $50 per share and the quarterly dividend
is $1.50 per share.
Regal's analysts are forecasting that over the next year the
airline stock will increase $2 per share and the insurance stock
will increase $3 per share.

This problem was solved by The Management Scientist giving the
following output:
===
OBJECTIVE FUNCTION VALUE =   5400.000

VARIABLE	VALUE	REDUCED COST
X1	1500.000	0.000
X2	800.000	0.000

CONSTRAINT	SLACK/SURPLUS	DUAL PRICES
1	0.000	0.050
2	0.000	0.010
3	100.000	0.000

OBJECTIVE COEFFICIENT RANGES

VARIABLE	LOWER LIMIT	CURRENT VALUE	UPPER LIMIT
X1	0.000	2.000	2.400
X2	2.500	3.000	NO UPPER LIMIT

RIGHTHAND SIDE RANGES

CONSTRAINT	LOWER LIMIT	CURRENT VALUE	UPPER LIMIT
1	96000.000	100000.000	NO UPPER LIMIT
2	20000.000	40000.000	100000.000
3	NO LOWER LIMIT	2600.000	2700.000
===

a) How should the client's money be invested to satisfy his restrictions?

b) Suppose Regal's estimate of the airline stock's appreciation is in error. Within what limits must the actual appreciation lie for the answer in (a) to remain optimal?

PROBLEM 6

A company produces two products made from aluminum and copper. The table below gives the unit requirements, the unit production man-hours required, the unit profit and the availability of the resources (in tons).

	Aluminum	Copper	Man-hours	Unit Profit
Product 1	1	0	2	50
Product 2	1	1	3	60
Available	10	6	24	

This problem was solved by The Management Scientist giving the following output:

```
================================================================
OBJECTIVE FUNCTION VALUE  =    540.000
```

VARIABLE	VALUE	REDUCED COST
X1	6.000	0.000
X2	4.000	0.000

CONSTRAINT	SLACK/SURPLUS	DUAL PRICES
1	0.000	30.000
2	2.000	0.000
3	0.000	10.000

OBJECTIVE COEFFICIENT RANGES

VARIABLE	LOWER LIMIT	CURRENT VALUE	UPPER LIMIT
X1	40.000	50.000	60.000
X2	50.000	60.000	75.000

RIGHTHAND SIDE RANGES

CONSTRAINT	LOWER LIMIT	CURRENT VALUE	UPPER LIMIT
1	9.000	10.000	12.000
2	4.000	6.000	NO UPPER LIMIT
3	20.000	24.000	26.000

a) What is the optimal production schedule?

b) Within what range for the profit on product 2 will the solution in (a) remain optimal? What is the optimal profit when C_2 = 70?

c) Suppose that simultaneously the unit profits on X1 and X2 changed from 50 to 55 and 60 to 65 respectively. Would the optimal solution change?

d) Explain the meaning of the "DUAL PRICES" column. Given the optimal solution, why should the dual price for copper be 0?

e) What is the increase in the value of the objective function for an extra unit of aluminum?

f) Man-hours were not figured into the unit profit as it must pay three workers for eight hours of work regardless of the number of man-hours used. What is the shadow price for man-hours? Interpret.

g) On the other hand, aluminum and copper are resources that are ordered as needed. The unit profit coefficients were determined by: (selling price per unit) - (cost of the resources per unit). The 10 units of aluminum cost the company $100. What is the most the company should be willing to pay for extra aluminum?

PROBLEM 7

A small company produces only two sizes of frames for stereo receivers: standard size and slim-line. The accounting department has provided the following analysis of the unit profit:

	STANDARD	SLIM-LINE
Selling Price	$6.00	$4.25
Raw Materials	$0.75	$0.50
	(1.5 units @ .50/unit)	(1 unit @ .50/unit)
Packaging	$0.25	$0.25
Labor*	0.40 hours	0.25 hours
Profit (excluding labor costs)	$5.00	$3.50

* Labor is considered a fixed cost as it is performed by salaried workers at the plant.

There are 350 units of the raw material and 300 packing boxes available daily. (Both products utilize the same packing boxes.) At most 10 workers (at 8 hrs./day) will be assigned to this project.

This problem was solved by The Management Scientist with output below:

```
================================================================
OBJECTIVE FUNCTION VALUE = 1100.000
```

VARIABLE	VALUE	REDUCED COST
X1	33.333	0.000
X2	266.667	0.000

CONSTRAINT	SLACK/SURPLUS	DUAL PRICES
1	33.333	0.000
2	0.000	1.000
3	0.000	10.000

OBJECTIVE COEFFICIENT RANGES

VARIABLE	LOWER LIMIT	CURRENT VALUE	UPPER LIMIT
X1	3.500	5.000	5.600
X2	3.125	3.500	5.000

RIGHTHAND SIDE RANGES

CONSTRAINT	LOWER LIMIT	CURRENT VALUE	UPPER LIMIT
1	316.667	350.000	NO UPPER LIMIT
2	200.000	300.000	320.000
3	75.000	80.000	90.000

```
================================================================
```

a) What is the optimal daily production plan?

b) What is the maximum selling price for standard models that will keep the same optimal solution as (a)?

c) What is the new optimal solution and optimal profit if an additional worker (8 additional hours) is assigned to the project? (Hint: The output states the current values for the right-hand sides of the constraints. Compare them with the resource data provided in the problem description to determine the constraint that corresponds with each resource.)

PROBLEM 8

Consider Problem 7 further.

a) Suppose C_1 was changed from 5 to 5.5. Would the optimal
   solution change?

b) Suppose C_2 was changed from 3.5 to 4. Would the optimal
   solution change?

c) Suppose simultaneously C_1 changed to 5.5 and C_2 changed to 4.
   Would the optimal solution change?

d) What is the shadow price for man-hours? Interpret.

e) What is the shadow price for the packaging? Interpret.

f) Suppose simultaneously the amount of material available
   increased from 350 to 500, the number of boxes available
   increased from 300 to 310 and the number of man-hours
   increased from 80 to 84. What conclusion can be drawn
   regarding the shadow prices?

PROBLEM 9

A client of an investment firm has $10,000 available for
investment. He has instructed that his money be invested in
three stocks so that no more than $5,000 is invested in any one
stock but at least $1,000 is invested in each stock. He has
further instructed the firm to use its current data and invest
in a manner that maximizes his expected overall gain during a
one-year period. The stocks, the current price per share, and
the firm's projected stock price a year from now are summarized
in the following table.

Stock	Current Price	Projected Price 1 Year Hence
James Industries	$25	$35
QM Inc.	$50	$60
Delicious Candy Co.	$100	$125

This problem was formulated as follows:

X1 = number of shares of James Industries to purchase,
X2 = number of shares of QM Inc. to purchase, and
X3 = number of shares of Delicious Candy Co. to purchase.

$$MAX \; Z = 10X_1 + 10X_2 + 25X_3$$

$$S.T. \quad 25X_1 + 50X_2 + 100X_3 \leq 10000 \quad (\$ \text{ available})$$

$$25X_1 \qquad\qquad\qquad \leq 5000 \quad (\text{max. } \$ \text{ stock 1})$$

$$50X_2 \qquad\qquad \leq 5000 \quad (\text{max. } \$ \text{ stock 2})$$

$$100X_3 \leq 5000 \quad (\text{max. } \$ \text{ stock 3})$$

$$25X_1 \qquad\qquad\qquad \geq 1000 \quad (\text{min. } \$ \text{ stock 1})$$

$$50X_2 \qquad\qquad \geq 1000 \quad (\text{min. } \$ \text{ stock 2})$$

$$100X_3 \geq 1000 \quad (\text{min. } \$ \text{ stock 3})$$

$$X_1, \; X_2, \; X_3 \geq 0$$

This problem was solved by The Management Scientist giving the following output:

```
================================================================
OBJECTIVE FUNCTION VALUE = 3200.000
```

VARIABLE	VALUE	REDUCED COST
X1	200.000	0.000
X2	20.000	0.000
X3	40.000	0.000

CONSTRAINT	SLACK/SURPLUS	DUAL PRICES
1	0.000	0.250
2	0.000	0.150
3	4000.000	0.000
4	1000.000	0.000
5	4000.000	0.000
6	0.000	-0.050
7	3000.000	0.000

OBJECTIVE COEFFICIENT RANGES

VARIABLE	LOWER LIMIT	CURRENT VALUE	UPPER LIMIT
X1	6.250	10.000	NO UPPER LIMIT
X2	NO LOWER LIMIT	10.000	12.500
X3	20.000	25.000	40.000

RIGHTHAND SIDE RANGES

CONSTRAINT	LOWER LIMIT	CURRENT VALUE	UPPER LIMIT
1	7000.000	10000.000	11000.000
2	4000.000	5000.000	8000.000
3	1000.000	5000.000	NO UPPER LIMIT
4	4000.000	5000.000	NO UPPER LIMIT
5	NO LOWER LIMIT	1000.000	5000.000
6	0.000	1000.000	4000.000
7	NO LOWER LIMIT	1000.000	4000.000

==

a) What is the optimal solution including the optimal value of the objective function?

b) How should the dual price for constraint 6 be interpreted?

c) If the client had an additional $1000 available for investing how much would the expected overall one-year gain increase?

d) If the client increased the allowed maximum investment amount to $6000 for such one stock, should it be Delicious Candy (the stock with the greatest gain)? Why?

e) Based on your stock choice in (d) above, how much would the objective function increase?

f) For your stock choice in (d) above, how much could the allowed maximum investment amount be raised before the optimal investment mix might change?

g) If the expected one-year gains on James Industries and QM Inc. each increased by $1.00, would the optimal investment mix change?

> **Note:** If the range of optimality (or range of feasibility) for an objective function coefficient (or right-hand side) involved in a simultaneous change is unlimited in the direction of the change, the change to this coefficient (or right-hand side) is of no concern.

TRUE/FALSE

10. Any change to an objective function coefficient of a variable which is positive in the optimal solution will change the optimal value of the objective function.

11. The shadow price for labor hours is $25. The profit coefficients c_1 and c_2 take into account a $10 per hour labor cost. Then the maximum value of an overtime hour is $35.

12. Ranges of optimality or feasibility are calculated for a single change only, and they assume no other coefficients in the problem have been changed.

13. Regarding the 100 percent rule, it is possible for the optimal solution to <u>not</u> change even though changes in the objective function coefficients exceed 100 percent.

14. If the range of feasibility for b_1 is between 16 and 37, then if b_1 = 22, the optimal solution will not change from the original optimal solution.

15. The 100 percent rule can be applied to changes in both objective function coefficients and right-hand sides at the same time.

16. Relevant costs should be reflected in the objective function, but sunk costs should not.

17. Dual price and shadow price are equivalent for maximization problems and are negative of each other for minimization problems.

18. For any constraint, either its slack/surplus value must be zero or its dual price must be zero.

19. For any decision variable, either its value must be zero or its reduced cost must be zero.

20. If the dual price for the right-hand side of a $\leq$ constraint is zero, there is no upper limit on its range of feasibility.

21. A $\leq$ constraint cannot have a negative dual price, regardless of whether it is a maximization or minimization problem.

22. Slack corresponds to $\leq$ constraints.

23. The Management Scientist can only be used to solve linear programs in two variables.

24. Shadow prices are only valid within the range of feasibility.

CHAPTER 4

Linear Programming Applications

KEY CONCEPTS

CONCEPT	ILLUSTRATED PROBLEMS	ANSWERED PROBLEMS
Programming Applications:		
Blending	1,4	14
Equipment Acquisition	2	10,15
Multiperiod Planning	3	11
Product Mix	4	12,13,14
Staff Scheduling	5	20
Portfolio Selection	6	16
Data Envelopment Analysis	7	19
Media Selection	8	17
Transportation	9	18
Computer Solutions	1,3,5,7,9	13,15,17,18,19

REVIEW

1. <u>Linear programming applications</u> include problems in production, marketing, finance, and numerous other business-related areas.

2. To develop a <u>good formulation</u>, one should strive to understand the problem thoroughly. Then one should: (1) define the decision variables (the inputs over which you have direct control); (2) define the objective (the goal that you wish to maximize or minimize); and, (3) define the constraints (the restrictions that deter you from even better values for the objective function.) Frequently it is advisable to write the objective function and constraints in English first before translating them into mathematical notation.

3. <u>Computer packages</u>, such as The Management Scientist may be used to solve linear programming problems giving the optimal solution and appropriate sensitivity analyses.

4. <u>Data Envelopment Analysis (DEA)</u> is an application of linear programming used to determine the relative operating efficiency of units with the same goals and objectives (e.g. banks, schools, company divisions, etc.)

5. DEA creates a fictitious <u>composite unit</u> made up of an optimal weighted average (W_1, W_2, etc.) of existing units. Then an individual unit, k, may be compared by determining E, the fraction of this unit's input resources required by the composite unit.

6. The <u>DEA model</u> is given by:

    MIN E

    S.T.   The sum of the weights = 1.

           Weighted outputs $\geq$ Unit k's output
                                (for each measured output)

           Weighted inputs $\leq$ E x (Unit k's input)
                                (for each measured input)

           E, weights, $\geq$ 0

7. In DEA, if the <u>optimal value of E</u> < 1, unit k is less efficient than the composite unit and can be judged relatively inefficient. If, however, E = 1, there is no evidence that unit k is inefficient, however, one cannot conclude that unit k is absolutely efficient.

ILLUSTRATED PROBLEMS

> **NOTE:** Students often confuse a constraint for the objective in a problem. If there is a limit imposed on an entity, it probably represents a constraint. (We are solving for the objective function's limit!)

> **NOTE:** A common dilemma is whether to use "=" or an inequality sign ($\leq$ or $\geq$) in a constraint. There is no simple, definitive answer; the correct answer is problem specific. The use of "=" when not necessary might result in an infeasible problem. Quite often, if you are choosing between "$\leq$" and "=", "$\leq$" will do no harm if you are maximizing ("$\geq$" if you are minimizing); equality is likely to be achieved if it is possible. Of course, using "$\leq$" when you should be using "$\geq$" is very harmful!

PROBLEM 1

Frederick's Feed Company receives four raw grains from which it blends its dry pet food. The per food advertises that each 8-ounce can meets the minimum daily requirements for vitamin C, protein and iron. The cost of each raw grain as well as the vitamin C, protein, and iron units per pound of each grain are summarized below.

Grain	Vitamin C Units/lb	Protein Units/lb	Iron Units/lb	Cost/lb
1	9	12	0	.75
2	16	10	14	.90
3	8	10	15	.80
4	10	8	7	.70

Frederick's is interested in producing the 8-ounce mixture at minimum cost while meeting the minimum daily requirements of 6 units of vitamin C, 5 units of protein, and 5 units of iron.

a) Formulate this problem as a linear program.

b) Solve for the optimal solution using a program such as The Management Scientist.

c) If the mixture costs 5.4 cents to can and Frederick's puts a 50% markup on the package to its retailers, how much will it charge its retailers for an 8-ounce can?

SOLUTION 1

a) <u>Define the decision variables</u>

X_j = the pounds of grain j (j = 1,2,3,4) used in the
8-ounce mixture

<u>Define the objective</u>

Minimize the total cost for an 8-ounce mixture:
MIN $.75X_1$ + $.90X_2$ + $.80X_3$ + $.70X_4$

<u>Define the constraints</u>

The total weight of the mixture (X_1 + X_2 + X_3 + X_4) is
8-ounces (.5 pounds):
(1) X_1 + X_2 + X_3 + X_4 = .5

Total amount of Vitamin C in the mixture is at least 6:
(2) $9X_1$ + $16X_2$ + $8X_3$ + $10X_4 \geq 6$

Total amount of protein in the mixture is at least 5:
(3) $12X_1$ + $10X_2$ + $10X_3$ + $8X_4 \geq 5$

Total amount of iron in the mixture is at least 5:
(4) $14X_2$ + $15X_3$ + $7X_4 \geq 5$

Nonnegativity of variables: $X_j \geq 0$ for all j

b) When solved by the Management Scientist the following output
was generated:

OBJECTIVE FUNCTION VALUE =   0.406

VARIABLE	VALUE	REDUCED COSTS
X1	0.099	0.000
X2	0.213	0.000
X3	0.088	0.000
X4	0.099	0.000

Thus, the optimal blend is about .10 lb. of grain 1, .21 lb.
of grain 2, .09 lb. of grain 3, and .10 lb. of grain 4.

c) The mixture costs Frederick's 40.6 cents. With 5.4 cents for
packaging, this brings their costs to 46 cents. A 50% markup
would mean it would charge retailers 1.5(46) = 69 cents per
can.

PROBLEM 2

Floataway Tours has $400,000 that may be used to purchase new
rental boats for hire during the summer. The boats my be
purchased from two different manufacturers. Pertinent data
concerning the boats are summarized below:

Boat	Manufacturer	Cost	Maximum Seating	Expected Daily Profit
Speedhawk	Sleekboat	$6000	3	$ 70
Silverbird	Sleekboat	$7000	5	$ 80
Catman	Racer	$5000	2	$ 50
Classy	Racer	$9000	6	$110

Floataway Tours would like to purchase at least 50 boats and
would like to purchase the same number from Sleekboat as from
Racer to maintain goodwill. At the same time, Floataway Tours
wishes to have a total seating capacity of at least 200.
     Formulate this problem as a linear program.

SOLUTION 2

Define the decision variables

X_1 = the number of Speedhawks ordered
X_2 = the number of Silverbirds ordered
X_3 = the number of Catmans ordered
X_4 = the number of Classys ordered

Define the objective function

Maximize total expected daily profit:
MAX (Expected daily profit per unit)(Number of units)
MAX $70X_1 + 80X_2 + 50X_3 + 110X_4$

Define the constraints

Spend no more than $400,000:
(1) $6000X_1 + 7000X_2 + 5000X_3 + 9000X_4 \leq 400,000$

Purchase at least 50 boats:
(2) $X_1 + X_2 + X_3 + X_4 \geq 50$

Same number of boats from each manufacturer:
(No. of boats from Sleekboat) = (No. of Boats from Racer)
(3) $X_1 + X_2 = X_3 + X_4$ or $X_1 + X_2 - X_3 - X_4 = 0$

Capacity at least 200:
(4) $3X_1 + 5X_2 + 2X_3 + 6X_4 \geq 200$

Nonnegativity of variables: $X_j \geq 0$, for j = 1,2,3,4

PROBLEM 3

Burt Wheeler is the production manager of Wheeler Wheels, Inc. Burt has just received orders for 1,000 standard wheels and 1,250 deluxe wheels next month and for 800 standard and 1,500 deluxe wheels the following month. All orders are to be filled.
   The cost of producing standard wheels is $10 and deluxe wheels is $16. Overtime rates are 50% higher. There are 1,000 hours of regular time and 500 hours of overtime available each month. The cost of storing one wheel from one month to the next is $2.
   Develop a two-month production schedule for Burt of standard and deluxe wheel production if it takes .5 hour to make a standard wheel and .6 hour to make a deluxe wheel and solve using a program such as the Management Scientist.

SOLUTION 3

Define the decision variables

We must determine how many of each type of wheel to make each month during regular time and overtime; also we must determine the number of each wheel stored from one month to the next. Thus we want to determine the production levels, X_j, as follows:

	Month 1		**Month 2**	
	Reg. Time	Overtime	Reg. Time	Overtime
Standard	X_1	X_2	X_5	X_6
Deluxe	X_3	X_4	X_7	X_8

Also let,
Y_1 = number of standard wheels stored from month 1 to month 2
Y_2 = number of deluxe wheels stored from month 1 to month 2.

Define the objective function

Minimize total production and storage costs:
MIN (cost per wheel)(number of wheels produced) + $2Y_1$ + $2Y_2$
MIN $10X_1$ + $15X_2$ + $16X_3$ + $24X_4$ + $10X_5$ + $15X_6$ + $16X_7$ + $24X_8$
    + $2Y_1$ + $2Y_2$

Define the constraints

Standard Wheel Product. Month 1 = (Requirements)+(Amount Stored)
(1) $X_1 + X_2 = 1,000 + Y_1$ or $X_1 + X_2 - Y_1 = 1,000$

Deluxe Wheel Production Month 1 = (Requirements)+(Amount Stored)
(2) $X_3 + X_4 = 1,250 + Y_2$ or $X_3 + X_4 - Y_2 = 1,250$

Standard Wheel Product. Month 2 = (Requirements)-(Amount Stored)
(3) $X_5 + X_6 = 800 - Y_1$ or $X_5 + X_6 + Y_1 = 800$

Deluxe Wheel Production Month 2 = (Requirements)-(Amount Stored)
(4) $X_7 + X_8 = 1,500 - Y_2$ or $X_7 + X_8 + Y_2 = 1,500$

Regular Hours Used Month 1 $\leq$ Regular Hours Available Month 1:
(5) $.5X_1 + .6X_3 \leq 1000$

Overtime Hours Used Month 1 $\leq$ Overtime Hours Avail. Month 1:
(6) $.5X_2 + .6X_4 \leq 500$

Regular Hours Used Month 2 $\leq$ Regular Hours Available Month 2:
(7) $.5X_5 + .6X_7 \leq 1000$

Overtime Hours Used Month 2 $\leq$ Overtime Hours Avail. Month 2:
(8) $.5X_6 + .6X_8 \leq 500$

Nonnegativity of variables:
$X_j \geq 0$, j = 1,,8 and $Y_j \geq 0$ j = 1,2

The Management Scientist provided the following solution:

OBJECTIVE FUNCTION VALUE = 67500.000

VARIABLE	VALUE	REDUCED COSTS
X1	500.000	0.000
X2	500.000	0.000
X3	1250.000	0.000
X4	0.000	2.000
X5	200.000	0.000
X6	600.000	0.000
X7	1500.000	0.000
X8	0.000	2.000
Y1	0.000	2.000
Y2	0.000	2.000

Thus, the following production schedule is recommended:

	Month 1		Month 2	
	Reg. Time	Overtime	Reg. Time	Overtime
Standard	500	500	200	600
Deluxe	1250	0	1500	0

No wheels are stored and the minimum total cost is $67,500.

PROBLEM 4

Target Shirt Company makes three varieties of shirts:
Collegiate, Traditional and European. These shirts are made
from different combinations of cotton and polyester.
   The cost per yard of unblended cotton is $5 and for unblended
polyester is $4. Target can receive up to 4,000 yards of raw
cotton and 3,000 yards of raw polyester fabric weekly.
   The table below pertinent data concerning the manufacture of
the shirts.

Shirt	Total Yards	Fabric Requirements	Weekly Contracts	Weekly Demand	Selling Price
Collegiate	1.00	At least 50% cotton	500	600	$14.00
Traditional	1.20	No more than 20% polyester	650	850	$15.00
European	.90	As much as 80% polyester	280	675	$18.00

Formulate a linear program that would give a manufacturing
policy for Target Shirt Company.

SOLUTION 4

Define the decision variables

Not only must we decide how many shirts to make and how much
fabric to purchase, we also need to decide how much of each
fabric is blended into each shirt.

Let,
T_j = the total number of shirt style j produced
F_i = the number of yards of material i purchased
X_{ij} = yards of fabric i blended into shirt style j

where i = 1 (cotton) or 2 (polyester) and
      j = 1 (collegiate), 2 (traditional), or 3 (European)

Define the objective

Maximize the overall profit.

To determine the profit function, subtract the cost of
purchasing the fabric from the revenue from the sale of the
shirts. Thus the objective function is :
MAX $14T_1 + 15T_2 + 18T_3 - 5F_1 - 4F_2$

Define the constraints

Definition of Total Number of Shirts of Each Style
Total Number of each style =
(Total Yardage used in making the style) / (Yardage/Shirt)
(1) Collegiate: $T_1 = (X_{11} + X_{21}) / 1$
(2) Traditional: $T_2 = (X_{12} + X_{22}) / 1.2$
(3) European: $T_3 = (X_{13} + X_{23}) / .9$

Definition of Total Yardage of Materials
(4) Cotton: $F_1 = X_{11} + X_{12} + X_{13}$
(5) Polyester: $F_2 = X_{21} + X_{22} + X_{23}$

Weekly Availability of the Resources
(6) Cotton: $F_1 \le 4000$
(7) Polyester: $F_2 \le 3000$

Meet Weekly Contracts
(8) Collegiate: $S_1 \ge 500$
(9) Traditional: $S_2 \ge 650$
(10) European: $S_3 \ge 280$

Do Not Exceed Weekly Demand
(11) Collegiate: $S_1 \le 600$
(12) Traditional: $S_2 \le 850$
(13) European: $S_3 \le 675$

Fabric Requirements
Collegiate At Least 50% Cotton:
(Total yds. of Cotton Used in Collegiate Shirts) $\ge$
[(.5(1.00) yds./shirt)(number of collegiate shirts)]
(14) $X_{11} \ge .5S_1$

Traditional At Most 20% Polyester:
(Total yds. Polyester Used in Traditional Shirts) $\le$
[.2(1.20) yds./shirt)(number of traditional shirts)]
(15) $X_{22} \le .24S_2$

European At Most 80% Polyester:
(Total yds. Polyester Used in European Shirts) $\le$
[.8(.90) yds./shirt)(number of European shirts)]
(16) $X_{32} \le .72S_3$

Nonnegativity of variables
S_j, F_i, $X_{ij} \ge 0$ for i = 1,2 and j = 1,2,3.

PROBLEM 5

The Accounting Department at Lenny's Restaurant requires information on the total number of employees it will be hiring for its new restaurant located across the street from a major university. Lenny's has broken down its requirements into 4-hour periods.

Time Period	Employees Required
7AM - 11AM	12
11AM - 3PM	20
3PM - 7PM	18
7PM - 11PM	22
11PM - 7AM	CLOSED

Staffing is done by hiring personnel for eight hour shifts commencing at 7AM, 11AM, and 3PM. Additionally there are enough students who wish to work the before and after school eight hour shift which includes 7PM - 11PM and 7AM - 11AM.

a) Formulate and solve for the minimum number of personnel the Accounting Department at Lenny's should expect for this new restaurant.

b) Based on the solution in part (a), determine the timing and amount of overstaffing that will occur.

SOLUTION 5

a) <u>Define</u> <u>the</u> <u>decision</u> <u>variables</u>

X_1 = number of workers hired <u>beginning</u> with 7AM shift
X_2 = number of workers hired <u>beginning</u> with 11AM shift
X_3 = number of workers hired <u>beginning</u> with 3PM shift
X_4 = number of workers hired <u>beginning</u> with 7PM shift and
     working 7PM - 11PM and 7AM - 11AM

<u>Define</u> <u>the</u> <u>objective</u>

Minimize the total number of personnel hired:
MIN $X_1 + X_2 + X_3 + X_4$

<u>Define</u> <u>the</u> <u>constraints</u>

Total personnel working during each 4-hour period must be greater than or equal to the number of employees required:
(1) $X_1 + X_4 \geq 12$
(2) $X_1 + X_2 \geq 20$
(3) $X_2 + X_3 \geq 18$
(4) $X_3 + X_4 \geq 22$

Nonnegativity of variables: $X_j \geq 0$ for j = 1,2,3,4

The Management Scientist provided the following solution:

OBJECTIVE FUNCTION VALUE   =   42.000

VARIABLE	VALUE	REDUCED COSTS
X1	20.000	0.000
X2	0.000	0.000
X3	18.000	0.000
X4	4.000	0.000

CONSTRAINT	SLACK/SURPLUS	DUAL PRICES
1	12.000	0.000
2	0.000	-1.000
3	0.000	0.000
4	0.000	-1.000

(There are alternate optimal solutions, one of which is:
X_1 = 12, X_2 = 8, X_3 = 22, and X_4 = 0.)

b) The timing and amount of overstaffing corresponds to the
   constraint surplus values shown in the computer output. The
   only four-hour period that is overstaffed is 7AM - 11AM.
   It is overstaffed by 12 workers. Thus, the total man-hours
   of overstaffing is 4(12) = 48.

PROBLEM 6

Winslow Savings has $20 million available for investment. It
wishes to invest over the next four months in such a way that it
will maximize the total interest earned over the four month
period as well as have at least $10 million available at the
start of the fifth month for a high rise building venture in
which it will be participating.
    For the time being, Winslow wishes to invest only in 2-month
government bonds (earning 2% over the 2-month period) and 3-
month construction loans (earning 6% over the 3-month period).
Each of these is available each month for investment. Funds not
invested in these two investments are liquid and earn 3/4 of 1%
per month when invested locally.
    Formulate a linear program that will help Winslow Savings
determine how to invest over the next four months if at no time
does it wish to have more than $8 million in either government
bonds or construction loans.

SOLUTION 6

Define the decision variables

G_j = amount of new investment in government bonds in month j
C_j = amount of new investment in construction loans in month j
L_j = amount invested locally in month j,   where j = 1,2,3,4

Define the objective

Maximize the total interest earned over the four-month period:
MAX (interest rate on investment)(amount invested)
MAX $.02G_1 + .02G_2 + .02G_3 + .02G_4 + .06C_1 + .06C_2 + .06C_3$
$+ .06C_4 + .0075L_1 + .0075L_2 + .0075L_3 + .0075L_4$

Define the constraints

Month 1's total investment amount limited to $20 million:
(1) $G_1 + C_1 + L_1 = 20,000,000$

Month 2's total investment amount limited to amount
(principle and interest) invested locally in Month 1:
(2) $G_2 + C_2 + L_2 = 1.0075L_1$ or $G_2 + C_2 - 1.0075L_1 + L_2 = 0$

Month 3's total investment amount limited to amounts (principle
and interest) invested in government bonds in Month 1 and
locally invested in Month 2:
(3) $G_3 + C_3 + L_3 = 1.02G_1 + 1.0075L_2$
or $- 1.02G_1 + G_3 + C_3 - 1.0075L_2 + L_3 = 0$

Month 4's total investment amount limited to amounts (principle
and interest) invested in construction loans in Month 1, in
government bonds in Month 2, and locally invested in Month 3:
(4) $G_4 + C_4 + L_4 = 1.06C_1 + 1.02G_2 + 1.0075L_3$
or $- 1.02G_2 + G_4 - 1.06C_1 + C_4 - 1.0075L_3 + L_4 = 0$

$10 million must be available at start of Month 5:
(5) $1.06C_2 + 1.02G_3 + 1.0075L_4 \geq 10,000,000$

No more than $8 million in government bonds at any time:
(6) $G_1 \leq 8,000,000$
(7) $G_1 + G_2 \leq 8,000,000$
(8) $G_2 + G_3 \leq 8,000,000$
(9) $G_3 + G_4 \leq 8,000,000$

No more than $8 million in construction loans at any time:
(10) $C_1 \leq 8,000,000$
(11) $C_1 + C_2 \leq 8,000,000$
(12) $C_1 + C_2 + C_3 \leq 8,000,000$
(13) $C_2 + C_3 + C_4 \leq 8,000,000$

Nonnegativity: $G_j, C_j, L_j \geq 0$ for j = 1,2,3,4

PROBLEM 7

The Langley County School District is trying to determine the relative efficiency of its three high schools. In particular, it wants to evaluate Roosevelt High School.

The district is evaluating performances on SAT scores, the number of seniors finishing high school, and the number of students who enter college as a function of the number of teachers teaching senior classes, the prorated budget for senior instruction, and the number of students in the senior class.

Input	Roosevelt	Linclon	Washington
Senior Faculty	37	25	23
Budget ($100,000's)	6.4	5.0	4.7
Senior Enrollments	850	700	600

Output	Roosevelt	Linclon	Washington
Average SAT Score	800	830	900
High School Graduates	450	500	400
College Admissions	140	250	370

a) Use data envelopment analysis to develop a linear program to determine the relative efficiency of Roosevelt High School.

b) Solve the linear program using the Management Scientist. Comment on the relative efficiency of Roosevelt High School for each of the output measures.

SOLUTION 7

a) The goal of data envelopment analysis is to compare Roosevelt High School to a fictitious composite high school developed by determining an optimal set of weights of all high schools in the Langley School District.

This set of weights minimizes the fraction, E, of Roosevelt High School's input resources required by the composite school.

If E = 1, the composite high school requires the same input resources as Roosevelt's and there would be no evidence that Roosevelt High School is inefficient. If E < 1, Roosevelt High School is operating inefficiently with its given inputs and further study of Roosevelt should be made to determine the reasons for this inefficiency.

Define the decision variables

E = Fraction of Roosevelt High School's input resources
     required by the composite high school
W_1 = Weight applied to Roosevelt High School's input/output
     resources by the composite high school
W_2 = Weight applied to Lincoln High School's input/output
     resources by the composite high school
W_3 = Weight applied to Washington High School's input/output
     resources by the composite high school

Define the objective

Minimize the fraction of Roosevelt High School's input
resources required by the composite high school:
MIN E

Define the constraints

Sum of the Weights is 1:
  (1) $W_1 + W_2 + W_3 = 1$

Output Constraints
   Since $W_1 = 1$ is possible, each output of the composite
   school must be at least as great as that of Roosevelt:
   (2) $800W_1 + 830W_2 + 900W_3 \geq 800$ (SAT Scores)

   (3) $450W_1 + 500W_2 + 400W_3 \geq 450$ (Graduates)

   (4) $140W_1 + 250W_2 + 370W_3 \geq 140$ (College Admissions)

Input Constraints
   The input resources available to the composite school is a
   fractional multiple, E, of the resources available to
   Roosevelt. Since the composite high school cannot use more
   input than that available to it, the input constraints are:
   (5) $37W_1 + 25W_2 + 23W_3 \leq 37E$ (Faculty)

   (6) $6.4W_1 + 5.0W_2 + 4.7W_3 \leq 6.4E$ (Budget)

   (7) $850W_1 + 700W_2 + 600W_3 \leq 850E$ (Seniors)

Nonnegativity of variables:
   $E, W_1, W_2, W_3 \geq 0$

b) The problem was solved by the Management Scientist and the
   output is on the next page.

The output shows that the composite high school is made up of equal weights of Lincoln High School and Washington High School. Roosevelt High School is 76.5% efficient compared to this composite high school when measured by college admissions (because of the 0 slack on this constraint (#4)).

It is even less than 76.5% efficient when using measures of SAT scores and high school graduates (because of the positive slack in these constraints (#2) and (#3).)

OBJECTIVE FUNCTION VALUE   =   0.765

VARIABLE	VALUE	REDUCED COSTS
E	0.765	0.000
W1	0.000	0.235
W2	0.500	0.000
W3	0.500	0.000

CONSTRAINT	SLACK/SURPLUS	DUAL PRICES
1	0.000	-0.235
2	65.000	0.000
3	0.000	-0.001
4	170.000	0.000
5	4.294	0.000
6	0.044	0.000
7	0.000	0.001

PROBLEM 8

The SMM Company, which is manufacturing a new instant salad machine, has $350,000 to spend on advertising. The product is only to be test marketed initially in the Dallas area. The money is to be spent on an advertising blitz during one weekend (Friday, Saturday, and Sunday) in January, and SMM is limited to television advertising.

The company has three options available: day time advertising, evening news advertising and the Super Bowl. Even though the Super Bowl is a national telecast, the Dallas Cowboys will be playing in it, and hence, the viewing audience will be especially large in the Dallas area. A mixture of one-minute TV spots is desired.

The table below gives pertinent data:

	Cost Per Ad	Estimated New Audience Reached With Each Ad
Day Time	$5,000	3000
Evening News	$7,000	4000
Super Bowl	$100,000	75,000

SMM has decided to take out at least one ad in each option.
Further, there are only two Super Bowl ad spots available.
There are 10 day time spots and 6 evening news spots available
daily. If SMM wants to have at least 5 ads per day, but spend
no more than $50,000 on Friday and no more than $75,000 on
Saturday, formulate a linear program to help SMM decide how the
company should advertise over the weekend.

SOLUTION 8

Define the decision variables

X_1 = the number of day ads on Friday
X_2 = the number of day ads on Saturday
X_3 = the number of day ads on Sunday
X_4 = the number of evening ads on Friday
X_5 = the number of evening ads on Saturday
X_6 = the number of evening ads on Sunday
X_7 = the number of Super Bowl ads

Define the objective

Maximize the estimated total new audience reached:
MAX (new audience reached per ad of each type)(number of ads of
each type)
MAX $3000X_1$ $+3000X_2$ $+3000X_3$ $+4000X_4$ $+4000X_5$ $+4000X_6$ $+75000X_7$

Define the constraints

Take out at least one ad of each type:
(1) $X_1 + X_2 + X_3 \geq 1$
(2) $X_4 + X_5 + X_6 \geq 1$
(3) $X_7 \geq 1$

10 daytime spots available:
(4) $X_1 \leq 10$
(5) $X_2 \leq 10$
(6) $X_3 \leq 10$

6 evening news spots available:
(7) $X_4 \leq 6$
(8) $X_5 \leq 6$
(9) $X_6 \leq 6$

Only two Super Bowl ad spots available:
(10) $X_7 \leq 2$

At least 5 ads per day:
(11) $X_1 + X_4 \geq 5$
(12) $X_2 + X_5 \geq 5$
(13) $X_3 + X_6 + X_7 \geq 5$

Spend no more than $50,000 on Friday:
(14) $5000X_1 + 7000X_4 \leq 50000$

Spend no more than $75,000 on Saturday:
(15) $5000X_2 + 7000X_5 \leq 75000$

Spend no more than $350,000 in total:
(16) $5000X_1 + 5000X_2 + 5000X_3 + 7000X_4 + 7000X_5 + 7000X_6 + 100000X_7 \leq 350000$

Nonnegativity:
$X_j \geq 0 \quad j = 1,\ldots,7$

PROBLEM 9

The Navy has 9,000 pounds of material in Albany Georgia which it wishes to ship to three installations: San Diego, Norfolk, and Pensacola. They require 4,000, 2,500, and 2,500 pounds respectively. The following gives the shipping costs per pound for truck, railroad, and airplane transit.

Mode	San Diego	Destination Norfolk	Pensacola
Truck	$12	$ 6	$ 5
Railroad	20	11	9
Airplane	30	26	28

Government regulations require equal distribution of shipping among the three carriers. Formulate and solve a linear program to determine the shipping arrangements (mode, destination, and quantity) that will minimize the total shipping cost.

SOLUTION 9

Define the decision variables

We want to determine the pounds of material, X_{ij}, to be shipped by mode i to destination j. The following table summarizes the decision variables:

	San Diego	Norfolk	Pensacola
Truck	X_{11}	X_{12}	X_{13}
Railroad	X_{21}	X_{22}	X_{23}
Airplane	X_{31}	X_{32}	X_{33}

Define the objective

Minimize the total shipping cost.
MIN (shipping cost per pound for each mode/destination pairing)
    X (number of pounds shipped by mode/destination pairing):
MIN $12X_{11} + 6X_{12} + 5X_{13} + 20X_{21} + 11X_{22} + 9X_{23} + 30X_{31} + 26X_{32} + 28X_{33}$

Define the constraints

Equal use of transportation modes:
(1) $X_{11} + X_{12} + X_{13} = 3000$
(2) $X_{21} + X_{22} + X_{23} = 3000$
(3) $X_{31} + X_{32} + X_{33} = 3000$

Destination material requirements:
(4) $X_{11} + X_{21} + X_{31} = 4000$
(5) $X_{12} + X_{22} + X_{32} = 2500$
(6) $X_{13} + X_{23} + X_{33} = 2500$

Nonnegativity of variables:
$X_{ij} \geq 0$, $i = 1,2,3$ and $j = 1,2,3$

The Management Scientist provided the following solution:

OBJECTIVE FUNCTION VALUE = 142000.000

VARIABLE	VALUE	REDUCED COSTS
X11	1000.000	0.000
X12	2000.000	0.000
X13	0.000	1.000
X21	0.000	3.000
X22	500.000	0.000
X23	2500.000	0.000
X31	3000.000	0.000
X32	0.000	2.000
X33	0.000	6.000

To summarize: San Diego will receive 1000 lbs. by truck and
3000 lbs. by airplane; Norfolk will receive 2000 lbs. by truck
and 500 lbs. by railroad; Pensacola will receive 2500 lbs. by
railroad. The total shipping cost will be $142,000.

NOTE: This problem is referred to as a transportation
problem. Transportation problems have a mathematical
structure that has enabled management scientists to
develop efficient, specialized procedures for solving
them. These procedures are covered in Chapter 7.

ANSWERED PROBLEMS

PROBLEM 10

Fullerton Trucking has $500,000 allocated to purchase at least
40 trucks. It will buy both Japanese and American-built trucks,
but keeping with its "BUY-AMERICAN" image, it wishes to purchase
at least twice as many American as Japanese-built trucks.
Fullerton has narrowed its choices to three American and three
Japanese models. It wishes to purchase at least 20 two-seat
models. The following table summarizes the data for each model:

Truck	Country	Cost	Capacity	Seats
Hauler	U.S.	$20,000	1.50 tons	2
Mauler	U.S.	$18,000	1.00	2
Bruiser	U.S.	$13,000	.75	1
Econotruck	Japan	$ 7,000	.50	1
T-150	Japan	$12,000	.75	2
Maxitruck	Japan	$15,000	1.00	2

a) Formulate this problem as a linear program with the objective
   of maximizing the overall trucking capacity.

b) Why is linear programming not the technically correct
   procedure to use to solve this problem?

PROBLEM 11

National Wing Company (NWC) is gearing up for the new B-48
contract. Currently NWC has 100 equally qualified workers.
Over the next three months NWC has made the following
commitments for wing production:

Month	Contract
May	20
June	24
July	30

Each worker can either be placed in production or can train new
recruits. A new recruit can be trained to be an apprentice in
one month. The next month, he, himself, becomes a qualified
worker (after two months from the start of training). Each
trainer can train two recruits. The production rate and salary
per employee is estimated below.

Employee	Production Rate (Wings/Month)	Salary Per Month
Production	.6	$3,000
Trainer	.3	$3,300
Apprentice	.4	$2,600
Recruit	.05	$2,200

At the end of July, NWC wishes to have no recruits or apprentices but have at least 140 full-time workers.

Formulate a linear program for NWC to accomplish this at minimum total cost.

PROBLEM 12

Triumph Trumpet Company makes two styles each of both trumpets and cornets: deluxe and professional models. Its unit profit on deluxe trumpets is $80 and on deluxe cornets is $60. The professional models realize twice the profit of the deluxe models.

Trumpets and cornets are made basically from two mixtures of two different brass alloys. The amount of each alloy (in pounds) required to produce each type of horn is summarized in the following table along with the monthly availability to Triumph of the alloys.

	Trumpets		Cornets		Monthly Availability
	Deluxe	Pro.	Deluxe	Pro.	
Alloy 1	2	1.5	1.5	1	2000
Alloy 2	1	1.5	1	1.5	1800

Triumph must fulfill contracts calling for at least 500 deluxe trumpets and 300 deluxe cornets monthly. Monthly demand for professional trumpets is not expected to exceed 150 and for professional cornets is not expected to exceed 100. Production set-ups are such that the company will produce exactly twice as many trumpets as cornets.

Formulate this problem as a linear program.

PROBLEM 13

Millard Construction is contemplating building a planned community with the help of federal funds. These funds are to be distributed only if Millard meets federal standards for low cost housing. There are three types of units -- houses, town-houses, and high rise condominiums. There are three styles each of the houses and town-houses -- low cost, standard, and deluxe. The high rise condominiums will have only standard and deluxe models.

The amount of total ground space (including allowances for parking and green belts) is given in the following table:

Ground Area (Sq. Ft.)

	Low Cost	Standard	Deluxe
Houses	1800	2200	3000
Town-Houses	740	1600	2230
Condominiums	X	1000	1500

The profit to Millard per unit is summarized in the following table:

Profit ($1000's)

	Low Cost	Standard	Deluxe
Houses	5	12	25
Town-Houses	4	10	18
Condominiums	X	9	16

Millard has 300,000 square feet for construction. To make the project "work", Millard wants houses and town-houses each to occupy between 25% and 40% of the total area while condominiums only need to occupy 10% to 25% of the total area.

The federal government requires that at least 25% of the total units built in the complex be low cost units.

a) Formulate this problem as a linear program.

b) Solve for the optimal solution using a computer package such as The Management Scientist.

c) Why is linear programming not the technically correct formulation procedure for this problem?

PROBLEM 14

Delicious Candy Company manufactures three types of candy bars--
Chompers, Smerks, and Delicious Chocolate. All three candies
come in a one-ounce size while Delicious Chocolate also comes in
a one-pound mini-bar bag.

The basic ingredients used are chocolate, peanuts, and
caramel. Delicious Chocolate is all chocolate, while Chompers
consists of chocolate and carmel, and Smerks consists of
chocolate, caramel and peanuts. Chompers' recipe allows for the
amount of caramel to be anywhere between 18% and 28% of the
candy bar's weight with chocolate making up the rest. Smerks'
recipe calls for an equal amount of caramel and peanuts, with
chocolate making up between 20% and 40% of the bar's weight.

For each one-ounce bar, labor and packaging costs $.012, while
labor and packaging for the one-pound bag costs $.039. The
company has production facilities for making up to 20,000 one-
ounce bars and up to 1000 one-pound bags daily.

Delicious has contracts to produce at least 3000 one-ounce
bars of each type of candy daily. Also, the difference between
the number of Chompers and the number of Smerks produced must be
less than 10% of the total number of Chompers and Smerks made.
The present prices for chocolate, caramel, and peanuts are
$1.60, $.95,, and $1.40 per pound respectively. The company has
contracts which will supply it with at least 1,000 pounds of
chocolate, exactly 350 pounds of caramel, and at most 500 pounds
of peanuts daily.

The company currently sells Chompers one-ounce bars for
$.14, Smerks one-ounce bars for $.16, Delicious Chocolate one-
ounce bars for $.15, and Delicious Chocolate one-pound bags for
$2.30. Formulate a linear program that would determine the
optimal daily production schedule and ingredients required.
(HINT: Variables must be established for each product type and
the amount of each ingredient in each product.)

PROBLEM 15

WeBuild Construction must decide how many small bulldozers to
purchase or lease for the coming year. Bulldozers may be
purchased for $40,000 each and their salvage value at the end of
a year is $20,000. WeBuild can also lease bulldozers for $8,000
per year payable in advance.

WeBuild has $1,000,000 available in its budget for purchase
and/or lease of bulldozers. Any monies not invested in
purchasing or leasing bulldozers will be invested at 8%.

There are 60 projects each requiring four bulldozers
throughout the year. Because of timing and reliability, each
new bulldozer will be available for eight projects, whereas each
leased bulldozer will be available for five projects.

Formulate and solve for the number of bulldozers WeBuild
should purchase and lease to minimize its total annual cost.

PROBLEM 16

John Sweeney is an investment advisor who is attempting to construct an "optimal portfolio" for a client who has $400,000 cash to invest. There are ten different investments, falling into four broad categories that John and his client have identified as potential candidates for this portfolio.
   The following table lists the investments and their important characteristics. Note that Unidyde Equities and Unidyde Debt are two separate investments, whereas First General REIT is a single investment that is considered both an equities and a real estate investment.

Category	Investment	Expected Annual After Tax Return	Liquidity Factor	Risk Factor
Equities	Unidyde Corporation	15.0%	100	60
	Col. Must. Restaurants	17.0%	100	70
	First General REIT	17.5%	100	75
Debt	Metropolitan Electric	11.8%	95	20
	Unidyde Corporation	12.2%	92	30
	Lemonville Transit	12.0%	79	22
Real Estate	Fairview Apartment Partnership	22.0%	0	50
	First General REIT	(See above)		
Money	T-Bill Account	9.6%	80	0
	Money Market Fund	10.5%	100	10
	All Saver's Certificate	12.6%	0	0

Formulate a linear program to accomplish John's objective as an investment advisor which is to construct a portfolio that maximizes his client's total expected after tax return over the next year, subject to a number of constraints placed upon him by the client for the portfolio:

1. Its (weighted) average liquidity factor must be at least 65.
2. The (weighted) average risk factor must be no greater than 55.
3. At most, $60,000 is to be invested in Unidyde Stocks or bonds.
4. No more than 40% of the investment can be in any one category except the money category.
5. No more than 20% of the investment can be in any one investment except the money market fund.
6. At least $1,000 must be invested in the money market fund.
7. The maximum investment in All Saver's Certificates is $15,000.
8. The minimum investment desired for debt is $90,000.
9. At least $10,000 must be placed in a T-Bill account.

PROBLEM 17

BP Cola must decide how much money to allocate for new soda and traditional soda advertising over the coming year. The advertising budget is $10,000,000.

Because BP wants to push its new sodas, at least one-half of the advertising budget is to be devoted to new soda advertising. However, at least $2,000,000 is to be spent on its traditional sodas. BP estimates that each dollar spent on traditional sodas will translate into 100 cans sold, whereas, because of the harder sell needed for new products, each dollar spent on new sodas will translate into 50 cans sold. To attract new customers BP has lowered its profit margin on new sodas to 2 cents per can as compared to 4 cents per can for traditional sodas.

How should BP allocate its advertising budget if it wants to maximize its profits while selling at least 750 million cans?

PROBLEM 18

Maybury Public School System has three high schools to serve a territory divided into five districts. The capacity of each high school, the student population in each district, and the distance (in miles) between each school and the center of each district are listed in the table below:

| | High School | | | |
District	McHale	McCallum	McBride	Student Population
Northeast	1.5	2.5	0.5	700
Southeast	4	1.5	3	1100
Southwest	2.5	3	3.5	900
Northwest	0.5	4	1.5	600
Central	1	2	1	800
Capacity	1500	1800	1100	

Formulate and solve a linear program to determine the school-student assignment that minimizes the total student-miles traveled per day.

PROBLEM 19

The June Company is a department store chain serving three states in the South: Georgia, Alabama, and Mississippi. Recently management has been concerned about the relative efficiency of its Alabama store.

The June Company tabulates the monthly gross sales of home appliances, clothing, home entertainment, and all other divisions and measures these outputs against inputs of store size, number of sales personnel for the store, and the population service area for each store (defined as the number of adults over 16 living within a 35 mile radius of the store.)

The tables below give the average monthly values for each of the inputs and outputs based on last year's data.

Inputs	Georgia	Alabama	Mississippi
Store Size (1000's sq. ft.)	25	24	18
Sales Personnel	250	210	180
Service Area Population (1000's)	600	750	375

Outputs: Average Monthly Sales ($mil.)	Georgia	Alabama	Mississippi
Appliances	1.2	0.8	0.6
Clothing	2.2	1.4	1.5
Home Entertainment	1.6	1.5	1.6
All Others	2.7	2.0	2.1

Based on last year's data, use data envelopment analysis to formulate and solve a linear program to help June Company determine the relative efficiency of its Alabama store.

PROBLEM 20

Niteton Power and Light Company (NPLC) wants to develop an efficient work schedule for its full- and part-time customer service clerks. The number of clerks needed to provide adequate service during each hour the office is open on a weekday is given below:

Hour	AM 8-9	9-10	10-11	11-12	PM 12-1	1-2	2-3	3-4	4-5	5-6
Clerks	5	4	6	8	10	9	7	4	7	5

A full-time clerk works 3 hours, has a 1-hour break, and then works another 3 hours. Part-time clerks work 4 consecutive hours. Full-timers get paid for their break. All clerks start work on the hour.

NPLC's office manager insists that at least one full-time clerk be on duty during all open hours and that a minimum of four full-time clerks are on the payroll. A full-time clerk costs NPLC $9.00 per hour, and a part-timer costs $6.50 per hour.

Formulate a linear program that will provide a schedule that will meet NPLC's customer service needs at a minimum labor cost. (Hint: there are 4 different full-time shifts and 7 different part-time shifts.)

TRUE/FALSE

21. Sunk costs should be viewed as relevant costs when developing the objective function for a linear programming model.

22. Double-subscript notation for decision variables should be avoided unless the number of decision variables exceeds nine.

23. Generating the data for large-scale LP models can be more time consuming than either the formulation of the model or the development of the computer solution.

24. Using minutes as the unit of measurement on the left-hand side of a constraint and using hours on the right-hand side is acceptable since both are a measure of time.

25. Using data envelopment analysis (DEA), the efficiency of a unit is compared to the most efficient unit in the reference group.

26. A company makes two products from steel; one requires 2 tons of steel and the other requires 3 tons. There are 100 tons of steel available daily. A constraint on daily production could be written as: $2X_1 + 3X_2 \leq 100$.

27. Using DEA, if a unit's optimal value of E is less than 1, the unit can be judged relatively inefficient.

28. DEA does not necessarily identify the operating units that are relatively efficient.

29. Using DEA to evaluate a large group of operating units, roughly one-fourth of the units can be identified as inefficient.

30. If a real-world problem is correctly formulated, it is impossible to have alternative optimal solutions.

31. A company makes two products; the first sells for $100 and the second for $90. The variable production costs are $30 per unit for the first product, $25 for the second. The company's objective could be written as: MAX $190X_1 - 55X_2$.

32. The primary limitation of linear programming's applicability is the requirement that all decision variables be nonnegative.

33. If an LP problem is not correctly formulated, the computer will indicate it is infeasible when trying to solve it.

34. The wide-spread use of linear programming is due largely to the fact that the nature of most business functions is linear.

35. A decision maker would be wise to not deviate from the optimal solution found by an LP model because it is the best solution.

CHAPTER

5

Linear Programming: The Simplex Method

KEY CONCEPTS

CONCEPT	ILLUSTRATED PROBLEMS	ANSWERED PROBLEMS
Problem Formulation	7	14
Standard Form	1,2,4,5,7	8,9,10,14,15
Tableau Form	1,2,4,5,7	8,9,10,14,15
Artificial Variables	4,5,7	9,10,11,15
Minimization Problems	2,4	8,10
Infeasibility	5	11
Unboundedness	5	11
Alternate Optimal Solutions	6	14
Degeneracy	--	13

REVIEW

1. The <u>simplex</u> <u>method</u> is an algebraic method for solving linear programs. (See description of algorithm on the next page.) The more recently developed Karmarkar method holds promise of solving large linear programs even more quickly than the simplex method.

2. The steps leading to the simplex method are as follows:

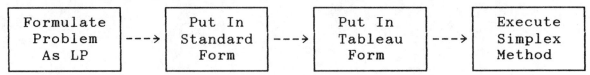

3. Putting an LP formulation into <u>standard</u> <u>form</u> involves adding slack and/or subtracting surplus variables, as discussed in Chapter 2.

4. The <u>simplex</u> <u>tableau</u> is a convenient means for performing the calculations required by the simplex method.

5. A set of equations is in <u>tableau</u> <u>form</u> if for each equation: (1) its right hand side (RHS) is non-negative and, (2) there is a <u>basic</u> <u>variable</u>. A basic variable for an equation is a variable whose coefficient in the equation is +1 and whose coefficient in all other equations of the problem is 0.

6. If a constraint is formulated with a <u>negative</u> <u>right-hand</u> <u>side</u>, multiply it by -1 before adding slack, surplus, or artificial variables.

7. To generate an initial tableau form, <u>artificial</u> <u>variables</u> must be added to all constraints which do not have a basic variable. These normally include "greater than or equal to" constraints and "equal to" constraints.

8. <u>Artificial</u> <u>variables</u> are given an objective function coefficient of -M in maximization problems (+M in minimization problems), where M is an extremely large number. Once an artificial variable becomes non-basic, it may be eliminated from further consideration by dropping its column.

9. If the problem has a <u>minimization</u> <u>objective</u>, multiply the objective function by -1 before solving by the simplex method.

10. A <u>basic</u> <u>feasible</u> <u>solution</u> for a problem in tableau form is found by setting the basic variables equal to the right hand side values of the equations and the other variables (the <u>non-basic</u> <u>variables</u>) to 0.

11. Basic feasible solutions are equivalent to <u>extreme points</u>, and for a linear program with an optimal solution, a basic feasible solution must be optimal.

12. The $\underline{C}_j - \underline{Z}_j$ row of a simplex tableau represents the amount the objective function will increase per unit increase in the corresponding column variable. For a maximization problem, the most positive entry in this row determines the <u>entering variable</u>.

13. A <u>tableau's</u> <u>right-hand</u> <u>side</u> gives the values of the current basic variables.

14. The minimizing ratio between the right hand side values and positive numbers in the column of the entering variable determines which current basic variable will reach zero first as the entering variable is increased. This variable is called the <u>leaving variable</u>.

15. <u>Infeasibility</u> is detected in the simplex method when an artificial variable remains positive in the final tableau.

16. A linear program has an <u>unbounded solution</u> if all entries in an entering column are non-positive.

17. A linear program has <u>alternate optimal solutions</u> if the final tableau has a $C_j - Z_j$ value equal to 0 for a non-basic variable.

18. A <u>degenerate solution</u> to a linear program is one in which at least one of the basic variables equals 0. This can occur at formulation or if there is a tie for the minimizing value in the ratio test to determine the leaving variable.

SETTING UP INITIAL SIMPLEX TABLEAU

Step 1: If the problem is a minimization problem, multiply the objective function by -1.

Step 2: If the problem formulation contains any constraints with negative right-hand sides, multiply each constraint by -1.

Step 3: Add a slack variable to each $\leq$ constraint.

Step 4: Subtract a surplus variable and add an artificial variable to each $\geq$ constraint.

Step 5: Add an artificial variable to each = constraint.

Step 6: Set each slack and surplus variable's coefficient in the objective function equal to zero.

Step 7: Set each artificial variable's coefficient in the objective function equal to -M, where M is a very large number.

Step 8: Each slack and artificial variable becomes one of the basic variables in the initial basic feasible solution.

FLOW CHART FOR
SETTING UP INITIAL SIMPLEX TABLEAU

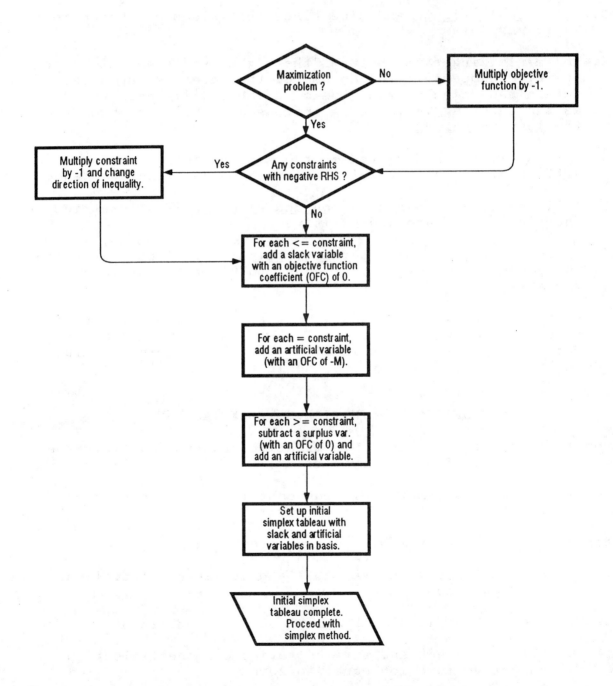

SIMPLEX METHOD

Starting with the initial simplex tableau:

Step 1: <u>Determine</u> <u>the</u> <u>entering</u> <u>variable</u>.
Identify the variable with the most positive value in the $C_j - Z_j$ row.

Step 2: <u>Determine</u> <u>the</u> <u>leaving</u> <u>variable</u>.
For each positive number in the entering column, compute the ratio of the right-hand side values divided by these entering column values.

If there are no positive values in the entering column, STOP; the problem is <u>unbounded</u>.

Otherwise, select the variable with the minimal ratio.

Step 3: <u>Generate</u> <u>the</u> <u>next</u> <u>tableau</u>.
(The entering column is called the <u>pivot</u> <u>column</u> and the leaving row is called the <u>pivot</u> <u>row</u>. The entry which is at the intersection of the pivot row and the pivot column is called the <u>pivot</u> <u>element</u>.)

(a) Divide the pivot row by the pivot element to get a new row. We designate this new row as (row *).

(b) Replace each non-pivot row i with:
[new row i] = [current row i] - [(a_{ij}) x (row *)],
where a_{ij} is the number in the entering column of row i

Step 4: <u>Calculate</u> <u>the</u> Z_j <u>row</u> <u>for</u> <u>the</u> <u>new</u> <u>tableau</u>.
For each column j, multiply the objective function coefficients of the basic variables by the corresponding numbers in column j and sum them.

Step 5: <u>Calculate</u> <u>the</u> $C_j - Z_j$ <u>row</u> <u>for</u> <u>the</u> <u>new</u> <u>tableau</u>.
For each column j, subtract the Z_j row from the C_j row in the tableau.

If all of the values in the $C_j - Z_j$ row are nonpositive, GO TO Step 1.

If there is an artificial variable in the basis with a positive value, the problem is infeasible. STOP.

Otherwise, an optimal solution has been found. The current values of the basic variables are optimal. The optimal values of the non-basic variables are all zero.

If any non-basic variable's $C_j - Z_j$ value is 0, alternate optimal solutions might exist. STOP.

FLOW CHART OF
SIMPLEX METHOD

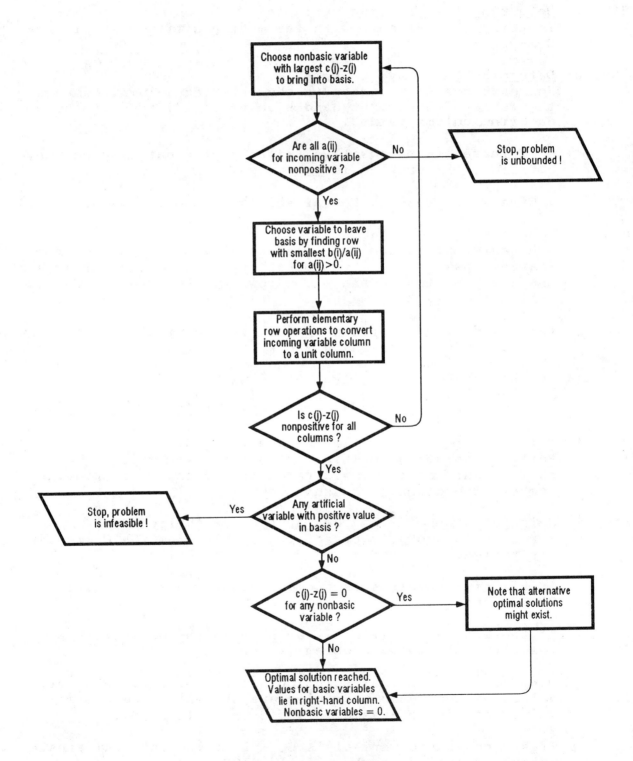

ILLUSTRATED PROBLEMS

PROBLEM 1

Solve the following problem by the simplex method:

$$MAX \ Z = 12X_1 + 18X_2 + 10X_3$$

$$S. \ T. \quad 2X_1 + 3X_2 + 4X_3 \leq 50$$

$$X_1 - X_2 - X_3 \geq 0$$

$$X_2 - 1.5X_3 \geq 0$$

$$X_1, \ X_2, \ X_3 \geq 0$$

SOLUTION 1

The first step is to write the problem in standard form. We can avoid introducing artificial variables to the second and third constraints by multiplying each by -1 (making them $\leq$ constraints). Thus, slack variables S_1, S_2, and S_3 are added to the three constraints, respectively.

$$MAX \ Z = 12X_1 + 18X_2 + 10X_3$$

$$S. \ T. \quad 2X_1 + 3X_2 + 4X_3 + S_1 \leq 50$$

$$X_1 - X_2 - X_3 + S_2 \geq 0$$

$$X_2 - 1.5X_3 + S_3 \geq 0$$

$$X_1, \ X_2, \ X_3, \ S_1, \ S_2, \ S_3 \geq 0$$

This gives the following first tableau:

Basis	C_B	X_1 12	X_2 18	X_3 10	S_1 0	S_2 0	S_3 0	
S_1	0	2	3	4	1	0	0	50
S_2	0	-1	1	1	0	1	0	0	(* row)
S_3	0	0	-1	1.5	0	0	1	0
Z_j		0	0	0	0	0	0	0
$C_j - Z_j$		12	18	10	0	0	0	

Iteration 1

(Step 1) The most positive $C_j - Z_j = 18$. Thus X_2 is the entering variable.

(Step 2) Take the ratio between the right hand side and positive numbers in the X_2 column:

$$50/3 = 16\ 2/3$$
$$0/1 = 0 \qquad \text{<==== minimum}$$

S_2 is the leaving variable and the 1 is the pivot element.

(Step 3) Divide the second row by 1, the pivot element. Call the "new" (in this case, unchanged) row the "* row".
Subtract 3 x (* row) from row 1.
Subtract -1 x (* row) from row 3.
New rows 1, 2, and 3 are shown in the tableau below.

(Step 4) The new Z_j row values are obtained by multiplying the C_B column by each column, element by element and summing. For example, $Z_1 = 5(0) + -1(18) + -1(0) = -18$.

(Step 5) The new C_j-Z_j row values are obtained by subtracting Z_j value in a column from the C_j value in the same column. For example, $C_1-Z_1 = 12 - (-18) = 30$.

Thus, the following tableau is derived with X_2 replacing S_2 as a basic variable.

Basis	C_B	X_1	X_2	X_3	S_1	S_2	S_3		
		12	18	10	0	0	0		
S_1	0	5	0	1	1	-3	0	50	(* row)
X_2	18	-1	1	1	0	1	0	0	
S_3	0	-1	0	2.5	0	1	1	0	
Z_j		-18	18	18	0	18	0	0	
$C_j - Z_j$		30	0	-8	0	-18	0		

Iteration 2

(Step 1) The most positive $C_j - Z_j = 30$. X_1 is the entering variable.

(Step 2) Take the ratio between the right hand side and positive numbers in the X_1 column:

$$10/5 = 2 \quad \text{<==== minimum}$$

There are no ratios for the second and third rows because their column elements (-1) are negative. Thus, S_1 (corresponding to row 1) is the leaving variable and 5 is the pivot element.

(Step 3) Divide row 1 by 5, the pivot element. (Call this new row 1 the "* row").
Subtract (-1) x (* row) from the second row.
Subtract (-1) x (* row) from the third row.
New rows 1, 2, and 3 are shown in the tableau below.

(Step 4) The new Z_j row values are obtained by multiplying the C_B column by each column, element by element and summing. For example, $Z_3 = .2(12) + 1.2(18) + .2(0) = 24$.

(Step 5) The new $C_j - Z_j$ row values are obtained by subtracting Z_j value in a column from the C_j value in the same column. For example, $C_3 - Z_3 = 10 - (24) = -14$.

Thus, the following tableau is derived with X_1 replacing S_1 as a basic variable.

Basis	C_B	X_1	X_2	X_3	S_1	S_2	S_3		
		12	18	10	0	0	0		
X_1	12	1	0	.2	.2	-.6	0	10	(* row)
X_2	18	0	1	1.2	.2	.4	0	10	
S_3	0	0	0	2.7	.2	.4	1	10	
Z_j		12	18	24	6	0	0	300	
$C_j - Z_j$		0	0	-14	-6	0	0		

Since there are no positive numbers in the $C_j - Z_j$ row, this tableau is optimal. The optimal solution is: $X_1 = 10$; $X_2 = 10$; $X_3 = 0$; $S_1 = 0$; $S_2 = 0$ $S_3 = 10$, and the optimal value of the objective function, $Z = 300$.

PROBLEM 2

Solve the following problem by the simplex method:

$$\text{MIN } Z = 8X_1 + 5X_2 + 4X_3$$

$$\text{S. T.} \quad X_1 + X_2 + \geq 10$$

$$X_2 + X_3 \geq 15$$

$$X_1 + X_3 \geq 12$$

$$20X_1 + 10X_2 + 15X_3 \leq 300$$

$$X_1,\ X_2,\ X_3 \geq 0$$

SOLUTION 2

First, write the problem in standard form. Constraints 1, 2, and 3 each require a surplus variable. Constraint 4 requires a slack variable.

$$\text{MIN } Z = 8X_1 + 5X_2 + 4X_3$$

$$\text{S. T.} \quad X_1 + X_2 + - S_1 \geq 10$$

$$X_2 + X_3 - S_2 \geq 15$$

$$X_1 + X_3 - S_3 \geq 12$$

$$20X_1 + 10X_2 + 15X_3 + S_4 \leq 300$$

$$X_1,\ X_2,\ X_3,\ S_1,\ S_2,\ S_3,\ S_4 \geq 0$$

To put in tableau form, add artificial variables A_1, A_2, and A_3 to the constraints 1, 2, and 3, respectively. Since this is a minimization problem, the A's have objective coefficients of +M.

$$\text{MIN } Z = 8X_1 + 5X_2 + 4X_3 + MA_1 + MA_2 + MA_3$$

$$\text{S. T.} \quad X_1 + X_2 + - S_1 \geq 10$$

$$X_2 + X_3 - S_2 \geq 15$$

$$X_1 + X_3 - S_3 \geq 12$$

$$20X_1 + 10X_2 + 15X_3 + S_4 \leq 300$$

$$X_1,\ X_2,\ X_3,\ S_1,\ S_2,\ S_3,\ S_4,\ A_1,\ A_2,\ A_3 \geq 0$$

Before beginning the simplex method, the objective function is converted to maximization by multiplying it by -1.

Iteration 1

Basis	C_B	X_1	X_2	X_3	S_1	S_2	S_3	S_4	A_1	A_2	A_3	
		-8	-5	-4	0	0	0	0	-M	-M	-M	
A_1	-M	1	1	0	-1	0	0	0	1	0	0	10
A_2	-M	0	1	1	0	-1	0	0	0	1	0	15
A_3	-M	1	0	1	0	0	-1	0	0	0	1	12
S_4	0	20	10	15	0	0	0	1	0	0	0	300
Z_j		-2M	-2M	-2M	M	M	M	0	-M	-M	-M	-37M
$C_j - Z_j$		2M-8	2M-5	2M-4	-M	-M	-M	0	0	0	0	

Iteration 2 (Drop the A_3 column)

Basis	C_B	X_1	X_2	X_3	S_1	S_2	S_3	S_4	A_1	A_2	
		-8	-5	-4	0	0	0	0	-M	-M	
A_1	-M	1	1	0	-1	0	0	0	1	0	10
A_2	-M	-1	1	0	0	-1	1	0	0	1	3
X_3	-4	1	0	1	0	0	-1	0	0	0	12
S_4	0	5	10	0	0	0	15	1	0	0	120
Z_j		-4	-2M	-4	M	M	-M+4	0	-M	-M	-13M -48
$C_j - Z_j$		-4	2M-5	0	-M	-M	M-4	0	0	0	

Iteration 3 (Drop the A_2 column)

Basis	C_B	X_1 -8	X_2 -5	X_3 -4	S_1 0	S_2 0	S_3 0	S_4 0	A_1 -M	
A_1	-M	2	0	0	-1	1	-1	0	1	7
X_2	-5	-1	1	0	0	-1	1	0	0	3
X_3	-4	1	0	1	0	0	-1	0	0	12
S_4	0	15	0	0	0	10	5	1	0	90
Z_j		-2M+1	-5	-4	M	-M+5	M-1	0	-M	-7M -63
$C_j - Z_j$		2M-9	0	0	-M	M-5	-M+1	0	0	

Iteration 4 (Drop the A_3 column)

Basis	C_B	X_1 -8	X_2 -5	X_3 -4	S_1 0	S_2 0	S_3 0	S_4 0	
X_1	-8	1	0	0	-1/2	1/2	-1/2	0	7/2
X_2	-5	0	1	0	-1/2	-1/2	1/2	0	13/2
X_3	-4	0	0	1	1/2	-1/2	-1/2	0	17/2
S_4	0	0	0	0	15/2	5/2	25/2	1	75/2
Z_j		-8	-5	-4	9/2	1/2	7/2	0	-189/2
$C_j - Z_j$		0	0	0	-9/2	-1/2	-7/2	0	

This is the optimal tableau. Thus the optimal solution is:

$$X_1 = 7/2 \qquad S_1 = 0$$
$$X_2 = 13/2 \qquad S_2 = 0$$
$$X_3 = 17/2 \qquad S_3 = 0$$
$$S_4 = 75/2$$

Because we multiplied the objective function by -1, the optimal maximization value of Z is 189/2 or 94.5.

PROBLEM 3

At some iteration of the simplex method, the tableau is the following:

Basis	C_B	X_1	X_2	S_1	S_2	S_3	S_4	
		10	6	0	0	0	0	
X_2	6	0	1	3	0	-2	0	7
S_2	0	0	0	4	1	3	0	8
X_1	10	1	0	-2	0	2	0	16
S_4	0	0	0	0	0	4	1	10
Z_j		10	6	-2	0	8	0	202
$C_j - Z_j$		0	0	2	0	-8	0	

a) Explain the meaning of each number in the tableau.

b) Note S_1 will be the entering variable. Explain why the ratio test is performed only on positive numbers in the S_1 column.

c) Use the simplex method to solve for the optimal solution.

SOLUTION 3

a) The C_j row gives the gross increase in Z per unit increase in the corresponding variable. The Z_j row gives the gross decrease in Z per unit increase in the corresponding variable. Thus, the $C_j - Z_j$ row gives the "net increase" in Z per unit increase in the corresponding variable.

The large matrix (the a_{ij}'s) give the amount the basic variable associated with row i will <u>decrease</u> per unit increase in the corresponding variable of column j.

The C_B column gives the objective function coefficients for the basic variables. The numbers on the right hand side give the current values of the basic variables, i.e. $X_2 = 7$, $S_2 = 8$, $X_1 = 16$, $S_4 = 10$. The bottom right number gives the value of Z = 202.

b) As noted in (a), the a_{ij}'s are the amount of decrease in the basic variable of row i per unit increase in the corresponding variable of column j. Hence, as for every unit S_1 is increased, X_2 decreases by 3, S_2 decreases by 4, and X_1 increases by 2. S_4 will not change as S_1 is increased. From one iteration to the next the variables must stay non-negative. Thus S_1 can increase to 7/3 before X_2 goes to 0 and to 2 (=8/4) before S_2 goes to 0. These are the only limiting factors.

c) (Step 1) The most positive $C_j - Z_j$ is 2. S_1 enters.

(Step 2) The ratio test on positive numbers in the S_1 column gives:

$$7/3 \;=\; 7/3$$
$$8/4 \;=\; 2 \qquad \texttt{<===== minimum}$$

S_2 leaves.

(Step 3) Divide row 2 by 4 to give a new (* row).
Subtract 3 x (* row) from row 1.
Subtract -2 x (* row) from row 3.
Leave row 4 as it is.

(Steps 4 and 5 are reflected in the tableau below.)

Basis	C_B	X_1 10	X_2 6	S_1 0	S_2 0	S_3 0	S_4 0		
X_2	6	0	1	0	-3/4	-17/4	0	1	
S_1	0	0	0	1	1/4	3/4	0	2	(* row)
X_1	10	1	0	0	1/2	7/2	0	20	
S_4	0	0	0	0	0	4	1	10	
Z_j		10	6	0	1/2	19/2	0	206	
$C_j - Z_j$		0	0	0	-1/2	-19/2	0		

Since the $C_j - Z_j$ row has no positive numbers, this is the optimal tableau and the optimal solution: $X_1 = 20$, $X_2 = 1$, $S_1 = 2$, $S_2 = 0$, $S_3 = 0$, $S_4 = 10$, and $Z = 206$.

PROBLEM 4

Given the following minimization problem:

$$\text{MIN } Z = 2X_1 - 3X_2 - 4X_3$$

$$\text{S.T.} \quad X_1 + X_2 + X_3 \leq 30$$

$$2X_1 + X_2 + 3X_3 \geq 60$$

$$X_1 - X_2 + 2X_3 = 20$$

$$X_j \geq 0 \quad j = 1,2,3$$

a) Write the problem in standard form. Explain why this is not tableau form.

b) Add artificial variables and amend the objective function appropriately to obtain the first tableau form.

c) Solve the problem by the simplex method.

SOLUTION 4

a)
$$\text{MIN } Z = 2X_1 - 3X_2 - 4X_3$$

$$\text{S.T.} \quad X_1 + X_2 + X_3 + S_1 \qquad = 30$$

$$2X_1 + X_2 + 3X_3 \qquad -S_2 = 60$$

$$X_1 - X_2 + 2X_3 \qquad = 20$$

$$X_j \geq 0 \quad j = 1,2,3; \quad S_j \geq 0 \quad j = 1,2$$

This is not tableau form because the second and third constraints do not have basic variables, i.e. variables whose coefficient in that constraint is +1, and whose coefficient in the other constraints is 0.

b) Add artificial variables A_2 and A_3 to the second and third constraints, respectively. Since this is a minimization problem, the A's objective function coefficients are +M.

$$\text{MIN } Z = 2X_1 - 3X_2 - 4X_3 \qquad\qquad + MA_2 + MA_3$$

$$\text{S.T.} \quad X_1 + X_2 + X_3 + S_1 \qquad\qquad\qquad = 30$$

$$2X_1 + X_2 + 3X_3 \qquad -S_2 + A_2 \qquad = 60$$

$$X_1 - X_2 + 2X_3 \qquad\qquad + A_3 = 20$$

$$X_j \geq 0 \quad j = 1,2,3; \quad S_j, A_j \geq 0 \quad j = 1,2$$

c) Before beginning the simplex method, the objective function is multiplied by -1, so that the maximization algorithm may be used.

Iteration 1

Basis	C_B	X_1	X_2	X_3	S_1	S_2	A_2	A_3	
		-2	3	4	0	0	-M	-M	
S_1	0	1	1	1	1	0	0	0	30
A_2	-M	2	1	3	0	-1	1	0	60
A_3	-M	1	-1	2	0	0	0	1	20
Z_j		-3M	0	-5M	0	M	-M	-M	-80M
$C_j - Z_j$		3M-2	3	5M+4	0	-M	0	0	

Iteration 2   (Drop the A_3 column)

Basis	C_B	X_1	X_2	X_3	S_1	S_2	A_2	
		-2	3	4	0	0	-M	
S_1	0	1/2	3/2	0	1	0	0	20
A_2	-M	1/2	5/2	0	0	-1	1	30
X_3	4	1/2	-1/2	1	0	0	0	10
Z_j		-(1/2M) +2	-(5/2)M -2	4	0	M	-M	-30M +40
$C_j - Z_j$		(1/2)M -4	(5/2)M +5	0	0	-M	0	

Iteration 3   (Drop the A_2 column)

Basis	C_B	X_1	X_2	X_3	S_1	S_2	
		-2	3	4	0	0	
S_1	0	1/5	0	0	1	3/5	2
X_2	3	1/5	1	0	0	-2/5	12
X_3	4	3/5	0	1	0	-1/5	16
Z_j		3	3	4	0	-2	100
$C_j - Z_j$		-5	0	0	0	2	

Iteration 4

Basis	C_B	X_1	X_2	X_3	S_1	S_2	
		-2	3	4	0	0	
S_2	0	1/3	0	0	5/3	1	10/3
X_2	3	1/3	1	0	2/3	0	40/3
X_3	4	2/3	0	1	1/3	0	50/3
Z_j		11/3	3	4	10/3	0	320/3
$C_j - Z_j$		-17/3	0	0	-10/3	0	

This is the optimal tableau. Thus the optimal solution is:

$$X_1 = 0$$
$$X_2 = 40/3$$
$$X_3 = 50/3$$
$$S_1 = 0$$
$$S_2 = 10/3$$

Because we multiplied the objective function by -1, the optimal minimization value of $Z = -320/3$.

PROBLEM 5

Solve problem #4 of Chapter 2 by the simplex method.

SOLUTION 5

For the first problem, the standard form is:

$$MAX \ Z = 2X_1 + 6X_2$$

$$S.T. \quad 4X_1 + 3X_2 + S_1 \qquad = 12$$

$$2X_1 + X_2 \qquad - S_2 = 8$$

$$X_1, \ X_2, \ S_1, \ S_2 \geq 0$$

Artificial variable A_2 is added to the second constraint to obtain the first tableau form. (A_2 has an objective function coefficient of $-M$.)

Iteration 1

Basis	C_B	X_1	X_2	S_1	S_2	A_2	
		2	6	0	0	$-M$	
S_1	0	4	3	1	0	0	12
A_2	$-M$	2	1	0	-1	1	8
Z_j		$-2M$	$-M$	0	M	$-M$	$-8M$
$C_j - Z_j$		$2M+2$	$6+M$	0	$-M$	0	

Iteration 2

Basis	C_B	X_1	X_2	S_1	S_2	A_2	
		2	6	0	0	$-M$	
X_1	2	1	$3/4$	$1/4$	0	0	3
A_2	$-M$	0	$-1/2$	$-1/2$	-1	1	2
Z_j		2	$(1/2)M+3/2$	$(1/2)M+1/2$	M	$-M$	$-2M+6$
$C_j - Z_j$		0	$-(1/2)M+9/2$	$-(1/2)M-1/2$	$-M$	0	

This is the last tableau since all $C_j - Z_j \leq 0$. But since an artificial variable is still positive, this indicates the problem is _infeasible_.

For the second problem the standard form is:

$$\text{MAX } Z = 3X_1 + 4X_2$$

$$\text{S.T.} \quad X_1 + X_2 - S_1 \qquad\quad = 5$$

$$3X_1 + X_2 \qquad - S_2 = 8$$

$$X_1, X_2, S_1, S_2 \geq 0$$

Artificial variables are added to both constraints to obtain the initial tableau form.

Iteration 1

		X_1	X_2	S_1	S_2	A_1	A_2	
Basis	C_B	3	4	0	0	-M	-M	
A_1	-M	1	1	-1	0	1	0	5
A_2	-M	3	1	0	-1	0	1	8
Z_j		-4M	-2M	M	M	-M	-M	-13M
$C_j - Z_j$		4M+3	2M+4	-M	-M	0	0	

Iteration 2 (Drop A_2)

		X_1	X_2	S_1	S_2	A_1	
Basis	C_B	3	4	0	0	-M	
A_1	-M	0	2/3	-1	1/3	1	7/3
X_1	3	1	1/3	0	-1/3	0	8/3
Z_j		3	-(2/3)M+1	M	-(1/3)M-1	-M	-(7/3)M+8
$C_j - Z_j$		0	(2/3)M+3	-M	(1/3)M+1	0	

Iteration 3   (Drop A_1)

Basis	C_B	X_1 3	X_2 4	S_1 0	S_2 0	
X_2	4	0	1	-3/2	1/2	7/2
X_1	3	1	0	1/2	-1/2	3/2
Z_j		3	4	-9/2	1/2	37/2
$C_j - Z_j$		0	0	9/2	-1/2	

Iteration 4

Basis	C_B	X_1 3	X_2 4	S_1 0	S_2 0	
X_2	4	3	1	0	-1	8
S_1	0	2	0	1	-1	3
Z_j		12	4	0	-4	32
$C_j - Z_j$		-9	0	0	4	

Note that $C_4 - Z_4 = 4$ (positive) but its column is all non-positive. This indicates that the problem is <u>unbounded</u>.

PROBLEM 6

Given the following optimal tableau for a linear programming problem:

Basis	C_B	X_1	X_2	X_3	S_1	S_2	S_3	S_4	
		2	4	6	0	0	0	0	
S_3	0	0	0	2	4	-2	1	0	8
X_2	4	0	1	2	2	-1	0	0	6
X_1	2	1	0	-1	1	2	0	0	4
S_4	0	0	0	1	3	2	0	1	12
Z_j		2	4	6	10	0	0	0	32
$C_j - Z_j$		0	0	0	-10	0	0	0	

a) Give the optimal solution associated with this tableau.

b) Give an optimal solution with X_3 replacing X_2 in the tableau.

c) Give an optimal solution with S_2 replacing X_1 in the tableau in part (a).

d) Take an arbitrary weighted average of the extreme points found in (a), (b), and (c), say .5, .3, .2 respectively. Show that this point is feasible by substituting into the equations defined by the above tableau, and demonstrate that it is optimal by showing its objective function value is 32. CONCLUSION: A weighted average of optimal solutions is also optimal.

SOLUTION 6

a) $X_1 = 4$
$X_2 = 6$
$X_3 = 0$
$S_1 = 0$
$S_2 = 0$
$S_3 = 8$
$S_4 = 12$
$Z = 32$

b) X_3 is non-basic and its $C_3 - Z_3 = 0$. This indicates that there are alternate optimal solutions. This 0 indicates that if X_3 were increased, the value of the objective function would not change.

Thus, another optimal solution may be found by choosing X_3 as the entering variable and performing one iteration of the simplex method. This gives the following tableau:

Basis	C_B	X_1 2	X_2 4	X_3 6	S_1 0	S_2 0	S_3 0	S_4 0	
S_3	0	0	-1	0	2	-1	1	0	2
X_3	6	0	1/2	1	1	-1/2	0	0	3
X_1	2	1	1/2	0	2	3/2	0	0	7
S_4	0	0	-1/2	0	2	5/2	0	1	9
Z_j		2	4	6	10	0	0	0	32
$C_j - Z_j$		0	0	0	-10	0	0	0	

$$X_1 = 7 \quad S_1 = 0 \quad Z = 32$$
$$X_2 = 0 \quad S_2 = 0$$
$$X_3 = 3 \quad S_3 = 2$$
$$S_4 = 9$$

c) Similarly doing an iteration of the simplex iteration using S_2 as the entering variable in the given tableau yields:

Basis	C_B	X_1 2	X_2 4	X_3 6	S_1 0	S_2 0	S_3 0	S_4 0	
S_3	0	1	0	1	5	0	1	0	12
X_2	4	1/2	1	3/2	5/2	0	0	0	8
S_2	0	1/2	0	-1/2	1/2	1	0	0	2
S_4	0	-1	0	2	2	0	0	1	8
Z_j		2	4	6	10	0	0	0	32
$C_j - Z_j$		0	0	0	-10	0	0	0	

This gives an optimal solution of:

$$
\begin{array}{lll}
X_1 = 0 & S_1 = 0 & Z = 32 \\
X_2 = 8 & S_2 = 2 & \\
X_3 = 0 & S_3 = 12 & \\
& S_4 = 8 &
\end{array}
$$

d) Take: .5 x (Values in part (a))
        + .3 x (Values in part (b))
        + .2 x (Values in part (c)).

This gives:

$$
\begin{array}{lll}
X_1 = .5(4) + .3(7) + .2(0) & = 4.1 \\
X_2 = .5(6) + .3(0) + .2(8) & = 4.6 \\
X_3 = .5(0) + .3(3) + .2(0) & = .9 \\
S_1 = .5(0) + .3(0) + .2(0) & = 0 \\
S_2 = .5(0) + .3(0) + .2(2) & = .4 \\
S_3 = .5(8) + .3(2) + .2(12) & = 7.0 \\
S_4 = .5(12)+ .3(9) + .2(8) & = 10.3
\end{array}
$$

Feasibility:

The first equation is: $2X_3 + 4S_1 - 2S_2 + S_3 = 8$
    Substituting, $2(.9) + 4(0) - 2(.4) + 7 \stackrel{?}{=} 8$

The second equation is: $X_2 + 2X_3 + 2S_1 - S_2 = 6$
    Substituting, $4.6 + 2(.9) + 2(0) - .4 \stackrel{?}{=} 6$

The third equation is: $X_1 - X_3 + S_1 + 2S_2 = 4$
    Substituting, $4.1 - .9 + 0 + 2(.4) \stackrel{?}{=} 4$

The fourth equation is: $X_3 + 3S_1 + 2S_2 + S_4 = 12$
    Substituting, $.9 + 3(0) + 2(.4) + 10.3 \stackrel{?}{=} 12$.

Therefore this solution is feasible.

Optimality:

$Z = 2X_1 + 4X_2 + 6X_3 = 2(4.1) + 4(4.6) + 6(.9) = 32$.

Thus, this is also an optimal solution.

PROBLEM 7

The Hondasaki Motorbike Company has the capability of making three kinds of motorbikes -- the C-90, the C-250, and the C-700.
   Although this is a small company, only three materials (denoted A, B, C) are in short enough supply to limit production. Daily supplies of materials A, B, and C are 400 lbs., 200 lbs., and 300 lbs. respectively. Whereas Hondasaki may have unused material B and C, all material A must be used daily for safety reasons.
   The profit per motorbike and the amount of material needed to make each motorbike are given in the following table.

Motorbike	Profit	Material A	Material B	Material C
C-90	$140	2	1	1
C-250	$300	8	1	0
C-700	$400	2	4	1

a) Solve for the optimal daily production of motorbikes?

b) How much of each of the materials A, B, and C are used daily?

SOLUTION 7

a) This problem can be formulated as follows:

X_1 = number of C-90's produced daily
X_2 = number of C-250's produced daily
X_3 = number of C-700's produced daily

$$MAX \quad Z = 140X_1 + 300X_2 + 400X_3$$

$$S.T. \quad 2X_1 + 8X_2 + 2X_3 = 400$$

$$X_1 + X_2 + 4X_3 \leq 200$$

$$X_1 + X_3 \leq 300$$

$$X_1, X_2, X_3 \geq 0$$

First add slack variables, S_2 and S_3, to the second and third constraints, respectively. Then add an artificial variable, A_1, to the first constraint. This will give the initial simplex tableau (on the next page).
   Using the simplex method, the optimal solution is to produce 40 C-250's and 40 C-700's daily for an optimal daily profit of $28,000. Note that because $C_1 - Z_1$ is zero, there are alternate optimal solutions.

b) From the optimal tableau, $S_2 = 0$, $S_3 = 260$. All of material A and B is used and 40 (= 300 - 260) of material C is used.

Iteration 1

Basis	C_B	X_1 140	X_2 300	X_3 400	S_2 0	S_3 0	A_1 -M	
A_1	-M	2	8	2	0	0	1	400
S_2	0	1	1	4	1	0	0	200
S_3	0	1	0	1	0	1	0	300
Z_j		-2M	-8M	-2M	0	0	-M	-400M
$C_j - Z_j$		2M+140	8M+300	2M+400	0	0	0	

Iteration 2 (Drop A_1).

Basis	C_B	X_1 140	X_2 300	X_3 400	S_2 0	S_3 0	
X_2	300	1/4	1	1/4	0	0	50
S_2	0	3/4	0	15/4	1	0	150
S_3	0	1	0	1	0	1	300
Z_j		75	300	75	0	0	15,000
$C_j - Z_j$		65	0	325	0	0	

Iteration 3

Basis	C_B	X_1 140	X_2 300	X_3 400	S_2 0	S_3 0	
X_2	300	1/5	1	0	-1/15	0	40
X_3	400	1/5	0	1	4/15	0	40
S_3	0	4/5	0	0	-4/15	1	260
Z_j		140	300	400	260/3	0	28,000
$C_j - Z_j$		0	0	0	-260/3	0	

This is the optimal tableau.

ANSWERED PROBLEMS

PROBLEM 8

Consider the following linear program:

$$MIN \ Z = 2X_1 + 3X_2 + 8X_3$$

$$S.T. \quad 4X_1 + 2X_2 + X_3 \geq 15$$

$$2X_1 + X_2 + 6X_3 \geq 30$$

$$X_1, \ X_2, \ X_3 \geq 0$$

a) Write the problem in standard form.

b) Why can you not multiply the equations in (a) by -1 to obtain a first tableau to begin the simplex method?

c) Solve the problem by the simplex method.

PROBLEM 9

Solve the following problem by the simplex method:

$$MAX \ Z = X_1 + 2X_2 - 3X_3$$

$$S.T. \quad X_1 \qquad\qquad\qquad \geq \quad 5$$

$$2X_1 + 3X_2 + 4X_3 \leq 24$$

$$3X_1 + 2X_2 + X_3 = 18$$

$$X_1, \ X_2, \ X_3 \geq 0$$

PROBLEM 10

Solve the following problem by the simplex method.

$$MIN \ Z = 3X_1 + 5X_2 + 1X_3$$

$$S.T. \quad 2X_1 + 4X_2 + 3X_3 \geq 20$$

$$5X_1 + 4X_2 + 6X_3 \leq 45$$

$$X_2 - .5X_3 \leq 0$$

$$X_1 \qquad\qquad\qquad \geq \quad 3$$

$$X_1, \ X_2, \ X_3 \geq 0$$

PROBLEM 11

Consider the following tableaus which have been generated at various times in different maximization linear programs. Give each tableau one of the following characterizations and perform the indicated operation consistent with the choice you have made.

Characterization	Operation

1. Tableau is optimal.

   Give the optimal solution.

2. Tableau is feasible but not yet optimal.

   Do one complete iteration of the simplex method.

3. Tableau indicates the entire problem is infeasible.

   State why.

4. Tableau is infeasible at this stage, but cannot yet state whether or not the problem is feasible.

   Do one complete iteration of the simplex method.

5. Tableau indicates the problem is unbounded.

   State why.

a)

Basis	C_B	X_1 10	X_2 8	X_3 6	S_1 0	S_2 0	S_3 0	A_2 -M	
S_1	0	2	3	4	1	0	0	0	24
A_2	-M	0	1	2	0	-1	0	1	16
S_3	0	1	1	2	0	0	1	0	10
Z_j		0	-M	-2M	0	M	0	-M	-16M
$C_j - Z_j$		10	M+8	2M+6	0	-M	0	0	

b)

Basis	C_B	X_1 4	X_2 6	X_3 10	S_1 0	S_2 0	
S_1	0	3	0	6	1	-1	18
X_2	6	1	1	2	0	2	14
Z_j		6	6	12	0	12	84
$C_j - Z_j$		-2	0	-2	0	-12	

c)

Basis	C_B	X_1 5	X_2 6	X_3 7	S_1 0	S_2 0	
X_1	5	1	0	0	4	0	6
S_2	0	0	0	-2	-2	1	16
X_2	6	0	1	-1	2	0	26
Z_j		5	6	-6	32	0	186
$C_j - Z_j$		0	0	13	-32	0	

d)

Basis	C_B	X_1 10	X_2 8	X_3 4	S_1 0	S_3 0	A_2 -M	
X_1	10	1	2	0	1	0	0	6
A_2	-M	0	-2	0	-1	-1	1	4
X_3	4	0	6	1	1	2	0	2
Z_j		10	2M+44	4	M+14	M+8	-M	-4M+68
$C_j - Z_j$		0	-2M-36	0	-M-14	-M-8	0	

e)

Basis	C_B	X_1 4	X_2 5	X_3 7	S_1 0	S_2 0	
X_3	7	0	0	1	0	0	12
S_2	0	0	2	0	0	1	14
S_1	0	0	3	0	1	0	18
X_1	4	1	-1	0	0	0	20
Z_j		4	-4	7	0	0	164
$C_j - Z_j$		0	9	0	0	0	

PROBLEM 12

Consider the following tableau at a particular iteration of the simplex method:

Basis	C_B	X_1	X_2	X_3	S_1	S_2	S_3	
		4	2	-1	0	0	0	
	0	1	-1	6	0	1		10
	0	0	4	2	1	1		20
	1	0	0	-3	0	1		30
Z_j								
$C_j - Z_j$								

a) Complete the tableau.

b) What is the current basic solution?

c) What would be the change in the objective function for each of the following cases:

   (1) X_3 were increased by 1
   (2) X_3 were increased by 3
   (3) S_1 were increased by 1.5
   (4) S_3 were increased by 2

d) What is the entering variable? Write the equations corresponding to the above tableau. Now, delete all the non-basic variables (since they are set to 0 anyway) except for the entering variable. Use this remaining set of three equations in four unknowns to justify why the ratio test is only performed on positive numbers in the entering column.

e) Explain why the entering variable could not be increased to 10 at this iteration.

f) To what value will the entering variable increase?

g) Use (d) and (f) to determine by how much the objective function will be increased in the next tableau. Use your equations in (d) to determine the values of the other basic variables in the next tableau.

h) Do one iteration of the simplex method to justify your answer in (g).

PROBLEM 13

Consider the following linear programming tableau:

Basis	C_B	X_1	X_2	X_3	S_1	S_2	S_3	
		5	2	1	0	0	0	
X_3	1	2	0	1	-6	1	0	8
X_2	2	1	1	0	4	0	0	4
S_3	0	4	0	0	3	-3	1	20
Z_j		4	2	1	2	1	0	16
$C_j - Z_j$		1	0	0	-2	-1	0	

a) Do one iteration of the simplex method by choosing the first row as the leaving row. What is the new basic solution? Based on the new $C_j - Z_j$ row, is this solution optimal?

b) Repeat (a), but this time choose the second row as the leaving row. What is the new basic solution? Does the new $C_j - Z_j$ row indicate that the solution is optimal?

c) Interpret the results of (a) and (b) by stating a conclusion concerning optimality when degeneracy occurs.

PROBLEM 14

The Doorco Company can produce three kinds of closet doors. Each door must go through two operations: production and finishing. There are 1,000 man-hours available in the production area weekly and 600 man-hours available in the finishing area weekly. Below is a chart which summarizes the number of hours each door must spend in each area as well as the unit profit per door.

Door	Production	Finishing	Profit
Basic	2	2	$3
Standard	3	2	$6
Deluxe	4	2	$8

a) Using the simplex method, show there is an optimal solution in which only one type of door is produced.

b) Using your resulting optimal tableau in (a), give another optimal solution in which two types of doors are produced.

PROBLEM 15

Given the following maximization problem:

$$\text{MAX } Z = 2X_1 + 5X_2 + 5X_3 + 3X_4$$

$$\text{S.T.} \quad 10X_1 + 12X_2 + 10X_3 + 9X_4 \leq 150$$

$$X_1 + X_2 + X_3 \geq 12$$

$$-X_1 + X_2 + X_3 - X_4 \leq 0$$

$$X_j \geq 0 \quad j = 1,2,3,4$$

a) Write the problem in standard form.
b) Set up the initial simplex tableau.
c) Solve the problem by the simplex method.

TRUE/FALSE

16. Once an artificial variable becomes non-basic, it can be dropped from the simplex tableau.

17. If the same slack variable enters the basis more than once, degeneracy exists.

18. Any tableau with a positive value for an artificial variable is infeasible.

19. Suppose X_4 is a non-basic variable in the optimal tableau in which all right-hand values are positive, but $C_4 - Z_4 = 0$. Then there exist optimal solutions with X_4 equal to 0 and also optimal solutions with X_4 positive.

20. One optimal solution to a linear program must be a basic feasible solution.

21. If X_4 is the entering variable and its corresponding column contains all non-positive entries, the problem is infeasible.

22. All elements in the $C_j - Z_j$ row of a simplex tableau must be ≤ 0 for the current solution to be optimal.

23. A problem with degenerate basic feasible solutions could theoretically cycle between non-optimal solutions without reaching the optimal solution.

24. The ratio test determines which current basic variable reaches zero first as the entering variable is increased from zero.

25. A basic solution can be either feasible or infeasible.

26. Writing an LP problem in standard form sometimes requires the introduction of one or more artificial variables.

27. The C_j row determines the "gross" increase, and the Z_j row determines the "gross" decrease, in the objective function per unit increase in the variables. Hence, the $C_j - Z_j$ row gives the "net" increase in the objective function per unit increase in the variables.

28. Degeneracy results from there being alternate optimal solutions to a problem.

29. If there are any slack or surplus variables in the basis, the solution is infeasible for the real-world problem.

30. The simplex method is applicable to maximization problems only

CHAPTER

6

Simplex Based Sensitivity Analyses and Duality

KEY CONCEPTS

CONCEPT	ILLUSTRATED PROBLEMS	ANSWERED PROBLEMS
Range of Optimality	1-3	7-11
Shadow Prices	1-4	7-11
Range of Feasibility	2,4	7,10,11
100% Rule	3	10
Relevant/Sunk Costs	3	8,9,10
Duality	5,6	12,13,14

REVIEW

1. The range of optimality for an objective function coefficient is the range of that coefficient for which the current optimal solution will remain optimal (keeping all other coefficients constant). The objective function value may change is that range.

2. Given an optimal tableau, the range of optimality for C_k can be calculated as follows:
   (a) Change the objective function coefficient to C_k in the C_j row.
   (b) If X_k is basic, then also change the objective function coefficient to C_k in the C_B column and recalculate the Z_j row in terms of C_k.
   (c) Recalculate the $C_j - Z_j$ row in terms of C_k. Determine the range of values for C_k that keep all entries in the $C_j - Z_j$ row less than or equal to 0.

3. If C_k changes to values outside the range of optimality, a new $C_j - Z_j$ row may be generated. The simplex method may then be continued to determine a new optimal solution.

4. A shadow price for a constraint is the increase in the objective function value resulting from a one unit increase in its right-hand side value.

5. Shadow prices are found in the optimal tableau as follows:
   (a) "less than or equal to" constraint -- Z_j value of the corresponding slack variable for the constraint
   (b) "greater than or equal to" constraint -- negative of the Z_j value of the corresponding surplus variable for the constraint
   (c) "equal to" constraint -- Z_j value of the corresponding artificial variable for the constraint.

6. Shadow prices and "DUAL PRICES" on The Management Scientist output are the same thing for maximization problems and negative of each other for minimization problems.

7. The range of feasibility for a right hand side coefficient is the range of that coefficient for which the shadow price remains unchanged. It is also the range for which the current set of basic variables remains the optimal set of basic variables (although their values change.)

8. The <u>range</u> <u>of</u> <u>feasibility</u> for a right-hand side coefficient of a "less than or equal to" constraint, b_k, is calculated as follows:

    (a) Express the right-hand side in terms of b_k by adding b_k times the column of the k-th slack variable to the current optimal right hand side.

    (b) Determine the range of b_k that keeps the right-hand side greater than or equal to 0.

    (c) Add the original right-hand side value b_k (from the <u>original</u> tableau) to these limits for b_k to determine the range of feasibility for b_k.

9. The <u>range</u> <u>of</u> <u>feasibility</u> for "greater than or equal to" constraints is similarly found except one subtracts b_k times the current column of the k-th surplus variable from the current right hand side in step (i) above. For equality constraints this range is similarly found by adding b_k times the current column of the k-th artificial variable to the current right hand side. Otherwise the procedure is the same.

10. For <u>simultaneous</u> <u>changes</u> of two or more objective function coefficients the <u>100%</u> <u>rule</u> provides a guide to whether the optimal solution changes. It states that as long as the sum of the percent changes in the coefficients from their current value to their maximum allowable increase or decrease does not exceed 100%, the solution will not change. Similarly, for shadow prices, the 100% rule can be applied to changes in the the right hand side coefficients.

11. Every linear program (called the <u>primal</u>) has associated with it another linear program called the <u>dual</u>.

12. A maximization linear program is said to be in <u>canonical</u> <u>form</u> if all constraints are "less than or equal to" constraints and the variables are non-negative. The constraints for a minimization problem in non-negative variables in canonical form are "greater than or equal to" constraints.

13. The <u>dual</u> of a maximization problem in canonical form is a minimization problem in canonical form. The rows and columns of the two programs are interchanged and hence the objective function coefficients of one are the right hand side values of the other and vice versa.

14. The optimal value of the objective function of the <u>primal</u> problem equals the optimal value of the objective function of the <u>dual</u> problem.

15. The <u>dual</u> <u>variables</u> are the "value per unit" of the corresponding primal resource, i.e. the shadow prices. Thus, they are found in the Z_j row of the optimal simplex tableau according to rule 5 on the previous page.

16. If the <u>dual</u> is solved, the <u>optimal</u> <u>primal</u> <u>solution</u> is found in Z_j row of the corresponding surplus variable in the optimal dual tableau. The optimal value of the primal's slack variables are the negative of the $C_j - Z_j$ entries in the optimal dual tableau for the dual variables.

17. <u>Convert</u> <u>any</u> <u>linear</u> <u>program</u> to a maximization problem in canonical form as follows:
    (a) minimization objective function -- multiply it by -1
    (b) "less than or equal to" constraint -- leave alone
    (c) "greater than or equal to" constraint -- multiply it by -1
    (d) "equal to" constraints -- form two constraints, one "less than or equal to", the other "greater or equal to"; then multiply this "greater than or equal to" constraint by -1.

18. By employing the rules of (17), the dual can be found to any linear program.

19. Solving the dual might be computationally <u>more</u> <u>efficient</u> when the primal has numerous constraints and few variables.

FLOW CHART FOR
PRIMAL–TO–DUAL CONVERSION

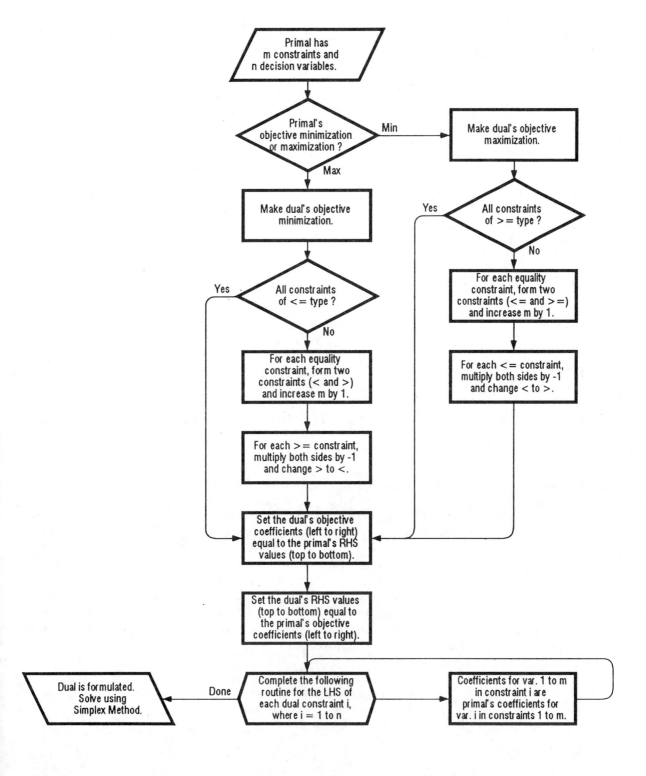

ILLUSTRATED PROBLEMS

PROBLEM 1

Consider the following optimal tableau in which S_1, S_2, and S_3 were the slack variables added to the original problem.

Basis	C_B	X_1	X_2	X_3	X_4	S_1	S_2	S_3	
		5	25	4	10	0	0	0	
X_4	10	0	2	1	1	1	0	-1	50
X_1	5	1	3	-1	0	-1	0	4	80
S_2	0	0	4	2	0	4	1	1	100
Z_j		5	35	5	10	5	0	10	900
$C_j - Z_j$		0	-10	-1	0	-5	0	-10	

a) What is the range of optimality of C_2 and what is the value of the objective function in this range?

b) What is the range of optimality of C_1 and what is the value of the objective function in this range?

c) What is the shadow price for the first resource? Interpret.

SOLUTION 1

a) Change the objective function coefficient C_2 in the coefficient row. Since X_2 is non-basic, there are no changes in the Z_j row. Thus, only $C_2 - Z_2$ changes to $C_2 - 35$. For the tableau to remain optimal, this quantity must be ≤ 0. Thus, $C_2 - 35 \leq 0$ or $C_2 \leq 35$. Since X_2 is 0, there is no change in the objective function value.

b) Replace the objective function coefficient for X_1 with C_1. Since X_1 is basic, change the coefficient in the C_B column for X_1 to C_1 and recalculate the Z_j and $C_j - Z_j$ rows. This gives the following tableau:

Basis	C_B	X_1 C_1	X_2 25	X_3 4	X_4 10	S_1 0	S_2 0	S_3 0	
X_4	10	0	2	1	1	1	0	-1	50
X_1	C_1	1	3	-1	0	-1	0	4	80
S_2	0	0	4	2	0	4	1	1	100
Z_j		C_1	$20+3C_1$	$10-C_1$	10	$10-C_1$	0	$-10+4C_1$	500 $+80C_1$
$C_j - Z_j$		0	$5-3C_1$	$-6+C_1$	0	$-10+C_1$	0	$10-4C_1$	

All $C_j - Z_j$ must remain ≤ 0 for the above tableau to remain optimal.

For $5 - 3C_1 \leq 0$, then $C_1 \geq 5/3$.
For $-6 + C_1 \leq 0$, then $C_1 \leq 6$.
For $-10 + C_1 \leq 0$, then $C_1 \leq 10$.
For $10 - 4C_1 \leq 0$, then $C_1 \geq 5/2$.

Combining all these inequalities, the range of optimality for C_2 is:

$$5/2 \leq C_1 \leq 6$$

As seen from above, in this range, the value of the objective function is $500+80C_1$.

c) The shadow price for the first resource is the Z_j value for S_1. Hence, the shadow price for the first resource is 5. It is the amount the objective function will increase per unit increase in the availability of the first resource available.

PROBLEM 2

Given the following linear program:

$$MAX \ Z = 2X_1 + X_2 + 3X_3$$

$$S.T. \qquad X_1 + 4X_2 + 4X_3 \leq 20$$

$$4X_1 + 4X_2 + X_3 \leq 20$$

$$X_1, \ X_2, \ X_3 \geq 0$$

a) Solve this linear program by the simplex method.

b) Calculate the range of optimality for each of the three decision variables.

c) Suppose a profit could be made on the slack of the first resource. What profit value on this slack would be sufficient to change the optimal solution?

d) By how much would the optimal value of the objective function change for a unit increase of the second resource?

e) Calculate the range of feasibility for b_2. Interpret.

SOLUTION 2

a)

Basis	C_B	X_1 2	X_2 1	X_3 3	S_1 0	S_2 0	
S_1	0	1	4	4	1	0	20
S_2	0	4	4	1	0	1	20
Z_j		0	0	0	0	0	0
$C_j - Z_j$		2	1	3	0	0	

Basis	C_B	X_1 2	X_2 1	X_3 3	S_1 0	S_2 0	
X_3	3	1/4	1	1	1/4	0	5
S_2	0	15/4	3	0	-1/4	1	15
Z_j		3/4	3	3	3/4	0	15
$C_j - Z_j$		5/4	-2	0	-3/4	0	

Basis	C_B	X_1	X_2	X_3	S_1	S_2	
		2	1	3	0	0	
X_3	3	0	4/5	1	4/15	-1/15	4
X_1	2	1	4/5	0	-1/15	4/15	4
Z_j		2	4	3	2/3	1/3	20
$C_j - Z_j$		0	-3	0	-2/3	-1/3	

Opt. solution: $X_1 = 4$, $X_2 = 0$, $X_3 = 4$, $S_1 = 0$, $S_2 = 0$, $Z = 20$

b) For C_1: Since X_1 is basic, change the objective function coefficient in the objective function row and C_B column. The Z_j row and $C_j - Z_j$ rows must be recalculated in terms of C_1.

Z_j	C_1	$\begin{array}{c}(12/5)\\+(4/5)C_1\end{array}$	3	$\begin{array}{c}(4/5)\\-(1/15)C_1\end{array}$	$\begin{array}{c}(-1/5)\\+(4/15)C_1\end{array}$	
$C_j - Z_j$	0	$\begin{array}{c}(-7/5)\\-(4/5)C_1\end{array}$	0	$\begin{array}{c}(-4/5)\\+(1/15)C_1\end{array}$	$\begin{array}{c}(1/5)\\-(4/15)C_1\end{array}$	

For $(-7/5) - (4/5)C_1 \leq 0$, then $C_1 \geq -7/4$.
For $(-4/5) + (1/15)C_1 \leq 0$, then $C_1 \leq 12$.
For $(1/5) - (4/15)C_1 \leq 0$, then $C_1 \geq 3/4$.

Thus $3/4 \leq C_1 \leq 12$.

For C_2: Since X_2 is a non-basic variable, only change X_2's objective function coefficient value to C_2. The Z_j value for X_2 remains 4. Hence its $C_j - Z_j$ value is $C_2 - 4$. Since this quantity must be ≤ 0, then $C_2 \leq 4$ is the only restriction.

For C_3: Since X_3 is basic, change the objective function coefficient in the objective function row and C_B column. The Z_j row and $C_j - Z_j$ rows must be recalculated in terms of C_3.

Z_j	2	$\begin{array}{c}(8/5)\\+(4/5)C_3\end{array}$	C_3	$\begin{array}{c}(-2/15)\\+(4/15)C_3\end{array}$	$\begin{array}{c}(8/15)\\-(1/15)C_3\end{array}$	
$C_j - Z_j$	0	$\begin{array}{c}(-3/5)\\-(4/5)C_3\end{array}$	0	$\begin{array}{c}(2/15)\\-(4/15)C_3\end{array}$	$\begin{array}{c}(-8/15)\\+(1/15)C_3\end{array}$	

For $(-3/5) - (4/5)C_3 \leq 0$, then $C_3 \geq -3/4$.
For $(2/15) - (4/15)C_3 \leq 0$, then $C_3 \geq 1/2$.
For $(-8/15) + (1/15)C_3 \leq 0$, then $C_3 \leq 8$.

Thus $1/2 \leq C_3 \leq 8$.

c) Change S_1's objective function coefficient to C_4. The only
other change would be in the C_j - Z_j row for S_1 and would be:
C_4 - 2/3. For optimality this quantity must be $\leq$ 0. Thus C_4
$\leq$ 2/3. If $C_4 \geq$ 2/3, then the optimal solution will change.

d) This is the shadow price for the second constraint. It is
found in the S_2 column in the Z_j row of the optimal tableau
and is 1/3.

e) The new RHS is altered by vb_2 x (the current S_2 column). To
maintain feasibility, the RHS must stay $\geq$ 0. Thus,
$$4 - (1/15)vb_2 \geq 0 \quad \text{or} \quad vb_2 \leq 60.$$
and, $4 + (4/15)vb_2 \geq 0 \quad$ or $\quad vb_2 \geq$ -15.

Thus, $-15 \leq vb_2 \leq$ 60, or since b_2 was originally 20, the
range of feasibility for b_2 is: $5 \leq b_2 \leq$ 80. Within this
range the shadow prices remain constant.

PROBLEM 3

Jonni's Toy Company produces stuffed toy animals and is gearing
up for the Christmas rush by hiring temporary workers giving it
a total production crew of 30 workers. Jonni's makes two sizes
of stuffed animals. The profit, the production time and the
material used per toy animal is summarized in the table below.
Workers work 8 hours per day and there are up to 2000 pounds of
material available daily.

Size	Profit	Production Time (hrs.)	Material (lbs.)
Small	$3	.10	1
Large	$8	.30	2

a) Find the optimal daily production level by the simplex
method.

b) Calculate the range of the profits on each of the animals
such that the solution in (a) does not change.

c) Will the solution change if the profit on small animals is
increased by $.75? Will the objective function value change?

d) Will the solution change if the profit on large animals is
increased by $.75? Will the objective function value change?

e) Will the solution change if the profits on both large and
small animals are increased by $.75?   Will the value of the
objective function change?

f) The unit profits do not include a per unit labor cost. Given
this, what is the maximum wage Jonni should pay for overtime?

SOLUTION 3

a) X_1 = number of small stuffed animals produced daily
X_2 = number of large stuffed animals produced daily

$$MAX \quad Z = 3X_1 + 8X_2$$

$$S.T. \qquad .1X_1 + .3X_2 \leq 240$$

$$X_1 + 2X_2 \leq 2000$$

$$X_1, \ X_2 \geq 0$$

Basis	C_B	X_1	X_2	S_1	S_2	
		3	8	0	0	
S_1	0	.1	.3	1	0	240
S_2	0	1	2	0	1	2000
Z_j		0	0	0	0	0
$C_j - Z_j$		3	8	0	0	

Basis	C_B	X_1	X_2	S_1	S_2	
		3	8	0	0	
X_2	8	1/3	1	10/3	0	800
S_2	0	1/3	0	-20/3	1	400
Z_j		8/3	8	80/3	0	6400
$C_j - Z_j$		1/3	0	-80/3	0	

Basis	C_B	X_1	X_2	S_1	S_2	
		3	8	0	0	
X_2	8	0	1	10	-1	400
X_1	3	1	0	-20	3	1200
Z_j		3	8	20	1	6,800
$C_j - Z_j$		0	0	-20	-1	

Produce 1200 small and 400 large stuffed animals daily for a daily profit of $6,800.

b) <u>Range of optimality for small stuffed animals</u> (C_1)
Replace 3 by C_1 in the objective function row and C_B column. Then recalculate Z_j and $C_j - Z_j$ rows.

Z_j	C_1	8	80	$-20C_1$	-8	$+3C_1$	$3200 + 1200C_1$
$C_j - Z_j$	0	0	-80	$+20C_1$	8	$-3C_1$	

For the $C_j - Z_j$ row to remain non-positive, $8/3 \le C_1 \le 4$

<u>Range of optimality for large stuffed animals</u> (C_2)
Replace 8 by C_2 in the objective function row and C_B column. Then recalculate Z_j and $C_j - Z_j$ rows.

Z_j	3	C_2	-60	$+10C_2$	9	$- C_2$	$3600 + 400C_2$
$C_j - Z_j$	0	0	60	$-10C_2$	-9	$+ C_2$	

For the $C_j - Z_j$ row to remain non-positive, $6 \le C_2 \le 9$

c) If the profit on small stuffed animals is changed to $3.75, this is within the range of optimality and the optimal solution will not change. However, since X_1 is a basic variable at positive value, changing its objective function coefficient will change the value of the objective function to $3200 + 1200(3.75) = 7700$.

d) If the profit on large stuffed animals is changed to $8.75, this is within the range of optimality and the optimal solution will not change. However, since X_2 is a basic variable at positive value, changing its objective function coefficient will change the value of the objective function to $3600 + 400(8.75) = 7100$.

e) If both the profits change by $.75, since the maximum increase for C_1 is $1 (from $3 to $4) and the maximum increase in C_2 is $1 (from $8 to $9), the overall sum of the percent changes is $(.75/1) + (.75/1) = 75\% + 75\% = 150\%$. This total is greater than 100%; both the optimal solution and the value of the objective function change.

f) Since the unit profits do not include a per unit labor cost, man-hours is a sunk cost. Thus the shadow price for man-hours gives the maximum worth of man-hours (overtime). This is found in the Z_j row in the S_1 column (since S_1 is the slack for man-hours) and is $20.

PROBLEM 4

Consider problem 7 of Chapter 5 in which three types of motorcycles were being produced with three constraining materials. Suppose one could purchase either material B or material C for $90 per pound. Which material(s) should be purchased if the per unit profits reflected a $15 per pound cost of material A, a $20 per pound cost of material B and a $25 per pound cost of material C? Within what limits of the material are you sure this would be a correct decision?
The optimal tableau was:

Basis	C_B	X_1 140	X_2 300	X_3 400	S_2 0	S_3 0	
X_2	300	1/5	1	0	-1/15	0	40
X_3	400	1/5	0	1	4/15	0	40
S_3	0	4/5	0	0	-4/15	1	260
Z_j		140	300	400	260/3	0	28,000
$C_j - Z_j$		0	0	0	-260/3	0	

SOLUTION 4

The shadow price for material B is the Z_j value of S_2 and is 260/3 = $86.67. In this problem, material costs are <u>relevant</u> costs and hence the shadow prices reflect the premium above the normal cost of the resource if it is positive. Thus since material B was figured at $20 per pound, its true value given this solution is $20 + $86.67 = $106.67, and would be worth the $90 per pound purchase. This price is valid within the range of feasibility.
To calculate the range of feasibility for b_2, determine the range of values for b_2 that keep:
(current RHS) + [b_2 x (S_2 column)] $\geq$ 0.

$$40 - 1/15 \ b_2 \geq 0 \quad \text{or} \quad b_2 \leq 600$$

$$40 + 4/15 \ b_2 \geq 0 \quad \text{or} \quad b_2 \geq -150$$

$$260 - 4/15 \ b_2 \geq 0 \quad \text{or} \quad b_2 \leq 975.$$

Thus we are sure this would be a correct decision for another 600 additional units of material B.

Since the shadow price for material C is 0, one should not purchase additional units of material C.

PROBLEM 5

Given the following linear program:

$$MAX\ Z = 4X_1 + 3X_2$$

$$S.T. \quad X_1 + X_2 \leq 8$$

$$3X_1 + 2X_2 \leq 18$$

$$2X_1 + 5X_2 \leq 15$$

$$5X_1 - X_2 \leq 10$$

$$X_1,\ X_2 \geq 0$$

a) Write the dual linear program.

b) Solve the dual problem.

c) From the optimal tableau of the dual, determine the optimal solution to the primal problem.

d) Verify the result in (c) by solving the primal graphically.

e) Why would solving the dual problem by the simplex method for this problem be more convenient than solving the primal problem by the simplex method?

> **NOTE:** To write the dual LP, essentially turn the primal LP on its side. That is, twist the primal 90 degrees counter-clockwise, with the exception of its objective coefficients; they become the dual's right-hand side.

SOLUTION 5

a) There are four variables and two constraints in the dual. The rows of the dual are formed from the columns of the primal:

$$MIN \quad Z = 8U_1 + 18U_2 + 15U_3 + 10U_4$$

$$S.T. \quad U_1 + 3U_2 + 2U_3 + 5U_4 \geq 4$$

$$U_1 + 2U_2 + 5U_3 - U_4 \geq 3$$

$$U_1,\ U_2,\ U_3,\ U_4 \geq 0$$

b) Put the problem in tableau form and change the objective function to a maximization by multiplying it by -1. Then solve it by the simplex method. This is done on the next page. The optimal dual solution is: $U_1 = 0$; $U_2 = 0$; $U_3 = 19/27$; $U_4 = 14/27$; with $Z = 425/27$.

Basis	C_B	U_1 -8	U_2 -18	U_3 -15	U_4 -10	S_1 0	S_2 0	A_1 $-M$	A_2 $-M$	
A_1	$-M$	1	3	2	5	-1	0	1	0	4
A_2	$-M$	1	2	5	-1	0	-1	0	1	3
Z_j		$-2M$	$-5M$	$-7M$	$-4M$	M	M	$-M$	$-M$	$-7M$
$C_j - Z_j$		$2M+8$	$5M+18$	$7M+15$	$4M+10$	$-M$	$-M$	0	0	

Basis	C_B	U_1 -8	U_2 -18	U_3 -15	U_4 -10	S_1 0	S_2 0	A_1 $-M$	
A_1	$-M$	3/5	11/5	0	27/5	-1	2/5	1	14/5
U_3	-15	1/5	2/5	1	$-1/5$	0	$-1/5$	0	3/5
Z_j		$-3/5M$ -3	$-11/5M$ -6	-15	$-27/5M$ $+3$	M	$-2/5M$ $+3$	$-M$	$-14/5M$ -9
$C_j - Z_j$		$3/5M$ -5	$11/5M$ -12	0	$27/5M$ -13	$-M$	$2/5M$ -3	0	

Basis	C_B	U_1 -8	U_2 -18	U_3 -15	U_4 -10	S_1 0	S_2 0	
U_4	-10	3/27	11/27	0	1	$-5/27$	2/27	14/27
U_3	-15	6/27	13/27	1	0	$-1/27$	$-5/27$	19/27
Z_j		$-120/27$	$-305/27$	-15	-10	$65/27$	$55/27$	$-425/27$
$C_j - Z_j$		$-96/27$	$-181/27$	0	0	$-65/27$	$-55/27$	

c) X_1 and X_2 are found in the Z_j row of the optimal tableau of the surplus variables, S_1 and S_2. Hence the optimal solution to the primal is $X_1 = 65/27$ and $X_2 = 55/27$, giving the same value of $Z = 425/27$.

d)

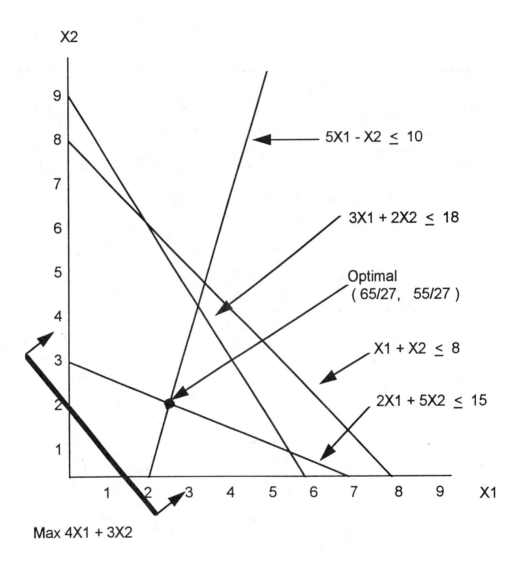

The optimal solution is at the intersection of $2X_1 + 5X_2 = 15$ and $5X_1 - X_2 = 10$. Solving these two equations in two unknowns gives $X_1 = 65/27$, $X_2 = 55/27$. The optimal value of the objective function $Z = 4(65/27) + 3(55/27) = 425/27$.

e) There are fewer constraints and hence one can expect fewer iterations and fewer computations per iteration.

PROBLEM 6

Given the following linear program:

$$MAX \ Z = 2X_1 + X_2 + 3X_3$$

$$S.T. \quad X_1 + 2X_2 + 3X_3 \leq 15$$

$$3X_1 + 4X_2 + 6X_3 \geq 24$$

$$X_1 + X_2 + X_3 = 10$$

$$X_1, X_2, X_3 \geq 0$$

a) Write the primal in canonical form.

b) Write the dual of the canonical primal.

c) Suppose the primal were solved by the simplex method. Explain where you would find the optimal value of the dual variables in the optimal primal tableau.

SOLUTION 6

a) Constraint (1) is a "$\leq$" constraint. Leave it alone. Constraint (2) is a "$\geq$" constraint. Multiply it by -1. Constraint (3) is an "=" constraint. Rewrite this as two constraints, one a "$\leq$", the other a "$\geq$" constraint. Then multiply the "$\geq$" constraint by -1.

$$MAX \ Z = 2X_1 + X_2 + 3X_3$$

$$S.T. \quad X_1 + 2X_2 + 3X_3 \leq 15$$

$$-3X_1 - 4X_2 - 6X_3 \leq -24$$

$$X_1 + X_2 + X_3 \leq 10$$

$$-X_1 - X_2 - X_3 \leq -10$$

$$X_1, X_2, X_3 \geq 0$$

b) There are four dual variables, U_1, U_2, U_3', U_3''. The objective function coefficients of the dual are the RHS of the primal. The RHS of the dual is the objective function coefficients of the primal. The rows of the dual are the columns of the primal. Thus the dual of the canonical primal is:

$$\text{MIN } Z = \ 15U_1 \ - \ 24U_2 \ + \ 10U_3{}' \ - \ 10U_3{}''$$

$$\text{S.T.} \qquad U_1 \ - \ 3U_2 \ + \ U_3{}' \ - \ U_3{}'' \ \geq \ 2$$

$$2U_1 \ - \ 4U_2 \ + \ U_3{}' \ - \ U_3{}'' \ \geq \ 1$$

$$3U_1 \ - \ 6U_2 \ + \ U_3{}' \ - \ U_3{}'' \ \geq \ 3$$

$$U_1, \ U_2, \ U_3{}', \ U_3{}'' \ \geq \ 0$$

c) The optimal solution to the dual is found in the Z_j row of the corresponding slack variable of the primal in the optimal tableau.

ANSWERED PROBLEMS

PROBLEM 7

Given the following LP: MAX $Z = 6X_1 + 5X_2$

S.T. $X_1 + X_2 \leq 6$

$2X_1 + X_2 \leq 8$

$X_1 \qquad \leq 3$

$X_1, X_2 \geq 0$

The optimal tableau is:

Basis	C_B	X_1	X_2	S_1	S_2	S_3	
		6	5	0	0	0	
S_3	0	0	0	1	-1	1	1
X_2	5	0	1	2	-1	0	4
X_1	6	1	0	-1	1	0	2
Z_j		6	5	4	1	0	32
$C_j - Z_j$		0	0	-4	-1	0	

a) What is the shadow price for the first constraint's resource? For what range of feasibility is this shadow price valid?

b) For what values of C_2 would the current solution remain optimal? What is the optimal profit when $C_2 = 4$?

PROBLEM 8

Consider the following LP: MAX $Z = 5X_1 + 2X_2 + 3X_3$
S.T. $X_1 + X_2 + X_3 \leq 10$
$2X_1 + 3X_2 + 4X_3 \leq 24$
$X_1, X_2, X_3 \geq 0$

a) Solve the LP and give the range of optimality for all of the objective function coefficients, including slack variables.

b) If you were offered another unit of the first resource for $4 would you accept the offer, considering the resource is a sunk cost for the problem. Would you pay $20 for five additional units?

PROBLEM 9

A small manufacturing firm makes three products from combinations of aluminum and steel. The manufacturing time as well as the amounts of each of the resources required to make one unit and the unit profits are summarized in the table below. There are 500 production hours, 600 lbs. of aluminum, and 900 lbs. of steel available each week.

Product	Profit	Production Hours	Aluminum	Steel
1	$40	1	2	1
2	$60	1	2	2
3	$80	2	2	3

a) Formulate and solve as a linear program.

b) What is the range of the profit on product 2 for which the solution in (a) remains optimal?

c) What is the profit if C_2 = 70?

d) Workers are currently paid $16 per hour. If they demand time and a half for overtime, should the firm schedule overtime? Discuss both in the context of labor being a sunk cost and labor being a relevant cost.

PROBLEM 10

Consider problem 9 above.

a) Management is considering cost cutting measures that would raise the unit profit on each product by an amount, x. What is the maximum value of x for which it is certain that the solution found in part (a) of problem 9 remains optimal?

b) Calculate the range of feasibility for aluminum and steel.

c) Explain in the context of this problem how aluminum and steel could be relevant costs and how they could be sunk costs. In each case, interpret the range of feasibility found in part (b).

d) A wholesale distribution company is selling packages containing one pound each of both aluminum and steel. What is the maximum number of these packages the manufacturing firm could purchase without affecting the shadow prices?

PROBLEM 11

Plant Electronics is considering producing three new computer boards on a daily basis. Each board will be produced from various combinations of plastic, copper, and transistors. The amount of each resource required per unit, the unit profitability, and the availability of the resources are summarized in the following table:

Chip Model	Plastic	Copper	Transistors	Profit
X12	2	1	1	$40
T7	1	2	1	$15
V8	1	1	1	$30
Daily Avail.	80	60	70	

The problem was solved with X_1, X_2, and X_3 representing the number of X12, T7, and V8 chips produced respectively giving the following optimal tableau:

Basis	C_B	X_1 40	X_2 15	X_3 30	S_1 0	S_2 0	S_3 0	
X_1	40	1	-1	0	1	-1	0	20
X_3	30	0	3	1	-1	2	0	40
S_3	0	0	-1	0	0	-1	1	10
Z_j		40	50	30	10	20	0	2000
$C_j - Z_j$		0	-35	0	-10	-20	0	

a) Give the optimal solution and the optimal daily profit.

b) A supplier is willing to sell Plant additional amounts of the resources. The following packages are available:

Resource	Quantity	Package Price
Plastic	30	$240
Copper	10	$150
Transistors	100	$100

If one of the above packages can be purchased, which one should be purchased? Explain. (Assume sunk costs for the resources.)

c) If management decides to raise the price of the T7 model so that its profit increases from $15 to $55, will the optimal product mix change? If so, what is the new optimal mix?

PROBLEM 12

Given the following linear program:

$$MAX \ Z = 10X_1 + 8X_2$$

$$\text{S.T.} \qquad X_1 + 3X_2 \leq 15$$

$$4X_1 + X_2 \leq 16$$

$$X_1, X_2 \geq 0$$

a) Formulate the dual linear program.

b) Solve both the primal and dual graphically.

c) Solve the primal by the simplex method. Show that the optimal value of the dual variables are, in fact, those determined in (b).

PROBLEM 13

Given the following linear program

$$MAX \ Z = 3X_1 + 2X_2 - 3X_3$$

$$\text{S.T.} \qquad X_1 + 3X_2 + 8X_3 \leq 56$$

$$2X_1 - X_2 - X_3 = 14$$

$$X_2 \geq 5$$

$$X_1, X_2, X_3 \geq 0$$

a) Write the problem in canonical form.

b) Write the dual to the canonical form.

c) Take the dual to this dual problem. Conclusion?

PROBLEM 14

Suppose in solving the primal problem, it is found that the primal problem is unbounded. Recalling that the objective function of the dual is a minimization objective function, what does this indicate about the solution to the dual problem?

TRUE/FALSE

15. Simplex-based sensitivity analysis is applicable to primal tableaus, but not dual tableaus.

16. The range of optimality for an objective function coefficient, C_k, is determined by finding the range of values of C_k that keep the $C_j - Z_j$ row less than or equal to 0.

17. In sensitivity analysis of the objective function coefficient, C_3, LINDO/PC states a maximum increase of 75 and an maximum decrease of 25. Currently C_3 is 130. If C_3 is changed to 150, the optimal solution does not change.

18. You cannot mix a right-hand side change and an objective function change when applying the 100 percent rule.

19. In the sensitivity analysis of the right-hand side coefficient, b_4, LINDO/PC states a maximum increase of 20 and maximum decrease of 10. Currently b_4 is 15. If b_4 changes to 25, the optimal solution does not change.

20. If the primal has few constraints, but relatively many variables, solving the dual is often faster.

21. Constraint 3 is a $\leq$ constraint and the optimal solution has $S_3 = 6$. Thus the shadow price for this constraint must be 0.

22. A shadow price for a resource is valid only in the range of feasibility for that resource.

23. Shadow prices are found in the Z_j row of the optimal tableau in the slack, surplus, or artificial variable columns.

24. The dual linear program for a maximization problem in canonical form seeks to maximize the value of the resources.

25. Dual variables and shadow prices are equivalent for problems of maximization and are negative of each other for minimization.

26. When the primal is unbounded, the dual is unbounded.

27. If simultaneous changes in the objective function violate the 100% rule (exceed 100%), the optimal solution will change.

28. The optimal values of the primal decision variables are given by the z_j entries for the surplus variables in the dual's optimal simplex tableau.

29. The primal and its dual cannot have the same optimal objective function value because one is a minimization problem and the other is a maximization.

CHAPTER

7

The Transportation, Assignment, and Transshipment Problems

KEY CONCEPTS

CONCEPT	ILLUSTRATED PROBLEMS	ANSWERED PROBLEMS
Transportation Problems		
Network Representation	1	8
Least Cost Starting Solution	1-3	8-11
MODI/Stepping Stone Solution	1-3	8-11
Dummy Rows/Columns	2,3	10
Maximization Problems	3	11
Unacceptable Routes	3	11
Degeneracy	3	9
Assignment Problem		
Network Representation	4	13
Hungarian Solution Procedure	4,5	12,13,14
Dummy Rows/Columns	4	13
Maximization Problems	5	12,14
Unacceptable Assignments	5	14
Transshipment Problem		
Network Representation	6,7	15
LP Formulation	6	15

REVIEW

1. A <u>network</u> <u>model</u> is one which can be represented by a set of nodes, a set of arcs, and functions (e.g. costs, supplies, demands, etc.) associated with the arcs and/or nodes.

2. Transportation, assignment, and transshipment problems of this chapter, as well as the shortest route, minimal spanning tree, and maximal flow problems (Chapter 9) and PERT/CPM problems (Chapter 10) are all examples of <u>network</u> <u>problems</u>.

3. Each of the three models of this chapter (transportation, assignment, and transshipment models) can be formulated as <u>linear</u> <u>programs</u> and solved by general purpose linear programming codes. However, there are many computer packages (including The Management Scientist) which contain separate computer codes for these models which take advantage of their network structure. This radically enhances the speed of solving particularly large problems.

4. For each of the three models in this chapter, if the right-hand side of the linear programming formulations are all integers, the optimal solution will be in terms of <u>integer</u> <u>values</u> for the decision variables.

TRANSPORTATION PROBLEM

1. The <u>transportation problem</u> seeks to minimize the total shipping costs of transporting goods from m origins (each with a supply s_i) to n destinations (each with a demand d_j), when the unit shipping cost from an origin, i, to a destination, j, is c_{ij}.

2. The <u>network representation</u> for a transportation problem with two sources and three destinations is given below:

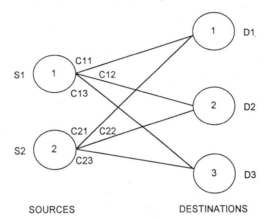

3. Transportation problems are special cases of linear programs. The <u>linear programming formulation</u> in terms of the amounts shipped from the origins to the destinations, x_{ij}, can be written as:

$$\text{MIN} \quad \sum_i \sum_j c_{ij} x_{ij}$$

$$\text{S.T.} \quad \sum_j x_{ij} \leq s_i \quad \text{for each origin i}$$

$$\sum_i x_{ij} = d_j \quad \text{for each destination j}$$

$$x_{ij} \geq 0 \quad \text{for all i and j.}$$

4. The following <u>special-case modifications</u> to the linear programming formulation can be made:
    (a) Minimum shipping guarantees from i to j: $x_{ij} \geq L_{ij}$
    (b) Maximum route capacity from i to j $x_{ij} \leq L_{ij}$
    (c) Unacceptable routes: delete the variable

5. To solve the transportation problem by its special <u>purpose algorithm</u>, it is required that the sum of the supplies at the origins equal the sum of the demands at the destinations. If the total supply is greater than the total demand, a <u>dummy destination</u> is added with demand equal to the excess supply, and shipping costs from all origins are zero. Similarly, if total supply is less than total demand, a <u>dummy origin</u> is added.

6. When solving a transportation problem by its special purpose algorithm, unacceptable shipping routes are given a cost of +M (a large number).

7. A transportation tableau giving a feasible solution and reduced costs is given below. Each cell represents a shipping route (which is an arc on the network and a decision variable in the LP formulation), and the unit shipping costs are given in an upper right hand box in the cell. If an arc is being used in the current solution, the cell is said to be occupied and the number in it represents its current value. If the arc is NOT being used the cell is unoccupied, its value is 0, and the circled number in the cell represents its reduced cost (the amount the objective function will change per unit increase in this variable).

	D1		D2		D3	
		4		4		2
O1	8		2		-5	
		7		3		6
O2	3		4		11	

The above tableau is equivalent to the following:

Shipping Route	Decision Variable	Value	Total Cost	Reduced Cost
O1-D1	X_{11}	8	8x5 = 40	0
O1-D2	X_{12}	2	2x4 = 8	0
O1-D3	X_{13}	0	0x2 = 0	-5
O2-D1	X_{21}	0	0x7 = 0	3
O2-D2	X_{22}	4	4x3 = 12	0
O2-D3	X_{23}	11	11x6 = 66	0

Total Cost = 126

8. The transportation problem is solved in two phases:
   Phase I -- Obtaining an initial feasible solution
   Phase II -- Moving toward optimality

9. In Phase I, a least cost starting procedure can be used to establish an initial basic feasible solution without doing numerous iterations of the simplex method. (See algorithm).

10. In Phase II, the stepping stone method, using the MODI method for evaluating the reduced costs may be used to move from the initial feasible solution to the optimal one. (See algorithm).

TRANSPORTATION ALGORITHM

It is assumed that the problem is a minimization problem and that dummy origins and destinations have been added so that the sum of the total supply equals the sum of the total demand.

Phase I - Least Cost Starting Solution

1. Select the cell with the least cost. Assign to this cell the minimum of its remaining row supply or remaining column demand.

2. Decrease the row and column availabilities by this amount and remove from consideration all other cells in the row or column with zero availability/demand. (If both are simultaneously reduced to 0, assign an allocation of 0 to any other unoccupied cell in the row or column before deleting both.) GO TO STEP 1.

Note: An equivalent greatest cost method is used for maximization.

Phase II - Stepping Stone Solution Procedure

1. For each unoccupied cell, calculate the reduced cost by the MODI method described below. Select the unoccupied cell with the most negative reduced cost. (For maximization problems select the unoccupied cell with the largest reduced cost.) If none, STOP.

2. For this unoccupied cell generate a stepping stone path by forming a closed loop with this cell and occupied cells by drawing connecting alternating horizontal and vertical lines between them. (Note that lines may cross and may go through other occupied or unoccupied cells.) Determine the minimum allocation where a subtraction is to be made along this path.

3. Add this allocation to all cells where additions are to be made, and subtract this allocation to all cells where subtractions are to be made along the stepping stone path. (Note: An occupied cell on the stepping stone path now becomes 0 (unoccupied). If more than one cell becomes 0, make only one unoccupied; make the others occupied with 0's.) GO TO STEP 1.

MODI METHOD FOR OBTAINING REDUCED COSTS

Associate a number, u_i, with each row and v_j with each column.

1. Set $u_1 = 0$.

2. Calculate the remaining u_i's and v_j's by solving the relationship $c_{ij} = u_i + v_j$ for occupied cells.

3. For unoccupied cells (i,j), the reduced cost $= c_{ij} - u_i - v_j$.

**FLOW CHART OF
TRANSPORTATION ALGORITHM, PHASE I
(MINIMUM COST METHOD)**

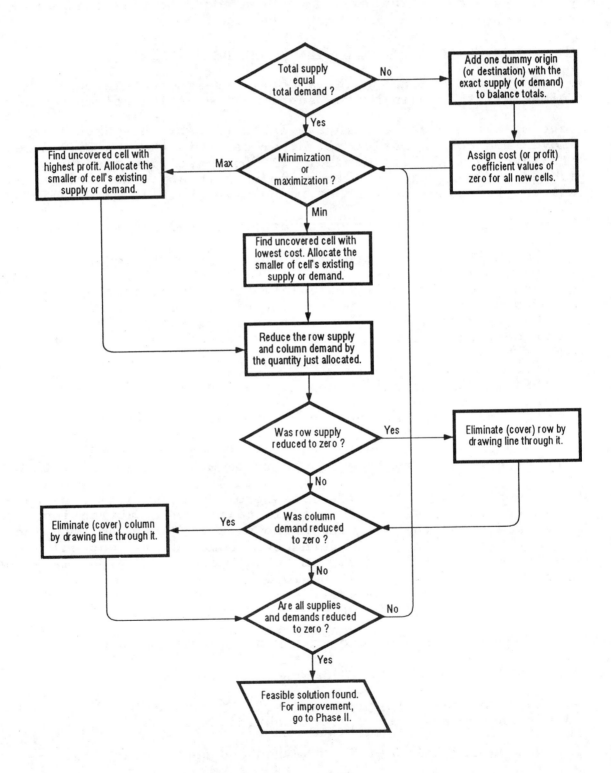

**FLOW CHART OF
TRANSPORTATION ALGORITHM, PHASE II
(STEPPING STONE METHOD)**

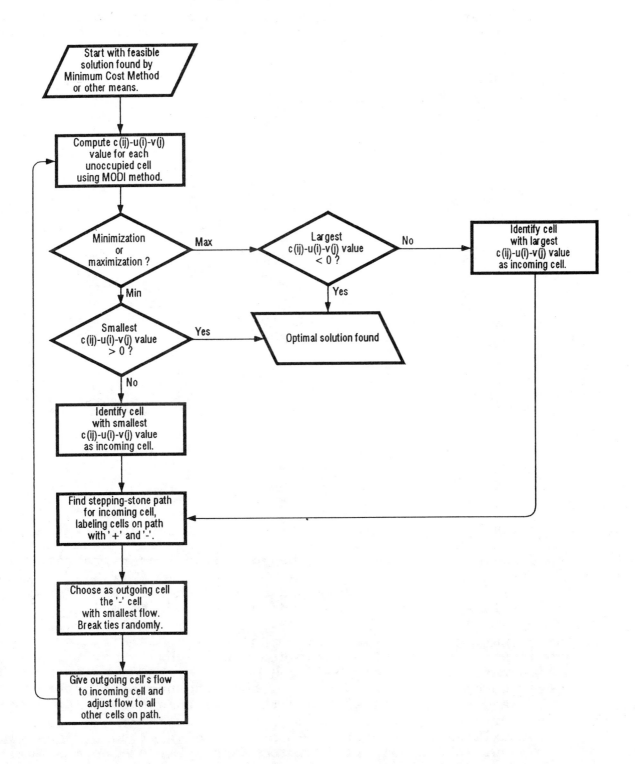

ASSIGNMENT PROBLEM

1. An <u>assignment</u> <u>problem</u> seeks to minimize the total cost assignment of m workers to m jobs, given that the cost of worker i performing job j is c_{ij}. It assumes all workers are assigned and each job is performed.

2. The <u>network</u> <u>representation</u> of an assignment problem with three workers and three jobs is:

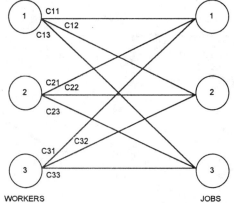

3. The <u>linear</u> <u>programming</u> <u>formulation</u> of the assignment problem using x_{ij} = 0 or 1 denoting whether worker i is assigned to job j is:

$$\text{MIN} \quad \sum_i \sum_j c_{ij} x_{ij}$$

$$\text{S.T.} \qquad \sum_j x_{ij} = 1 \quad \text{for each worker i}$$

$$\sum_i x_{ij} = 1 \quad \text{for each job j}$$

$$x_{ij} \geq 0 \text{ for all i and j.}$$

4. An assignment problem is a <u>special</u> <u>case</u> <u>of</u> <u>a</u> <u>transportation</u> <u>problem</u> in which all supplies and all demands are equal to 1; hence assignment problems may be solved as linear programs.

5. A modification to the <u>right-hand</u> <u>side</u> of the linear program can be made if a worker is permitted to work more than 1 job.

6. The <u>Hungarian</u> <u>method</u> (see next page) solves minimization assignment problems with m workers and m jobs. Special considerations can include:
     (a) number of workers does not equal the number of jobs --
          add dummy workers/jobs with 0 assignment costs as needed
     (b) worker i cannot do job j -- assign c_{ij} = +M.
     (c) maximization objective -- create an <u>opportunity</u> <u>loss</u> <u>matri</u>
          subtracting all profits for each job from the maximum
          profit for that job before beginning the Hungarian method

HUNGARIAN METHOD

It is assumed that the problem is a minimization problem and that dummy workers/jobs have been added so that the total number of workers equals the total number of jobs.

1. For each row, subtract the minimum number in that row from all numbers in that row.

2. Then, for each column, subtract the minimum number in that column from all numbers in that column.

3. Draw the minimum number of lines to cover all zeroes (see below.) If this number = m, STOP -- an assignment can be made.

4. Determine the minimum uncovered number (call it d.)
   (a) Subtract d from uncovered numbers.
   (b) Add d to numbers covered by two lines.
   (c) Numbers covered by one line remain the same.
   Then, GO TO STEP 3.

Finding the Minimum Number of Lines and Determining the Optimal Solution

1. Find a row or column with only one unlined zero and circle it. (If all rows/columns have two or more unlined zeroes choose an arbitrary zero and circle it.)

2. If the circle is in a row with one zero, draw a line through its column. If the circle is in a column with one zero, draw a line through its row. A heuristic approach when all rows and columns have two or more zeroes is to draw a line through one with the most zeroes, breaking ties arbitrarily.

3. Repeat step 2 until all circles are lined.

This determines the minimum number of lines. If this minimum number equals m, the circles provide the optimal assignment.

FLOW CHART OF
HUNGARIAN METHOD

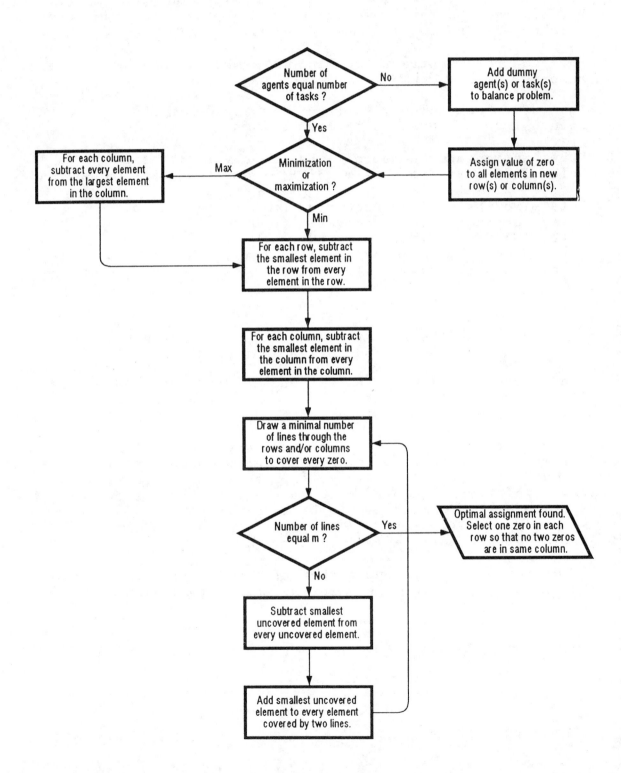

TRANSSHIPMENT PROBLEM

1. <u>Transshipment</u> <u>problems</u> are transportation problems in which a shipment may move through intermediate nodes (transshipment nodes) before reaching a particular destination node.

2. The <u>network</u> <u>representation</u> for a transshipment problem with two sources, three intermediate nodes, and two destinations is given below:

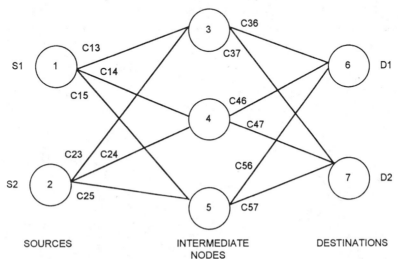

3. The <u>linear</u> <u>programming</u> <u>formulation</u> for the transshipment problem with x_{ij} representing the shipment from node i to node j is:

$$\text{MIN} \quad \sum_i \sum_j c_{ij} x_{ij}$$

$$\text{S.T.} \quad \sum_j x_{ij} \leq s_i \qquad \text{for each origin i}$$

$$\sum_i x_{ik} - \sum_j ?x_{kj} = 0 \qquad \text{for each intermediate node k}$$

$$\sum_i x_{ij} = d_j \qquad \text{for each destination j}$$

$$x_{ij} \geq 0 \qquad \text{for all i and j.}$$

4. <u>Conversion</u> of transshipment problems to large transportation problems for solution, but for computer programs without such codes, they may be solved by general purpose linear programming codes.

ILLUSTRATED PROBLEMS

> **NOTE:** The coefficient values used in dummy rows and
> dummy columns in transportation tables and assignment
> matrices are always zero, regardless of whether you
> are maximizing or minimizing.
>   In the case of infeasible (unallowed) shipments or
> assignments, use as your coefficients a very large
> negative number when maximizing and a very large
> positive number when minimizing.

PROBLEM 1

Given the following minimum cost transportation network:

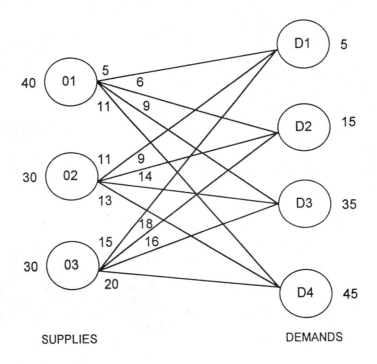

SUPPLIES   DEMANDS

a) Use the Least Cost Method to get an initial solution.

b) Use the MODI Method to determine the reduced costs of the
   unoccupied cells.

c) What is the value of the current solution?

d) By how much will the next transportation tableau improve the
   value of the objective function over this solution?

e) Solve the problem by the stepping stone method.

SOLUTION 1

Let us first develop the transportation tableau:

	D1	D2	D3	D4	Supply
O1	5	6	9	11	40
O2	11	9	14	13	30
O3	15	18	16	20	30
Demand	5	15	35	45	

a) Least Cost Method:

Iteration 1

	D1	D2	D3	D4	S_i
O1	5	6	9	11	40
O2	11	9	14	13	30
O3	15	18	16	20	30
D_j	5	15	35	45	

Least cost is 5 for O1-D1.
Remaining supply for O1 = 40.
Remaining demand for D1 = 5.
Assign 5 units to O1-D1.
Reduce S_1 by 5 to 35.
Eliminate the D1 column.

Iteration 2

	D1	D2	D3	D4	S_i
O1		6	9	11	35
O2		9	14	13	30
O3		18	16	20	30
D_j		15	35	45	

Least cost is 6 for O1-D2.
Remaining S_1 = 35.
Remaining D_2 = 15.
Assign 15 units to O1-D2.
Reduce S_1 by 15 to 20.
Eliminate the D2 column.

Iteration 3

	D1	D2	D3	D4	S_i
O1			9	11	20
O2			14	13	30
O3			16	20	30
D_j			35	45	

Least cost is 9 for O1-D3.
Remaining S_1 = 20.
Remaining D_3 = 35.
Assign 20 units to O1-D3.
Eliminate the O1 row.
Reduce D_3 by 20 to 15.

Iteration 4

	D1	D2	D3	D4	S_i
O1					
O2			14	13	30
O3			16	20	30
D_j			15	45	

Least Cost is 13 for O2-D4.
Remaining S_2 = 30.
Remaining D_4 = 45.
Assign 30 units to O2-D4.
Eliminate the O2 row.
Reduce D_4 by 30 to 15.

Iteration 5

This leaves the one row O3 with $S_3 = 30$. Assign 15 to O3-D3 and 15 to O3-D4 to complete the least cost assignment.

	D1	D2	D3	D4
O1	5 / 5	6 / 15	9 / 20	11
O2	11	9	14	13 / 30
O3	15	18	16 / 15	20 / 15

b) To calculate the reduced costs for the unoccupied cells, first calculate the u_i's and the v_j's.

1. Set $u_1 = 0$.

2. Since $u_1 + v_j = c_{1j}$ for occupied cells in row 1, $v_1 = 5$, $v_2 = 6$, and $v_3 = 9$.

3. Now since $u_3 + v_3 = c_{33}$ for occupied cell (3,3), $u_3 + 9 = 16$ or $u_3 = 7$.

4. Now since $u_3 + v_4 = c_{34}$ for occupied cell (3,4), $7 + v_4 = 20$ or $v_4 = 13$.

5. Finally since $u_2 + v_4 = c_{24}$ for occupied cell (2,4), $u_2 + 13 = 13$ or $u_2 = 0$.

Now the reduced costs can be calculated for the unoccupied cells by:

Unoccupied Cell	Reduced Cost = $c_{ij} - u_i - v_j$
(1,4)	11 - 0 - 13 = -2
(2,1)	11 - 0 - 5 = 6
(2,2)	9 - 0 - 6 = 3
(2,3)	14 - 0 - 9 = 5
(3,1)	15 - 7 - 5 = 3
(3,2)	18 - 7 - 6 = 5

Thus the tableau at this iteration is:

	D1	D2	D3	D4	u_i
01	5 5	6 15	9 20	11 -2	0
02	11 6	9 3	14 5	13 30	0
03	15 3	18 5	16 15	20 15	7
v_j	5	6	9	13	

c) The value of the current solution is the sum of the allocations times the unit costs:

   Z = 5(5) + 15(6) + 20(9) + 30(13) + 15(16) + 15(20) = $1225.

d) The unoccupied cell with the most negative reduced cost is cell (1,4), with a reduced cost of -2. The stepping stone path would be to add to cell (1,4) subtract from occupied cell (3,4), add to occupied cell (3,3) and subtract from occupied cell (1,3). Along this path subtractions are made from cells (3,4) and (1,3). The allocations X_{34} = 15 and X_{13} = 20. The minimum is 15, and so the total cost will change by (-$2)x15 = -$30, i.e. a $30 reduction.

e) (c) and (d) are the first two steps of the transportation stepping stone algorithm. Thus, all shipments at the corners of the stepping stone path will be changed by subtracting 15 from the subtraction cells and adding 15 to the addition cells. Thus the changes are:

   X_{14} = 0 + 15 = 15
   X_{34} = 15 - 15 = 0 (blank for next tableau)
   X_{33} = 15 + 15 = 30
   X_{13} = 20 - 15 = 5

The resulting tableau is:

	D1	D2	D3	D4	u_i
O1	5 / 5	6 / 15	9 / 5	11 / 15	0
O2	11 / +4	9 / +1	14 / +3	13 / 30	2
O3	15 / +3	18 / +5	16 / 30	20 / +2	7
v_j	5	6	9	11	

In this tableau, the circled numbers are the reduced costs calculated as follows:

1. Set $u_1 = 0$.

2. Since all cells in row 1 are occupied and $u_1 + v_j = c_{ij}$ for occupied cells, $v_1 = 5$; $v_2 = 6$; $v_3 = 9$; $v_4 = 11$.

3. Since $v_4 = 11$ and cell (2,4) is occupied, $u_2 + 11 = 13$ or $u_2 = 2$.

4. Since $v_3 = 9$ and cell (3,3) is occupied, $u_3 + 9 = 16$ or $u_3 = 7$.

Now the reduced costs can be calculated for the unoccupied cells by:

Unoccupied Cell	Reduced Cost = $c_{ij} - u_i - v_j$	Unoccupied Cell	Reduced Cost = $c_{ij} - u_i - v_j$
(2,1)	11 - 2 - 5 = 4	(3,1)	15 - 7 - 5 = 3
(2,2)	9 - 2 - 6 = 1	(3,2)	18 - 7 - 6 = 5
(2,3)	14 - 2 - 9 = 3	(3,4)	20 - 7 - 11 = 2

Since all the reduced costs are non-negative, this tableau is optimal. To summarize, the optimal solution is:

From	To	Shipment	Cost
O1	D1	5	25
O1	D2	15	90
O1	D3	5	45
O1	D4	15	165
O2	D4	30	390
O3	D3	30	480
	Total Cost	=	$1,195

PROBLEM 2

Building Brick Company (BBC) has orders for 80 tons of bricks at three suburban locations as follows: Northwood -- 25 tons, Westwood -- 45 tons, and Eastwood -- 10 tons. BBC has two plants, each of which can produce 50 tons per week. How should end of week shipments be made to fill the above orders given the following delivery cost per ton:

	Northwood	Westwood	Eastwood
Plant 1	24	30	40
Plant 2	30	40	42

SOLUTION 2

Since total supply = 100 and total demand = 80, a dummy destination is created with demand of 20 and 0 unit costs.

	Northwood	Westwood	Eastwood	Dummy	Supply
Plant 1	24	30	40	0	50
Plant 2	30	40	42	0	50
Demand	25	45	10	20	

Least Cost Starting Procedure: (See problem 1 for more details.)

1. Tie for least cost (0), arbitrarily select X_{14}. Allocate 20. Reduce S_1 by 20 to 30 and delete the Dummy column.

2. Of the remaining cells the least cost is 24 for X_{11}. Allocate 25. Reduce S_1 by 25 to 5 and eliminate the Northwood column.

3. Of the remaining cells the least cost is 30 for X_{12}. Allocate 5. Reduce the Westwood column to 40 and eliminate the Plant 1 row.

4. Since there is only one row with two cells left, make the final allocations of 40 and 10 to X_{22} and X_{23} respectively.

Thus, the initial tableau is on the next page. To determine the u_i's and v_j's using the MODI method:

Iteration 1

1. Set $u_1 = 0$

2. Since $u_1 + v_j = c_{1j}$ for occupied cells in row 1, then
   $v_1 = 24$, $v_2 = 30$, $v_4 = 0$.

3. Since $u_i + v_2 = c_{i2}$ for occupied cells in column 2, then
   $u_2 + 30 = 40$, hence $u_2 = 10$.

4. Since $u_2 + v_j = c_{2j}$ for occupied cells in row 2, then
   $10 + v_3 = 42$, hence $v_3 = 32$.

Calculate the reduced costs (circled numbers) by $c_{ij} - u_i + v_j$.

Unoccupied Cell	Reduced Cost
(1,3)	40 - 0 - 32 = 8
(2,1)	30 - 24 - 10 = -4
(2,4)	0 - 10 - 0 = -10

	Northwood	Westwood	Eastwood	Dummy	u_i
Plant 1	24 25	30 5	40 +8	0 20	0
Plant 2	30 -4	40 40	42 10	0 -10	10
v_j	24	30	32	0	

The stepping stone path for cell (2,4) is (2,4), (1,4), (1,2), (2,2). The allocations in the subtraction cells are 20 and 40, respectively. The minimum is 20, and hence reallocate 20 along this path. Thus for the next tableau:

$$X_{24} = 0 + 20 = 20 \quad \text{(0 is its current allocation)}$$
$$X_{14} = 20 - 20 = 0 \quad \text{(blank for the next tableau)}$$
$$X_{12} = 5 + 20 = 25$$
$$X_{22} = 40 - 20 = 20$$

The other occupied cells remain the same.

Iteration 2

The reduced costs are found by calculating the u_i's and v_j's for this tableau.

1. Set $u_1 = 0$.

2. Since $u_1 + v_j = c_{ij}$ for occupied cells in row 1, then $v_1 = 24$, $v_2 = 30$.

3. Since $u_i + v_2 = c_{i2}$ for occupied cells in column 2, then $u_2 + 30 = 40$, or $u_2 = 10$.

4. Since $u_2 + v_j = c_{2j}$ for occupied cells in row 2, then $10 + v_3 = 42$ or $v_3 = 32$; and, $10 + v_4 = 0$ or $v_4 = -10$.

Calculate the reduced costs (circled numbers) by $c_{ij} - u_i + v_j$.

Unoccupied Cell	Reduced Cost
(1,3)	40 − 0 − 32 = 8
(1,4)	0 − 0 − (−10) = 10
(2,1)	30 − 10 − 24 = −4

	Northwood	Westwood	Eastwood	Dummy	u_i
Plant 1	24 25	30 25	40 +8	0 +10	0
Plant 2	30 −4	40 20	42 10	0 20	10
v_j	24	30	36	−6	

The most negative reduced cost is = −4 determined by X_{21}. The stepping stone path for this cell is (2,1),(1,1),(1,2),(2,2). The allocations in the subtraction cells are 25 and 20 respectively. Thus the new solution is obtained by reallocating 20 on the stepping stone path. Thus for the next tableau:

$$X_{21} = \ \ 0 + 20 = 20 \quad \text{(0 is its current allocation)}$$
$$X_{11} = 25 - 20 = \ \ 5$$
$$X_{12} = 25 + 20 = 45$$
$$X_{22} = 20 - 20 = \ \ 0 \quad \text{(blank for the next tableau)}$$

The other occupied cells remain the same.

Iteration 3

The reduced costs are found by calculating the u_i's and v_j's for this tableau.

1. Set $u_1 = 0$

2. Since $u_1 + v_j = c_{1j}$ for occupied cells in row 1, then $v_1 = 24$ and $v_2 = 30$.

3. Since $u_i + v_1 = c_{i1}$ for occupied cells in column 2, then $u_2 + 24 = 30$ or $u_2 = 6$.

4. Since $u_2 + v_j = c_{2j}$ for occupied cells in row 2, then $6 + v_3 = 42$ or $v_3 = 36$, and $6 + v_4 = 0$ or $v_4 = -6$.

Calculate the reduced costs (circled numbers) by $c_{ij} - u_i + v_j$.

Unoccupied Cell	Reduced Cost
(1,3)	40 - 0 - 36 = 4
(1,4)	0 - 0 - (-6) = 6
(2,2)	40 - 6 - 30 = 4

This gives the tableau on the next page. Since all the reduced costs are non-negative, this is the optimal tableau.

	Northwood	Westwood	Eastwood	Dummy	u_i
Plant 1	24 5	30 45	40 +4	0 +6	0
Plant 2	30 20	40 +4	42 10	0 20	6
v_j	24	30	36	-6	

Thus the optimal solution is:

From	To	Amount	Cost
Plant 1	Northwood	5	120
Plant 1	Westwood	45	1,350
Plant 2	Northwood	20	600
Plant 2	Eastwood	10	420

	Total Cost	=	$2,490

PROBLEM 3

Telly's Toy Company produces three kinds of dolls called Bertha, Holly, and Shari. Maximum production quantities for the dolls are 1,000, 2,000, and 2,000 per week respectively. These dolls are purchased by three large department stores: Shears, Nichols and Words. Each department store wishes 1,500 total dolls per week form Telly's. However, Words does not want any Bertha dolls.

Because of past commitments and the sizes of other orders from Telly's, unit profits per doll vary from store to store for each style of doll. These are summarized as follows:

	Shears	Nichols	Words
Bertha	$ 5	$10	X
Holly	$16	$ 8	$ 9
Shari	$12	$ 9	$11

a) Set the problem up as a maximization transportation problem.

b) Give the "highest profit" starting solution.

c) Solve the problem using MODI to determine the reduced costs.

SOLUTION 3

a) The origins are the dolls, the destinations are the stores. Since potential supply exceeds demand by 500, a dummy destination is added with a demand of 500 and with unit profits of 0. The profit for shipment from Bertha - Words is -M (a large negative number.) The shipments will be in terms of hundreds of dolls shipped.

b) Starting solution: (See problems 1 and 2 for more details)

Iteration	Maximum Profit	Cell	Assignment	Eliminate
1	16	(H,S)	15	S column
2	11	(S,W)	15	W column
3	10	(B,N)	10	B row
4	9	(S,N)	5	S row & N col.

(Degeneracy! Also assign a 0 anywhere left in Shari row or Nichols column before they are deleted, say, in (S,D).)

| 5 | 0 | (H,D) | 5 | Finished |

Thus the first assignment tableau becomes:

	Shears	Nichols	Words	Dummy
Bertha	5	10	-M	0
		10		
Holly	16	8	9	0
	15			5
Shari	12	9	11	0
		5	15	0

Calculate the u_i's and v_j's (See problems 1 & 2 for details):
1. $u_1 = 0$.
2. Since $u_1 = 0$, then $v_2 = 10$.
3. Since $v_2 = 10$, then $u_3 = -1$.
4. Since $u_3 = -1$, then $v_3 = 12$ and $v_4 = 1$.
5. Since $v_4 = 1$, then $u_2 = -1$.
6. Since $u_2 = -1$, then $v_1 = 17$.

Calculate the reduced costs $(c_{ij} - u_i - v_j)$ for unoccupied cells. The resulting transportation tableau is:

	Shears	Nichols	Words	Dummy	u_i
Bertha	5	10	-M	0	0
	-12	10	-M	-1	
Holly	16	8	9	0	-1
	15	-1	-2	5	
Shari	12	9	11	0	-1
	-4	5	15	0	
d_j	17	10	12	1	

In a maximization problem we choose the unoccupied cell with the highest reduced cost. There are no occupied cells with positive reduced costs, so this gives the optimal solution:

Dolls	Store	Shipment	Profit	
Bertha	Nichols	1000	$10,000	
Holly	Shears	1500	$24,000	
Shari	Nichols	500	$ 4,500	Total Profit
Shari	Words	1500	$16,500	= $55,000

PROBLEM 4

A contractor pays his subcontractors a fixed fee plus mileage for work performed. On a given day the contractor is faced with three electrical jobs associated with various projects. He has four electrical subcontractors which are located at various places throughout the area. Given below are the distances between the subcontractors and the projects.

		Project		
		A	B	C
Subcontractors	Westside	50	36	16
	Federated	28	30	18
	Goliath	35	32	20
	Universal	25	25	14

How should the contractors be assigned to minimize total costs?

SOLUTION 4

This is an assignment problem that needs a dummy job (column).

Now let us draw the network representation of this problem:

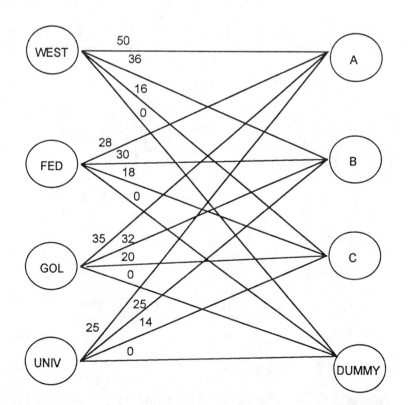

Since the Hungarian algorithm requires that there be the same number of rows as columns, add a Dummy column so that the first tableau is:

	A	B	C	Dummy
Westside	50	36	16	0
Federated	28	30	18	0
Goliath	35	32	20	0
Universal	25	25	14	0

Step 1: Subtract minimum number in each row from all numbers in that row. Since each row has a zero, we would simply generate the same matrix above.

Step 2: Subtract the minimum number in each column from all numbers in the column. For A it is 25, for B it is 25, for C it is 14, for Dummy it is 0. This yields:

	A	B	C	Dummy
Westside	25	11	2	0
Federated	3	5	4	0
Goliath	10	7	6	0
Universal	0	0	0	0

Step 3: Draw the minimum number of lines to cover all zeroes.

Although one can "eyeball" this minimum, use the following algorithm. If a "remaining" row has only one zero, draw a line through the column. If a remaining column has only one zero in it, draw a line through the row.

Note that row W has one 0, (column D); draw a line through column D. Then column A has one "remaining" 0, (row U); draw a line through row U. Now there are no more zeros uncovered.

	A	B	C	Dummy
Westside	25	11	2	0
Federated	3	5	4	0
Goliath	10	7	6	0
Universal	— 0 —	0 —	0 —	0 —

Step 4: The minimum uncovered number is 2 (circled above).

Step 5: Subtract 2 from uncovered numbers; add 2 to all numbers covered by two lines. This gives:

	A	B	C	Dummy
Westside	23	9	0	0
Federated	1	3	2	0
Goliath	8	5	4	0
Universal	0	0	0	2

Step 3: Draw the minimum number of lines to cover all zeroes. Column A has one 0 (row U) -- draw a line through row U. Row F has one 0 remaining (column D) -- draw a line through column D. Column C has one 0 remaining (row W) -- draw a line through row W.

	A	B	C	Dummy
Westside	— 23 —	9 —	0 —	0 —
Federated	1	3	2	0
Goliath	8	5	4	0
Universal	— 0 —	0 —	0 —	2 —

Step 4: The minimum uncovered number is 1 (circled).

Step 5: Subtract 1 from uncovered numbers. Add 1 to numbers covered by two lines. This gives:

	A	B	C	Dummy
Westside	23	9	0	1
Federated	0	2	1	0
Goliath	7	4	3	0
Universal	0	0	0	3

Step 4: The minimum number of lines to cover all 0's is four. Thus, there is a minimum-cost assignment of 0's with this tableau. The optimal assignment is:

Subcontractor	Project	Distance
Westside	C	16
Federated	A	28
Universal	B	25
(Goliath	(unassigned)	--

Total Distance = 69 miles

PROBLEM 5

A foreman is trying to assign crews to produce the maximum
number of parts per hour of a certain product. He has three
crews and four possible work centers. The estimated number of
parts per hour for each crew at each work center is summarized
below:

	Work Center			
	WC1	WC2	WC3	WC4
Crew 1	15	20	18	30
Crew 2	20	22	26	30
Crew 3	25	26	27	30

Solve for the optimal assignment of crews to work centers.

SOLUTION 5

This is a maximization assignment problem with fewer rows than
columns. First add a row of zeroes (dummy crew). Then
construct an opportunity loss matrix as follows. Find the
maximum number in each column, 25 for column 1, 26 for column 2,
27 for column 3 and 30 for column 4. Then for each number in a
column, replace it with the difference between that number and
the corresponding maximum number in that column. This yields:

	WC1	WC2	WC3	WC4
Crew 1	10	6	9	0
Crew 2	5	4	1	0
Crew 3	0	0	0	0
Dummy	25	26	27	30

Now apply the Hungarian algorithm.

Step 1: Subtract the minimum number in each row from all numbers
in that row. Note that only the bottom row is changed.

	WC1	WC2	WC3	WC4
Crew 1	10	6	9	0
Crew 2	5	4	1	0
Crew 3	0	0	0	0
Dummy	0	1	2	5

Step 2: Subtract the minimum number in each column from all
numbers in the corresponding column. Since there is a
zero in each column the above matrix is left unchanged.

Step 3: Draw the minimum number of lines to cover all 0's.

	WC1	WC2	WC3	WC4
Crew 1	10	6	9	0
Crew 2	5	4	1	0
Crew 3	0	0	0	0
Dummy	0	1	2	5

Step 4: The minimum uncovered number is 1.

Step 5: Subtract 1 from uncovered numbers. Add 1 to numbers covered by two lines. This yields:

	WC1	WC2	WC3	WC4
Crew 1	10	5	8	0
Crew 2	5	3	0	0
Crew 3	1	0	0	1
Dummy	0	0	1	5

It will now take four lines to cover all 0's and an optimal solution is:

Crew	Work Center	Parts/Hour
Crew 1	WC4	30
Crew 2	WC3	26
Crew 3	WC2	26
----	WC1	--

Total Parts Per Hour = 82

PROBLEM 6

Thomas Industries and Washburn Corporation supply three firms (Zrox, Hewes, Rockwright) with customized shelving for its offices. They both order shelving from the same two manufacturers, Arnold Manufacturers and Supershelf, Inc. Because of long standing contracts based on past orders, unit costs from the manufacturers to the suppliers are given below:

	Thomas	Washburn
Arnold	5	8
Supershelf	7	4

The chart below gives the cost to install the shelving at the various locations:

	Zrox	Hewes	Rockwright
Thomas	1	5	8
Washburn	3	4	4

Currently weekly demands by the users are 50 for Zrox, 60 for Hewes, and 40 for Rockwright. Both Arnold and Supershelf can supply at most 75 units to its customers.

a) Draw the network representation for this problem.

b) Formulate this problem as a transshipment linear program.

SOLUTION 6

a) Arnold Manufacturers and Supershelf are manufacturers (origins) and Zrox, Hewes, and Rockwright are customers (destinations). Thomas and Washburn represent transshipment points (middlemen) supplying Arnold and Supershelf products to their customers. The network representation is on the next page.

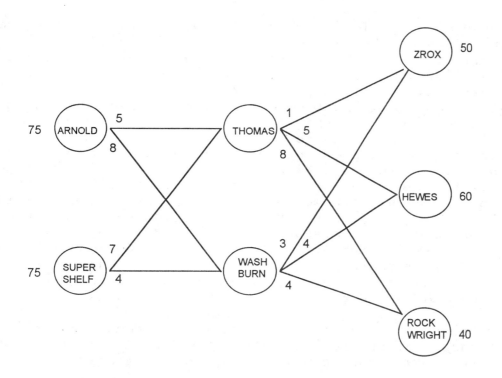

b) Linear Programming Formulation

Define the decision variables:
    X_{ij} = amount shipped from manufacturer i to supplier j
    X_{jk} = amount shipped from supplier j to customer k
        i = 1(Arnold), 2(Supershelf)
        j = 3(Thomas), 4(Washburn)
        k = 5(Zrox), 6(Hewes), 7(Rockwright)

Define Objective: Minimize Overall Shipping Costs:
    MIN $5X_{13}$ + $8X_{14}$ + $7X_{23}$ + $4X_{24}$ + $1X_{35}$ + $5X_{36}$ + $8X_{37}$ + $3X_{45}$
         + $4X_{46}$ + $4X_{47}$

Define the constraints:
    Amount Out of Arnold: $X_{13} + X_{14} \leq 75$
    Amount Out of Supershelf: $X_{23} + X_{24} \leq 75$

    Amount Through Thomas: $X_{13} + X_{23} - X_{35} - X_{36} - X_{37} = 0$
    Amount Through Washburn: $X_{14} + X_{24} - X_{45} - X_{46} - X_{47} = 0$

    Amount Into Zrox: $X_{35} + X_{45} = 50$
    Amount Into Hewes: $X_{36} + X_{46} = 60$
    Amount Into Rockwright: $X_{37} + X_{47} = 40$

Non-negativity of Variables: $X_{ij} \geq 0$, for all i and j.

PROBLEM 7

Fodak must schedule its production of camera film for the first
four months of the year. Film demand (in 000s of rolls) in
January, February, March and April is expected to be 300, 500,
650 and 400, respectively. Fodak's production capacity is 500
thousand rolls of film per month.

Film produced in month i can be used to meet demand in month i
or can be held in inventory to meet demand in month i+1 or month
i+2 (but not later due to the film's limited shelflife). There
is no film in inventory at the start of January.

The film business is highly competitive, so Fodak cannot
afford to lose sales or keep its customers waiting. Meeting
month i's demand with month i+1's production is unacceptable.

The film's production and delivery cost per thousand rolls
will be $500 in January and February. This cost will increase
to $600 in March and April due to a new labor contract. Any
film put in inventory requires additional transport costing $100
per thousand rolls. Film held in inventory from one month to
the next costs $50 per month per thousand rolls.

a) Modeling this least-cost production scheduling problem as a
   transportation problem, develop the transportation tableau
   (overlooking the need for a dummy row or column).

b) Modeling this same problem as a transshipment problem, draw
   the network representation.

c) How might the network in (b) be changed if there was no limit
   on the length of time film could be held in inventory?

SOLUTION 7
a)

	Jan. Demand	Feb. Demand	Mar. Demand	Apr. Demand	Production Capacity
January Production	500	650	700	+M	500
February Production	+M	500	650	700	500
March Production	+M	+M	500	650	500
April Production	+M	+M	+M	500	500
Demand	300	500	650	400	

Note in the above tableau that there are numerous unacceptable "routes", resulting from two restrictions: 1) demand cannot be kept waiting, and 2) film cannot be held in inventory more than two months. We use +M as the cost for an unacceptable route since our objective is cost minimization.

b) The source nodes in this transshipment problem are the four months of production. The destination nodes are the four months of demand. The intermediate nodes are the first three months' ending inventory (there is no reason to be holding any inventory at the end of April).

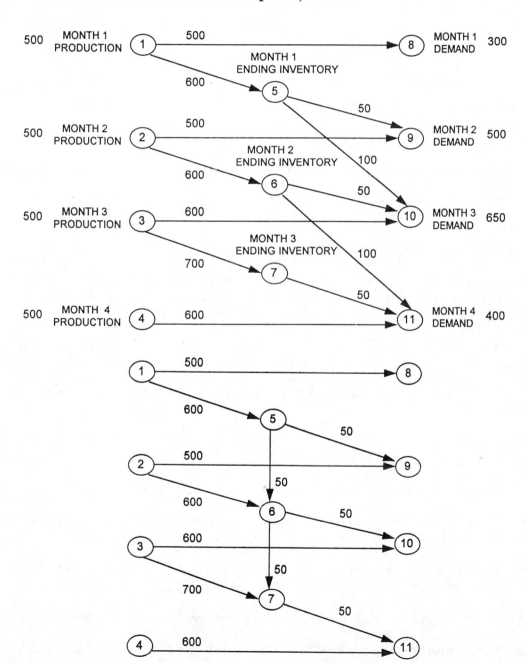

c)

ANSWERED PROBLEMS

PROBLEM 8

The Navy has 9,000 pounds of material in Albany, Georgia which it wishes to ship to three installations: San Diego, Norfolk, and Pensacola. They require 4,000, 2,500, and 2,500 pounds, respectively. The following gives the shipping costs per pound for truck, railroad, and airplane transit.

	San Diego	Norfolk	Pensacola
Truck	$12	$ 6	$ 5
Railroad	$20	$11	$ 9
Airplane	$30	$26	$28

Laws require equal allotment of shipping among the 3 carriers.

a) Draw the network representation of this problem.

b) Give the least cost starting solution for this problem.

c) Solve using the transportation algorithm.

PROBLEM 9

There are four marketing research firms (MR1, MR2, MR3, MR4) that Hairways has faith in to advertise its products. Hairways has just come out with a new hairspray and they wish to have 30 newspaper ads, 15 television ads, and 25 radio ads available within three months. Given the size of the firms it is expected that MR1 can produce 15 total ads, MR2 can produce 25 total ads, MR3 can produce 10 total ads, and MR4 can produce 20 total ads. The bids submitted (in thousands of dollars per ad) are:

	MR1	MR2	MR3	MR4
Newspaper	16	10	12	12
Television	26	20	30	21
Radio	22	15	23	14

a) Formulate this problem as a linear program and show that it fits the structure of a transportation problem.

b) Solve as a transportation problem and give a solution with six media-firm combinations.

c) Give another solution with five media-firm combinations.

d) Give another solution with seven media-firm combinations.

PROBLEM 10

The city of Francene has 25 contracts up for bids in each of
four different departments: Sanitation, Police Services, Parks
Department, and Administration.   Three different consulting
firms are bidding on the contracts: Ace Consulting, Band
Corporation, and QM Associates. Ace has personnel for 40
contracts, Band for 40, and QM for 30.   Because contracts are
similar within each department, each firm is able to set a fixed
bid per contract for each department.   The bid price (in $1000s
per contract) is summarized below:

	Sanitation	Police	Parks	Administration
Ace	10	15	14	16
Band	15	18	8	10
QM	12	12	12	12

How should the contracts be awarded and how much will the city
spend?

PROBLEM 11

Independent Auditors (IA) has committed 100 of its auditors in
three locations (35 from its Los Angeles branch, 30 from its
Chicago branch, and 35 from its New York branch) to audit firms
in three cities: 25 for Denver, 35 for Atlanta, and 40 for New
York.   Because of possible charges of conflicts of interest, no
New York based IA auditor will audit a New York firm. Taking
into account all costs and revenues, and the following profit
table giving the average profit per auditor (in $1000's), solve
for IA's optimal distribution of auditors.

	Denver	Atlanta	New York
Los Angeles	25	18	10
Chicago	30	35	20
New York	14	24	X

PROBLEM 12

Emily Rodd, manager of Camp Pinnacle, must assign her five head counselors to cabins for the summer. The counselors have cabin assignment preferences (based on cabin size, location, condition and other factors). The counselors' cabin preference ratings on a 1-to-9 scale (9 being most favorable) are listed below:

	Cabin				
	1	2	3	4	5
Abbey	3	9	7	5	5
Babbs	6	8	3	5	7
Carla	2	8	5	2	7
Diane	7	4	2	2	9
Ellsa	6	8	5	2	5

Help Emily make the counselor-cabin assignments that will maximize the sum of the preference ratings achieved.

PROBLEM 13

In addition to Pine City's established microcomputer firm, Local Computer, there are three new microcomputer firms that have opened up in the area. In an effort to establish good relations, Manny's Manufacturing plans on buying one computer system from each of the new firms and two from Local Computer. Manny's has five plants, each with different needs, and hence Manny needs to install five different systems. The bids (in $1,000's) from the firms are:

	Plant				
	P1	P2	P3	P4	P5
Computer Town	10	12	14	18	20
Computer World	11	13	15	14	18
Universal Comp	6	14	24	20	19
Local Computer	14	15	16	22	25

a) Give a network representation for this problem.

b) Solve the problem using the Hungarian Method.

c) Suppose Computer World did not have the system needed by P5. How would this have affected the first assignment matrix? How would this have affected the optimal solution?

d) Suppose Computer World did not have the systems needed by P4 or P5. How would this have affected the first assignment matrix? How would this have affected the optimal solution?

PROBLEM 14

A plant manager for a sporting goods manufacturer is in charge
of assigning the manufacture of four new aluminum products to
four different departments. Because of varying expertise and
workloads, the different departments can produce the new
products at various rates. If only one product is to be
produced by each department and the daily output rates are given
in the table below, which department should manufacture which
product to maximize total daily product output? (Note:
Department 1 does not have the facilities to produce golf clubs.)

Department	Bats	Tennis Rackets	Golf Clubs	Racquetball Rackets
1	100	60	X	80
2	100	80	140	100
3	110	75	150	120
4	85	50	100	75

PROBLEM 15

RVW (Restored Volkswagens) buys 15 used VW's at each of two car
auctions each week held at different locations. It then
transports the cars to repair shops it contracts with. When
they are restored to RVW's specifications, RVW sells 10 each to
three different used car lots. There are various costs
associated with the average purchase and transportation prices
from each auction to each repair shop. Also there are
transportation costs from the repair shops to the used car lots.
RVW is concerned with minimizing its total cost given the costs
in the table below.

a) Given the costs below, draw a network representation for this
   problem.

	Repair Shops			Used Car Lots		
	S1	S2		L1	L2	L3
Auction 1	550	500	S1	250	300	500
Auction 2	600	450	S2	350	650	450

b) Formulate this problem as a transshipment linear programming
   model.

TRUE/FALSE

16. In order to use the special solution procedures for the transportation problem (Stepping Stone and MODI), it is assumed that the cost per unit of shipment between an origin and a destination is independent of the number of items shipped.

17. If a transportation problem has four origins and five destinations, the LP formulation of the problem will have nine constraints.

18. In a transportation problem, if the total supply is greater than the total demand, a dummy origin is added prior to using its special purpose algorithm.

19. The transportation, assignment, and transshipment problems are all special cases of linear programming models known as network models and can be solved by the simplex method.

20. In the stepping stone method, when two cells are simultaneously reduced to zero, degeneracy occurs and one of the two cells must stay occupied with a zero quantity.

21. In a transportation problem with total supply equal to total demand, if there are four origins and seven destinations, and there is a unique optimal solution, the optimal solution will utilize 11 shipping routes.

22. If the optimal transportation tableau has an occupied cell with a zero allocation, then there are alternate optimal solutions.

23. Before using the Hungarian method for a maximization problem with three workers and four jobs to be assigned, first an opportunity cost matrix would be calculated and then a row of zeroes would be added.

24. A transshipment problem is a generalization of the transportation problem in which certain nodes are neither supply nodes nor destination nodes.

25. The assignment problem is a special case of the transportation problem in which all supply and demand values equal one.

26. The stepping stone procedure does not always improve the solution found in the first phase of the transportation simplex method.

27. An opportunity loss matrix in an assignment problem is obtained by subtracting each element in the matrix from the largest element in the matrix.

28. All of the transportation costs associated with a dummy origin or a dummy destination are zero, regardless of whether you are maximizing or minimizing.

29. The optimal solution to a transportation problem will never include a shipment from a dummy origin.

30. Transshipment problem allows shipments both in and out of some nodes while transportation problems do not.

CHAPTER

8

Integer Linear Programming

KEY CONCEPTS

CONCEPT	ILLUSTRATED PROBLEMS	ANSWERED PROBLEMS
All-Integer Linear Program	1,2	6,7,11,13
Mixed-Integer Linear Program	2	11,13
ILP: Maximization	1,3	6,7,8,12
ILP: Minimization	2	11,13
Rounding LP Solution	1	6,12
Graphical Solution	1,2	7
Branch-and-Bound Algorithm	1,2,5	8,11
0-1 Integer Linear Program	3,4,5	9,10
Special 0-1 Constraints	3	9

REVIEW

1. A linear program in which all the variables are restricted to be integers is called an <u>integer linear program (ILP)</u>. If only a subset of the variables are restricted to be integers, the problem is called a <u>mixed integer linear program (MILP)</u>.

2. <u>Binary variables</u> are variables whose values are restricted to be 0 or 1. If all variables are restricted to be 0 or 1, the problem is called a <u>0-1</u> <u>or</u> <u>binary integer program</u>.

3. Many practical applications involve only binary integer variables and hence many computer codes are written only for this case (such as LINDO/PC). <u>Binary expansion</u> is a mathematical technique which may be used to convert any integer variable into the sum of binary variables.

4. The <u>branch and bound algorithm</u> may be used to solve ILPs or MILPs. (See algorithm on the next page.)

5. <u>Rounding</u> the values of the variables obtained by solving the linear programming problem may yield an infeasible solution or a solution that might be feasible but not optimal for the ILP or MILP.

6. For problems in which X_i and and X_j represent binary variables designating whether projects i and j have been completed, the following <u>special constraints</u> may be formulated:

   (a) At most <u>k</u> <u>out</u> <u>of</u> <u>n</u> projects will be completed: $\sum_j X_j \leq k$

   (b) Project j is <u>conditional</u> on project i: $X_j - X_i \leq 0$

   (c) Project i is a <u>corequisite</u> for project j: $X_j - X_i = 0$

   (d) Projects i and j are <u>mutually exclusive</u>: $X_i + X_j \leq 1$.

7. <u>Sensitivity analysis</u> information for integer linear programming does not have the same connotation as that for linear programming and should be either discarded or used with great caution. In fact, small changes in the coefficients of an integer program can cause large changes in its optimal solution or even cause the problem to be infeasible.

BRANCH AND BOUND PROCEDURE
FOR THE ALL-INTEGER LINEAR PROGRAM

The following is for a <u>maximization problem</u>. For a minimization
problem the roles of the upper bound and lower bound would be
reversed.

1. Solve the problem as a linear program.
   If the solution satisfies the integer constraints, STOP.
   Otherwise the solution is an <u>upper bound (UB)</u> for the problem.
   Construct an initial node giving this solution.

2. Find any solution that satisfies all the constraints.
   This provides an initial <u>lower bound (LB)</u> for the problem.
   (If none initially can be found, set LB = $-\infty$).

3. Consider the node with the largest z value in which an integer
   variable, X_j, has a non-integer value, x_j.
   If none exists, an optimal solution can be identified. STOP.
   Otherwise, create two branches:
   (1) one with this added constraint: $X_j \leq [x_j]$;
   (2) the other with this added constraint: $X_j \geq [x_j] + 1$.
       ($[x_j]$ means the integer part of x_j.)

4. Solve the two linear programs (each with one of the constraints
   added in the previous step).
   Add two new nodes at the end of the branches with the solutions.

5. (1) If the branch gives an <u>infeasible solution</u>, do not consider
       this branch further. GO TO STEP 6.
   (2) If the branch gives an <u>integer solution</u>, do not consider
       this branch further. GO TO STEP 6.
   (3) If the branch gives a <u>feasible solution</u> <u>to the linear
       program, but not an integer</u> solution, GO TO STEP 7.

6. For the integer solution, with objective function value = Z,
   (1) If Z = UB, it is optimal. STOP.
   (2) If LB < Z < UB, set LB = Z. GO TO STEP 3.
   (3) If Z < LB, do not change either the UB or LB, GO TO STEP 3.

7. Consider all <u>descendent nodes</u> with non-integer values.
   (1) For any node in which Z $\leq$ LB, do not consider this branch
       further.
   (2) Consider all nodes with Z > LB.
       Set UB to the maximum Z value of any of these nodes.
       If UB = LB, STOP.
       Otherwise GO TO STEP 3.

[Note: There is a flow chart of this procedure in your textbook.]

ILLUSTRATED PROBLEMS

PROBLEM 1

Given the following all-integer linear program:

$$\text{MAX} \quad Z = 3X_1 + 2X_2$$

$$\text{S.T.} \quad 3X_1 + X_2 \leq 9$$

$$X_1 + 3X_2 \leq 7$$

$$-X_1 + X_2 \leq 1$$

$$X_1, X_2 \geq 0 \text{ and integer}$$

a) Solve the problem as a linear program ignoring the integer constraints. Show that the optimal solution to the linear program gives fractional values for both X_1 and X_2.

b) What is the solution obtained by rounding fractions greater than of equal to 1/2 to the next larger number? Show that this solution is not a feasible solution.

c) What is the solution obtained by rounding down all fractions? Is it feasible?

d) Enumerate all points in the linear programming feasible region in which both X_1 and X_2 are integers, and show that the feasible solution obtained in (c) is not optimal and that in fact the optimal integer is not obtained by any form of rounding.

e) Solve the above problem by the branch and bound method and show that the optimal solution obtained by this method is the same as that enumerated in (d).

SOLUTION 1

a) From the graph on the next page, the optimal solution to the linear program is $X_1 = 2.5$, $X_2 = 1.5$, $Z = 10.5$.

b) By rounding the optimal solution of $X_1 = 2.5$, $X_2 = 1.5$ to $X_1 = 3$, $X_2 = 2$, this point lies outside the feasible region.

c) By rounding the optimal solution down to $X_1 = 2$, $X_2 = 1$, we see that this solution indeed is an integer solution within the feasible region, and substituting in the the objective function, it gives $Z = 8$.

d) There are eight feasible integer solutions in the linear
programming feasible region with Z values as follows:

	X_1	X_2	Z	
1.	0	0	0	
2.	1	0	3	
3.	2	0	6	
4.	3	0	9	<==== optimal
5.	0	1	2	
6.	1	1	5	
7.	2	1	8	<==== part (c) solution
8.	1	2	7	

$X_1 = 3$, $X_2 = 0$ is the optimal solution. Rounding the LP
solution ($X_1 = 2.5$, $X_2 = 1.5$) would not have been optimal.

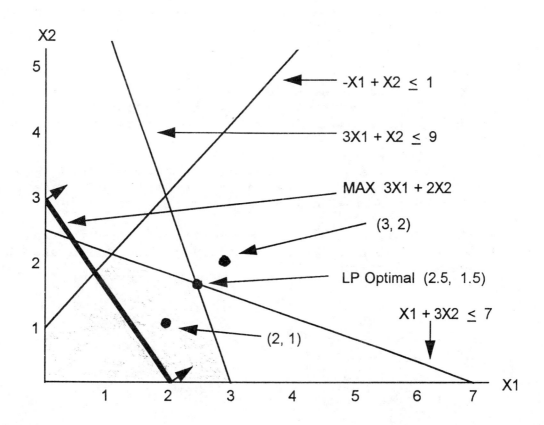

e) Solve by branch and bound.

Iteration 1
_____

1. Solving as a linear program gives $X_1 = 2.5$, $X_2 = 1.5$,
   $Z = 10.5$. This is an initial upper bound (UB = 10.5).

2. Rounding to $X_1 = 2$, $X_2 = 1$, $Z = 8$, is a feasible integer
   solution. Hence this provides a lower bound (LB = 8).

UB = 10.5
LB = 8

Inside node 1:
$X_1 = 2.5$
$X_2 = 1.5$
$Z = 10.5$

3. Branch on X_1, solve two linear programs, one with $X_1 \leq 2$
   added to the original constraints of node 1, the other
   with $X_1 \geq 3$ added to the original constraints of node 1.
   This is done on the next page.

4. Form nodes with these solutions.

5. Note node 2 gives a feasible but not integer solution to
   the linear program. Follow the procedure at step 7.
   Node 3 gives an integer solution. Follow the procedure at
   step 6.

6. At node 3, $Z = 9$; since this integer solution gives an
   objective function value greater than the current LB, set
   the LB = 9. Do not branch further from node 3.

7. At node 2, $Z = 9\ 1/3$. Since this is the maximum of all
   descendent nodes, set UB = 9 1/3, and go to step 3 for
   next iteration.

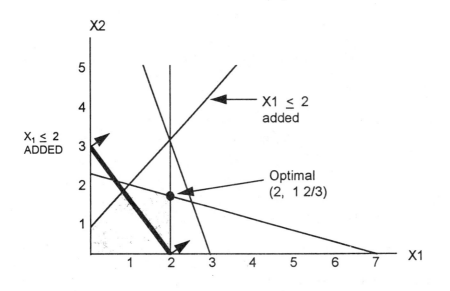

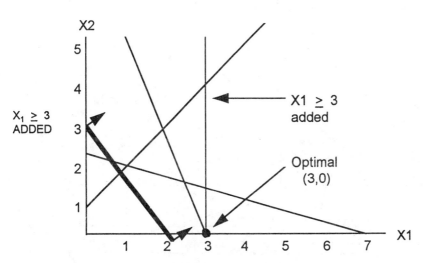

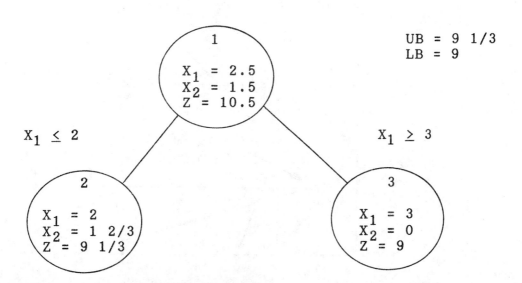

Iteration 2
_____

3. Branch from node 2 on $X_2 \leq 1$ and $X_2 \geq 2$, added to the
    constraints at node 2 respectively (see below) to create
    nodes 4 and 5 (see next page).

4. Form nodes 4 and 5 with these solutions.

5. Node 4 gives an integer solution as does node 5.
    Proceed to step 6.

6. For node 4, $Z = 8$; for node 5, $Z = 7$. Since these are
    both less than the current LB, do not change the LB, and
    do not consider these branches further.

7. The maximum Z value of the descendent nodes is 9. Thus
    change the UB to 9. Since the LB = UB, STOP. The optimal
    $Z = 9$, determined by $X_1 = 3$, $X_2 = 0$. See next page for
    final solution tree.

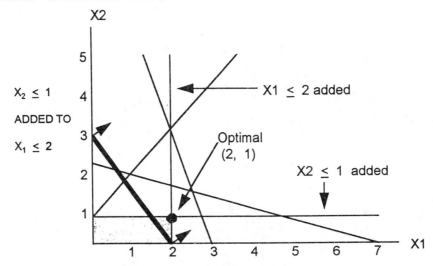

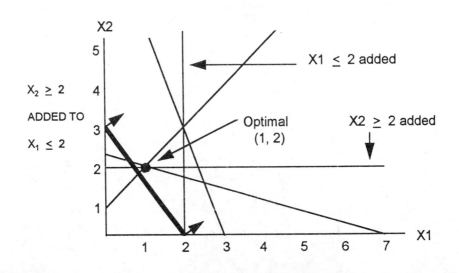

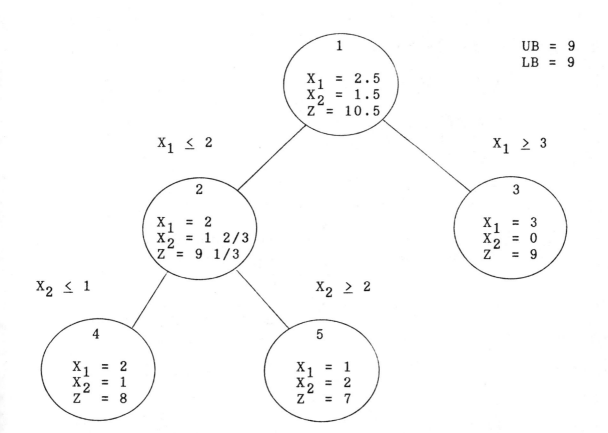

UB = 9
LB = 9

Node 1:
$X_1 = 2.5$
$X_2 = 1.5$
$Z = 10.5$

$X_1 \leq 2$

$X_1 \geq 3$

Node 2:
$X_1 = 2$
$X_2 = 1\ 2/3$
$Z = 9\ 1/3$

Node 3:
$X_1 = 3$
$X_2 = 0$
$Z = 9$

$X_2 \leq 1$

$X_2 \geq 2$

Node 4:
$X_1 = 2$
$X_2 = 1$
$Z = 8$

Node 5:
$X_1 = 1$
$X_2 = 2$
$Z = 7$

PROBLEM 2

Given the following problem:

$$\text{MIN } Z = 2X_1 + X_2$$

$$\text{S.T.} \quad X_1 + 3X_2 \geq 5$$

$$8X_1 + 3X_2 \geq 17$$

$$X_1, X_2 \geq 0$$

a) Solve for the optimal solution to the linear program.

b) Suppose only X_2 were restricted to be an integer. Use the branch-and-bound method to determine the optimal solution to this mixed integer linear program.

c) Suppose both X_1 and X_2 were restricted to be integers. Determine the optimal solution to the all-integer linear program.

SOLUTION 2

a)

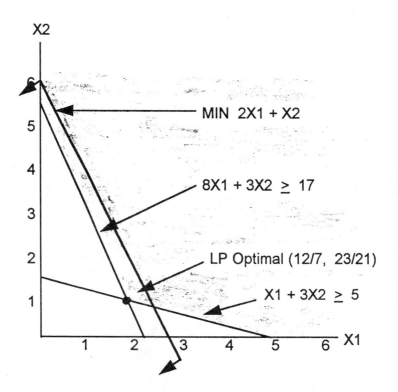

The optimal solution is $X_1 = 1 \ 5/7$, $X_2 = 1 \ 2/21$, $Z = 4 \ 11/21$.

b) Since only X_2 must be integer we will branch on this.

1. The initial <u>lower</u> <u>bound</u>, LB = 4 11/21, is the optimal solution to the LP (since this is a minimization).

2. Rounding <u>up</u> X_2 to 2, gives a solution of X_1 = 12/7, X_2 = 2, Z = 5 3/7.

$$\begin{array}{c}
1 \\
X_1 = 1\ 5/7 \\
X_2 = 1\ 2/21 \\
Z = 4\ 11/21
\end{array}$$

LB = 4 11/21
UB = 5 3/7

3. Branch from node 1 on $X_2 \leq 1$, and $X_2 \geq 2$ respectively.

$X_2 \leq 1$ ADDED

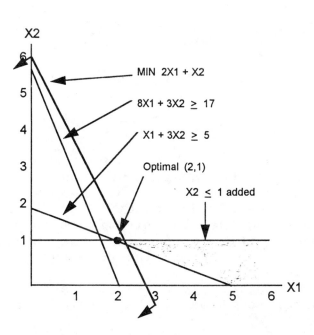

X_1 = 2, X_2 = 1, Z = 5

$X_2 \geq 2$ ADDED

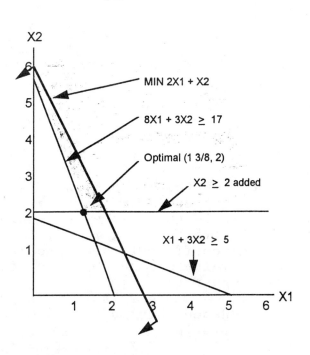

X_1 = 1 3/8, X_2 = 2, Z = 4 3/4

4. Form nodes 2 and 3 respectively.

5. Node 2 gives $X_1 = 2$, $X_2 = 1$, $Z = 5$. Node 3 gives
    $X_1 = 1\ 3/8$, $X_2 = 2$, $Z = 4\ 3/4$. Both are integer in X_2.
    Proceed to step 6.

6. Since both of these nodes have integer values for X_2, they
    both provide UBs for the problem (since it is a
    minimization). Thus the new UB = 4 3/4.

7. Considering all descendent nodes (2 and 3), the LB = 4 3/4
    (since this is a minimization). Since the LB = UB, STOP.
    The optimal mixed integer solution is $X_1 = 1\ 3/8$, $X_2 = 2$,
    $Z = 4\ 3/4$.

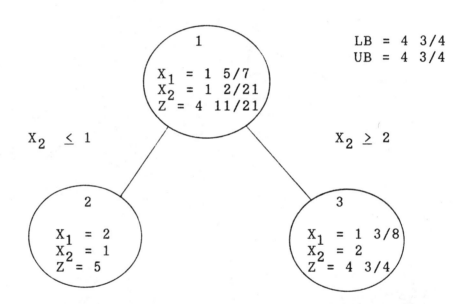

c) Now that both X_1 and X_2 must both be integers, we could
    proceed from above by branching on X_1 in node 3. However,
    note that since the optimal value of the objective function
    with X_2 integer only is 4 3/4 and the objective function
    coefficients are also integers, this implies that the optimal
    value of the objective function in the all-integer problem
    must be $\geq$ 5.
      At node 2, an all-integer solution giving Z = 5 was found.
    Hence this must be the optimal solution to the all-integer
    problem:

$$X_1 = 2, \quad X_2 = 1; \quad Z = 5.$$

PROBLEM 3

Metropolitan Microwaves, Inc. is planning to expand its operations into other electronic appliances. The company has identified seven new product lines it can carry. The required initial investment and floor space and the expected rate of return on each line.

Product Line	Initial Investment	Floor Space (Sq.Ft.)	Expected Rate Of Return
1. Black & White TVs	$ 6,000	125	8.1%
2. Color TVs	12,000	150	9.0
3. Large Screen TVs	20,000	200	11.0
4. VHS VCRs	14,000	40	10.2
5. Beta VCRs	15,000	40	10.5
6. Video Games	2,000	20	14.1
7. Home Computers	32,000	100	13.2

Metropolitan has decided that they should not stock large screen televisions unless they stock either b&w or color televisions. Also, they will not stock both types of VCRs, and they will stock video games if they stock color televisions. Finally, the company wishes to introduce at least three new product lines.

If the company has $45,000 to invest and 420 sq. ft. of floor space available, formulate an integer linear program for Metropolitan to maximize its overall expected rate of return.

SOLUTION 3

Define variables: X_j = 0 or 1 depending on whether or not product line j is introduced.

Define objective: Maximize total overall expected return:
$$MAX \; .081(6000)X_1 + .09(12000)X_2 + .11(20000)X_3 + .102(14000)X_4$$
$$+ .105(15000)X_5 + .141(2000)X_6 + .132(32000)X_7$$

Define constraints:
1) Money: $6X_1 + 12X_2 + 20X_3 + 14X_4 + 15X_5 + 2X_6 + 32X_7 \leq 45$

2) Space: $125X_1 + 150X_2 + 200X_3 + 40X_4 + 40X_5 + 20X_6 + 100X_7 \leq 420$

3) Stock large screen TVs only if stock b&w or color TVs:
   $X_1 + X_2 \geq X_3$ or $X_1 + X_2 - X_3 \geq 0$

4) Not stock both types of VCRs: $X_4 + X_5 \leq 1$

5) Stock video games if they stock color TV's: $X_2 - X_6 \geq 0$.

6) At least 3 new lines: $X_1 + X_2 + X_3 + X_4 + X_5 + X_6 + X_7 \geq 3$

7) Variables are 0 or 1: X_j = 0 or 1 for j = 1,,,7.

PROBLEM 4

Tom's Tailoring has five idle tailors and four custom garments
to make. The estimated time (in hours) it would take each
tailor to make each garment is listed below. (An 'X' in the
table indicates an unacceptable tailor-garment assignment.)

	Tailor				
Garment	1	2	3	4	5
Wedding gown	19	23	20	21	18
Clown costume	11	14	X	12	10
Admiral's uniform	12	8	11	X	9
Bullfighter's outfit	X	20	20	18	21

Formulate an integer program for determining the tailor-garment
assignments that minimize the total estimated time spent making
the four garments. No tailor is to be assigned more than one
garment and each garment is to be worked on by only one tailor.

SOLUTION 4

This is a classic assignment problem. A specialized solution
procedure for this type of problem is covered in Chapter 7.
Here we will formulate it as a 0-1 integer program. Note: the
LP solution to this problem will automatically be integer.

Define the decision variables:
X_{ij} = 0 or 1 depending on whether or not garment i is assigned
to tailor j. Number of decision variables =
[(number of garments)(number of tailors)] - (number of
unacceptable assignments) = [4(5)] - 3 = 17.

Define the objective:
Minimize total time spent making garments:
$$\text{MIN } 19X_{11} + 23X_{12} + 20X_{13} + 21X_{14} + 18X_{15} + 11X_{21} + 14X_{22}$$
$$+ 12X_{24} + 10X_{25} + 12X_{31} + 8X_{32} + 11X_{33} + 9X_{35} + 20X_{42}$$
$$+ 20X_{43} + 18X_{44} + 21X_{45}$$

Define the constraints:
Only one tailor per garment:
$$(1)\ X_{11} + X_{12} + X_{13} + X_{14} + X_{15} = 1$$
$$(2)\ X_{21} + X_{22} + X_{24} + X_{25} = 1$$
$$(3)\ X_{31} + X_{32} + X_{33} + X_{35} = 1$$
$$(4)\ X_{42} + X_{43} + X_{44} + X_{45} = 1$$
No more than one garment per tailor:
$$(5)\ X_{11} + X_{21} + X_{31} \leq 1$$
$$(6)\ X_{21} + X_{22} + X_{23} + X_{24} \leq 1$$
$$(7)\ X_{31} + X_{33} + X_{34} \leq 1$$
$$(8)\ X_{41} + X_{42} + X_{44} \leq 1$$
$$(9)\ X_{51} + X_{52} + X_{53} + X_{54} \leq 1$$

Nonnegativity: $X_{ij} \geq 0$ for i = 1,..,4 and j = 1,...,5

PROBLEM 5

Given the following 0-1 integer program:

$$\text{MAX} \quad Z = 3.1X_1 + 2.4X_2 + 4.4X_3 + 2.9X_4$$

$$\text{S.T.} \qquad X_1 + X_2 + X_3 + X_4 \leq 2$$

$$3X_1 + 8X_2 + 5X_3 + 6X_4 \leq 18$$

$$X_1 \qquad\qquad - X_4 \leq 0$$

$$X_1, X_2\ X_3, X_4 = 0 \text{ or } 1$$

Solve this problem using the branch-and-bound algorithm.

SOLUTION 5

> **NOTE:** To apply the branch-and-bound procedure covered in this chapter to a 0-1 integer programming problem, a constraint of the type $X \leq 1$ must be added to the program for each 0-1 variable. Also, 0-1 branching variable X_i is treated as a constant; the branching constraints introduced will be $X_i = 0$ and $X_i = 1$.

Following the noted instruction above, four constraints are added to the problem formulation: $X_i \leq 1$ for i = 1,2,3,4.

Iteration 1

(Step 1) Solving as a LP gives $X_1 = .5$, $X_2 = 0$, $X_3 = 1$, $X_4 = .5$, $Z = 7.4$. This is an initial upper bound (UB = 7.4).

(Step 2) Rounding to $X_1 = 0$, $X_2 = 0$, $X_3 = 1$, $X_4 = 0$, $Z = 4.4$ is a feasible 0-1 solution. This provides a lower bound (LB = 4.4).

```
        1
   X₁=.5   X₃=1
   X₂=0    X₄=.5
        Z=7.4
```

UB = 7.4
LB = 4.4

(Step 3) Branch on X_1 creating two branches, one with the constraint $X_1 = 0$ replacing $X_1 \leq 1$ and the other with the constraint $X_1 = 1$ replacing $X_1 \leq 1$.

(Step 4) Solve the two linear programs resulting from Step 3 and form two new nodes with the solutions.

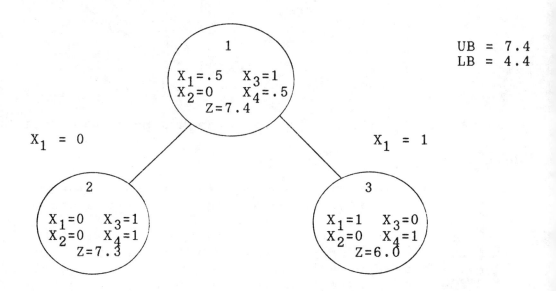

(Step 5) Both node 2 and node 3 give 0-1 solutions. Go to Step 6 for both nodes.

(Step 6) At node 2, $Z = 7.3$; since this 0-1 solution gives an objective function value greater than the current LB, set the LB = 7.3. Do not branch further from node 2.

At node 3, $Z = 6.0$; since this 0-1 solution gives an objective function value less than the current LB, do not change the LB. Do not branch further from node 3.

Go to Step 3.

(Step 3) There are no descendent nodes with any 0-1 variables having values other than 0 or 1. The optimal solution has been reached; it corresponds to the LB of 7.3. Thus, the optimal solution is $X_1 = 0$, $X_2 = 0$, $X_3 = 1$, $X_4 = 1$, $Z = 7.3$.

ANSWERED PROBLEMS

PROBLEM 6

Given the following all-integer linear program:

$$MAX \ Z = 15X_1 + 2X_2$$

$$S.T. \qquad 7X_1 + X_2 \leq 23$$

$$3X_1 - X_2 \leq 5$$

$$X_1, X_2 \geq 0 \text{ and integer}$$

a) Solve the problem as an LP, ignoring the integer constraints.

b) What solution is obtained by rounding up fractions greater than or equal to 1/2? Is this the optimal integer solution?

c) What solution is obtained by rounding down all fractions? Is this the optimal integer solution? Explain.

d) Show that the optimal solution to the all-integer problem gives a lower Z value than the optimal Z value for the LP.

e) Explain why the optimal Z value for the ILP problem is always less than or equal to the corresponding LP's optimal Z value. When would they be equal? What can you say about the MILP's optimal Z value compared to the corresponding LP and ILP.

PROBLEM 7

Given the following all-integer linear programming problem:

$$MAX \ Z = 3X_1 + 10X_2$$

$$S.T. \qquad 2X_1 + X_2 \leq 5$$

$$X_1 + 6X_2 \leq 9$$

$$X_1 - X_2 \geq 2$$

$$X_1, X_2 \geq 0 \text{ and integer}$$

a) Solve the problem graphically as a linear program.

b) Show that there is only one integer point and it is optimal.

c) Suppose the third constraint were changed to $X_1 - X_2 \geq 2.1$. What is the new optimal solution to the LP? ILP?

PROBLEM 8

Given the following all-integer linear programming problem:

$$\text{MAX } Z = 5X_1 + 4X_2$$

$$\text{S.T.} \quad 4X_1 + X_2 \leq 10$$

$$5X_1 + 3X_2 \leq 15$$

$$X_1 + X_2 \leq 4$$

$$X_1, X_2 \geq 0 \text{ and integer}$$

a) Solve this problem using the branch and bound algorithm.

b) Suppose the objective function were changed to:
MAX $Z = 5X_1 + 3X_2$. Using the same branch and bound tree calculated in (a), re-evaluate the optimal solution to the all-integer problem.

PROBLEM 9

Tower Engineering Corporation is considering undertaking several proposed projects for the next fiscal year. The projects, the number of engineers and the number of support personnel required for each project, and the expected profits for each project are summarized in the following table:

	Project					
	1	2	3	4	5	6
Engineers Required	20	55	47	38	90	63
Support Personnel Required	15	45	50	40	70	70
Profit ($1,000,000s)	1.0	1.8	2.0	1.5	3.6	2.2

Formulate an integer program that maximizes Tower's profit subject to the following management constraints:

(1) Use no more than 175 engineers

(2) Use no more than 150 support personnel

(3) If either project 6 or project 4 is done, both must be done

(4) Project 2 can be done only if project 1 is done

(5) If project 5 is done, project 3 must not be done and vice versa

(6) No more than three projects are to be done.

PROBLEM 10

Kloos Industries has projected the availability of capital over each of the next three years to be $850,000, $1,000,000, and $1,200,000 respectively. It is considering four options for the disposition of the capital:

(1) Research and development of a promising new product
(2) Plant expansion
(3) Modernization of its current facilities
(4) Investment in a valuable piece of nearly real estate

Monies not invested in these projects in a given year will NOT be available for following year's investment in the projects.
   The expected benefits three years hence from each of the four projects and the yearly capital outlays of the four options are summarized in the table below in $1,000,000's.
   In addition, Kloos has decided to undertake exactly two of the projects, and if plant expansion is selected, it will also modernize its current facilities.

Options	Capital Outlays Year 1	Year 2	Year 3	Projected Benefits
New Product R&D	.35	.55	.75	5.2
Plant Expansion	.50	.50	0	3.6
Modernization	.35	.40	.45	3.2
Real Estate	.50	0	0	2.8

Formulate this problem as a binary programming problem.

PROBLEM 11

Given the following problem:

$$MIN\ Z = 5X_1 + 8X_2$$

$$S.T.\qquad X_1 + X_2 \geq 7.2$$

$$X_1 + 4X_2 \geq 20$$

$$5X_1 + 3X_2 \leq 34$$

$$X_1,\ X_2 \geq 0$$

a) Solve the mixed-integer problem where X_1 must be integer.

b) Solve the problem where both X_1 and X_2 must be integer.

PROBLEM 12

A business manager for a grain distributor is asked to decide
how many containers of each of two grains to purchase to fill
its 1,600 pound capacity warehouse. The table below summarizes
the container size, availability, and expected profit per
container upon distribution.

Grain	Container Size	Containers Available	Container Profit
A	500 lbs.	3	$1,200
B	600 lbs.	2	$1,500

a) Formulate as a linear program with the decision variables
representing the number of containers purchased of each
grain. Solve for the optimal solution.

b) What would be the optimal solution if you were not allowed
to purchase fractional containers?

c) Consider the possible effects of rounding an LP solution to
obtain an integer solution. There are three cases:
   (1) the rounded linear programming optimal solution will be
       the optimal integer programming solution;
   (2) the rounded linear programming optimal solution gives a
       feasible, but not optimal integer solution;
   (3) the rounded linear programming optimal solution is an
       infeasible integer solution.
For this problem (i) round down all fractions; (ii) round up
all fractions; (iii) round off all fractions (NOTE: Two of
these are equivalent.) Which case above occurred under each
rounding method?

PROBLEM 13

Given the following problem:

$$\text{MIN } Z = 4X_1 + 7X_2$$

$$\text{S.T.} \quad X_1 + 6X_2 \geq 14$$

$$2X_1 + 5X_2 \geq 22$$

$$3X_1 + X_2 \geq 10$$

$$X_1, X_2 \geq 0$$

a) Solve the mixed integer problem where X_1 is required to be
integer.

b) Using (a), solve the all-integer linear program.

TRUE/FALSE

14. The optimal solution to a linear program gave X_1 = 2.58 and X_2 = 1.32. If X_1 and X_2 were restricted to be integers, then X_1 = 3, X_2 = 1 will give a feasible solution, but not necessarily an optimal integer solution.

15. The objective function coefficients are all integers for an ILP. The optimal solution to the linear program is X_1 = 2.58, X_2 = 1.32, and z = 14.28. The solution was rounded to X_1 = 3, X_2 = 1 and z = 14, and this is a feasible solution. Then this must be the optimal solution to the ILP.

16. Project 5 must be completed before project 6 is started. The constraint would be: $X_5 - X_6 \leq 0$.

17. In the branch and bound procedure for a maximization problem, the objective function value at a descendent node can never be greater than the objective function value at a previous node on the branch.

18. In the branch and bound procedure for a maximization problem, when a node yields integer values for all variables required to be integers, its objective function value provides an upper bound for the optimal value of the objective function.

19. The optimal solution to an integer linear program still must occur at an extreme point of the feasible region formed by the functional constraints.

20. If at most three of five projects are to be completed, the constraint would be: $X_1 + X_2 + X_3 + X_4 + X_5 \leq 3$.

21. In the branch and bound procedure for a maximization problem with an established LB = 15, a certain node has X_1 = 3.52, X_2 = 3, z = 14.78. Descendent nodes would be created with branches by adding the constraints: $X_1 \leq 3$ and $X_1 \geq 4$ respectively.

22. When using the branch-and-bound procedure on a maximization problem, the lower bound value tends to decrease as more branching occurs.

23. An optimal integer solution of X_1 = 3, X_2 = 5, z = 150 has been found for an ILP. For the linear programming formulation, the range of optimality for C_1 was between 15 and 30 with a current C_1 = 20. Then if C_1 is increased to 21 in the ILP, the new optimal value of the objective function must be 153.

24. For a minimization ILP, a lower bound is found when any integer solution is determined.

25. The branch-and-bound solution procedure can be used for both all-integer and mixed-integer linear programs.

26. The value of the optimal solution to any mixed-integer linear program involving minimization will be less than or equal to the solution to its LP relaxation.

27. Generally, the optimal solution to an integer linear program is less sensitive to the constraint coefficients than is a linear program.

28. Using the branch-and-bound procedure, an optimal solution has been reached when the upper bound equals the lower bound.

CHAPTER

9

Network Models

KEY CONCEPTS

CONCEPT	ILLUSTRATED PROBLEMS	ANSWERED PROBLEMS
Shortest Route Problem	1,2	7,10,12
Minimal Spanning Tree Problem	3	6,9,11
Maximal Flow Problem	4	5,8,13

REVIEW

1. The shortest-route problem is concerned with finding the shortest path in a network from one node (or set of nodes) to another node (or set of nodes).

2. If all arcs in the network have nonnegative values then a labeling algorithm can be used to find the shortest paths from a particular node to all other nodes in the network. (See next page.)

3. A tree is a set of connected arcs that does not form a cycle.

4. A spanning tree is a tree that connects all nodes of a network.

5. The minimal spanning tree problem seeks to determine the minimum sum of arc lengths necessary to connect all nodes in a network. It can be solved by a greedy algorithm. (The algorithm is presented at the end of this section.)

6. The maximal flow problem is concerned with determining the maximal volume of flow from one node (called the source) to another node (called the sink).

7. In the maximal flow problem, each arc has a maximum arc flow capacity which limits the flow through the arc. It is possible that an arc, (i,j), may have a different flow capacity from i to j than from j to i. The maximal flow algorithm is used to solve this problem. (See next page.)

8. Computer codes for specific network problems (e.g. shortest route, minimal spanning tree, and maximal flow) are extremely efficient and can solve even large problems relatively quickly. The Management Scientist contains computer codes for each of these problems.

SHORTEST ROUTE ALGORITHM

Note: We use the notation [ ] to represent a <u>permanent</u> <u>label</u> and
       ( ) to represent a <u>tentative</u> <u>label</u>.

1. Assign node 1 the permanent label [0,S]. The first number is
   the distance from node 1; the second number is the preceding
   node. Since node 1 has no preceding node, it is labeled S for
   the starting node.

2. Compute tentative labels, (d,n), for the nodes that can be
   reached directly from node 1. d = the direct distance from node
   1 to the node in question -- this is called the <u>distance</u> <u>value</u>.
   n indicates the preceding node on the route from node 1 --
   this is called the <u>preceding</u> <u>node</u> <u>value</u>. (All nodes labeled in
   this step have n = 1.)

3. Identify the tentatively labeled node with the smallest
   distance value. Suppose it is <u>node k</u>. Node k is now
   <u>permanently</u> <u>labelled</u> (using [,] brackets). If all nodes are
   permanently labeled GO TO STEP 5.

4. Consider all nodes (i) <u>without</u> <u>permanent</u> <u>labels</u> that can be
   reached directly from the node k identified in step 3. For
   each, calculate the quantity t as follows:

   t = (arc distance from node k to node i)
       + (distance value at node k).

   If the non-permanently labeled node has a tentative label:
       Compare t with the current distance value at the tentatively
       labeled node in question.
           If t < distance value of the tentatively labeled node:
               Replace the tentative label in question with (t,k).
           If t $\geq$ distance value of the tentatively labeled node:
               Keep the current tentative label.

   If the non-permanently labeled node does not have a tentative
   label:
       Create a tentative label of (t,k) for the node in question.

   In either case GO TO STEP 3.

5. The permanent labels identify the shortest distance from node 1
   to each node as well as the preceding node on the shortest
   route. The shortest route to a given node can be found by
   working backwards by starting at the given node and moving to
   its preceding node. Continuing this procedure from the
   preceding node will provide the shortest route from node 1 to
   the node in question.

FLOW CHART OF
SHORTEST−ROUTE ALGORITHM

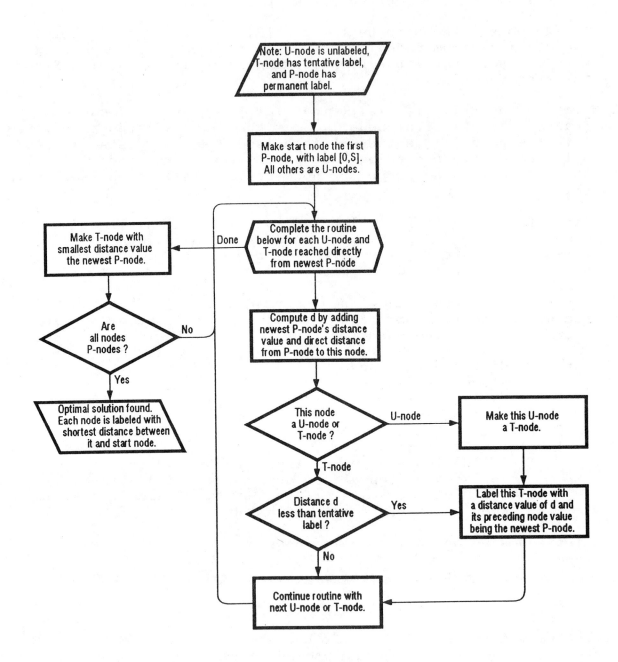

MINIMAL SPANNING TREE ALGORITHM

1. Arbitrarily begin at any node and connect it to the closest node. The two nodes are referred to as <u>connected nodes</u>, and the remaining nodes are referred to as <u>unconnected nodes</u>.

2. Identify the unconnected node that is closest to one of the connected nodes (break ties arbitrarily). Add this new node to the set of connected nodes. Repeat this step until all nodes have been connected.

> **NOTE:** The criterion to be minimized in the minimal spanning tree algorithm and the shortest-route algorithm is not limited to distance even though the terms "closest" and "shortest" are used in describing the procedures. Other criteria include time and cost. (Neither time nor cost are necessarily linearly related to distance.)

MAXIMAL FLOW ALGORITHM

1. Find any path from the source node to the sink node that has positive flow capacities (in the direction of the flow) for <u>all</u> arcs on the path. If no path is available, then the optimal solution has been found.

2. Find the smallest arc capacity, P_f, on the path selected in step 1. Increase the flow through the network by sending the amount, P_f, over this path.

3. For the path selected in step 1 reduce all arc flow capacities in the direction of the flow by P_f and increase all arc flows in the opposite direction of the flow by P_f. Go to step 1.

> **NOTE:** Students often ask if it is necessary to increase the arc flow capacities in the opposite direction of the flow (latter part of step 3), since it appears to be a wasted effort. The answer is 'yes' it is necessary.
>
> This creation of fictitious capacity allows us to alter a previous flow assignment if we need to (which is illustrated in an upcoming problem). Otherwise, we might have to terminate the algorithm before reaching an optimal solution.

FLOW CHART FOR
MAXIMAL FLOW ALGORITHM

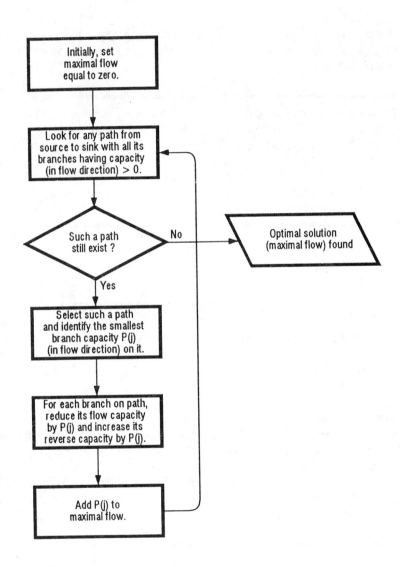

ILLUSTRATED PROBLEMS

PROBLEM 1

Find the shortest route from node 1 to all other nodes in the network below.

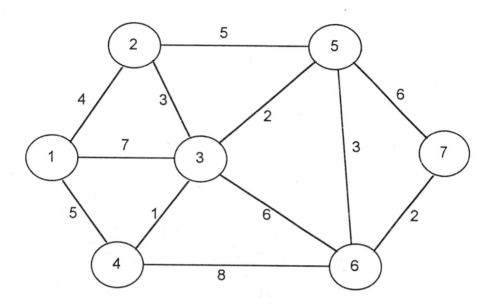

SOLUTION 1

Iteration 1

1. Assign node 1 the permanent label [0,S].

2. Since nodes 2, 3, and 4 are connected to node 1 by only one arc assign the tentative labels of (4,1) to node 2; (7,1) to node 3; (5,1) to node 4. The first part of this tentative label indicates the distance between node 1 and the node in question. The second part of the label indicates that the preceding node was node 1.

3. Node 2 is the tentatively labelled node with the smallest distance (4) , and hence becomes the new permanently labelled node. The network should now appear as follows:

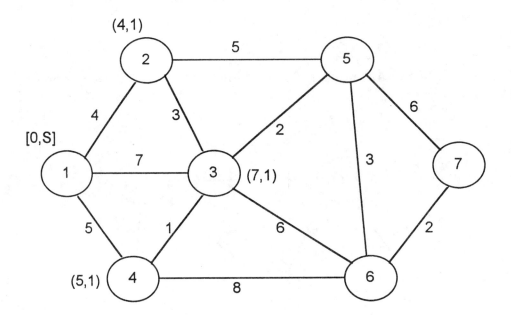

4. For each node with a tentative label which is connected to
   node 2 by just one arc, compute the sum of its arc length
   plus the distance value of node 2 (which is 4).

   Node 3:   3 + 4 = 7   (not smaller than current label; do not
                          change.)
   Node 5:   5 + 4 = 9   (assign tentative label to node 5 of
                          (9,2) since node 5 had no label.)

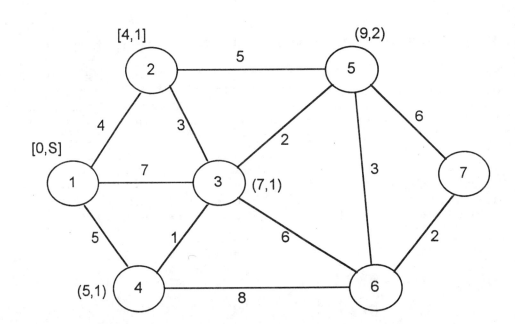

Iteration 2

3. Node 4 has the smallest tentative label distance (5). It now becomes the <u>new permanently labelled node</u>.

4. For each node with a tentative label which is connected to node 4 by just one arc, compute the sum of its arc length plus the distance value of node 4 (which is 5).

   Node 3:   1 + 5 = 6   (replace the tentative label of node 3 by (6,4) since 6 < 7, the current distance.)
   Node 6:   8 + 5 = 13 (assign tentative label to node 6 of (13,4) since node 6 had no label.)

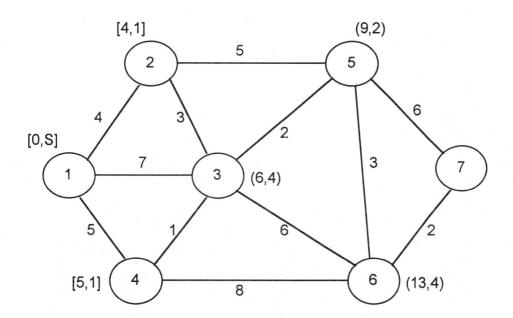

Iteration 3

3. Node 3 has the smallest tentative distance label (6). It now becomes the new permanently labelled node.

4. For each node with a tentative label which is connected to node 3 by just one arc, compute the sum of its arc length plus the distance to node 3 (which is 6).

   Node 5:   2 + 6 = 8   (replace the tentative label of node 5 with (8,3) since 8 < 9, the current distance)
   Node 6:   6 + 6 = 12 (replace the tentative label of node 6 with (12,3) since 12 < 13, the current distance)

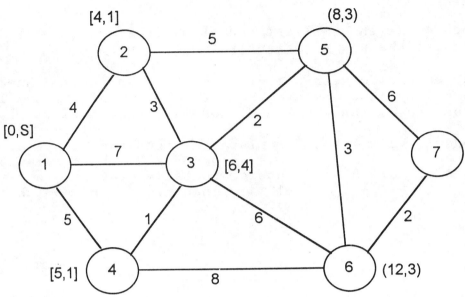

Iteration 4

3. Node 5 has the smallest tentative label distance (8). It now
becomes the new permanently labelled node.

4. For each node with a tentative label which is connected to
node 5 by just one arc, compute the sum of its arc length plus
the distance value of node 5 (which is 8).

Node 6: 3 + 8 = 11 (replace the tentative label of node 6
with (11,5) since 11 < 12, the current
distance)
Node 7: 6 + 8 = 14 (assign tentative label to node 7 of
(14,5) since node 7 had no label.)

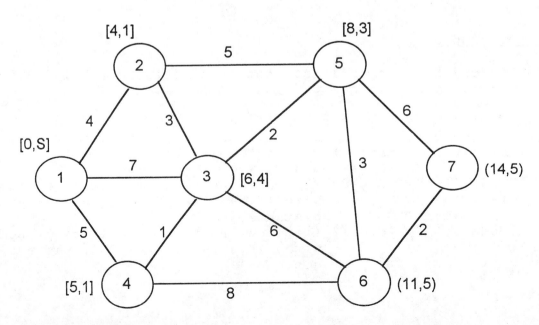

Iteration 5

3. Node 6 has the smallest tentative label distance (11). It
   now becomes the new permanently labelled node.

4. For each node with a tentative label which is connected to
   node 6 by just one arc, compute the sum of its arc length
   plus the distance value of node 6 (which is 11).

   Node 7: 2 + 11 = 13 (replace the tentative label of node 7
                         with (13,6) since 13 < 14, the current
                         distance)

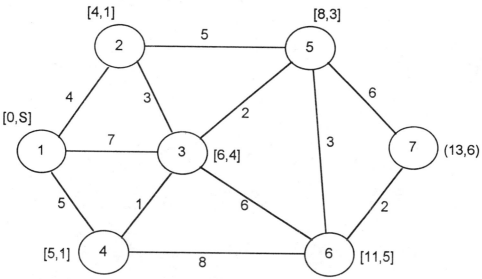

Iteration 6

3. Node 7 becomes permanently labelled, and hence all nodes are
   now permanently labelled. Thus proceed to summarize in
   Step 5.

5. Summarizing by tracing the shortest routes backwards through
   the permanent labels:

Node	Minimum Distance	Shortest Route
2	4	1-2
3	6	1-4-3
4	5	1-4
5	8	1-4-3-5
6	11	1-4-3-5-6
7	13	1-4-3-5-6-7

PROBLEM 2

Susan Winslow has an important business meeting in Paducah this evening. She has a number of alternate routes by which she can travel from the company headquarters in Lewisburg (city 1) to Paducah (city 6). The network below summarizes the various routes.

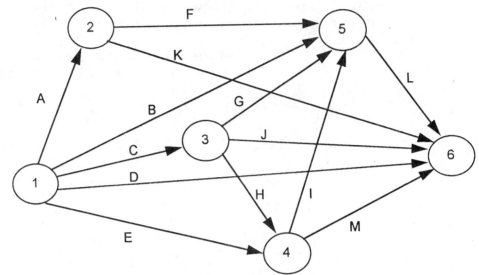

The following table gives the method of travel, travel time, and ticket cost associated with each of the branches of the network.

Route	Method	Time (hours)	Ticket Cost
A	Train	4	$ 20
B	Plane	1	$115
C	Bus	2	$ 10
D	Taxi	6	$ 90
E	Train	3 1/3	$ 30
F	Bus	3	$ 15
G	Bus	4 2/3	$ 20
H	Taxi	1	$ 15
I	Train	2 1/3	$ 15
J	Bus	6 1/3	$ 25
K	Taxi	3 1/3	$ 50
L	Train	1 1/3	$ 10
M	Bus	4 2/3	$ 20

If Susan earns a salary of $15 per hour, what route should she take to minimize the total overall travel costs?

SOLUTION 2

First determine the appropriate values for the arcs. As Susan is interested in minimizing her total travel costs, each arc value would represent the total cost of traveling over that arc.

Thus: Arc Cost = $15 x (Travel Time) + (Ticket cost)

This results in the following cost network:

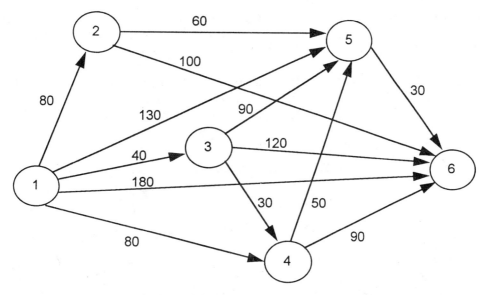

Now solve this problem by the shortest route algorithm using
these costs for the "distances".

Iteration 1

1. Assign node 1 the permanent label [0,S].

2. Nodes 2, 3, 4, 5, and 6 are connected to node 1 by one arc.
   Assign a tentative label of (80,1) to node 2; (40,1) to
   node 3; (80,1) to node 4; (130,1) to node 5; and, (180,1) to
   node 6.

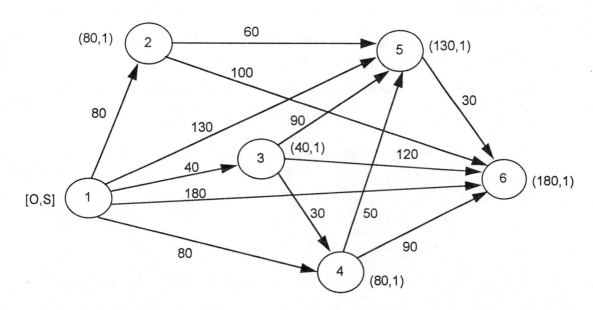

3. Node 3 has the tentatively labeled node with the smallest distance (40), and hence becomes the new permanently labeled node.

4. For each node with a tentative label which is connected to node 3 by just one arc, compute the sum of its arc length plus the distance value of node 3 (which is 40).

Node 4: 30 + 40 = 70 (Replace tentative label with (70,3))
Node 5: 90 + 40 = 130 (Leave the current tentative label)
Node 6: 120 + 40 = 160 (Replace tentative label with (160,3))

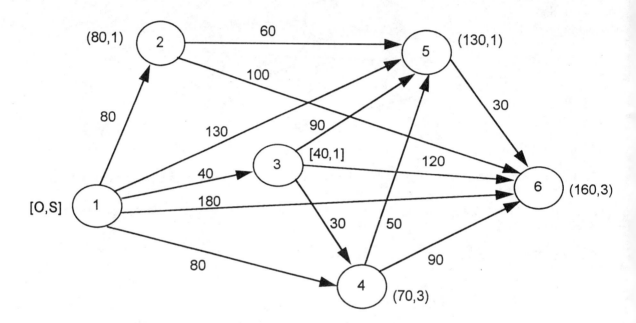

Iteration 2

3. Node 4 has the smallest tentative label distance (70). It now becomes the new permanently labeled node.

4. For each node with a tentative label which is connected to node 4 by just one arc, compute the sum of its arc length plus the distance of node 4 (which is 70).

Node 5: 50 + 70 = 120 (replace tentative label with (120,4))
Node 6: 90 + 70 = 160 (leave the current tentative label)

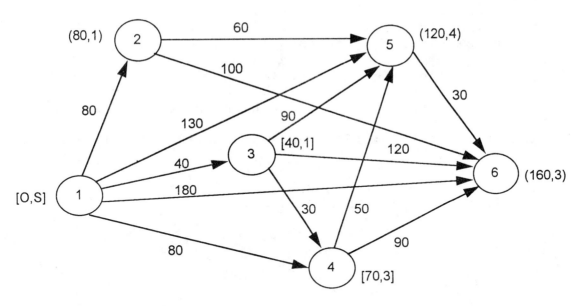

Iteration 3

3. Node 2 has the smallest tentative label distance (80). It now becomes the new permanently labelled node.

4. For each node with a tentative label which is connected to node 2 by just one arc, compute the sum of its arc length plus the distance value of node 2 (which is 80).

   Node 5: 60 + 80 = 140 (leave the current tentative label)
   Node 6: 100 + 80 = 180 (leave the current tentative label)

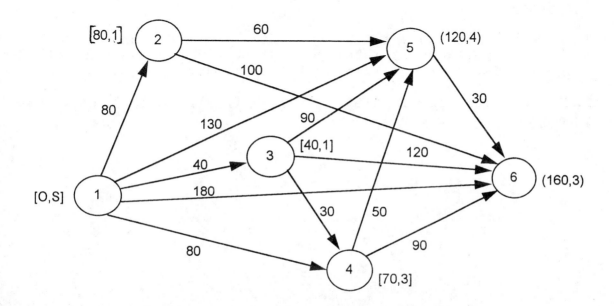

Iteration 4

3. Node 5 has the smallest tentative label distance (120). It
   now becomes the new permanently labeled node.

4. For each node with a tentative label which is connected to
   node 5 by just one arc, compute the sum of its arc length
   plus the distance of node 5 (which is 120).

   Node 6: 30 + 120 = 150 (replace tentative label with (150,5))

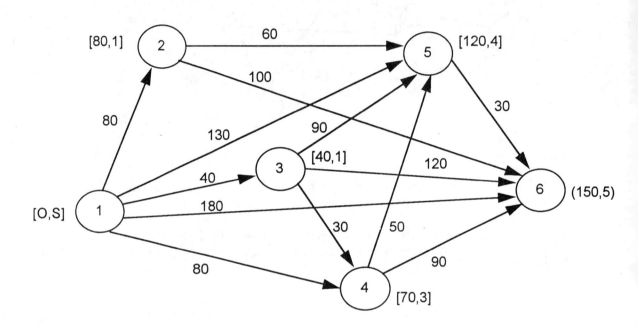

Iteration 5

3. Node 6 is the only tentatively labelled node, and hence it
   becomes permanently labelled. Since all nodes are labelled,
   go to STEP 5 -- determining the optimal solution.

5. The minimum cost is $150. Tracing the route backwards, the
   minimum cost route is:

                1 - 3 - 4 - 5 - 6   or

        C (bus) - H (taxi) - I (train) - L (train).

PROBLEM 3

Find the minimal spanning tree in the following network:

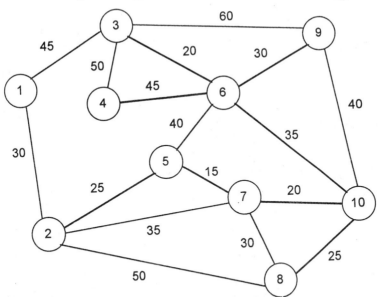

Arbitrarily selecting node 1, we see that its closest node is
node 2 (distance = 30). Therefore, initially we have:
  Connected nodes: 1,2   Unconnected nodes: 3,4,5,6,7,8,9,10
  Chosen arcs: 1-2

Now, the closest unconnected node to a connected node is node 5
(distance = 25 to node 2).   Node 5 becomes a connected node.
  Connected nodes: 1,2,5   Unconnected nodes: 3,4,6,7,8,9,10
  Chosen arcs: 1-2, 2-5

Now, the closest unconnected node to a connected node is node 7
(distance = 15 to node 5).   Node 7 becomes a connected node.
  Connected nodes: 1,2,5,7   Unconnected nodes: 3,4,6,8,9,10
  Chosen arcs: 1-2, 2-5, 5-7

Now, the closest unconnected node to a connected node is node 10
(distance = 20 to node 7).   Node 10 becomes a connected node.
  Connected nodes: 1,2,5,7,10   Unconnected nodes: 3,4,6,8,9
  Chosen arcs: 1-2, 2-5, 5-7, 7-10

Now, the closest unconnected node to a connected node is node 8
(distance = 25 to node 10).   Node 8 becomes a connected node.
  Connected nodes: 1,2,5,7,10,8   Unconnected nodes: 3,4,6,9
  Chosen arcs: 1-2, 2-5, 5-7, 7-10, 10-8

Now, the closest unconnected node to a connected node is node 6
(distance = 35 to node 10).   Node 6 becomes a connected node.
  Connected nodes: 1,2,5,7,10,8,6   Unconnected nodes: 3,4,9
  Chosen arcs: 1-2, 2-5, 5-7, 7-10, 10-8, 10-6

Now, the closest unconnected node to a connected node is node 3
(distance = 20 to node 6).   Node 3 becomes a connected node.
   Connected nodes: 1,2,5,7,10,8,6,3   Unconnected nodes: 4,9
   Chosen arcs: 1-2, 2-5, 5-7, 7-10, 10-8, 10-6, 6-3

Now, the closest unconnected node to a connected node is node 9
(distance = 30 to node 6).   Node 9 becomes a connected node.
   Connected nodes: 1,2,5,7,10,8,6,3,9   Unconnected nodes: 4
   Chosen arcs: 1-2, 2-5, 5-7, 7-10, 10-8, 10-6, 6-3, 6-9

The only remaining unconnected node is node 4.   It is closest to
connected node 6 (distance = 45).

Thus, the minimal spanning tree (displayed below) consists of:

Arcs: 1-2, 2-5, 5-7, 7-10, 10-8, 10-6, 6-3, 6-9, 6-4

Values: 30 + 25 + 15 + 20 + 25 + 35 + 20 + 30 + 45 = 245

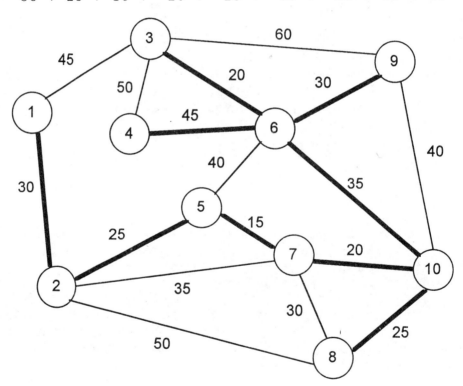

NOTE: The minimal spanning tree algorithm can be
executed with minimal writing effort. Assuming you
have drawn a network representation of the problem,
simply darken the minimum-value arcs you are
choosing to connect one node with another. The
unconnected nodes will always be evident and the
solution, when you reach it, will also be clear.

PROBLEM 4

Find the maximal flow from node 1 to node 7 in the following network:

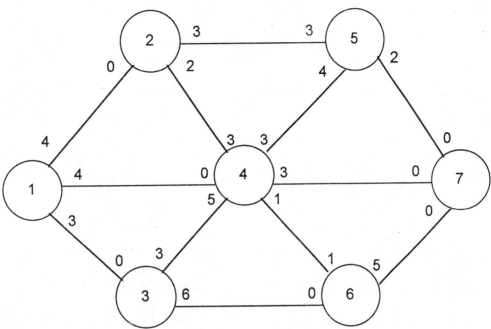

SOLUTION 4

Iteration 1

1. Find a path from the source node, 1, to the sink node, 7, that has flow capacities greater than zero on all arcs of the path. One such path is 1-2-5-7.

2. The smallest arc flow capacity on the path 1-2-5-7 is the minimum of {4, 3, 2} = 2.

3. Reduce all arc flows in the direction of the flow by 2 on this path and increase all arc flows in the reverse direction by 2:

        (1-2)   4 - 2 = 2   (2-1)   0 + 2 = 2
        (2-5)   3 - 2 = 1   (5-2)   3 + 2 = 5
        (5-7)   2 - 2 = 0   (7-5)   0 + 2 = 2

The new network is as follows:

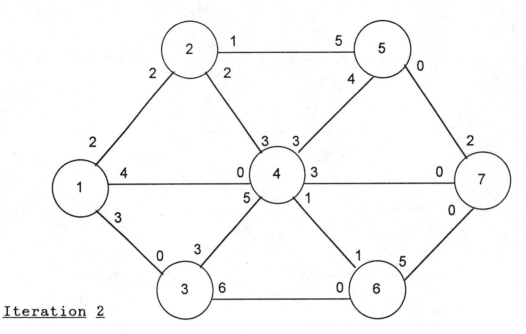

Iteration 2

1. Path 1-4-7 has flow capacity greater than zero on all arcs.

2. The minimum arc flow capacity on 1-4-7 is 3.

3. Reduce the arc flow capacities on the path in the direction of the flow by 3, and increase these capacities in the reverse direction by 3:

   (1-4)   4 - 3 = 1   (4-1)   0 + 3 = 3
   (4-7)   3 - 3 = 0   (7-4)   0 + 3 = 3

The new network is:

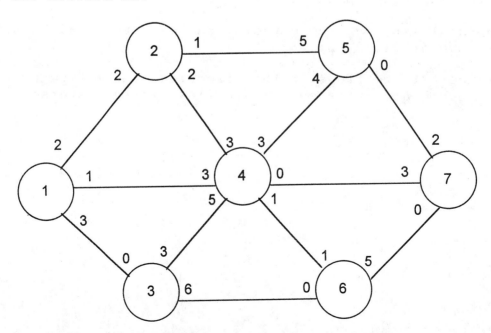

Iteration 3

1. Path 1-3-4-6-7 has flow capacity greater than zero on all arcs.

2. The minimum arc flow capacity on 1-3-4-6-7 is 1.

3. Reduce the arc flow capacities on the path in the direction of the flow by 1 and increase the arc flow capacities in the reverse direction of the flow by 1:

        (1-3)   3 - 1 = 2   (3-1)   0 + 1 = 1
        (3-4)   3 - 1 = 2   (4-3)   5 + 1 = 6
        (4-6)   1 - 1 = 0   (6-4)   1 + 1 = 2
        (6-7)   5 - 1 = 4   (7-6)   0 + 1 = 1

This gives the following network:

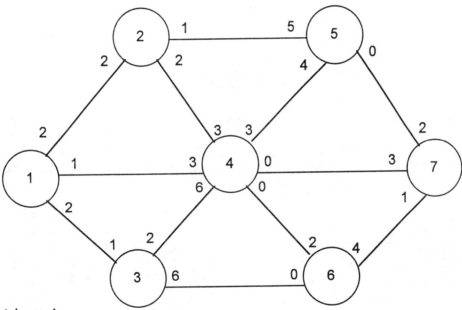

Iteration 4

1. Path 1-3-6-7 has flow capacity greater than zero on all arcs.

2. The minimum arc flow capacity on 1-3-6-7 is 2.

3. Reduce all arc flow capacities on the path in the direction of the flow by 2 and increase the arc flow capacities in the reverse direction by 2:

        (1-3)   2 - 2 = 0   (3-1)   1 + 2 = 3
        (3-6)   6 - 2 = 4   (6-3)   0 + 2 = 2
        (6-7)   4 - 2 = 2   (7-6)   1 + 2 = 3

This gives:

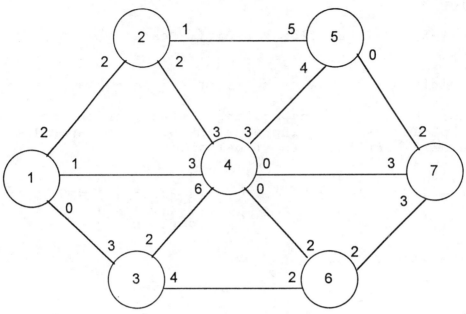

Iteration 5

1. Using the shortest route algorithm, the shortest route from
    node 1 to node 7 is 1-2-4-3-6-7.

2. The smallest arc flow capacity on 1-2-4-3-6-7 is 2.

3. Reduce the arc flow capacities on the path in the direction
    of the flow by 2 and increase these capacities in the reverse
    direction of the flow by 2:

(1-2)	2 - 2 = 0	(2-1)	2 + 2 = 4
(2-4)	2 - 2 = 0	(4-2)	3 + 2 = 5
(4-3)	6 - 2 = 4	(3-4)	2 + 2 = 4
(3-6)	4 - 2 = 2	(6-3)	2 + 2 = 4
(6-7)	2 - 2 = 0	(7-6)	3 + 2 = 5

> **NOTE:** Arc 3-4 is a case where in iteration 3 flow of
> 1 unit was directed from node 3 to node 4.   In
> iteration 5 flow of 2 units was directed from node 4
> to node 3.   By subtracting the assigned flow from
> the capacity of the "sending" end of the arc and
> adding it to the "receiving" end of the arc, the net
> effect of the oppositely directed flow assignments
> is readily known.

This gives the following network:

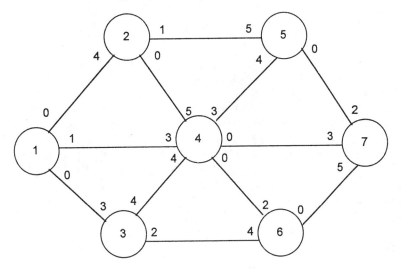

Note there are no arcs with positive flow into the sink node 7.
Thus, the maximal possible flow from node 1 to node 7 has been
found. To identify the maximal flow amount and how it is to be
achieved (directed), compare the original capacities with the
adjusted capacities of each arc in both directions. If the
adjusted capacity is less than the original capacity, the
difference represents the flow amount for that arc.

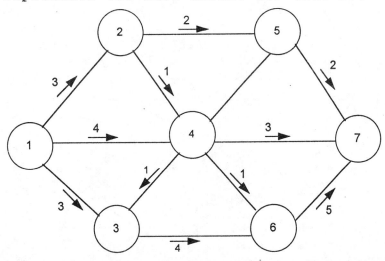

NOTE: There is a degree of randomness to the maximal
flow algorithm. (Recall that Step 1 states "find
any path ...") As long as you follow the algorithm
you will reach an optimal solution, regardless of
your path choice in each iteration. Two people
solving the same problem might get the same optimal
solution or their solutions might differ in regard
to flow routings, but the maximal flows will be the
same.

ANSWERED PROBLEMS

PROBLEM 5

Federated Express operates a fleet of cargo planes and is in the package delivery business. FedEx is interested in knowing what is the maximum it could transport in one day indirectly from Los Angeles to Tampa (via Denver, St. Louis, and/or Houston) if its direct flight was out of service. FedEx's indirect routes from Los Angeles to Tampa, along with their respective estimated excess shipping capacities (measured in hundreds of cubic feet per day), are shown in the network below.

  Is there sufficient excess capacity to indirectly ship 5000 cubic feet of packages in one day? What is the maximum FedEx could ship and how would it be routed?

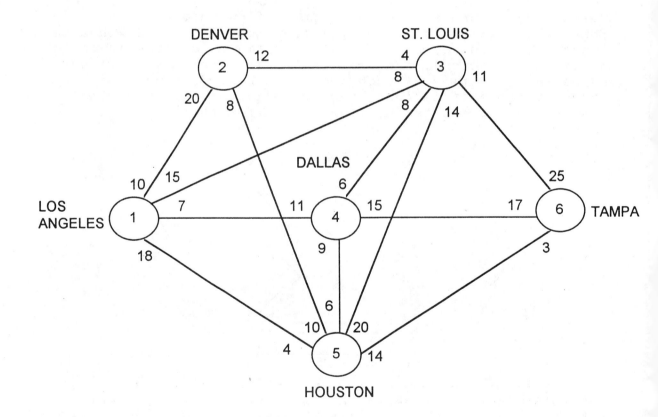

PROBLEM 6

Griffith's Cherry Preserve is a combination wild animal habitat and amusement park. Besides their phenomenally successful wild animal safari tour, there are eight different theme areas in the amusement park.

One problem encountered by management is to develop a method by which people can efficiently travel between each area of the park. Management has learned that a people mover can be constructed at a cost of $50 per foot.

If the following network represents the distances (in feet) between each area of the park for which a people mover is possible, determine the minimum cost for such a system.

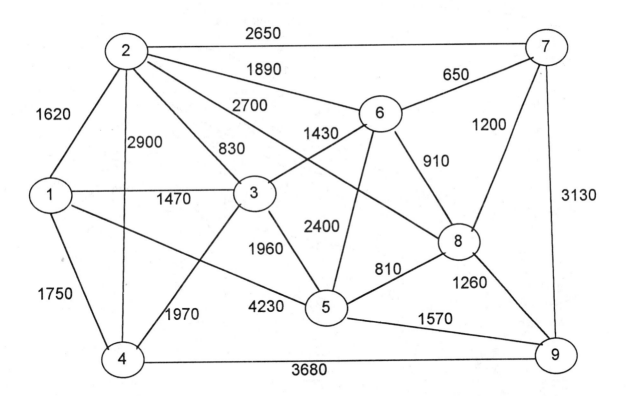

PROBLEM 7

Harvey Hubbell is a graduate student in statistics at a major East Coast university. Harvey believes he has devised a new system for gambling and wishes to spend his summer in Las Vegas testing out his theory.

Harvey has obtained information on one-way discount airfares between relevant pairs of cities. This is given in the network below.

If Harvey's objective is to fly from his home in Philadelphia to Las Vegas for the minimum total cost airfare, what route should he travel?

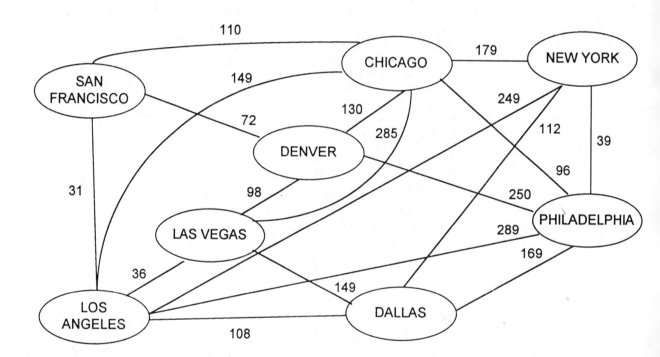

PROBLEM 8

Northeast Energy Consortium is a cooperative venture of eight
electrical utility companies. The network below gives a
representation of the electrical capacity among these companies
over their major transmission lines for a typical day in July.
    If the numbers on the arcs represent megawatt capacity over
the links between the companies, what is the maximum amount of
electricity that can flow from utility A to utility B?

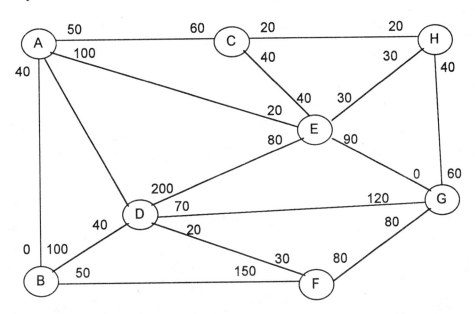

PROBLEM 9

Watkins Industries is planning to create the "office of the
future" for its executive branch. The company plans to install
two word processors, two printers, a laser copier, and a
facsimile transmission machine. All will be interconnected
using an ethernet system.
    The cost of connecting these devices will depend on how the
ethernet cable is routed between the machines. Ethernet cable
costs $25 per foot to install. The table below gives the
approximate direct routing distance in feet between various
pairs of machines.

	WP1	WP2	P1	P2	LC	FT
WP1	0	46	16	23	100	29
WP2		0	81	44	67	98
P1			0	45	57	36
P2				0	38	73
LC					0	52

a) Use the minimal spanning tree algorithm to determine the
   least cost method of connecting all machines.

b) How much cheaper would it be if the company decided not to
   hook up the second printer to this system?

PROBLEM 10

Consider problem 2. Which path should Susan Winslow take to travel from Lewisburg to Paducah if she earned only $6 per hour? What would be the answer if she earned $60 per hour?

PROBLEM 11

Wondercamp is planning a new resort for the urban professional who wishes to "get back to nature". For a hefty fee, it plans to transport clients up the Crocodile River by canoe and then have their clients camp at one of eight designated camp sites.
   They must build a 1000 yard trail from the river to the first camp site as there are no feasible alternatives. It then wishes to build a sequence of trails (of minimum total length) so that every camp site can be reached from any other camp site. A study of the terrain of the area has yielded the following possibilities for trails between campsites. Which trails should be built?

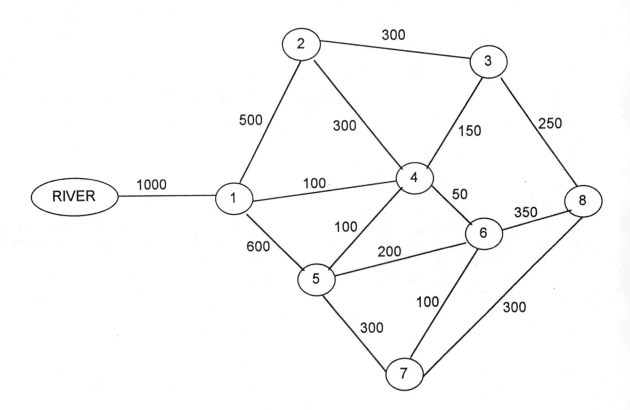

PROBLEM 12

Quicksilver Messenger Service needs to get an important package from Flatsburg (node 1) to Peakston (node 8) as quickly as possible. The network below is a model of the highways that lie between Flatsburg and Peakston. The arc values are travel times in minutes. Which route should Quicksilver take?

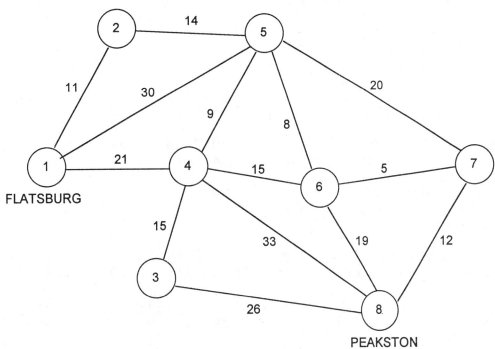

PROBLEM 13

Trans Oceanic Shipping Company has 5 cargo ships which sail between New York and Tel Aviv. Trans Oceanic has been offered a contract to ship up to 120,000 pounds of Jaffa oranges from Tel Aviv to New York in April. After a careful analysis, management has determined the following relevant ship capacities (in 1000's of pounds) during April. How many pounds of oranges can Trans Oceanic ship?

| | | TO | | | | |
		Athens	Rome	Paris	London	New York
	Tel Aviv	60	20	40	--	--
	Athens	--	15	40	--	20
FROM	Rome	10	--	20	40	--
	Paris	40	30	--	30	40
	London	--	10	25	--	60

TRUE/FALSE

14. If one wishes to find the shortest distance necessary to interconnect all nodes in a network one should use the shortest-route algorithm.

15. If the unique shortest path from node 1 to node 8 goes from node 1 to node 3 to node 5 to node 9 to node 8, then the shortest path from node 1 to node 9 must go through node 3.

16. In the solution to the maximal flow algorithm, the flow from all sources must equal the flow into all sinks.

17. In order to use the maximal flow algorithm, each arc's capacity must be the same in both direction.

18. It is possible for shortest-route, minimal spanning tree, and maximal flow problems to have alternative optimal solutions.

19. In the shortest-route algorithm, once a node is given a permanent label one can find the shortest route to that node from node 1.

20. In the maximal flow algorithm, the optimal solution is obtained when no additional paths with positive flow can be found.

21. If the shortest route between two nodes in a network passes through every node in the network, then this must also be the minimal spanning tree for the network.

22. Using the shortest-route algorithm, it is possible for a permanently labeled node to have its label values change.

23. At each iteration of the minimal spanning tree algorithm, the number of connected nodes is increased by one.

24. The maximum amount that can flow from source to sink along a path is equal to the total of the arc capacities on that path.

25. The minimal spanning tree algorithm is unusual for a greedy algorithm in that it is optimal.

26. The solution found by the shortest-route algorithm shows the shortest distance between any pair of nodes in the network.

27. The number of iterations required to solve a shortest-route problem depends on the amount of tentative labeling done.

28. The number of arcs in a minimal spanning tree depends only on the number of nodes in the network and not on distances.

CHAPTER

10

Project Scheduling: PERT/CPM

KEY CONCEPTS

CONCEPT	ILLUSTRATED PROBLEMS	ANSWERED PROBLEMS
Construction of PERT Networks	1,2	6,8,12,13
PERT Analysis with Certain Times	1	6,7,9
PERT Analysis with Uncertain Times	2,4	8,10,11
Activity Earliest/Latest Times	1,2,5	7,9
Time/Cost Analysis	3,4	9-13
LP Formulation for Crashing	3	12,13
PERT/Cost	5	14

REVIEW

1. <u>PERT</u> (Program Evaluation Review Technique) is used to plan the scheduling of individual activities that make up a project.

2. A <u>PERT</u> <u>network</u> can be constructed to model the <u>precedence</u> of the activities. The <u>arcs</u> of the network represent the activities. The <u>nodes</u> of the network represent points in time when an activity or a group of activities have been completed. The nodes are numbered so that each activity begins at a lower numbered node and ends at a higher numbered node. <u>Dummy</u> <u>activities</u> having 0 completion times can be created to help indicate that the proper set of activities has been completed prior to the start of another activity.

3. PERT can be used to determine the earliest/latest start and finish times for each activity, the entire project completion time and the <u>slack</u> <u>time</u> for each activity. (See algorithm at the end of the Review.)

4. A <u>critical</u> <u>path</u> for the network is a path consisting of activities with <u>zero</u> <u>slack</u>.

5. In the <u>three-time</u> <u>estimate</u> <u>approach</u>, the time to complete an activity is assumed to follow a <u>Beta</u> <u>distribution</u>. Its mean is $t = (a + 4m + b)/6$, and its variance is $\sigma^2 = ((b-a)/6)^2$. Here a = the <u>optimistic</u> completion time estimate, b = the <u>pessimistic</u> completion time estimate , and m = the <u>most</u> <u>likely</u> completion time estimate.

6. In the three-time estimate approach, the <u>critical</u> <u>path</u> is determined as if the mean times for the activities were fixed times. The overall project completion time is assumed to have a normal distribution with mean equal to the sum of the means along the critical path and variance equal to the sum of the variances along the critical path.

7. In <u>CPM</u> (Critical Path Method) approach to project scheduling, it is assumed that the normal time to complete an activity, t_j, which can be met at a normal cost, c_j, can be <u>crashed</u> to a reduced time, t_j', under maximum crashing for an increased cost, c_j'.

8. Using CPM, activity j's maximum <u>time</u> <u>reduction</u>, M_j, may be calculated by: $M_j = t_j - t_j'$. It is assumed that its cost per unit reduction, K_j, is linear and can be calculated by: $K_j = (c_j' - c_j)/M_j$.

9. <u>Linear</u> <u>programming</u> may be used to solve a CPM problem to
    minimize the crashing costs needed to complete a project within
    a specified time limit. (See formulation at the end of the
    Review.)

10. <u>PERT/COST</u> is a technique for monitoring costs during a project.
    <u>Work</u> <u>packages</u> (groups of related activities) with estimated
    budgets and completion times are evaluated.

11. A <u>cost</u> <u>status</u> <u>report</u> may be calculated by determining the cost
    overrun or underrun for each work package. These are
    calculated by subtracting the <u>budgeted</u> <u>cost</u> from the <u>actual</u>
    <u>cost</u> of the work package. For work in progress, these may be
    determined by subtracting the prorated budget cost from the
    actual cost to date. The overall project <u>cost</u> <u>overrun</u> <u>or</u>
    <u>underrun</u> at a particular time during a project is determined by
    summing the individual cost overruns and underruns to date of
    the work packages.

PERT ANALYSIS ALGORITHM

PERT networks assume all activities are directed from lower numbered nodes to higher numbered nodes.

1. Make a forward pass through the network as follows: Move sequentially from node 1 to node 2 to node 3, etc. At a given node i, consider all activities beginning at node i. For each of these activities, (i,j), beginning at node i:
    (a) Earliest Start Time = the maximum of all earliest finish times ending at node i. (For node 1 this is 0.)
    (b) Earliest Finish Time = (Earliest Start Time) + (Time to complete activity (i,j)).
The project completion time is the maximum of the Earliest Finish Times at the completion node.

2. Make a backwards pass through the network as follows: Move sequentially backwards from the last node, N, to node N-1, to node N-2, etc. At a given node, j, consider all activities ending at node j. For each of these activities, (i,j):
    (a) Latest Finish Time = the minimum of the latest start times beginning at node j. (For node N, this is the project completion time.)
    (b) Latest Start Time = (Latest Finish Time) - (Time to complete activity (i,j)).

3. Calculate the slack time for each activity by: (Latest Start) - (Earliest Start) or (Latest Finish) - (Earliest Finish).
A critical path is a path of activities, from node 1 to N, with 0 slack times.

LINEAR PROGRAM FOR PROJECT CRASHING

Notation (Note: activity ij starts at node i, ends at node j)
     T = required completion time of the project
     x_i = time represented by node i
     y_{ij} = the amount activity ij is crashed
     M_{ij} = maximum amount activity ij can be crashed
     K_{ij} = cost per time unit to crash activity ij
     τ_{ij} = normal time to complete activity ij

Formulation   MIN $\underset{ij}{\Sigma\Sigma} K_{ij}y_{ij}$

S.T. $x_N \leq T$ where N is the completion node

$y_{ij} \leq M_{ij}$ for each activity ij

$-x_i + x_j + y_{ij} \geq \tau_{ij}$ for each activity ij

$x_i, y_{ij} \geq 0$

FLOW CHART FOR
PROJECT CRASHING

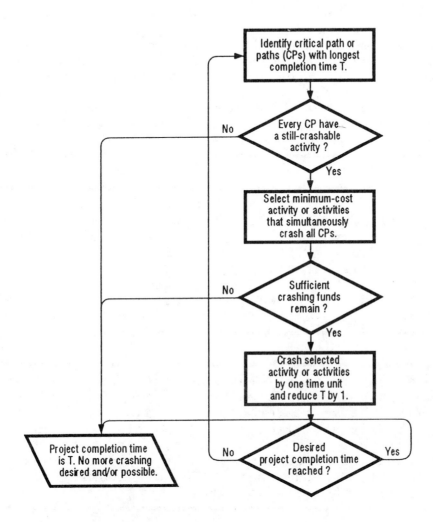

ILLUSTRATED PROBLEMS

NOTE: Two reasons for using dummy activities in project networks are:
(1) Two (or more) arcs should not have both a common starting node <u>and</u> a common finish node because many PERT/CPM computer programs will erroneously treat these multiple arcs as one.
(2) An arc must not enter node i unless it is a prerequisite to <u>every</u> arc exiting node i; otherwise, precedence is inaccurately depicted.

NOTE: One way to partially check the accuracy of your activity earliest/latest time calculations is to compute every activity's slack two ways:
$$\text{Slack} = (EF - ES) = (LF - LS)$$
If the above is not true, you have an error!
   Also, the number of different values in your slack column should not exceed (but does not have to equal) the number of paths in the project network.

NOTE: If you are only interested in identifying the critical path and expected project completion time, there might be an easier approach than determining every activity's earliest start and finish times.
   List (if there are not too many) every path in the network and, for each one, sum the expected times of the activities on that path. You are looking for the path with the largest sum.

PROBLEM 1

Kraft's Kustom Kars is in the business of producing custom automobile assemblies. In particular, Kraft operates a shop that builds and assembles the body and frame of the cars.

Kraft's operations begin with the processing of initial paperwork. This must be done before any other operations are commenced. Once the paperwork has been completed, the body of the car can be built in Room A and the frame of the car can be built in Room B. When the body is built, it is transferred to Room C for finishing work. Similarly, when the frame is built, it is transferred to Room D for finishing work.

When both are built, although not necessarily finished, the final paperwork can be completed. When both the body and frame are finished, they are transported to the assembly Room E, where the body is mounted to the frame.

In the frame building room, Room B, certain chemicals are used which must be completely eliminated by a thorough washdown to prevent gaseous fumes from becoming a health hazard. The project is considered complete when the final paperwork has been completed, the body has been mounted to the frame, and Room B has been completely washed down.

The table below gives the expected completion times in hours for each activity of the project.

Activity	Description	Completion Time
A	Initial Paperwork	3
B	Build Body	3
C	Build Frame	2
D	Finish Body	3
E	Finish Frame	7
F	Final Paperwork	3
G	Mount Body to Frame	6
H	Room B Washdown	2

a) Draw the PERT network that corresponds to this problem.

b) Find the earliest and latest start and finish times for each activity of the project. How long should the project take?

c) Which activities must not be delayed if the project is to be completed in the time calculated in part (b)?

d) Suppose the body finish operation (D) were delayed four hours. By how much would the entire project be delayed?

SOLUTION 1

Before constructing the PERT network, summarize in the following table the immediate predecessor activities for each activity.

Activity	Immediate Predecessors	Completion Times (Hrs.)
A	--	3
B	A	3
C	A	2
D	B	3
E	C	7
F	B,C	3
G	D,E	6
H	C	2

To construct a PERT network, there must be a node for the completion of each distinct entry in the immediate predecessor column as well as a beginning node and and ending node. (There could be others.) Number the nodes such that arrows point from a lower number node to a higher number node.

The result is:

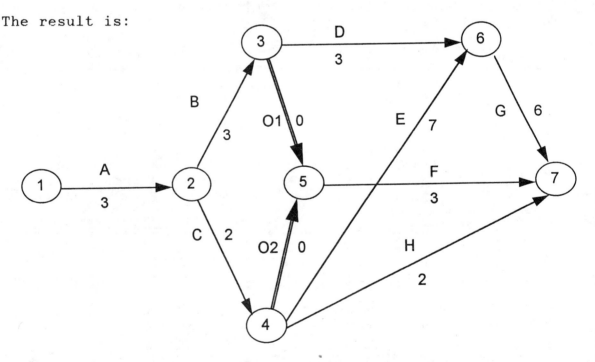

(NOTE: Node 5 represents the time point when both B and C are completed, since node 3 is the time point when only B is completed and node 4 is the time point when only C is completed. Thus, dummy activities, O1 and O2, were created to connect nodes 3 and 5, and nodes 4 and 5 respectively to give the proper precedence relation meaning to node 5. They both have a 0 completion time.)

b) The earliest start time (ES) for activities from node 1 is 0. Then the earliest finish time (EF) for an activity is given by: EF = ES + (completion time). Then ES for an activity = max (EF for all activities into its start node. These are represented on the top of the arrow as [ES,EF].

The <u>forward</u> <u>pass</u> <u>to</u> <u>calculate</u> <u>ES</u> <u>and</u> <u>EF</u>:

Start Node	Activity	Earliest Start (ES)	Earliest Finish(EF)
1	A	0	0 + 3 = 3
2	B	3	3 + 3 = 6
	C	3	3 + 2 = 5
3	D	6	6 + 3 = 9
	O1	6	6 + 0 = 6
4	O2	5	5 + 0 = 5
	E	5	5 + 7 = 12
	H	5	5 + 2 = 7
5	F	MAX(5,6)=6	6 + 3 = 9
6	G	MAX(9,12)=12	12 + 6 = 18

The max(EF at node 7) = 18; Thus, the completion time of the project is 18.

The <u>backwards</u> <u>pass</u> <u>to</u> <u>calculate</u> <u>LF</u> <u>and</u> <u>LS</u>:

End Node	Activity	Latest Finish (LF)	Latest Start (LS)
7	H	18	18 - 2 = 16
	G	18	18 - 6 = 12
	F	18	18 - 3 = 15
6	E	12	12 - 7 = 5
	D	12	12 - 3 = 9
5	O1	15	15 - 0 = 15
	O2	15	15 - 0 = 15
4	C	MIN(15,5,16)=5	5 - 2 = 3
3	B	MIN(9,15)=9	9 - 3 = 6
2	A	MIN(6,3)=3	3 - 3 = 0

This gives the completed network at the top of the next page.

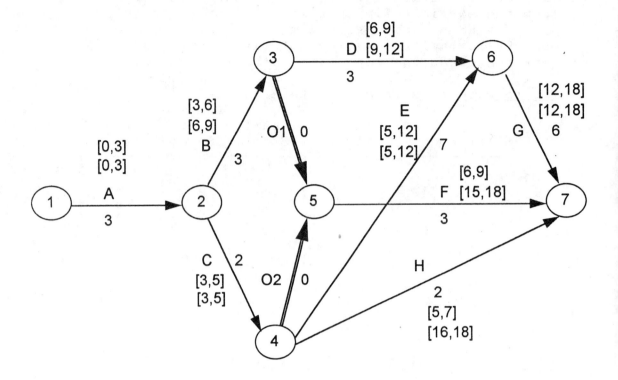

The slack time for each activity (LS - ES) is summarized below:

Activity	ES	EF	LS	LF	Slack
A	0	3	0	3	0
B	3	6	6	9	3
C	3	5	3	5	0
D	6	9	9	12	3
E	5	12	5	12	0
F	6	9	15	18	9
G	12	18	12	18	0
H	5	7	16	18	11

c) Activities A, C, E, G have 0 slack times -- they form the critical path.

d) Activity D has a slack of 3. Hence a 4 hour delay in D would delay the entire project 4 - 3 = 1 hour.

PROBLEM 2

The following project has been analyzed:

Activity	Immediate Predecessors	Optimistic Time (Hrs.)	Most Likely Time (Hrs.)	Pessimistic Time (Hrs.)
A	--	4	6	8
B	--	1	4.5	5
C	A	3	3	3
D	A	4	5	6
E	A	0.5	1	1.5
F	B,C	3	4	5
G	B,C	1	1.5	5
H	E,F	5	6	7
I	E,F	2	5	8
J	D,H	2.5	2.75	4.5
K	G,I	3	5	7

a) Construct the PERT network for this problem.

b) Solve for the expected earliest and latest start and finish times for each activity.

c) Identify the critical path and give the estimated project completion time.

d) What is the probability the project will be completed within one day (24 hours)?

SOLUTION 2

a) Nodes are needed for the start node, the finish node, the completion of A, completion of B, completion of C, completion of E and F, completion of D and H, and the completion of G and I:

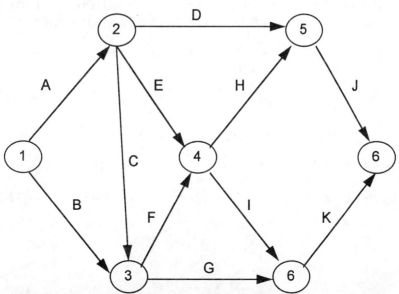

b) Calculate the expected times, t, and variances, σ^2, for each activity by:

$$t = (a + 4m + b)/6 \qquad \sigma^2 = ((b-a)/6)^2$$

Activity	Expected Time	Variance
A	6	4/9
B	4	4/9
C	3	0
D	5	1/9
E	1	1/36
F	4	1/9
G	2	4/9
H	6	1/9
I	5	1
J	3	1/9
K	5	4/9

Thus, using the algorithm illustrated in problem 1, we have:

Activity	ES	EF	LS	LF	Slack
A	0	6	0	6	0
B	0	4	5	9	5
C	6	9	6	9	0
D	6	11	15	20	9
E	6	7	12	13	6
F	9	13	9	13	0
G	9	11	16	18	7
H	13	19	14	20	1
I	13	18	13	18	0
J	19	22	20	23	1
K	18	23	18	23	0

c) The critical path is the path of 0 slack = A-C-F-I-K. The estimated project completion time is the Max EF at node 7 = 23.

d) $z = (24 - 23)/\sigma$.

Here, $\sigma^2 = \sigma^2_A + \sigma^2_C + \sigma^2_F + \sigma^2_H + \sigma^2_K$

$= 4/9 + 0 + 1/9 + 1 + 4/9 = 2.$

Hence, $\sigma = 1.414$. Thus $z = (24-23)/1.414 = .71$.

From appendix B, $P(z < .71) = .5 + .2612 = .7612$.

PROBLEM 3

National Business Machines (NBM) has just developed a new
microcomputer it plans to put into full scale production in a
few months. The table and the PERT network below show the
precedence relations and give the activity times and costs under
normal operations and maximum crashing for a daily operation
production of 1000 microcomputers at its local plant.
   NBM plans three eight-hour shifts per day and desires to know
the minimum cost of producing the 1000 microcomputers within the
24-hour period. Set up a linear program, which when solved,
would yield this information.

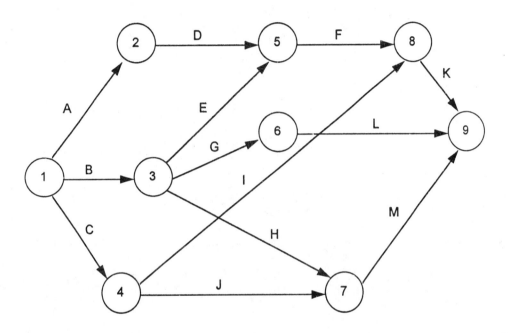

Activity*		Normal		Crash	
		Time	Cost	Time	Cost
12	(A)	2	$2,000	1.5	$3,000
13	(B)	4	3,000	3	3,500
14	(C)	1	1,500	1	1,500
25	(D)	4	5,300	2.5	8,000
35	(E)	6	5,400	5	7,000
58	(F)	10	6,000	8	9,000
36	(G)	8	4,800	5	9,900
37	(H)	2	2,800	1	2,900
48	(I)	5	4,500	4	5,000
47	(J)	12	6,000	6	9,600
89	(K)	7	7,000	4	9,700
69	(L)	11	8,800	9	9,200
79	(M)	4	1,000	1	7,000

* Activity 12 starts at node 1 and ends at node 2, etc.

SOLUTION 3

First prepare a chart giving maximum crashing,
  M = (Normal Time) - (Time Under Maximum Crashing)
and the marginal cost per hour for crashing,
  K = ([Cost Under Maximum Crashing] - [Normal Cost])/M

Activity		M	K
12	(A)	0.5	2000
13	(B)	1	500
14	(C)	0	0
25	(D)	1.5	1800
35	(E)	1	1600
58	(F)	2	1500
36	(G)	3	1700
37	(H)	1	100
48	(I)	1	500
47	(J)	6	600
89	(K)	3	900
69	(L)	2	200
79	(M)	3	2000

Define,
  x_i = time represented by node i
  y_{ij} = time activity ij is crashed

The linear program must minimize the total extra cost:

MIN $2000y_{12} + 500y_{13} + 0y_{14} + 1800y_{25} + 1600y_{35} + 1500y_{58}$
  $+ 1700y_{36} + 100y_{37} + 500y_{48} + 600y_{47} + 900y_{89} + 200y_{69}$
  $+ 2000y_{79}$

Subject to:

(1) The project must be completed within 24 hours: $x_9 \leq 24$

(2) The amount an activity is crashed cannot exceed its
    maximum crashing:

$$y_{12} \leq 0.5$$
$$y_{13} \leq 1$$
$$y_{14} \leq 0$$
$$y_{25} \leq 1.5$$
$$y_{35} \leq 1$$
$$y_{58} \leq 2$$
$$y_{36} \leq 3$$
$$y_{37} \leq 1$$
$$y_{48} \leq 1$$
$$y_{47} \leq 6$$
$$y_{89} \leq 3$$
$$y_{69} \leq 2$$
$$y_{79} \leq 3$$

(3) For each activity,
    (Time at end node) $\geq$ (Time at Start Node) + [(Normal
    Activity Time) - (Amount of Time the Activity is crashed)]

$$x_9 \geq x_7 + 4 - y_{79}$$
$$x_9 \geq x_6 + 11 - y_{69}$$
$$x_9 \geq x_8 + 7 - y_{89}$$

$$x_8 \geq x_4 + 5 - y_{48}$$
$$x_8 \geq x_5 + 10 - y_{58}$$

$$x_7 \geq x_4 + 12 - y_{47}$$
$$x_7 \geq x_3 + 2 - y_{37}$$

$$x_6 \geq x_3 + 8 - y_{36}$$

$$x_5 \geq x_3 + 6 - y_{35}$$
$$x_5 \geq x_2 + 4 - y_{25}$$

$$x_4 \geq x_1 + 1 - y_{14}$$

$$x_3 \geq x_1 + 4 - y_{13}$$

$$x_2 \geq x_1 + 2 - y_{12}$$

(4) Non-negativity of the variables:

$$x_i \geq 0 \quad \text{for all } i$$
$$y_{ij} \geq 0 \quad \text{for all } j$$

PROBLEM 4

Given the following PERT network for Gus's Painters:

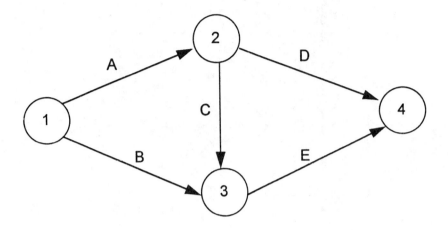

The following means and standard deviations were calculated for the activities:

Activity	t	σ
A	6	2
B	3	1
C	6	1
D	15	2
E	12	2

There is a $100,000 bonus for completing the project in 26 weeks. Currently activity E is assigned to Wilson Brothers. Gus has the option of hiring Jones Inc. for activity E. Their expected completion time for activity E is 8 weeks (with a standard deviation of 2), but they will cost Gus $15,000 more to do E than Wilson Brothers. Should Gus hire Jones, Inc.?

SOLUTION 4

Analysis using Wilson Brothers to do E:

Activity	ES	EF	LS	LF
A	0	6	0	6
B	0	3	9	12
C	6	12	6	12
D	6	21	9	21
E	12	24	12	24

Hence the critical path is A - C - E and the overall expected project completion time is 24. The variance of the critical path is:

$$\sigma^2 = \sigma^2_A + \sigma^2_C + \sigma^2_E = (2)^2 + (1)^2 + (2)^2 = 9. \quad \text{Thus } \sigma = 3.$$

To find the probability of completing the project in 26 weeks, calculate,

$$z = (26 - 24)/3 = .67.$$

Thus the probability of finishing in 26 weeks is $P(Z < .67)$. From appendix A, the table gives the $P(0 < Z < .67) = .2486$. Therefore the probability of completing the project within 26 weeks is $.5 + .2486 = .7486$.

Thus the expected bonus using Wilson Brothers to do E is: $(.7486)(100,000) + (.2514)(0) = \$74,860$.

Analysis using Jones, Inc. do E:

Activity	ES	EF	LS	LF
A	0	6	0	6
B	0	3	10	13
C	6	12	7	13
D	6	21	6	21
E	12	20	13	21

Hence the critical path is A - D and the overall expected project completion time is 21. The variance of the critical path is:

$$\sigma^2 = \sigma^2_A + \sigma^2_D = (2)^2 + (2)^2 = 8. \quad \text{Thus } \sigma = 2.828.$$

To find the probability of completing the project in 26 weeks, calculate,

$$z = (26 - 21)/2.828 = 1.77.$$

Thus the probability of finishing in 26 weeks is $P(Z < 1.77)$. From appendix A, the table gives the $P(0 < Z < 1.77) = .4616$. Therefore the probability of completing the project within 26 weeks is $.5 + .4616 = .9616$.

Thus the expected bonus using Jones, Inc. to do E is: $(.9616)(100,000) + (.0384)(0) = \$96,160$.

Decision:

The difference in expected returns between the two firms is: $\$96,160 - \$74,860 = \$21,300$. Since this is greater than the $\$15,000$ cost to hire Jones, Inc., Gus should hire Jones, Inc.

PROBLEM 5

For the PERT network below, the project cost of each activity
was $6000. After the eleventh week the following data has been
forwarded to management concerning the project status:

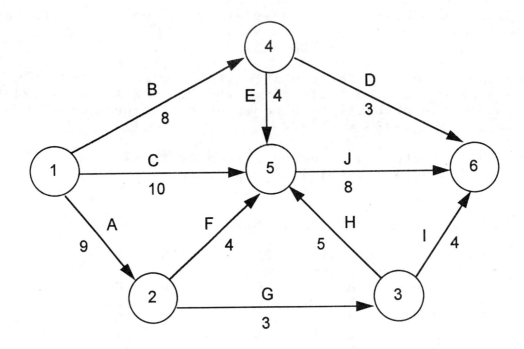

Activity	Actual Cost	% Complete
A	$6,200	100%
B	$5,700	100%
C	$5,600	90%
D	0	0%
E	$1,000	25%
F	$5,000	75%
G	$2,000	50%
H	0	0%
I	0	0%
J	0	0%

a) Solve for the earliest and latest start and finish times for
each activity as well as the expected overall completion
time.

b) Do the total expenditures to date represent an overall cost
overrun or overall cost underrun?

c) Is the project being completed on time?

d) What corrective action, if any, do you recommend?

SOLUTION 5

a) Solving the PERT network for the ES, EF, LS, LF, and slack
   times by the method illustrated in problem 1, we can
   summarize:

Activity	ES	EF	LS	LF	Slack
A	0	9	0	9	0
B	0	8	5	13	5
C	0	10	7	17	7
D	8	11	22	25	14
E	8	12	13	17	5
F	9	13	13	17	4
G	9	12	9	12	0
H	12	17	12	17	0
I	12	16	21	25	9
J	17	25	17	25	0

The overall project completion time is 25 weeks.

b) Use the following formula for each activity:

Value = (proportion complete) X (amount budgeted).

This gives the following table of costs:

Activity	Actual Cost	Value		Difference
A	$6,200	(1.00)x6000	= 6000	$ 200
B	5,700	(1.00)x6000	= 6000	- 300
C	5,600	(.90)x6000	= 5400	200
D	0	0		0
E	1,000	(.25)x6000	= 1500	- 500
F	5,000	(.75)x6000	= 4500	500
G	2,000	(.50)x6000	= 3000	-1000
H	0	0		0
I	0	0		0
J	0	0		0
TOTALS	$25,500	$26,400		-$ 900

Based on these values, the project is currently experiencing
a $900 cost underrun.

c) Consider the PERT diagram at week 11. The times reflect that 11 weeks have already passed and the activity completion times are the times remaining for each activity. For instance, activity C is 90% complete, and thus has 10% of 10 (= 1) week remaining. The PERT diagram then is:

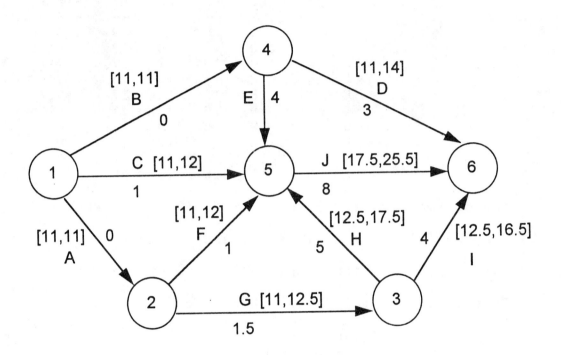

Note that the overall completion time is now 25.5 weeks or a .5 week delay.

d) Management should consider using some of the $900 cost savings and apply it to activity G to assist in a more rapid completion of this activity (and hence the entire project).

ANSWERED PROBLEMS

PROBLEM 6

Consider a project which has been modeled as follows:

Activity	Immediate Predecessors	Completion Time (hrs.)
A	---	7
B	---	10
C	A	4
D	A	30
E	A	7
F	B,C	12
G	B,C	15
H	E,F	11
I	E,F	25
J	E,F	6
K	D,H	21
L	G,J	25

a) Draw the PERT network for this project and determine project's expected completion time and its critical path.

b) Can activities E and G be performed simultaneously without delaying the minimum project completion time?

c) Can one person perform A, G, and I without delaying the project?

d) By how much can activities G and L be delayed without delaying the entire project?

e) How much would the project be delayed if activity G were delayed by 7 hours and activity L by 4 hours? Explain.

PROBLEM 7

Given the following PERT network of tasks with completion times in hours for scheduling interns in a hospital:

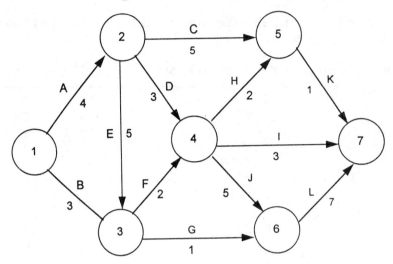

a) Given that interns start at midnight (00:00), construct a chart giving the ES, EF, LS, LF, and slack for each activity.

b) What is the critical path and project completion time?

c) If an intern can do any job and works a 24-hour shift, show that all the jobs can be completed by two interns. (Hint: One intern is assigned the critical path jobs, but be sure to schedule the remaining activities within the limits in (a).)

PROBLEM 8

A project consists of five activities. Naturally the paint mixing precedes the painting activities. Also, both ceiling painting and floor sanding must be done prior to floor buffing.

Activity	Optimistic Time (hrs.)	Most Likely Time (hrs.)	Pessimistic Time (hrs.)
Floor sanding	3	4	5
Floor buffing	1	2	3
Paint mixing	0.5	1	1.5
Wall painting	1	2	9
Ceiling painting	1	5.5	7

a) Construct a PERT network for this problem.

b) What is the expected completion time of this project?

c) What is the probability that the project can be completed within nine hours?

PROBLEM 9

Given the following PERT network modeling new home construction
by Bonanza Development:

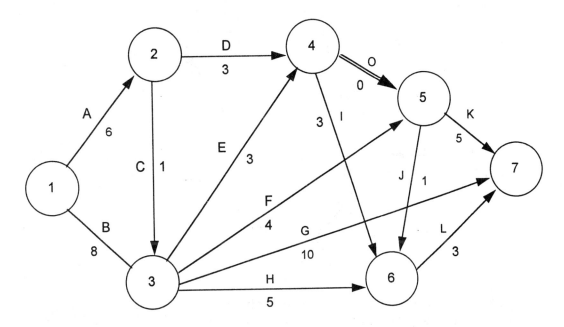

a) Prepare a table of the earliest and latest start and finish
   times and slack times for each activity in Bonanza's project.

b) What is the critical path and the expected project completion
   time?

c) Reliable Plumbers, the subcontractor performing activity J,
   is going to be delayed 5 weeks. If the project is delayed,
   it will cost Bonanza $2000 per week of delay of the entire
   project. Reliable is charging $3000 for the plumbing.

   Bonanza has three options:
   (1) Keep Reliable Plumbers.
   (2) Cancel the contract with Reliable Plumbers and hire Local
       Plumbers, Inc. Local Plumbers, however, will take two
       weeks to do activity J, and will charge $7000.
   (3) Bonanza can train its own employees who are currently
       performing activity E to do the work. This involves a
       two-week training period as soon as activity E is done.
       Then it is expected it will take them three weeks to
       perform activity J. The cost of the training is $800 per
       week and the cost of them doing activity J is $1,000 per
       week.

   Which alternative do you recommend to Bonanza? Explain.

PROBLEM 10

Consider the following PERT network with estimated times in weeks. The project is scheduled to begin on May 1.

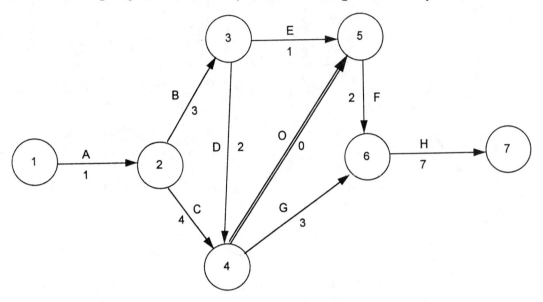

The three-time estimate approach was used to calculate the expected times (on the arcs) and the following table gives the variance for each activity:

Activity	Variance
A	1.1
B	.5
C	1.2
D	.8
E	.3
F	.6
G	.6
H	1.0

a) Give the expected project project completion <u>date</u> and the critical path.

b) By what <u>date</u> are you 99% sure the project will be completed?

c) The project has a target completion date of August 28 (17 weeks). If the project is completed by August 28, the profit on the project will be $10,000. If work is not completed by August 28, a $5,000 penalty will be incurred, reducing the project's profit to $5,000. For $2,000 more than is currently being spent for a firm to do activity H, a more experienced firm can complete the activity in just 5 weeks. Should this offer be accepted? (Assume the variance for activity H will not change.)

PROBLEM 11

Consider the following PERT network.

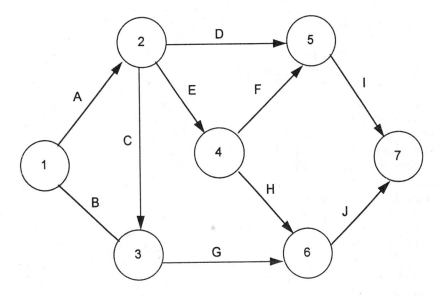

The following chart has been prepared giving the optimistic time (a), the most likely time (m), and the pessimistic time (b), in weeks for each activity.

Activity	a	m	b
A	2	8	14
B	3	12	21
C	2	5	8
D	4	5	12
E	1	3	17
F	2	3	10
G	3	9	15
H	7	8	9
I	3	11	13
J	7	10	13

a) Determine the critical path, expected project completion time, and standard deviation of the project completion time.

b) Management insists that the project be completed in 36 weeks and will be charged a $100,000 fine for any time overrun. If, at a cost of $3,000, the expected completion time of activity A could be reduced by 2 weeks, should the extra money be spent? (Assume A's variance does not change.)

c) Why is considering only critical path activities for project completion time not always a good assumption in probabilistic cases? (HINT: Consider activity E.)

PROBLEM 12

Plane, Inc. is a manufacturer of heavy equipment and is considering introducing a new line of small steamrollers. Development is to proceed as follows.

A feasibility study will first be performed. Upon receiving a successful feasibility report, a manufacturing building is to be secured and a project leader hired. Once the building is secured, Plane will be committed to the project. Therefore an advertising group will be selected and the raw materials for the manufacturing process will be purchased. When, in addition to securing the building, a project leader has been named, a manufacturing staff will be recruited.

After the manufacturing staff has been selected and the raw materials purchased, a prototype model of the steamroller will be produced. Following the completion of the prototype, work will begin on a production run of 100 steamrollers. When both the prototype model has been built and the advertising staff selected, an intensive advertising campaign will be launched.

The development phase of this project will be complete with the production of the first 100 steamrollers and the initiation of the advertising campaign.

Two separate costs analyses have been prepared. One is effective under current (normal) conditions, while the other is effective if the development phase of the activities is "crashed". These are summarized below. (Times are in weeks.)

Activity	Normal		Crash	
	Time	Cost	Time	Cost
Feasibility Study (A)	6	$ 80,000	5	$100,000
Building Purchased (B)	4	100,000	4	100,000
Project Leader Hired (C)	3	50,000	2	100,000
Advertising Staff Selected (D)	6	150,000	3	300,000
Materials Purchased (E)	3	180,000	2	250,000
Manufacturing Staff Hired (F)	10	300,000	7	480,000
Prototype Manufactured (G)	2	100,000	2	100,000
Production Run of 100 (H)	6	450,000	5	800,000
Advertising Campaign (I)	8	350,000	4	650,000

a) Draw the PERT network for this problem.

b) Write a linear program for determining the minimum cost of completing this project in half a year (=26 weeks).

c) What assumptions are made in calculating the "marginal" costs for the activities?

d) Interpret the meaning of the shadow price that would be associated with the constraint that set the maximum completion time to 26 weeks.

PROBLEM 13

Joseph King has ambitions to be mayor of Williston, North Dakota. Joe has determined the breakdown of the steps to the nomination and has estimated normal and crash costs and times for the campaign as follows (times are in weeks):

| | | Normal | | Crash | | Immediate |
	Activity	Time	Cost	Time	Cost	Predecessors
A.	Solicit Volunteers	6	$5,000	2	$10,000	--
B.	Initial "Free" Exposure	3	$4,000	3	$ 4,000	--
C.	Raise Money	10	$4,000	6	$12,000	A
D.	Organize and co-ordinate Schedule	4	$1,000	2	$ 2,000	A
E.	Hire Advertising Firm	2	$1,500	1	$ 2,000	B
F.	Arrange Major TV Interview	3	$4,000	1	$ 8,000	B
G.	Advertising Campaign	5	$7,000	4	$12,000	C,E
H.	Personal Campaigning	7	$8,000	5	$20,000	D,F

a) Joe King is not a wealthy man and would like to organize a four month (16 week) campaign at minimum cost. Write a linear program that, when solved, would accomplish this task.

b) Dan Wetzel is an independent who is also trying to make a bid to become mayor of Williston. He has promised a clean campaign, one that he will initially finance on his own. He has $50,000 to invest in his campaign. Being a student of recent successful political campaigns, he knows that his best chance to win is be a "fresh new face" at nomination time. Hence he wishes to keep the entire campaign from beginning to end at a minimum. Write a linear program that, when solved, will minimize the total time of the campaign while keeping expenditures to a maximum of $50,000.

PROBLEM 14

Consider the following PERT network:

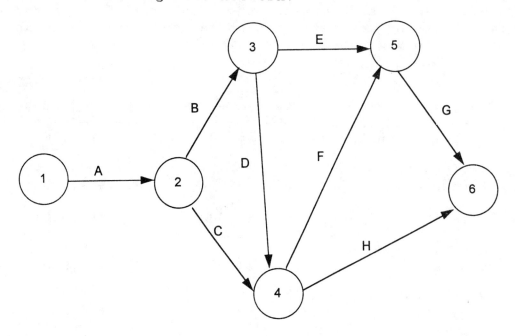

The estimated times (in weeks) and costs to do each activity are summarized below along with the actual status after 12 weeks.

Activity	Time	Expected Cost	Cost Through 12 Weeks	Percent Complete In 12 Weeks
A	4	$200	$200	100%
B	3	$600	$525	100%
C	4	$500	$480	100%
D	2	$500	$515	100%
E	5	$725	$600	60%
F	2	$250	$130	50%
G	5	$800	$ 0	0%
H	6	$780	$400	50%

a) Given the current status of the project, does it appear as if the project will be completed in its minimum expected time?

b) Is the project currently in a cost overrun or cost underrun posture?

c) What corrective action, if any, do you recommend? Should the project leader report to management that an overall cost overrun is inevitable?

TRUE/FALSE

15. The only purpose of dummy activities in PERT is to keep the precedence relations correct.

16. In PERT, it is assumed that the amount of time to complete any one activity is independent of the amount of time to complete any other activity in the project.

17. In PERT, an activity's most likely time is the same as its expected time.

18. In PERT, it is assumed that the underlying distribution for each activity in the three-time estimate approach is a normal distribution.

19. In a given PERT problem, activities F and G are on the critical path. If each is delayed two weeks, then in all cases, the project will be delayed four weeks.

20. The difference between an activity's earliest finish and latest finish equals the difference between its earliest start and latest start.

21. In a given PERT problem, activities F and G are not on the critical path and each has two weeks slack time. If both are delayed by two weeks each, then in all cases, the project will not be delayed.

22. An activity originating at a node can be started as soon as any one of the activities terminating at that node is finished.

23. In a given PERT problem, activity F is on the critical path. If its time is reduced by five weeks, then in all cases, the overall project completion time will be reduced by five weeks.

24. In PERT, the critical path is the path of longest distance through the network.

25. In CPM, the marginal cost per week's saving of an activity's completion time is valid only between its normal time and the time after maximum crashing.

26. It is possible to have more than one critical path at a time.

27. In CPM, if activity B's normal completion time is 8 weeks and normal cost is $10,000, and its completion time after maximum crashing is 5 weeks at a cost of $15,000, then the assumption is that if $13,000 is spent on activity B, its completion time is 6.8 weeks.

28. Work package G is 80% completed and it has been budgeted for $50,000. To date $45,000 has been expended on this work package. Work package G is in a cost underrun situation.

29. A critical activity can be part of a noncritical path.

CHAPTER

11
Inventory Models

KEY CONCEPTS

CONCEPT	ILLUSTRATED PROBLEMS	ANSWERED PROBLEMS
Economic Order Quantity Model	1	10,11,14,20
Economic Production Lot Size Model	2	11,12,20,21
Planned Shortage Model	3	13,14,22
Quantity Discount Model	4	15,26,28
EOQ Model With Stochastic Demand	5	16,29
Reorder Point Based on Service Level	5	16,23,29

Single Period Inventory Model:
  Normal Demand Distribution
  Uniform Demand Distribution
	6
	7
		17,24
		25

Periodic Review Systems	8	18,30
Material Requirements Planning	9	19,27

REVIEW

1. The study of inventory models is concerned with <u>two</u> <u>basic</u> <u>questions</u>: (1) <u>how</u> <u>much</u> should be ordered each time, and (2) <u>when</u> should the reordering occur. The objective is to minimize total variable cost over a specified time period (assumed to be annual in the following review).

2. Potential <u>variable</u> <u>costs</u> include:
   (1) <u>Ordering</u> <u>cost</u> -- salaries and expenses of processing an order, regardless of the order quantity
   (2) <u>Holding</u> <u>cost</u> -- usually a percentage of the value of the item assessed for keeping an item in inventory (including finance costs, insurance, security costs, taxes, warehouse overhead, and other related variable expenses)
   (3) <u>Backorder</u> <u>cost</u> -- costs associated with being out of stock when an item is demanded (including lost goodwill)
   (4) <u>Purchase</u> <u>cost</u> -- the actual price of the items
   (5) Other Costs

3. The simplest inventory models assume demand and the other parameters of the problem to be deterministic and constant. The <u>deterministic</u> <u>models</u> covered in this chapter are: a) economic order quantity (EOQ), b) economic production lot size, c) EOQ with planned shortages, and d) EOQ with quantity discounts.

4. The most basic of the deterministic inventory models is the <u>economic</u> <u>order</u> <u>quantity</u> <u>(EOQ)</u>. The variable costs in this model are annual holding cost and annual ordering cost. For the EOQ, these two costs are equal.

5. The <u>economic</u> <u>production</u> <u>lot</u> <u>size</u> model is a variation of the basic EOQ model. A replenishment order is not received in one lump sum as it is in the basic EOQ model. Instead, inventory is replenished gradually as the order is produced (which requires the production rate to be greater than the demand rate). This model's variable costs are annual holding cost and annual set-up cost (equivalent to ordering cost). For the optimal lot size, these two costs are equal.

6. A <u>stockout</u> (or <u>shortage</u>) is a demand that cannot be immediately satisfied. A <u>backorder</u> is a stockout in which the customer waits until the next replenishment order arrives and then the demand is satisfied.

7. With the EOQ with planned shortages model, a replenishment
   order does not arrive at or before the inventory position drops
   to zero. Instead, shortages occur until a predetermined
   backorder quantity is reached, at which time the replenishment
   order arrives. The variable costs in this model are annual
   holding, backorder, and ordering. For the optimal order and
   backorder quantity combination, the sum of the annual holding
   and backordering costs equals the annual ordering cost

8. The EOQ with quantity discounts model is applicable where a
   supplier offers a lower purchase cost when an item is ordered
   in larger quantities. This model's variable costs are annual
   holding, ordering and purchase costs.

9. EOQ-based inventory models give results that are rather
   insensitive to changes in the parameters. Small and sometimes
   even moderate changes in costs, demands, etc. will have only
   minor effects on overall total costs.

10. The decision maker must determine if a set of assumptions is
    appropriate for his particular problem. If the assumptions are
    approximately correct, employing them will simplify the
    solution procedure, but the results should only be used as
    guidelines for an inventory policy.

11. There may be reasons, not built into the model, for modifying
    the results of a model (such as rounding a reorder time from
    12.8 days to 2 weeks to simplify reordering and make
    bookkeeping control easier).

12. In many cases demand (or some other factor) is not known with a
    high degree of certainty and a probabilistic inventory model
    should actually be used. These models tend to be more complex
    than deterministic models. The probabilistic models covered in
    this chapter are: a) single-period order quantity, b) reorder-
    point quantity, and c) periodic-review order quantity.

13. A single-period order quantity model (sometimes called the
    newsboy problem) deals with a situation in which only one order
    is placed for the item and the demand is probabilistic. If the
    period's demand exceeds the order quantity, the demand is not
    backordered and revenue (profit) will be lost. If demand is
    less than the order quantity, the surplus stock is sold at the
    end of the period (usually for less than the original purchase
    price).

14. A firm's inventory position consists of the on-hand inventory
    plus on-order inventory (all amounts previously ordered but not
    yet received). An inventory item is reordered when the item's
    inventory position reaches a predetermined value, referred to
    as the reorder point.

15. The <u>reorder point</u> represents the quantity available to meet demand during lead time. <u>Lead time</u> is the time span starting when the replenishment order is placed and ending when the order arrives.

16. Under deterministic conditions, when both demand and lead time are constant, the reorder point associated with EOQ-based models is relatively simple to determine. The reorder point is set equal to <u>lead time demand</u>.

17. Under probabilistic conditions, when demand and/or lead time varies, the reorder point often includes safety stock. <u>Safety stock</u> is the amount by which the reorder point exceeds the expected (average) lead time demand.

18. The amount of safety stock in a reorder point determines the odds (chance) of a stockout during lead time. The complement of this chance is called the service level. <u>Service level</u>, in this context, is defined as the probability of not incurring a stockout during any one lead time. Also, it is the long-run proportion of lead times in which no stockouts occur.

19. A <u>periodic review system</u> is one in which the inventory level is checked and reordering is done only at specified points in time (at fixed intervals usually). Assuming the demand rate varies, the order quantity will vary from one review period to another. This is in contrast to the <u>continuous review system</u> in which inventory is monitored continuously and an order (of a fixed amount) can be placed whenever the reorder point is reached.

20. At the time a <u>periodic-review order quantity</u> is being decided, the concern is that the on-hand inventory and the quantity being ordered is enough to satisfy demand from the time this order is placed until the next order is received (not placed).

21. In manufacturing there is often a <u>dependent-demand</u> relationship between inventory items. For example, the demand for a certain component is dependent on the demand for the subassembly in which the component is installed, and the subassembly's demand is dependent on the demand for the finished good in which it is installed.

22. <u>Material Requirements Planning(MRP)</u> is used to control <u>manufacturing inventory</u>. MRP is a part of a data processing system and its major function is to translate the demand for finished goods into detailed inventory requirements for all their components.

23. MRP determines material requirement dates by a procedure called <u>time phasing</u>. In time phasing, a production plan for parts is developed by working backwards from the desired completion date of the finished product through the manufacturing stages.

24. One <u>MRP</u> <u>system</u> <u>input</u> is the <u>master</u> <u>production</u> <u>schedule</u> which summarizes requirements and deadlines for finished goods. Another input is the <u>bill</u> <u>of</u> <u>materials</u> which is a structured parts list detailing the sequencing of the assembly of the product. A third input is <u>inventory</u> <u>information</u> including on-hand amounts, lead times, safety stock requirements, lot sizes, and much more.

25. <u>Just-in-time</u> <u>(JIT)</u> inventory management reflects a philosophy whose objective is to eliminate all sources of waste including unnecessary inventory. In order for JIT to function effectively, changes in the design of the production layout and the material flow process may be required as well as a reduction in setup times.

26. A key component in a JIT system production is a visual signaling system called <u>Kanban</u> (the Japanese word for "card".) The type and number of units required by the production process are written on Kanbans which are used to indicate withdrawal and production of units through the production process. In this manner the entire manufacturing operation is synchronized to the final assembly stage.

27. In a JIT system, <u>lot</u> <u>sizes</u> <u>are</u> <u>small</u> and <u>inventory</u> <u>levels</u> <u>are</u> <u>minimal</u>. There is little or no safety stock to replace nonconforming or defective units, so a trusting partnership between suppliers and the manufacturer is required in order to obtain materials on time and with zero defects.

DETERMINISTIC INVENTORY MODELS -- ASSUMPTIONS/RESULTS

I.   ECONOMIC ORDER QUANTITY (EOQ)

Assumptions

1. Demand is constant throughout the year at D items per year.
2. Ordering cost: $\$C_o$ per order.
3. Holding cost: $\$C_h$ per item in inventory per year.
4. Purchase cost per unit is constant (no quantity discount).
5. Delivery time (lead time) is constant.
6. Planned shortages are not permitted.

Results

1. Optimal order quantity: $Q^* = \sqrt{2DC_o/C_h}$

2. Number of orders per year: D/Q^*

3. Time between orders (cycle time): Q^*/D years

4. Total annual cost: $[(1/2)Q^*C_h] + [DC_o/Q^*]$
   (holding + ordering)

II.   ECONOMIC PRODUCTION LOT SIZE

Assumptions

1. Demand occurs at a constant rate of D items per year.
2. Production rate is P items per year (and P>D).
3. Set-up cost: $\$C_o$ per run.
4. Holding cost: $\$C_h$ per item in inventory per year.
5. Purchase cost per unit is constant (no quantity discount).
6. Set-up time (lead time) is constant.
7. Planned shortages are not permitted.

Results

1. Optimal production lot-size: $Q^* = \sqrt{\dfrac{2DC_o}{(1-D/P)C_h}}$

2. Number of production runs per year: D/Q^*

3. Time between set-ups (cycle time): Q^*/D years

4. Total annual cost: $[(1/2)(1-D/P)Q^*C_h] + [DC_o/Q^*]$
   (holding + ordering)

III. PLANNED-SHORTAGE ORDER QUANTITY

Assumptions

1. Demand occurs at a constant rate of D items per year.
2. Ordering cost: $\$C_o$ per order.
3. Holding cost: $\$C_h$ per item in inventory per year.
4. Backorder cost: $\$C_b$ per item backordered per year.
5. Purchase cost per unit is constant (no quantity discount).
6. Set-up time (lead time) is constant.
7. Planned shortages are permitted (backordered demand units are
    withdrawn from a replenishment order when it is delivered).

Results

1. Optimal order quantity: $Q^* = \sqrt{\dfrac{2DC_o}{C_h} \dfrac{C_h+C_b}{C_b}}$

2. Maximum number of backorders: $S^* = Q^*(C_h/(C_h+C_b))$

3. Number of orders per year: D/Q^*

4. Time between orders (cycle time): Q^*/D years

5. Total annual cost: $[C_h(Q^*-S^*)^2/2Q^*] + [DC_o/Q^*] + [S^{*2}C_b/2Q^*]$
   (holding + ordering + backordering)

IV. QUANTITY-DISCOUNT ORDER QUANTITY

Assumptions

1. Demand occurs at a constant rate of D items per year.
2. Ordering Cost: $\$C_o$ per order.
3 Holding Cost: $\$C_h = \$C_i I$ per item in inventory per year
    (note holding cost is based on the cost of the item, C_i).
4. Purchase Cost: $\$C_1$ per item if the quantity ordered is between
    0 and X_1, $\$C_2$ if the order quantity is between X_1 and X_2, etc.
5. Delivery time (lead time) is constant.
6. Planned shortages are not permitted.

Results

1. Optimal order quantity: use the procedure on the next page
                            to determine Q^*

2. Number of orders per year: D/Q^*

3. Time between orders (cycle time): Q^*/D years

4. Total annual cost: $[(1/2)Q^*C_h] + [DC_o/Q^*] + DC$
   (holding + ordering + purchase)

FLOW CHART OF
QUANTITY DISCOUNT PROCEDURE

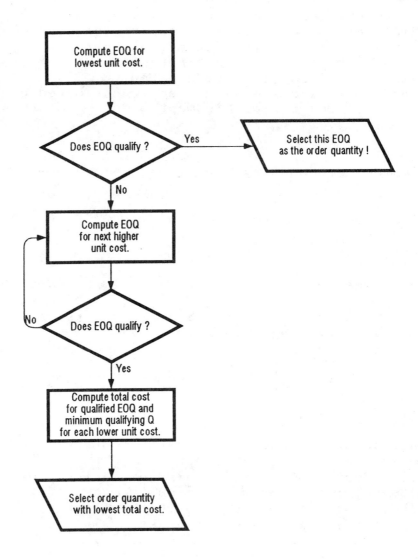

PROBABILISTIC INVENTORY MODELS -- ASSUMPTIONS/RESULTS

I.   SINGLE-PERIOD ORDER QUANTITY

Assumptions

1. Period demand follows a known probability distribution.
   a. normal: mean is μ, standard deviation is σ
   b. uniform: minimum is a, maximum is b
2. Cost of overestimating demand: $\$c_o$
3. Cost of underestimating demand: $\$c_u$
4. Shortages are not backordered.
5. Period-end stock is sold for salvage (not held in inventory).

Results

1. Optimal probability of no shortage: $P(\text{demand} \leq Q^*) = c_u/(c_u+c_o)$

2. Optimal probability of shortage: $P(\text{demand} > Q^*) = 1 - c_u/(c_u+c_o)$

3. Optimal order quantity, based on demand distribution --
   a) normal: $Q^* = \mu + z\sigma$
   b) uniform: $Q^* = a + P(\text{demand} \leq Q^*)(b-a)$

II.   REORDER POINT

Assumptions

1. Lead-time demand is normally distributed
   with mean μ and standard deviation σ.
2. Approximate optimal order quantity: EOQ
3. Service level is defined in terms of the probability of
   no stockouts during lead time and is reflected in z.
4. Shortages are not backordered.
5. Inventory position is reviewed continuously.

Results

1. Reorder point: $r = \mu + z\sigma$
2. Safety stock: $z\sigma$
3. Average inventory: $1/2(Q) + z\sigma$
4. Total annual cost: $[(1/2)Q^*C_h] + [z\sigma C_h] + [DC_o/Q^*]$
   (holding(normal) + holding(safety) + ordering)

III. PERIODIC-REVIEW ORDER QUANTITY

Assumptions

1. Inventory position is reviewed at constant intervals (periods).
2. Demand during review period plus lead time period
   is normally distributed with mean μ and standard deviation σ.
3. Service level is defined in terms of the probability of
   no stockouts during a review period and is reflected in z.
4. On-hand inventory at ordering time: I
4. Shortages are not backordered.
5. Lead time is less than the length of the review period.

Results

1. Replenishment level: $M = \mu + z\sigma$
2. Order quantity: $Q = M - I$

DEPENDENT-DEMAND INVENTORY SYSTEM

MATERIAL REQUIREMENTS PLANNING

Assumptions

1. Gross requirement in period i: GR_i
2. Scheduled receipts in period i: SR_i
3. On-hand inventory in period i: OH_i

Results

1. Net requirement in period i: $NR_i = GR_i - SR_i - OH_i$

ILLUSTRATED PROBLEMS

PROBLEM 1

Bart's Barometer Business (BBB) is a retail outlet which deals exclusively with weather equipment. Currently BBB is trying to decide on an inventory and reorder policy for home barometers. These cost BBB $50 each and demand is about 500 per year distributed fairly evenly throughout the year. Reordering costs are $80 per order and holding costs are figured at 20% of the cost of the item. BBB is open 300 days a year (6 days a week and closed two weeks in August). Lead time is 60 working days.

a) Develop a total variable cost model for this system.

b) What is the optimal reorder quantity and reorder point?

c) How many times per year would BBB reorder?

d) What total annual variable cost does the model give?

e) Given your answer to parts (b) and (c), choose a more convenient order quantity. What is the total annual cost of this decision? Compare this with (d) and comment.

SOLUTION 1

a) Total Costs = (Holding Cost) + (Ordering Cost)
$$TC = [C_h(Q/2)] + [C_o(D/Q)] = [.2(50)(Q/2)] + [80(500/Q)]$$

$$= 5Q + (40,000/Q)$$

b) $Q^* = \sqrt{\dfrac{2DC_o}{C_h}} = \sqrt{\dfrac{2(500)(80)}{10}} = 89.44 \cong 90$

Lead time is m = 60 days, and daily demand is d = 500/300 or 1.667. Thus the reorder point r = (1.667)(60) = 100. Bart should reorder 90 barometers when his inventory position reaches 100, i.e. 10 on hand and one outstanding order.

c) Number of reorder times per year = (500/90) = 5.56 or once every (300/5.56) = 54 working days -- about every 9 weeks.

d) TC = 5(90) + (40,000/90) = 450 + 444 = $894.

e) It might be more convenient to order 100 at a time and order 5 times per year (every 10 weeks). This total cost is:

TC = 5(100) + (40,000/100) = 500 + 400 = $900. This $6 difference represents only a 0.6% change in total cost.

PROBLEM 2

Non-Slip Tile Company (NST) has been using production runs of 100,000 tiles, 10 times per year to meet the demand of 1,000,000 tiles annually. The set-up cost is $5,000 per run and holding cost is estimated at 10% of the manufacturing cost of $1 per tile. The production capacity of the machine is 500,000 tiles per month. The factory is open 365 days per year.

a) Develop a mathematical model for the total annual variable cost for this problem.

b) What production schedule do you recommend?

c) How much is NST losing annually by using their present production schedule?

d) How long is the machine idle between production runs?

e) What is the maximum number of tiles in inventory under the current policy? under the optimal policy?

f) What fraction of time is the machine producing tiles?

SOLUTION 2

This is an economic production lot size problem with $D = 1,000,000$, $P = 6,000,000$, $C_h = .10$, $C_o = 5,000$.

a) TC = (Holding Costs) + (Set-Up Costs)
$$= [C_h(Q/2)(1 - D/P)] + [DC_o/Q] = .04167Q + 5,000,000,000/Q$$

b) $$Q^* = \sqrt{\frac{2DC_o}{C_h (1 -D/P)}} = \sqrt{\frac{2(1,000,000)(5,000)}{(.1)(1 - 1/6)}} = 346,410$$

The number of runs per year = D/Q^* = 2.89 times per year

c) Optimal TC = .04167(346,410) + 5,000,000,000/346,410 = $28,868
   Current TC = .04167(100,000) + 5,000,000,000/100,000 = $54,167
   Difference = 54,167 - 28,868 = $25,299

d) There are 2.89 cycles per year. Thus, each cycle lasts (365/2.89) = 126.3 days. The time to produce 346,410 per run = (346,410/6,000,000)365 = 21.1 days. Thus, the machine is idle for 126.3 - 21.1 = 105.2 days between runs.

e) Current maximum inventory = $(1-D/P)Q^*$ = (1-1/6)100,000
$$\approx 83,333.$$
   Optimal maximum inventory = (1-1/6)346,410 = 288,675.

f) The machine is producing tiles D/P = 1/6 of the time.

PROBLEM 3

Hervis Rent-a-Car has a fleet of 2,500 Rockets serving the Los Angeles area. All Rockets are maintained at a central garage. On the average, eight Rockets per month require a new engine. Engines cost $850 each. There is also a $120 order cost (independent of the number of engines ordered).

Hervis has an annual holding cost rate of 30% on engines. It takes two weeks to obtain the engines after they are ordered. For each week a car is out of service, Hervis loses $40 profit.

a) Determine Hervis' optimal order policy for engines.

b) How many days after receiving an order does Hervis run out of engines? How long is Hervis without any engines per cycle?

SOLUTION 3

This can be modeled as a planned shortage model with the following annual data: $D = 8 \times 12 = 96$; $C_o = \$120$; $C_h = .30(850) = \$255$; $C_b = 40 \times 52 = \$2080$.

a) $Q^* = \sqrt{\dfrac{2DC_o}{C_h} \dfrac{C_h + C_b}{C_b}} = \sqrt{\dfrac{2(96)(120)}{255} \dfrac{255+2080}{2080}} = 10.07 \cong 10$

$S^* = Q^*(C_h/(C_h+C_b)) = 10(255/(255+2080)) = 1.09 \cong 1$

Demand is 8 per month or 2 per week. Since lead time is 2 weeks, lead time demand is 4. Thus, since the optimal policy is to order 10 to arrive when there is one backorder, the order should be placed when there are 3 engines remaining in inventory.

b) Inventory exists for $C_b/(C_b+C_h) = 2080/(255+2080) = .8908$ of the order cycle. (Note, $(Q^*-S^*)/Q^* = .8908$ also, before Q^* and S^* are rounded.) An order cycle is $Q^*/D = .1049$ years = 38.3 days. Thus, Hervis runs out of engines $.8908(38.3) = 34$ days after receiving an order. Hervis is out of stock for approximately $38 - 34 = 4$ days.

PROBLEM 4

Nick's Camera Shop carries Zodiac instant print film. The film normally costs Nick $3.20 per roll, and he sells it for $5.25.

Zodiac film has a shelf life of 18 months. Nick's average sales are 21 rolls per week. His annual inventory holding cost rate is 25% and it costs Nick $20 to place an order with Zodiac.

If Zodiac offers a 7% discount on orders of 400 rolls or more, a 10% discount for 900 rolls or more, and a 15% discount for 2000 rolls or more, determine Nick's optimal order quantity.

SOLUTION 4

This can be modeled as a quantity discount problem with the following annual data: $D = 21(52) = 1092$; $C_h = .25(C_i)$; $C_o = 20$.
For each unit-price, starting with the lowest and working up, determine the most economical, <u>feasible</u> order quantity.

For $C_4 = .85(3.20) = \$2.72$:

To receive a 15% discount Nick must order at least 2,000 rolls. Unfortunately, the film's shelf life is 18 months. The demand in 18 months (78 weeks) is 78 X 21 = 1638 rolls of film, if he ordered 2,000 rolls he would have to scrap 372 of them. This would cost more than the 15% discount would save.

For $C_3 = .90(3.20) = \$2.88$:

$$Q_3{}^* = \sqrt{\frac{2DC_o}{C_h}} = \sqrt{\frac{2(1092)(20)}{.25(2.88)}} = 246.31 \text{ (not feasible)}$$

The most economical, feasible quantity for C_3 is $Q_3{}^* = 900$.

For $C_2 = .93(3.20) = \$2.976$:

$$Q_2{}^* = \sqrt{\frac{2DC_o}{C_h}} = \sqrt{\frac{2(1092)(20)}{.25(2.976)}} = 242.30 \text{ (not feasible)}$$

The most economical, feasible quantity for C_2 is $Q_2{}^* = 400$.

For $C_1 = 1.00(3.20) = \$3.20$ (no discount):

$$Q_1{}^* = \sqrt{\frac{2DC_o}{C_h}} = \sqrt{\frac{2(1092)(20)}{.25(3.20)}} = 233.67 \text{ (feasible, so we}$$
stop computing Q's. In this problem we have no more to compute anyway.)

Compute the total cost for the most economical, feasible order quantity in each price category for which a Q^* was computed.
$$TC_i = (1/2)(Q_i{}^*C_h) + (DC_o/Q_i{}^*) + DC_i$$

$TC_3 = (1/2)(900)(.72) + ((1092)(20)/900) + (1092)(2.88) = \$3493$

$TC_2 = (1/2)(400)(.744) + ((1092)(20)/400) + (1092)(2.976) = \$345$

$TC_1 = (1/2)(234)(.80) + ((1092)(20)/234) + (1092)(3.20) = \$3681$

Comparing the total costs for 234, 400 and 900, the lowest total annual cost is $3453. Nick should order 400 rolls at a time.

PROBLEM 5

Robert's Drugs is a drug wholesaler supplying 55 independent drug stores. Roberts wishes to determine an optimal inventory policy for COMFORT brand headache remedy. Sales of COMFORT are relatively constant as the past 10 weeks of data indicate:

Week	Sales (cases)	Week	Sales (cases)
1	110	6	120
2	115	7	130
3	125	8	115
4	120	9	110
5	125	10	130

a) Each case of COMFORT costs Roberts $10 and Roberts uses a 14% annual holding cost rate for its inventory. If the cost to prepare a purchase order for COMFORT is $12, determine the optimal inventory ordering quantity for COMFORT.

b) The lead time for a delivery of COMFORT has averaged four working days. Lead time has therefore been estimated as having a normal distribution with a mean of 80 cases and a standard deviation of 10 cases. Roberts wants at most a 2% probability of selling out of COMFORT during this lead time. What should be Roberts' reorder point?

c) On the basis of parts (a) and (b) determine the total annual inventory cost for COMFORT.

SOLUTION 5

a) The average sales over the 10 week period is 120 cases. Hence D = 120 X 52 = 6,240 cases per year; C_h = (.14)(10) = 1.40; C_o = 12.

$$Q^* = \sqrt{\frac{2DC_o}{C_h}} = \sqrt{\frac{(2)(6240)(12)}{1.40}} = 327$$

b) Lead time demand is normally distributed with m = 80, s = 10. Since Roberts wants at most a 2% probability of selling out of COMFORT, the corresponding z value (see Appendix A) is 2.06. That is, P(z > 2.06) = .0197 (about .02). Hence Roberts should reorder COMFORT when supply reaches m + zs = 80 + 2.06(10) = 101 cases. The safety stock is 21 cases.

c) The total annual cost of this solution is:

Ordering: (DC_o/Q^*) = ((6240)(12)/327)	=	$229
Holding--Normal: $(1/2)Q^*C_o$ = (1/2)(327)(1.40)	=	$229
Holding--Safety Stock: $C_h(21)$ = (1.40)(21)	=	$ 29
TOTAL	=	$487

PROBLEM 6

The publishers of the <u>Fast</u> <u>Food</u> <u>Restaurant</u> <u>Menu</u> <u>Book</u> wish to determine how many copies to print. There is a fixed cost of $5,000 to produce the book and the incremental profit per copy is $.45. Sales for this edition are estimated to be normally distributed. The most likely sales volume is 12,000 copies and they believe there is a 5% chance that sales will exceed 20,000.

a) If any unsold copies of the book can be sold at salvage at a $.55 loss, how many copies should be printed?

b) If any unsold copies of the book can be sold at salvage at a $.65 loss, how many copies should be printed? Comment.

SOLUTION 6

a) $m = 12,000$. To find s note that $z = 1.65$ corresponds to a 5% tail probability. Therefore, $(20,000 - 12,000) = 1.65\sigma$ or $\sigma = 4848$.

Using incremental analysis with $C_o = .55$ and $C_u = .45$, $(C_u/(C_u+C_o)) = .45/(.45+.55) = .45$.

Find Q^* such that $P(D \leq Q^*) = .45$. From Appendix A, $z = -.12$ gives this probability. Thus, $Q^* = 12,000 - .12(4848) = 11,418$ books.

b) Again using incremental analysis as above but with $C_o = .65$, $(C_u/(C_u + C_o)) = .45/(.45 + .65) = .4091$.

Find Q^* such that $P(D \leq Q^*) = .4091$. From Appendix A, $z = -.23$ gives this probability. Thus, $Q^* = 12,000 - .23(4848) = 10,885$ books.

However, since this is less than the breakeven volume of 11,111 books (= 5000/.45), NO COPIES SHOULD BE PRINTED because if the company produced only 10,885 copies it will not recoup its $5,000 fixed cost of producing the book.

> **NOTE:** A common mistake is thinking that the probability of having a stockout in some period is equivalent to the portion of the period's demand that will be backordered or lost, when demand is stochastic.
> A .10 stockout probability does NOT mean that ninety percent of demand will be satisfied. This point applies to all of the stochastic models in this chapter.

PROBLEM 7

Joe Walsh is a salesman for the Ace Brush Company. Every three weeks he contacts Dollar Department Store so that they may place an order to replenish their stock.
  Weekly demand for Ace brushes at Dollar approximately follows a normal distribution with a mean of 60 brushes and a standard deviation of 9 brushes. Once Joe submits an order, the lead time until Dollar receives the brushes is one week.
  Dollar would like at most a 2% chance of running out of stock during any replenishment period. If Dollar has 75 brushes in stock when Joe contacts them, how many should they order?

SOLUTION 7

This can be modeled as a periodic review problem with probabilistic demand. The review period plus the following lead time totals 4 weeks. This is the amount of time that will elapse before the next shipment of brushes will arrive.

Weekly demand is normally distributed with:
        Mean weekly demand, μ =   60
        Weekly standard deviation, σ =   9
        Weekly variance, σ^2 =   81

Thus the distribution of demand for 4 weeks is normal with
        Mean demand over 4 weeks, μ = 4x60 = 240
        Variance of demand over 4 weeks, σ^2 = 4x81 = 324
        Standard deviation over 4 weeks, σ = $(324)^{1/2}$ = 18

The replenishment level, M, is given by the formula $M = \mu + z\sigma$ where z is determined by the desired stockout probability. For a 2% stockout probability (2% tail area in Appendix A), z = 2.05. Thus, M = 240 + 2.05(18) = 277.

As the store currently has 75 brushes in stock, Dollar should order: 277 - 75 = <u>202</u> brushes from Joe. The safety stock is $z\sigma$ = (2.05)(18) = 37 brushes.

NOTE: The standard deviation (SD) of the "whole" does NOT equal the sum of the SDs of the "parts". For example, if the SD of daily demand equals 10, the SD of two-day demand does NOT equal 20.
  However, the variance (VAR) of the "whole" does equal the sum of the VARs of the "parts". So, for the above example, the VAR of two-day demand is 200 and the SD of two-day demand equals $\sqrt{200}$ = 14.14 or $10\sqrt{2}$ days = 14.14.

PROBLEM 8

Columbia Mopeds has just received an order for 10,000 mopeds
from Shears Department Stores. To meet the contract
requirements the mopeds must be completed in 10 weeks. The
following is a bill of materials chart for the Columbia moped.

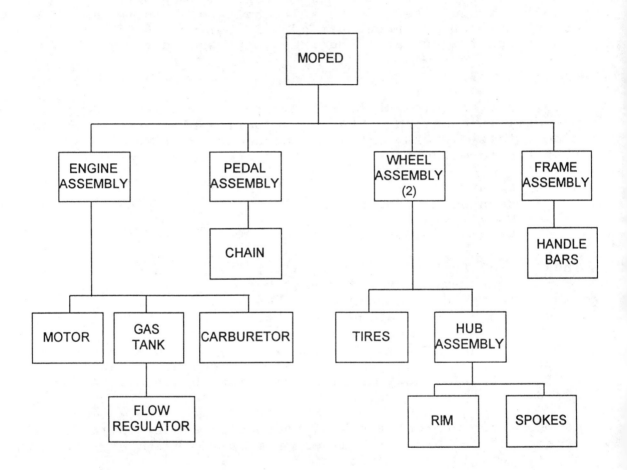

The table on the next page gives the current inventory and lead
times necessary for each component in the manufacturing process.
On the basis of this information, use MRP to determine the net
requirements and order times for each component.

Component	Units in Inventory (per moped)	Lead Time (in weeks)
Moped	2,200	1
Engine Assembly	1,500	2
Motor	900	5
Gas Tank	2,000	1
Carburetor	800	4
Flow Regulator	1,600	3
Pedal Assembly	600	6
Chain	900	3
Wheel Assembly	9,500	4
Tires	1,000	4
Hub Assembly	2,000	1
Rims	6,000	3
Spoke Assembly	3,200	2
Frame Assembly	8,000	4
Handle Bars	600	7

(Note that each moped requires two wheel assemblies)

SOLUTION 8

The contract calls for 10,000 mopeds, but the company has only 2,200 in stock. Therefore, it needs to manufacture 7,800 mopeds. Using the formula:

(Net component requirements) = (Gross component requirements) − (Number of components in inventory)

we have the following net component requirements:

Engine Assemblies	7,800 − 1,500	= 6,300
Motor	6,300 − 900	= 5,400
Gas Tank	6,300 − 2,000	= 4,300
Carburetor	6,300 − 800	= 5,500
Flow Regulator	4,300 − 1,600	= 2,700
Pedal Assembly	7,800 − 600	= 7,200
Chain	7,200 − 900	= 6,300
Wheel Assembly	2 x(7,800)− 9,500	= 6,100
Tire	6,100 − 1,000	= 5,100
Hub Assembly	6,100 − 2,000	= 4,100
Rim	4,100 − 6,000	= 0*
Spoke Assembly	4,100 − 3,200	900
Frame Assembly	6,300 − 8,000	= 0*
Handle Bars	0* − 600	= 0*

(* = current inventory exceeds demand requirements.)

For example, in order to deliver the 10,000 mopeds it will be
necessary to produce 6,300 chains which will bring the total
number of chains available to 7,200. These 7,200 chains will be
used to manufacture 7,200 pedal assemblies. This will bring the
total number of pedal assemblies available to 7,800 which will
allow the 7,800 mopeds to be built.

To determine the order times we work backwards. Since the order
must be completed in 10 weeks, the moped assembly must begin by
week 9 (= 10 - 1). Continuing in this fashion of subtracting
the lead times from the completion dates for each component to
determine the week that the order must be placed we have:

Component	Completion Date	Lead Time	Place Order
Engine Assembly	9	2	7
Motor	7	5	2
Gas Tank	7	1	6
Flow Regulator	6	3	3
Carburetor	7	4	3
Pedal Assembly	9	6	3
Chain	3	3	0 (immediately)
Wheel Assembly	9	4	5
Tire	5	4	1
Hub Assembly	5	1	4
Spoke Assembly	4	2	2

Note that it is not necessary to calculate the order placement
date for rims, frames, or handle bars since current inventory
exceeds the demand requirements. Thus, summarizing,

Component	Net Requirements	Lead Time (in weeks)	Order Date (in weeks)
Moped	7,800	1	9
Engine Assembly	6,300	2	7
Motor	5,400	5	2
Gas Tank	4,300	1	6
Carburetor	5,500	4	3
Flow Regulator	2,700	3	3
Pedal Assembly	7,200	6	3
Chain	6,300	3	0
Wheel Assembly	6,100	4	5
Tires	5,100	4	1
Hub Assembly	4,100	1	4
Rim	0	3	-
Spoke Assembly	900	2	2
Frame Assembly	0	4	-
Handle Bars	0	7	-

PROBLEM 9

   Mark Hall manages a small greeting card shop that sells
artificial Christmas trees during the six weeks prior to
Christmas. Based on past experience and current circumstances,
Mark estimates that he will sell somewhere between 20 and 80
trees and that the actual number is equally likely to fall
anywhere in that range.
   A tree costs Mark $28.00 and he sells it for $46.00. Due to
very limited storage space, Mark is forced to sell any trees
that remain after Christmas at half price ($23.00).

a) What is the optimal probability of stocking out (having more
   demand than supply)?

b) How many trees should Mark order?

c) Based on your order quantity in (b), what is the probability
   that Mark will have ten or more trees to sell at a discount
   after Christmas?

SOLUTION 9

   This can be modeled as a single-period problem with uniform
demand. The demand limits are a = 20 and b = 80.
C_u = 46 - 28 = $18. C_o = 28 - 23 = $5.

a) Using incremental analysis, the optimal probability of NOT
   running out of stock is:

$$P(D \leq Q^*) = C_u/(C_u+C_o) = 18/(18+5) = .7826$$

   Thus, the optimal probability of stocking out is:

$$P(D > Q^*) = 1 - P(D \leq Q^*) = 1 - .7826 = .2174$$

b) The optimal order quantity is:

$$Q^* = a + P(D \leq Q^*)(b-a) = 20 + .7826(80-20)$$
$$= 20 + 46.956 = 67 \text{ trees.}$$

c) If Mark orders 67 trees and later is left with ten or more
   of them, demand would have to be less than or equal to 57
   trees. The probability of this is:
$$P(D \leq 57) = (57-a)/(b-a) = (57-20)/(80-20)$$
$$= 37/60 = .6167 \doteq 62$$

ANSWERED PROBLEMS

PROBLEM 10

Terri's Tie Shop (TTS) is the exclusive retail outlet for Trophy
Ties. Although demand is slightly higher in December
(Christmas) and June (Father's Day), it is relatively constant
throughout the year as last year's sales figures show:

Month	Demand	Month	Demand
JAN	75	JUL	68
FEB	70	AUG	75
MAR	72	SEP	74
APR	76	OCT	70
MAY	69	NOV	76
JUN	85	DEC	90

The average cost of a Trophy Tie is $4 to TTS. TTS figures
inventory costs at 15% yearly and reorder costs are $25 per
order. There is no reason to assume demand will change much
this year.

a) What is the average monthly demand?

b) Assume demand is constant throughout the year and the lead
   time is two months. Determine an optimal inventory policy
   for the model.

c) What is the total annual variable costs of the model?

d) Make some suggestions to modify the inventory policy of the
   model to fit the "real" problem. Comment.

PROBLEM 11

One decision faced by many manufacturing firms is whether to
make or buy a particular component of the manufacturing process.
  Harrison Sound Corporation manufactures stereo systems. The
company has a choice of either manufacturing the digital display
unit for the Model 243 receiver themselves or purchasing the
unit from Allied Electronics.
  Allied will charge Harrison $7.50 per unit and Harrison
estimates the cost of placing an order with Allied at $48.
  On the other hand, if Harrison manufactures the units
themselves, there will be a set-up cost for production of
$1,600, an annual production rate of 50,000 units a year is
possible, and the per unit production cost will be $7.00 (in
addition to the set-up cost).

a) If Harrison expects the annual demand for these display
   units to be about 10,000, and the holding cost rate is 20%,
   determine the total annual variable costs of both policies.

b) Which policy would you recommend to management? Why?

PROBLEM 12

National Business Machines (NBM) is trying to develop the
effective use of one of its production lines which produces
transistors for circuits of computers. In general, allowing for
defectives, NBM needs 1,000,000 transistors per year for their
NBM 470 series. A production rate of 3,000,000 per year is
possible if the production line were in continuous operation 24
hours a day, 365 days a year. The cost of storing a transistor
is $1 per year. Production set-up costs $4,000 and takes two
weeks.

a) What is the optimal number of transistors NBM should make per
   production run?

b) What will be the number of production runs per year?

c) What is the duration of a production run?

d) If workers have (and must take) vacation between the end of
   one production run and the start-up of another, how much
   vacation time do they get per year. (Note they participate
   in the set-up).

PROBLEM 13

Andy's Auto Parts has been stocking an unusually fine grade of
racing oil on which it makes a $.10 per quart profit. Demand
has been 2,000 quarts per week. Storage costs are $.01 per
quart per week. Reorder costs are $10 per order. If Andy
allows backorders, he figures his demand will drop to 1,900
quarts per week. Andy will, however, give a $.03 per week
discount per can backordered.

a) Derive an optimal inventory policy for Andy.

b) Based on your answer in (a), what is the maximum time a
   backordered customer would have to wait?

PROBLEM 14

Wiley's TV Town sells Apex large screen TV's. Weekly demand has
averaged 20 Apex TV's per week. Wiley makes a gross profit of
$50 per TV sold (not including inventory costs). Holding costs
are $260 per TV per year and reorder costs are $32 per order.
Lead time is 1 week.

a) Determine: (1) the optimal number of TV's Wiley should
   order; (2) his reorder point; and, (3) his yearly net
   profit.

b) Wiley is considering allowing backorders. Wiley intends to
   offer customers a discount of $20 per week for each week the
   customer must wait for his TV. Wiley estimates that this
   policy will result in a drop in demand to 19 TV's per week.
   Order and holding costs will remain the same. Should Wiley
   adopt this policy? Why or why not?

PROBLEM 15

Rosato's Pizza Parlor uses tomato sauce at a fairly constant
rate of 3600 cans per year. It costs Rosato $40 to place an
order for tomato sauce. The holding cost rate is 30 percent per
can per year.
   Shipping cost, based on weight, must be paid by Rosato and a
can of tomato paste weighs 15 pounds. Both the shipping cost
and the purchase cost depend on the order quantity. Using the
information below, determine the most economical number of cans
to order at one time. (Hint: Start by converting the shipping
cost discount schedule from pounds to cans.)

Shipping Cost		Purchase Cost	
Pounds	Cost/Pound	Quantity	Cost/Can
1 - 1799	$0.26	1 - 149	$17.80
1800 - 4499	0.23	150 - 349	17.50
4500 or more	0.20	350 or more	17.40

NOTE: A common mistake is to think that the EOQ
equation (square-root equation) ALWAYS determines the
optimal order quantity. This is not true for quantity
discount problems. Recall that an optimal solution
must be a feasible solution. With quantity discounts,
an EOQ-derived order quantity must be checked to see
if it is feasible (falls in the required range).

PROBLEM 16

Kelly's Service Station does a large business in tune-ups. Demand has been averaging 210 spark plugs per week. Holding costs are $.01 per plug per week and reorder costs are estimated at $10 per order. Kelly does not want to be out of stock on more than 1% of his orders. There is a one day delivery time. The standard deviation of demand is five plugs per day. Assume a normal distribution of demand during lead time and a 7-day work week.

a) What inventory policy do you suggest for Kelly's station?

b) What is the average amount of safety stock for the reorder point in (a)?

c) What are the total variable weekly costs including safety stock costs?

PROBLEM 17

Winkies Donuts is a small chain of donut shops in Lemon County. Winkies' success is built largely around its jelly donut. Recently, Winkies management has received a number of complaints concerning store #17 running out of jelly donuts late in the afternoon. Thus, Winkies has undertaken a study of the store's operations. The study has indicated the following:

(1) Afternoon demand for jelly donuts is approximately normally distributed with mean 150 and standard deviation 30 donuts.
(2) The cost to manufacture a jelly donut is $.09.
(3) The selling price is $.20.
(4) Donuts unsold at the end of the day are given to a charity which gives Winkies a tax savings of $.03 per donut.

Winkies management feels there is a goodwill loss of $.75 for each sale lost when it is out of stock of jelly donuts. Based on this information, how many jelly donuts should the baker prepare for the afternoon?

PROBLEM 18

A lawn and garden shop that is open for business seven days a week orders bags of grass seed every OTHER Monday. Lead time for seed orders is 5 days. On Monday, at ordering time, a clerk found 112 bags of seed in stock, and so he ordered 198 bags.
   Daily demand for grass seed is normally distributed with a mean of 15 bags and a standard deviation of four bags.
   The manager would like to know what the probability is that a grass seed stockout will occur before the NEXT order arrives.

PROBLEM 19

Innovative Products Inc. manufactures "charcoal" barbecue grills
for indoor use. Innovative has been asked to give a bid on an
order from Shears Department Stores for 5,000 grills. Because
this grill will have to be specially made for Shears, Innovative
estimates that there will be a fixed cost of $40,000 involved in
setting up the production line. The accounting department
estimates the variable production cost per unit to be $12.

Suppose Innovative wins the bid. The diagram below represents
the bill of materials (or how the barbecues are to be
assembled).

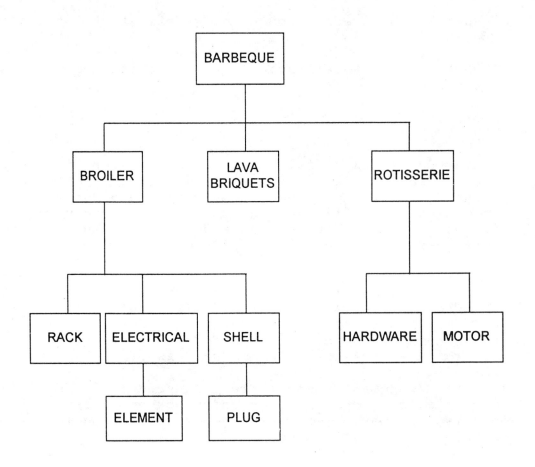

Innovative makes some of the items required in manufacturing the
barbecues itself, while it purchases other items from outside
suppliers. In the case where Innovative manufactures the part
itself, the lead time is given in days per unit quantity. In
the case where Innovative purchases the part from an outside
supplier, the lead time is for the total amount needed. The
following table gives the current inventory and lead time for
the parts.

Item	Quantity on Hand	Lead Times
Barbecue	0	1 week per 2500 units
Broiler	0	1 week per 2500 units
Rack	3,000	1 week per 1000 units
Electrical	2,000	1 week per 1500 units
Shell	0	1 week per 1000 units
Element	3,700	5 weeks
Plug	900	3 weeks
Rotisserie	3,000	1 week per 500 units
Hardware	1,000	1 week per 250 units
Motor	2,500	10 weeks
Lava Briquets	2,000	6 weeks

For example, if Innovative needs to produce 2,000 shells it will take two weeks. Regardless of how many elements must be ordered, the lead time is five weeks, etc.

Using this information, determine how many weeks it will take for Innovative to produce 5,000 barbecues.

PROBLEM 20

Zak's Zippers is contemplating manufacturing their own zippers rather than distributing the zippers it receives from ZZZ, Inc. Zak's figures it must sell the zipper at the same price or else the yearly demand of 4,000 dozen zippers will be greatly affected.

Presently the purchase cost per dozen zippers is $10, whereas the proposed manufacturing cost for labor and raw materials is estimated at $8 per dozen. In any event, the holding costs are estimated at 20% of the purchase or manufacturing cost of the item.

Reorder costs are currently $40 per order. However, set-up costs for each production cycle are estimated at $400.

If Zak's can lease a machine with production capacity of 8,000 dozen zippers per year at an annual cost of $5,000, should Zak's convert to manufacturing their own zippers?

PROBLEM 21

Rancher Jim's Luncheon Meat Company produces fresh luncheon meats. Demand is for 300,000 pounds of meat annually. Rancher Jim has his choice of two machines to process the meats. The annual lease costs and annual processing capacities are given below:

	Annual Lease Cost	Annual Processing Capacity
Machine I	$10,000	250,000 lbs.
Machine II	$12,000	1,000,000 lbs.

Set-up costs are $1,000 per run and holding costs are $.10 per pound per year. Rancher Jim's gross profit is $.20 per pound (not including annual lease, set-up or holding costs).

a) Show that Machine II gives the maximum profit for processing.

b) Why would you likely recommend machine I for Rancher Jim?

PROBLEM 22

Honest Archie's Appliance Co. has a policy of giving loaner TV's to customers who purchase a set from Archie when he is out of stock of they model they want. As soon as Archie gets the set in stock, he delivers the new set and picks up the loaner from the customer.

Demand at Archie's for the Apex 19-inch remote control TV is 5 units per week. The sets have an annual holding cost of $55. The cost to place an order for the sets is $80, and it typically takes three weeks for the sets to arrive after the order is placed.

a) If the loaner TV's cost Archie $3 per week to rent, determine his optimal order policy.

b) What is the total annual variable cost of this policy?

PROBLEM 23

Clearview Optical gives a customer a complimentary carrying case with each pair of eye glasses purchased. Lead time demand for these cases is normally distributed with a mean of 230 cases and a standard deviation of 42 cases.

a) If Clearview reorders cases when inventory reaches 285 cases, what is the probability that there will be a stockout during lead time?

b) If Clearview desires a .05 probability of a stockout during lead time, what should the reorder point be for glass cases?

PROBLEM 24

Amazing Bakers sells bread to 40 supermarkets. It costs Amazing $1,250 per day to operate its plant. The profit per loaf of bread sold in the supermarket is $.025. Any unsold bread is returned to be sold at the Amazing Thrift store at a loss of $.015.

a) If sales follow a normal distribution with μ = 70,000 and σ = 5,000 per day, how many loaves should Amazing bake daily?

b) Amazing is considering a different sales plan for which the profit per loaf of bread sold in the supermarket is $.03 and the loss per loaf bread returned is $.018. If μ = 60,000 and σ = 4,000 per day, how many loaves should Amazing bake daily?

PROBLEM 25

Every year in early October Steven King buys pumpkins of one size from a farmer in Maine and then hires an artist to carve bewitching faces in them. He then tries to sell them at his produce stand in a public market in Boston.

The farmer charges Steven $2.50 per pumpkin and the artist is paid $2.00 per carved pumpkin. Steven sells a carved pumpkin for $8.00. Any pumpkins not sold by 5:00 p.m. on Halloween are donated to Steven's favorite children's hospital. Steven pays the artist $0.75 per pumpkin to rush the pumpkins to the hospital for the youngsters to enjoy.

Steven estimates the demand for his pumpkins this season to be uniformly distributed within a range of 30 to 70.

a) How many pumpkins should Steven have available for sale?

b) Based on your answer to (a), what is the probability that Steven will be short five or more pumpkins?

PROBLEM 26

Bank Drugs sells Jami Michelle lipstick. The Jami Michelle Company offers a 6% discount on orders of at least 500 tubes, a 10% discount on orders of at least 1,000 tubes, a 12% discount on orders of at least 1,800 tubes and a 15% discount on orders at least 2,500 tubes.

Bank sells an average of 40 tubes of Jami Michelle lipstick weekly. The normal price paid by Bank drugs is $1 per tube. If it costs Bank $30 to place an order, and Bank's annual holding cost rate is 27%, determine the optimal order policy for Bank Drugs.

PROBLEM 27

Weber Appliance is gearing up for Christmas production of its La Guillotine food processor. The following is a bill of material chart for the food processor.

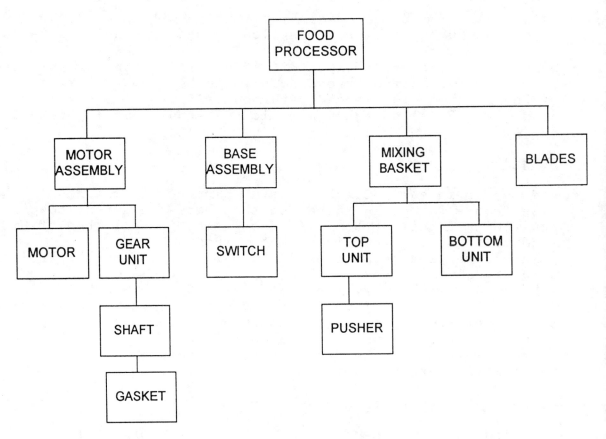

The company wishes to manufacture 15,000 additional units within
the next 13 weeks. The following table gives the current
inventory and lead time for each component in the food
processor.

Component	Current Inventory	Lead Time (in weeks)
Food Processor	0	1
Motor Assembly	5,000	2
Motor	2,000	5
Gear Unit	6,000	3
Shaft	1,000	4
Gasket	4,000	5
Base Assembly	3,000	4
Switch	3,000	3
Mixing Basket	5,000	1
Top Unit	2,000	9
Pusher	1,000	2
Bottom Unit	4,000	8
Blades	7,000	10

Use MRP to determine the net requirements and order times for
each component.

PROBLEM 28

A company has the following choices for purchasing a product for which demand is 100 per week.

Option	Purchase Cost/Item	Quantity
I	$10.00	0 - 599
II	$ 9.80	600 or more
III	$ 9.90	exactly 100

Under option III, the ordering company will have no paperwork as the 100 items will be delivered every week automatically. Thus under option III, the only work associated with an order is in filing an invoice which is assumed to have zero cost.
   Otherwise reorder costs are $75 per order. If holding costs are figured at .5% per week, what is the optimal order quantity?

PROBLEM 29

Demand for the Kansas Systems Model 402 printer at the Computer Town chain of computer stores has averaged 35 units per week with a standard deviation of 10 units per week.
   The units cost Computer Town $910 each and there is a $500 order cost. Computer Town's an annual holding cost rate is 20%.
   The lead time for these printers is approximately a month with lead time demand being normally distributed with a mean of 140 units and a standard deviation of 20 units.

a) If Computer Town wants to experience an average of at most one stockout per year on these printers, determine an optimal inventory policy for the store.

b) Determine the annual cost of the policy for Computer Town.

c) If Computer Town was just starting to stock printers, use the data above to determine how many printers they should order.

PROBLEM 30

Chez Paul Restaurant orders special styrofoam "doggy bags" for its customers once a month and lead time is one week. Weekly demand for doggy bags is approximately normally distributed with an average of 120 bags and a standard deviation of 25.
   Chez Paul wants at most a 3% chance of running out of doggy bags during the replenishment period. If he has 150 bags in stock when he places an order, how many additional bags should he order? What is the safety stock in this case?

TRUE/FALSE

31. At the optimal order quantity, Q^*, in the EOQ model, annual order costs equal annual holding costs.

32. If an item's per-unit backorder cost is greater than its per-unit holding cost, no intentional shortage should be planned.

33. At the optimal order quantity for the quantity discount model, the sum of the annual holding and ordering costs is minimized.

34. As lead time for an item increases, the cycle time increases.

35. If an item's per-unit backorder cost equals one-half of its per-unit holding cost, it is optimal to plan to incur the first shortage one-third of the way through the order cycle.

36. If the annual production rate for an item increases, then the optimal production lot size, Q^*, will also increase.

37. In an MRP system, it is possible that one should order a component before ordering one of the subcomponents making up that component.

38. If the cost of underestimating demand, C_u, is greater than the cost of overestimating demand, C_o, the optimal single-period order quantity is greater than expected demand.

39. In an MRP system, if a particular subcomponent has a lead time of ten weeks, then the finished good could not be completed in less than ten weeks.

40. In the EOQ model, an item's optimal order quantity, Q^*, cannot be greater than its annual demand, D.

41. One of the few drawbacks of the just-in-time approach to inventory management is its sizable safety stock requirement.

42. Material requirements planning (MRP) uses gross-to-net logic to handle the "how much to order" question and uses reorder point logic to handle the "when to order" question.

43. To avoid a stockout of a periodic-review item, the item's order quantity plus inventory on hand at ordering time must last until the time the item can be ordered again.

44. If the optimal production lot size Q^* decreases, average inventory increases.

45. In the EOQ model, the doubling of both the ordering and holding costs would result in no change in the optimal order quantity.

CHAPTER

12
Waiting Line Models

KEY CONCEPTS

CONCEPT	ILLUSTRATED PROBLEMS*	ANSWERED PROBLEMS
Poisson Arrival Process	1	10
Exponential Service Time Distribution	1	10
M/M/1 System	1,4,5	10-15,17
M/M/k System	2,3	11,15,16,18
M/M/1 System with Finite Calling Population	6	23
M/G/1 System	7	19
M/G/k System with Blocked Customers Cleared	8	20,21
M/D/1 System	9	22
Economic Analysis of Queuing Systems	3,4,5	11,14,16,17

* Note: <u>Unless</u> <u>otherwise</u> <u>stated</u>, all problems in this chapter assume a Poisson arrival process, an exponential service time distribution, a first-come-first-served queue discipline and an unlimited potential queue length.

REVIEW

1. Queuing theory is the study of waiting lines. Four characteristics of a queuing system are: (1) the manner in which customers arrive; (2) the time required for service; (3) the priority determining the order of service; and (4) the number and configuration of servers in the system.

2. In general, the arrival of customers into the system is a random event. Frequently the arrival pattern is modeled as a Poisson process. The Poisson distribution defines the probability of x arrivals during a specified time period as:

$$P(x) = \frac{\lambda^x e^{-\lambda}}{x!}$$

Here λ is the mean number of arrivals during the specified period and e = 2.71828... Appendix C provides a table of the quantity e^- for specified values of λ. Sample data should be collected to determine the appropriateness of using the Poisson distribution as well as estimating the value for λ.

3. Service time is also usually a random variable. A distribution commonly used to describe this time is the exponential distribution. The exponential distribution has a probability density function:

$$f(t) = \mu e^{-\mu t}$$

Here μ is the mean number of customers that can be served in a specified time period.

4. For the exponential distribution, the cumulative probability:

$$P(t \leq T) = 1 - e^{-\mu T}$$

Thus the probability of a service taking longer than T is $e^{-\mu T}$.

5. The most common queue discipline is first come, first served (FCFS). An elevator is an example of last come, first served (LCFS) queue discipline.

6. A three part code of the form A/D/k is used to describe various queueing systems. Here, A identifies the arrival distribution, D the service (departure) distribution and k the number of servers for the system.
    Frequently used symbols for the arrival and service processes are: M - Markov distributions (Poisson/exponential), D - Deterministic (constant) and G - General distribution (with a known mean and variance).

Thus the notation, <u>M/M/k</u> refers to a queuing situation in which arrivals occur according to a Poisson distribution, service times follow an exponential distribution and there are k servers each working at an identical service rate.

7. In order for an M/M/k system not to have an <u>infinitely large queue</u>, λ must be less than $k\mu$, where λ is the mean arrival rate and μ is the mean service rate for each server.

8. For a single server system, one defines the ratio λ/μ as the <u>utilization factor</u> for the queue. This can be thought of as the long run proportion of time the server is busy, the probability there is someone in the system, or the probability that an arriving customer must wait for service.

9. In determining the most economical queuing system configuration or evaluating service parameters for the system, one is frequently interested in long run or <u>steady state</u> results. For steady state results to exist, $\lambda < \mu$ for an M/M/1 or an M/G/1 queue, and $\lambda < k\mu$ for an M/M/k queue.

10. Notation used for various queue measures are as follows:

P_0 = <u>probability</u> the service facility is idle
P_n = <u>probability</u> of n units in the system
P_w = <u>probability</u> an arriving unit must wait for service
L_q = average <u>number</u> <u>of</u> <u>units</u> in the queue awaiting service
L = average <u>number</u> <u>of</u> <u>units</u> in the system
W_q = average <u>time</u> a unit spends in the queue awaiting service
W = average <u>time</u> a unit spends in the system
λ = the average arrival <u>rate</u>
μ = the average service <u>rate</u> for each server
$1/\lambda$ = the average <u>time</u> between arrivals
$1/\mu$ = the average service <u>time</u>
σ = the standard deviation of the service <u>time</u>

11. For nearly all queuing systems, there is a relationship between the average time a unit spends in the system or queue and the average number of units in the system or queue. These relationships, known as <u>Little's flow equations</u> are:

$$L = \lambda W \quad \text{and} \quad L_q = \lambda W_q$$

12. When the queue discipline is FCFS, <u>analytical formulas</u> have been derived for several different queuing models including the following: M/M/1, M/M/k, M/G/1, M/G/k with blocked customers cleared, and M/M/1 with with a finite calling population. These formulas are presented on the next pages.

13. Analytical formulas are not available for all possible queuing systems. In this event, insights may be gained through a <u>simulation</u> of the system.

STEADY STATE RESULTS

Quantity	M/M/1 Queues	M/M/k Queues
P_0	$1 - \lambda/\mu$	$\dfrac{1}{\left[\displaystyle\sum_{n=0}^{k-1} (1/n!)(\lambda/\mu)^n\right] + \dfrac{1}{k!}(\lambda/\mu)^k \dfrac{k\mu}{k\mu-\lambda}}$
P_n	$(\lambda/\mu)^n P_0$	$\dfrac{1}{k!\,k^{n-k}}(\lambda/\mu)^n P_0 \quad \text{for } n > k$ $\dfrac{1}{n!}(\lambda/\mu)^n P_0 \quad \text{for } n \leq k$
L_q	$\dfrac{\lambda^2}{\mu(\mu - \lambda)}$	$\dfrac{\lambda\mu(\lambda/\mu)^k}{(k-1)!(k\mu - \lambda)^2} P_0$
L	$\lambda/(\mu - \lambda)$ or $L_q + (\lambda/\mu)$	$L_q + (\lambda/\mu)$
W_q	$\lambda/[\mu(\mu - \lambda)]$ or L_q/λ	L_q/λ
W	$1/(\mu - \lambda)$ or L/λ	L/λ
P_w	$1 - P_0$ or λ/μ	$\dfrac{1}{k!}(\lambda/\mu)^k \dfrac{k\mu}{k\mu-\lambda} P_0$

STEADY STATE RESULTS

Quantity	M/G/1 Queues*	M/G/k Queues With Blocked Customers Cleared	M/M/1 Queues** With Finite Calling Population (Size N)
P_0	$1 - \lambda/\mu$	$\dfrac{1}{\displaystyle\sum_{i=0}^{k} (\lambda/\mu)^i/i!}$	$\dfrac{1}{\displaystyle\sum_{i=0}^{N} \dfrac{N!}{(N-i)!} (\lambda/\mu)^i}$
P_n	No formula	$\dfrac{(\lambda/\mu)^n}{n!} P_0$ for n=0,1,2,..k	$\dfrac{N!}{(N-n)!} (\lambda/\mu)^n P_0$ for n=1,2,..N
L_q	$\dfrac{\lambda^2\sigma^2 + (\lambda/\mu)^2}{2(1-\lambda/\mu)}$	No queue	$N - \dfrac{\lambda+\mu}{\lambda} (1-P_0)$
L	$L_q + (\lambda/\mu)$	$(\lambda/\mu)(1 - P_k)$	$N - \left[(\mu+\lambda)/\lambda\right](1-P_0)$
W_q	L_q/λ	No queue	$L_q/(N-L)\lambda$
W	L/λ	$(1 - P_k)/\mu$	$L/(N-L)\lambda$
P_w	λ/μ	No waiting	$1 - P_0$

NOTES:

* In the M/G/1 queue, if G is the exponential distribution, then $\sigma = 1/\mu$ and the above formulas reduce to those given for the M/M/1 queue

** In the finite calling population model, λ represents the mean arrival rate for each unit.

ILLUSTRATED PROBLEMS

> **NOTE:** Students frequently confuse <u>rates</u> and <u>times</u> in this chapter. They are not the same; they have an inverse relationship. The equations throughout the chapter assume λ and μ are <u>rates</u>. If you are given average interarrival time or service time, use the inverse.
>
> Also, λ and μ should be stated in the same unit of time (per hour, for example). Finally, be careful converting the standard deviation of service times σ from one unit of time to another. (It might be easier to convert the arrival rate's time basis to that of the service rate.

> **NOTE:** Economic analysis of queuing systems usually involves a tradeoff between the cost of service and the <u>cost</u> of <u>waiting</u>. To get the latter, you might be inclined to multiple the waiting cost per unit per time period, c_w, by the average wait time in the system, W. If you take this approach you are not finished until you also multiply by the average number of units entering the system per hour, λ. You get the same results by simply multiplying c_w by L, the average number of units in the system.

PROBLEM 1

Joe Ferris is a stock trader on the floor of the New York Stock Exchange for the firm of Smith, Jones, Johnson, and Thomas, Inc. Stock transactions arrive at a mean rate of 20 per hour. Each order received by Joe requires an average of two minutes to process.

a) What is the probability that no orders are received within a 15-minute period?

b) What is the probability that exactly 3 orders are received within a 15-minute period?

c) What is the probability that more than 6 orders arrive within a 15-minute period?

d) What is the mean service rate per hour?

e) What percentage of the orders will take less than one minute to process?

f) What percentage of the orders will be completed in exactly 3 minutes?

g) What percentage of the orders will require more than 3 minutes to process?

h) What is the average time an order must wait from the time Joe receives the order until it is finished being processed (i.e. its turnaround time)?

i) What is the average number of orders Joe has waiting to be processed?

j) What percentage of the time is Joe processing orders?

SOLUTION 1

Orders arrive at a mean rate of 20 per hour or one order every 3 minutes. Therefore, in a 15 minute interval the average number of orders arriving will be λ = 15/3 = 5. From Appendix C note that e^{-5} = .0067.

a) $P(x = 0) = (5^0 e^{-5})/0! = e^{-5} = .0067$.

b) $P(x = 3) = (5^3 e^{-5})/3! = 125(.0067)/6 = .1396$.

c) $P(x > 6) = 1 - P(x = 0) - P(x = 1) - P(x = 2) - P(x = 3) -$
$P(x = 4) - P(x = 5) - P(x = 6) = 1 - .762 = .238$.

d) Since Joe Ferris can process an order in average time of 2 minutes (= 2/60 hr.), then the mean service rate, μ, is μ = 1/(mean service time), or 60/2 = 30/hr.

e) Since the units are expressed in hours, $P(T \le 1$ minute) = $P(T \le 1/60$ hour). Using the exponential distribution, $P(T \le t) = 1 - e^{-\mu t}$. Hence,

$P(T \le 1/60) = 1 - e^{-30(1/60)} = 1 - e^{-.5} = 1 - .6065 = .3935$.

f) Since the exponential distribution is a continuous distribution, the probability a service time exactly equals any specific quantity is 0.

g) The percentage of orders requiring more than 3 minutes to process is:

$P(T > 3/60) = e^{-30(3/60)} = e^{-1.5} = .2231$.

h) This is an M/M/1 queue with g = 20 per hour and m = 30 per hour. The average time an order waits in the system is:

$W = 1/(\mu - \lambda) = 1/(30 - 20) = 1/10$ hour or 6 minutes.

i) The average number of orders waiting in the queue is:

$$L_q = \lambda^2/[\mu(\mu - \lambda)]$$

$$= (20)^2 /[(30)(30-20)] = 400/300 = 4/3.$$

j) The percentage of time Joe is processing orders is equivalent to the utilization factor, g/m. Thus, the percentage of time he is processing orders is:

$$\lambda/\mu = 20/30 = 2/3 \text{ or } 66 \text{ } 2/3\%.$$

PROBLEM 2

Smith, Jones, Johnson, and Thomas, Inc. (see problem 1) has begun a major advertising campaign which it believes will increase its business 50%. To handle the increased volume, the company has hired an additional floor trader, Fred Hanson, who works at the same speed as Joe Ferris?

a) Why will Joe Ferris alone not be able to handle the increase in orders?

b) What is the probability that neither Joe nor Fred will be working on an order at any point in time?

c) What is the average turnaround time for an order with both Joe and Fred working?

d) What is the average number of orders waiting to be filled with both Joe and Fred working?

SOLUTION 2

We first note that the new arrival rate of orders, , is 50% higher than that of problem 1. Thus, $\lambda = 1.5(20) = 30$ per hour.

a) Since Joe Ferris processes orders at a mean rate of $\mu = 30$ per hour, then $\lambda = \mu = 30$ and the utilization factor is 1. This implies the queue of orders will grow infinitely large. Hence, Joe alone cannot handle this increase in demand.

b) This is now an M/M/2 queueing system with $\lambda = 30$, $\mu = 30$, k = 2 and $(\lambda/\mu) = 1$. The probability that neither Joe nor Fred will be working is:

$$P_0 = \cfrac{1}{\left[\displaystyle\sum_{n=0}^{k-1} (1/n!)(\lambda/\mu)^n\right] + \cfrac{1}{k!}(\lambda/\mu)^k \cfrac{k\mu}{k\mu-\lambda}}$$

$$= \cfrac{1}{[(1 + (1/1!)(30/30)^1] + [(1/2!)(1)^2][2(30)/(2(30)-30)]}$$

$$= 1/(1 + 1 + 1)$$

$$= 1/3$$

c) The average turnaround time is the average waiting time in the system, W. W = L/ and L = L_q + (/μ). Now,

$$L_q = \cfrac{\lambda\mu(\lambda/\mu)^k}{(k-1)!(k\mu - \lambda)^2} P_0$$

$$= \cfrac{(30)(30)(30/30)^2}{(1!)((2)(30)-30))^2} (1/3)$$

$$= 1/3$$

Hence, L = 1/3 + (30/30) = 4/3.

W = (4/3)/30 = 4/90 hr. = 2.67 min.

d) The average number of orders waiting to be filled is L_q. This was calculated above in part (c) as 1/3.

PROBLEM 3

The advertising campaign of Smith, Jones, Johnson and Thomas, Inc. (see problems 1 and 2) was so successful that business actually doubled. The mean rate of stock orders arriving at the exchange is now 40 per hour and the company must decide how many floor traders to employ. Each floor trader hired can process an order in an average time of 2 minutes.

Based on a number of factors the brokerage firm has determined the average waiting cost per minute for an order to be $.50. Floor traders hired will earn $20 per hour in wages and benefits. Using this information compare the total hourly cost of hiring 2 traders with that of hiring 3 traders.

SOLUTION 3

The hourly cost can be modeled as (Total Salary Cost Per Hour) + (Total Hourly Cost for Orders in the System) = ($20 per trader per hour)x(Number of Traders) + ($30 waiting cost per hour) x (average number of orders in the system) = 20k + 30L.

Thus, L must be determined for k = 2 traders and for k = 3 traders with λ = 40/hr. and m = 30/hr. (since the average service time is 2 minutes (1/30 hr.).

k = 2
___

$$P_0 = \cfrac{1}{\left[\sum_{n=0}^{k-1} (1/n!)(\lambda/\mu)^n \right] + \cfrac{1}{k!} (\lambda/\mu)^k \cfrac{k\mu}{k\mu-\lambda}}$$

$$= \cfrac{1}{[1+(1/1!)(40/30)]+[(1/2!)(40/30)^2(60/(60-40))]}$$

$$= \cfrac{1}{1 + (4/3) + (8/3)} = 1/5$$

Thus,

$$L_q = \cfrac{\lambda\mu(\lambda/\mu)^k}{(k-1)!(k\mu - \lambda)^2} P_0 = \cfrac{(40)(30)(40/30)^2}{1!(60-40)^2} (1/5) = 16/15$$

Hence, $L = L_q + (\lambda/\mu) = 16/15 + 4/3 = 12/5$.

Thus, the total Cost = (20)(2) + 30(12/5) = $112.00 per hour

k = 3
___

Using the same formulas for k = 3:

$$P_0 = \cfrac{1}{\substack{[1+(1/1!)(40/30)+(1/2!)(40/30)^2]+ \\ [(1/3!)(40/30)^3(90/(90-40))]}}$$

$$= \cfrac{1}{[1 + 4/3 + 8/9] + [32/45]}$$

$$= 15/59$$

Hence, $L_q = \dfrac{(30)(40)(40/30)^3}{(2!)(3(30)-40)^2}$ (15/59) = 128/885 (=.1446)

Thus, L = 128/885 + 40/30 = 1308/885 (= 1.4780)
Total Cost = (20)(3) + 30(1308/885) = \$104.35 per hour

Thus, the cost of having 3 traders is less than that of 2 traders.

PROBLEM 4

Frederick's Auto Company currently receives an average of 22 letters a day and has a typist who can type a letter in an average time of 20 minutes. It is considering taking some relief action to ease the typist's workload. It can either hire an additional typist (who also works at an average rate of one letter per 20 minutes) at a cost of \$40 per day or it can lease one of three models of word processing systems listed below:

Model	Cost Per Day	Increase in Typist's Efficiency
I	\$37	50%
II	\$39	75%
III	\$43	150%

Frederick's has determined that the cost of a letter waiting to be mailed out is \$.80 per hour. If typists work 8 hours per day, what action should the company take?

SOLUTION 4

For each of the 5 alternatives, determine the average number of letters in the system and the total daily cost. The total daily cost = (Extra typist cost or Lease Cost) + 6.40L, where \$6.40 is the hourly cost of \$.80 times 8 hours per day.

Another Typist
This is an M/M/2 system with λ = 22, μ = 24 and k = 2. Using the formulas from the review section we compute P_0 = .3714 and L = 1.16. Hence Total Cost = 40 + (6.40)(1.16) = \$47.42.

Lease Machine 1
This is an M/M/1 system with λ = 22 and μ = (1.5)(24) = 36.
Using the formulas from the review section for an M/M/1 system, L = 22/(36-22) = 1.57. Total Cost = 37 + (6.40)(1.57) = \$47.05.

Lease Machine 2
This is an M/M/1 system with λ = 22 and μ = (1.75)(24) = 42.
L = 22/(42-22) = 1.1. Total cost = 39 + (6.40)(1.1) = 46.04.

Lease Machine 3
This is an M/M/1 system with λ = 22 and μ = (2.5)(24) = 60.
L = 22/(60-22) = .58.   Total cost = 43 + (6.40)(.58) = 46.71.

No Action
This is an M/M/1 system with λ = 22 and μ = 24.
L = 22/(24-22) = 11.   Total cost = 0 + (6.40)(11) = $70.40.

Thus the best course of action is to lease Machine II.

PROBLEM 5

Jerry's Jewelry Store is seeking a salesman for its evening
shift.   Three applicants with former experience have applied for
the position, each demanding different salaries.   Jerry has
contacted the former supervisor of each who has supplied him
with information on average service times for each applicant.
The applicant's salary demands and average service times are as
follows:

| | Hourly | Average |
Applicant	Wage	Service Time
Martha Miller	$ 6	6 min.
Ken Weeks	$10	5 min.
Eddie Smith	$14	4 min.

Customers arrive to the store at the average rate of 8 per hour
and you have estimated the cost of having a customer in the
store to be $4 per customer per hour (for security, customer
relations, etc.)   Which applicant should Jerry hire?

SOLUTION 5

For each applicant calculate the total hourly cost = (Hourly
Wage) + 4L, where L is the average number of customers in the
system.   Each case is an M/M/1 queueing system with   = 8.

Martha Miller
Since the average service time is 6 min., the average service
rate, μ = 1/6 per minute or 10 per hour.

L = 8/(10-8) = 4.   Thus total hourly cost = 6 + (4)(4) = $22.

Ken Weeks
Since the average service time is 5 min., the average service
rate, μ = 1/5 per minute or 12 per hour.

L = 8/(12-8) = 2.   Thus total hourly cost = 10 + (4)(2) = $18.

Eddie Smith
Since the average service time is 4 min., the average service
rate, μ = 1/4 per minute or 15 per hour.
L = 8/(15-8) = 8/7.   Total hourly cost = 14 + (4)(8/7) = \$18.56.

Based on this study, hire Ken Weeks.

PROBLEM 6

Biff Smith is in charge of maintenance for four of the rides at
the Algorithmland Amusement Park: the Pivot, the Traveling
Salesman's Adventure, Minimax Regret, and the CPM Crash. On the
average, each ride operates four hours before needing repair.
When repair is needed, the average repair time is 10 minutes.
   Assuming that the time between machine repairs and the service
times follow exponential distributions, determine the following:

a) the proportion of time Biff is idle

b) the average time a ride is "down" for repairs

> **NOTE:** For an M/M/1 system with a finite calling
> population, the arrival rate is the average number
> of times <u>one</u> unit from the finite population arrives
> per time period, not the average number of total
> arrivals per time period.

SOLUTION 6

This problem can be modeled as an M/M/1 queue with a finite
calling population of size N = 4 (rides). Here

$$\lambda = 1/(4 \text{ hours}) = .25 \text{ per hour}$$
$$\mu = 60/(10 \text{ minutes}) = 6 \text{ per hour.}$$
$$\lambda/\mu = .25/6 = 1/24$$

a) The proportion of time Biff is idle is P_0:

$$P_0 = \cfrac{1}{\displaystyle\sum_{i=0}^{N} \frac{N!}{(N-i)!} (\lambda/\mu)^i}$$

$$P_0 = \cfrac{1}{\dfrac{4!}{4!}(1/24)^0 + \dfrac{4!}{3!}(1/24)^1 + \dfrac{4!}{2!}(1/24)^2 + \dfrac{4!}{1!}(1/24)^3 + \dfrac{4!}{0!}(1/24)^4}$$

$$= \frac{1}{1 + 4(1/24)^1 + 12(1/24)^2 + 24(1/24)^3 + 24(1/24)^4}$$

$$= .840825$$

Hence, Biff is idle approximately 84% of the time.

b) To find the average time a ride is "down" for repairs we need to calculate W. This is given by the formula:

$$W = \frac{N}{(N-L)\lambda} - \frac{(\lambda + \mu)(1 - P_0)}{(N - L)\lambda^2} + \frac{1}{\mu}$$

where $L = N - (\mu/\lambda)(1-P_0)$.

Substituting the appropriate values gives:

$$L = 4 - (6/.25)(1-.840825) = .1798$$

and,
$$W = \frac{4}{(4-.1798)(.25)} - \frac{(.25+6)(1-.840825)}{(4-.1798)(.25)^2} + \frac{1}{6}$$

$$= .188 \text{ hours or } 11.3 \text{ minutes.}$$

PROBLEM 7

The Bowmar University Student Union has one self service copying machine. On the average, 12 customers per hour arrive to make copies. (The arrival process follows a Poisson distribution.) The time to copy documents follows approximately a _normal_ distribution with a mean of two and one-half minutes and a standard deviation of 30 seconds.
The Union president has received several complaints from students regarding the long lines at the copying machine. On the basis of this information determine:

a) the average number of customers waiting or using the copy machine

b) the probability an arriving customer must wait in line

c) the proportion of time the copy machine is idle

d) the average time a customer must wait in line before using the copy machine

SOLUTION 7

This situation can be modeled as an M/G/1 system with

$$\lambda = 12 \text{ per hour} = 12/60 = .2/\text{minute}$$
$$1/\mu = 2.5 \text{ minutes}$$
$$\mu = 1/(2.5) = .4 \text{ per minute}$$
$$\sigma = 30 \text{ seconds} = .5 \text{ minutes}$$

a) The average number of customers waiting or using the copy machine is:

$$L = \frac{\sigma^2 + (\lambda/\mu)^2}{2(1 - \lambda/\mu)} + \frac{\lambda}{\mu} = \frac{(.2)^2(.5)^2 + (.2/.4)^2}{2(1 - .2/.4)} + \frac{.2}{.4} = .76$$

b) The probability an arriving customer must wait in line is:

$$P_w = \lambda/\mu = .2/.4 = .5$$

c) The proportion of time the copy machine is idle is:

$$P_0 = 1 - \lambda/\mu = 1 - .2/.4 = .5$$

d) The average time a customer must wait in line before using the copy machine is:

$$W_q = \frac{\sigma^2 + \lambda/\mu^2}{2(1 - \lambda/\mu)} = \frac{.2(.5)^2 + .2/(.4)^2}{2(1 - .2/.4)} = 1.3 \text{ minutes}$$

PROBLEM 8

Several firms are over the counter (OTC) market makers of Probabillistics stock. A broker wishing to trade this stock for a client will call on these firms to execute the order. If the market maker's phone line is busy, a broker will immediately try calling another market maker to transact the order.

Richardson and Company is one such OTC market maker. It estimates that on the average, a broker will try to call to execute a stock transaction every two minutes. The time required to complete the transaction averages 75 seconds. The firm has four traders staffing its phones.

Assume calls arrive according to a Poisson distribution.

a) What percentage of its potential business will be lost by Richardson?

b) What percentage of its potential business would be lost if only three traders staffed its phones?

SOLUTION 8

This problem can be modeled as an M/G/k system with block customers cleared with:

$$1/\lambda = 2 \text{ minutes} = 2/60 \text{ hour}$$
$$\lambda = 60/2 = 30 \text{ per hour}$$
$$1/\mu = 75 \text{ seconds} = 75/60 \text{ minutes} = 75/3600 \text{ hours}$$
$$\mu = 3600/75 = 48 \text{ per hour}$$

a) As there are four traders staffing the phones, k = 4, and the system will be blocked when there are four customers in the system. Hence, the answer is P_4. To find P_4, first find P_0 by:

$$P_0 = \frac{1}{\sum\limits_{i=0}^{4} (\lambda/\mu)^i/i!}$$

$$= \frac{1}{1 + (30/48) + (30/48)^2/2! + (30/48)^3/3! + (30/48)^4/4!}$$

$$= \frac{1}{1 + (.625) + (.625)^2/2 + (.625)^3/6 + (.625)^4/24}$$

$$= .536$$

Now, $$P_4 = \frac{(\lambda/\mu)^4}{4!} P_0 = \frac{(30/48)^4}{24} (.536) = .003$$

Thus with four traders 0.3% of the potential customers are lost.

b) In this case k = 3, and the answer is P_3. Recalculate P_0:

$$P_0 = \frac{1}{\sum\limits_{i=0}^{3} (\lambda/\mu)^i/i!}$$

$$= \frac{1}{1 + (30/48) + (30/48)^2/2! + (30/48)^3/3!} = .537$$

Now, $P_3 = \dfrac{(\lambda/\mu)^3}{3!} P_0 = \dfrac{(30/48)^3}{6} (.537) = .022$

Thus with three traders 2.2% of the potential customers are lost.

PROBLEM 9

The long distance viewing scope at the scenic rest stop on Interstate 20 provides two minutes of viewing for $.25. People wanting to use the scope arrive according to a Poisson distribution with a mean rate of 15 per hour.

a) What fraction of time is the scope idle?

b) What is the average number of sightseers waiting to use the scope?

c) What is the average time a sightseer waits to use the scope?

SOLUTION 9

This situation can modeled as an M/D/1 system with

$$\lambda = 15 \text{ per hour}$$
$$1/\mu = 2 \text{ minutes} = 2/60 \text{ hour}$$
$$\mu = 60/2 = 30 \text{ per hour}$$
$$\sigma = 0$$

a) The fraction of time the scope is idle is the complement of the utilization factor:

$1 - \lambda/\mu = 1 - 15/30 = .5$

b) The average number of customers waiting in line is:

$$L_q = \dfrac{(\lambda/\mu)^2}{2(1 - \lambda/\mu)} = \dfrac{(15/30)^2}{2(1- 15/30)} = .25 \text{ people}$$

c) The average time a customer must wait to use the scope is:

$W_q = L_q/\lambda = .25/15 = .01667 \text{ hours or } 1.0 \text{ minutes.}$

ANSWERED PROBLEMS

PROBLEM 10

Customers arrive at the Roney Tax Preparation office at an average rate of one per hour. The average time it takes Ms. Roney to prepare a customer's income tax form is 45 minutes.

a) What is the probability of no customers arriving in 2 hours?

b) What is the probability that an income tax form is finished within 45 minutes from the time it is started?

c) What is the average time a customer spends waiting to see Ms. Roney?

d) What is the probability Ms. Roney has 3 customers in the office (i.e. 2 waiting customers plus the one being served)?

PROBLEM 11

Ms. Roney is contemplating a computer system to help her with her income tax preparation (see problem 9). She estimates that such a system will reduce the average time to prepare a return from 45 minutes to 30 minutes. The computer leases for $40 per day.
   Ms. Roney estimates the average cost to her of having a waiting customer (due to good will, lost sales, etc. is $3 per hour. She is open 10 hours per day.

a) Should she lease the computer?

b) If Ms. Roney has the option of hiring another tax preparer for $60 per day who works at the same speed she does, should she do this rather than lease the computer?

PROBLEM 12

The postmaster at the Oak Hill Post Office expects the mean arrival rate of people to her customer counter will soon increase by fifty percent due to a large apartment complex being built.
   Currently, the mean arrival rate is 15 people per hour. The postmaster can serve an average of 25 people per hour.
   By what percentage must the postmaster's mean service rate increase when the apartment complex is completed in order that the average time spent at the post office remains at its current value?

PROBLEM 13

Cars travel down Main Street at the rate of 20,000 per hour.
The probability of any of these cars stopping at the drive-in
window of the Burger Prince Restaurant is .002. Cars at Burger
Prince are serviced at the mean rate of 60 per hour.

a) What is the average arrival rate to the drive-in window?

b) What is the average number of cars waiting to be served?

c) What is the average number of cars both being served and
   waiting to be served?

d) What is the probability an arriving car to the Burger Prince
   Restaurant must wait for service?

e) Management believes that if the number of cars waiting to be
   served was reduced to less than 1, the probability a car
   would stop at the drive-in window would increase to .003 and
   is contemplating implementing changes to speed up service.
   Given the increased arrival rate, what is the minimum value
   of the service rate that will meet management's objective?

PROBLEM 14

Cabinet Crafters manufactures specially designed kitchen
cabinets and bathroom vanities. One piece of machinery used on
most projects is a stationary router. The average number of
times carpenters use the router daily is 20 and the average time
required for each use is 15 minutes.
   The company is planning to purchase a digital router which
should reduce the average time required for each use to 12
minutes. The digital router will cost an an additional $60 per
day. If carpenters earn an average of $20 per hour and work 9
hours per day, determine whether or not Cabinet Crafters should
purchase the digital router.

PROBLEM 15

Shear's Department Store has 2 catalog order desks, one at each
entrance to the store. On the average, a customer arrives at
each order desk every 12 minutes. The service rate at each
order desk is an average of 8 customers per hour.
   Shear's is considering consolidating its two desks into one
location staffed by two order clerks. They would continue to
serve customers at the mean rate of 8 customers per hour.
Shear's figures it would not lose customers under this
arrangement and hence arrivals to this single desk would occur
every 6 minutes on the average.

For each configuration of the catalog order desks determine:

a) the average number of customers waiting to be served

b) the probability no customers are present in the entire
system

c) the average time a customer spends at the order desk
(waiting time plus service time)

d) the probability both clerks are busy

e) should Shear's consolidate its catalog order desks? Explain.

PROBLEM 16

The insurance department at Shear's has two agents, each working
at a mean speed of 8 customers per hour. Customers arrive at
the insurance desk at a mean rate of one every six minutes and
form a single queue.
   Management feels that some customers are going to find the
wait at the desk too long and take their business to Word's,
Shear's competitor. In order to reduce the time required by an
agent to serve a customer Shear's is contemplating installing
one of two minicomputer systems: System A which leases for $18
per day and will increase an agent's efficiency by 25%; or,
System B which leases for $23 per day and will increase an
agent's efficiency by 50%. Agents work 8-hour days.
   If Shear's estimates its cost of having a customer in the
system at $3 per hour, determine if Shear's should install a new
minicomputer system, and if so, which one.

PROBLEM 17

A company has tool cribs where workmen draw parts. Two men have
applied for the position of distributing parts to the workmen.
George Fuller is fresh out of trade school and expects a $6 per
hour salary. His average service time is 4 minutes. John Cox
is a veteran who expects $12 per hour. His average service time
is 2 minutes. A workman's time is figured at $10 per hour.
Workmen arrive to draw parts at an average rate of 12 per
hour.

a) What is the average waiting time a workman would spend in the
system under each applicant?

b) Which applicant should be hired?

PROBLEM 18

Dollar Supermarkets currently has 5 checkout positions. On the average, one customer per minute enters the store and spends an average of 55 minutes choosing his items. Each checker can check out a customer in an average of 4 minutes.

a) What is the average time a customer will spend in the store?

b) Management is considering reducing the number of checkout positions to 3 and hiring baggers. This would reduce the average time required to check out a customer to 2.5 minutes. Would this reduce the average waiting time?

PROBLEM 19

Ted "Tank" Fuller operates a small Texxon gas station that has one gas pump. The arrival rate of vehicles to the pump follows a Poisson probability distribution having a mean of 10 per hour. The time it takes Tank to service a vehicle follows a normal distribution with a mean of 4 minutes and a standard deviation of 1.5 minutes.

a) What is the utilization factor for the gas pump?

b) What is the average length of time a gas customer spends waiting for service to begin?

c) What is the average number of full-service vehicles at the gas station?

d) What is the probability that the servicing of a vehicle will take no more than 7 minutes (excluding the queue wait)?

PROBLEM 20

Tom's Towing Service operates three tow trucks and relies solely on towing requests from the city police department. If Tom has a truck available when the police need one, Tom is always their first choice. However, if he does not have a truck available, the police will select an alternative company rather than wait.
   On the average, the police request a tow truck once every 50 minutes. Tom estimates his average tow job takes 90 minutes.

a) Is Tom achieving at least 50 percent utilization of his fleet of tow trucks? (HINT: start by determining the average number of his trucks being used.)

b) What percentage of the police department's towing business is Tom losing because he has only three trucks?

PROBLEM 21

   Quick Clean Rooter cleans out clogged drains. Due to the
competitive nature of the drain cleaning business, if a customer
calls Quick Clean and finds the line busy, they immediately try
another company and Quick Clean loses the business.
   Quick Clean management estimates that on the average, a
customer tries to call Quick Clean every three minutes and the
average time to take a service order is 200 seconds. The
company wishes to hire enough operators so that at most 4% of
its potential customers get the busy signal.

   a) How many operators should be hired to meet this objective?

   b) Given your answer to a), what is the probability that all the
      operators are idle?

PROBLEM 22

The Quick Snap photo machine at the Lemon County bus station
takes four snapshots in exactly 75 seconds. Customers arrive at
the machine according to a Poisson distribution at the mean rate
of 20 per hour.
   On the basis of this information, determine the following:

   a) the average number of customers waiting to use the photo
      machine

   b) the average time a customer spends in the system

   c) the probability an arriving customer must wait for service.

PROBLEM 23

Andy Archer, Ph.D., is a training consultant for six mid-sized
manufacturing firms. On the average, each of his six clients
calls him for consulting assistance once every 25 days. Andy
typically spends an average of five days at the client's firm
during each consultation.
   Assuming that the time between client calls follows an
exponential distribution, determine the following:

   a) the average number of clients Andy has on backlog

   b) the average time a client must wait before Andy arrives to it

   c) the proportion of the time Andy is busy.

TRUE/FALSE

24. For a single server queue, the average time a customer spends in the system is equal to the average time a customer spends in the waiting line plus the average service time.

25. In order to obtain analytical results for a queuing problem one must assume an exponential service time.

26. For a single server queuing system, the average number of customers in the waiting line is always one less than the average number of customers in the system.

27. In queuing notation L_q is the average time a customer spends in the waiting line.

28. Little's flow equations apply to any queuing system regardless of the arrival distribution, service time distribution, and number of channels.

29. For an M/M/1 queuing problem, the sum of the utilization factor plus P_0 equals 1.

30. Queue discipline refers to the assumption that a customer has the patience to remain in a slow moving queue.

31. For an M/M/2 system, the probability that the system is empty plus the probability an arriving customer must wait for service equals 1.

32. If some maximum number of customers are allowed in a queuing system at one time, the system has a finite calling population.

33. Assuming the same arrival rates, the average number of customers in the system for an M/M/1 system is the same as that for an M/M/2 system if the average service time in the M/M/2 system is twice as long as for the M/M/1 system.

34. For an M/M/k system, the average number of customers in the system equals the customer arrival rate times the average time a customer spends waiting in the system.

35. Simulation may be used to obtain results for queuing systems.

36. For an M/M/1 queuing system, if the service rate, μ, is doubled, the average wait in the system, W, is cut in half.

37. A multiple-channel system has more than one waiting line.

38. Even when the mean service rate of the queuing system cannot be increased, a reduction in the service time variation will reduce the average length of the waiting line.

CHAPTER

13

Computer Simulation

KEY CONCEPTS

CONCEPT	ILLUSTRATED PROBLEMS	ANSWERED PROBLEMS
Simulation of:		
One Event	1,2	9
Two Events	3	7,8,10,11,14
Multiple Events	4	13,15
Comparison of Expected and Simulated Outcomes	1,6	9,10
Simulation of Decision Alternatives	2	7,10,11,14
Simulation Applications:		
Inventory Systems	2	10,11,13
Waiting Lines	3,4	8,12,15
Markov Processes	5	16
Project Times	6	9

REVIEW

1. <u>Computer</u> <u>simulation</u> is one of the most frequently employed management science techniques. It is typically used to model random processes that are too complex to be solved by analytical methods.

2. One begins a computer simulation by developing a <u>mathematical</u> <u>statement</u> of the problem. The model should be realistic yet solvable within the speed and storage constraints of the computer system being used. Input values for the model as well as probability estimates for the random variables must then be determined.

3. Random variable values are utilized in the model through a technique known as <u>Monte Carlo</u> <u>simulation</u>. Here each random variable is mapped to a set of numbers so that each time one number in that set is generated, the corresponding value of the random variable is given as an input to the model. The mapping is done in such a way that the likelihood that a particular number is chosen is the same as the probability that the corresponding value of the random variable occurs.

4. Because a computer program generates random numbers for the mapping according to some formula, the numbers are not truly generated in a random fashion. However, using standard statistical tests, the numbers can be shown to appear to be drawn from a random process. These numbers are called <u>pseudo-random</u> <u>numbers</u>. Appendix B is a table of pseudo-random digits.

5. In a <u>fixed</u> <u>time</u> simulation model, time periods are incremented by a fixed amount. For each time period a different set of data from the input sequence is used to calculate the effects on the model.

6. In a <u>next</u> <u>event</u> simulation model, time periods are not fixed but are determined by the data values from the input sequence.

7. The computer program that performs the simulation is called a <u>simulator</u>. Flowcharts can be useful in writing such a program. While this program can be written in any general purpose language (e.g. BASIC, FORTRAN, PL/1, etc.) <u>special</u> <u>languages</u> which reduce the amount of code which must be written to perform the simulation have been developed. Some of these are SIMSCRIPT, GASP, DYNAMO, and SLAM.

8. <u>Validation</u> of both the model and the method used by the computer to carry out the calculations is extremely important. Models which do not accurately reflect real world behavior cannot be expected to generate meaningful results. Likewise, errors in programming can result in nonsensical results.

9. <u>Validation</u> is generally done by having an expert review the model and the computer code for errors. If possible, the simulation should be run using actual past data. Predictions from the simulation model should be compared with historical results.

10. <u>Experimental</u> <u>design</u> is an important consideration in the simulation process. Issues such as the length of time of the simulation and the treatment of initial data outputs from the model must be addressed prior to collecting and analyzing output data. Through careful development of the simulation model, one can reduce the time required for the computer run without sacrificing the accuracy of the results.

11. Normally one is interested in results for the <u>steady</u> <u>state</u> (long run) operation of the system being modelled. Hence, the initial data inputs to the simulation generally represent a start-up period for the process and it may be important that the data outputs for this start-up period be neglected for predicting this long run behavior.

12. For each policy under consideration by the decision maker, the simulation is run by considering a long sequence of input data values (given by a pseudo-random number generator). Whenever possible, different policies should be compared by using the <u>same</u> <u>sequence</u> <u>of</u> <u>input</u> <u>data</u>.

13. Among the <u>advantages</u> of computer simulation is the ability to gain insights into the model solution which may be impossible to attain through other techniques. Also, once the simulation has been developed, it provides a convenient experimental laboratory to perform <u>"what</u> <u>if"</u> <u>and</u> <u>sensitivity</u> <u>analyses</u>.

14. Two major <u>disadvantages</u> of simulation are: (1) a large amount of time may be required to develop the simulation; and, (2) there is no guarantee that the solution obtained will actually be optimal. Simulation is, in effect, a <u>trial</u> <u>and</u> <u>error</u> <u>method</u> of comparing different policy inputs. It does not determine if some input which was not considered could have provided a better solution for the model.

FLOW CHART OF
COMPUTER SIMULATION PROCESS

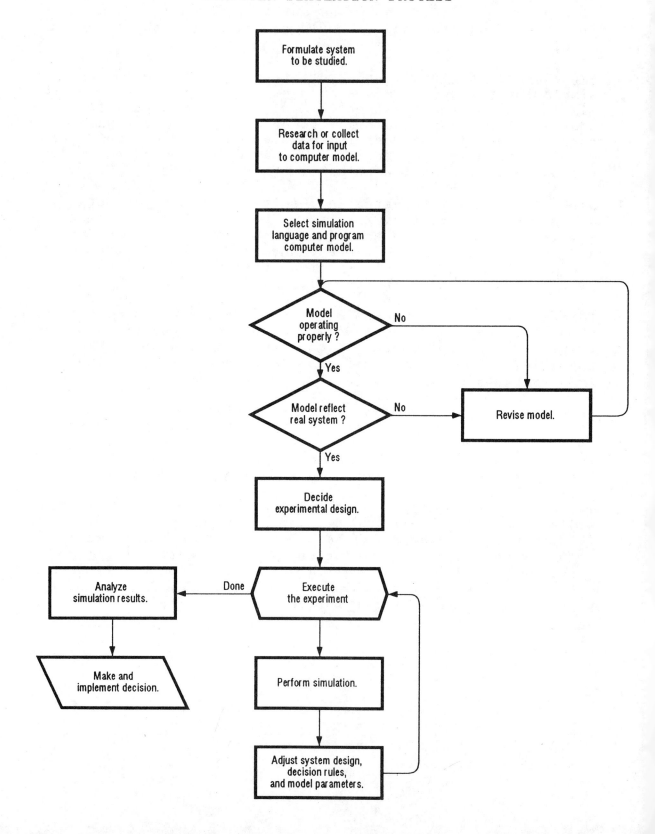

ILLUSTRATED PROBLEMS

NOTE: Several of the problems in this chapter relate
to topics of other chapters such as inventory, waiting lines, markov processes, and projects. Where
applicable, you are encouraged to compare your
simulation results with those of analytic procedures
covered in other chapters. However, you might find
significant differences that are due most likely to
the small number of simulation trials performed.

PROBLEM 1

The price change of shares of Probablistics, Inc. has been
observed over the past 50 trades. The frequency distribution is
as follows:

Price Change	Frequency (Number of Trades)
-3/8	4
-1/4	2
-1/8	8
0	20
+1/8	10
+1/4	3
+3/8	2
+1/2	1
TOTAL	50

a) Develop a relative frequency distribution for this data.

b) If the current price per share of Probablistics is 23, use
   random numbers to simulate the price per share over the next
   20 trades. (For your random numbers, use the first two
   numbers at the bottom of column 1 of Appendix B and move up.)

c) Compare this price with the expected price one would obtain
   based on the probability distribution.

SOLUTION 1

a) To develop a relative frequency distribution for this data,
   divide the frequency of each price by the total number of
   trades. The results are shown in the table below.

b) To develop a simulation for the future prices, assign a
   random number to each price change so that the probability of
   seeing a certain price corresponds to its probability
   (relative frequency). One such assignment of numbers is:

Price Change	Relative Frequency	Random Numbers
-3/8	.08	00 - 07
-1/4	.04	08 - 11
-1/8	.16	12 - 27
0	.40	28 - 67
+1/8	.20	68 - 87
+1/4	.06	88 - 93
+3/8	.04	94 - 97
+1/2	.02	98 - 99

TOTAL   1.00

According to the instructions, the first random number will be 21, the second 84, etc. The simulated results are:

Trade Number	Random Number	Price Change	Stock Price
1	21	-1/8	22 7/8
2	84	+1/8	23
3	07	-3/8	22 5/8
4	30	0	22 5/8
5	94	+3/8	23
6	57	0	23
7	57	0	23
8	19	-1/8	22 7/8
9	84	+1/8	23
10	84	+1/8	23 1/8
11	62	0	23 1/8
12	32	0	23 1/8
13	71	+1/8	23 1/4
14	94	+3/8	23 5/8
15	04	-3/8	23 1/4
16	97	+3/8	23 5/8
17	58	0	23 5/8
18	67	0	23 5/8
19	78	+1/8	23 3/4
20	14	-1/8	23 5/8

c) Based on the probability distribution, the expected price change per trade can be calculated by:

$$(.08)(-3/8) + (.04)(-1/4) + (.16)(-1/8) + (.40)(0) +$$
$$(.20)(1/8) + (.06)(1/4) + (.04)(3/8) + (.02)(1/2) = .005$$

The expected price change for 20 trades is (20)(.005) = .10. Hence, the expected stock price after 20 trades is 23 + .10 = 23.10. This is lower than the simulated price of 23.625.

PROBLEM 2

Shelly's Supermarket has just installed a postage stamp vending
machine. Based on one month of operation, Shelly's estimates
the number of postage stamps sold per day can be approximated by
the following distribution:

Number Sold Per Day	Probability
20	.10
30	.15
40	.20
50	.25
60	.20
70	.10

Shelly's makes a $.02 profit per postage stamp. The vending
machine holds 230 stamps and it costs Shelly's $2.00 in labor to
fill the machine.

a) Determine the mean number of stamps sold per day.

b) Determine the mean time until the machine is empty.

c) Assume that Shelly's adopts the following policy. It will
   fill the machine at the beginning of every n-th day, where n
   is the answer found in part (b). Conduct a 20-day simulation
   and determine the expected profit per day. Assume the
   machine must be filled on the first day. (Use the first two
   numbers of column 3 of Appendix B, beginning at the top for
   the random numbers.)

d) Suppose fills the machine every (n-1)-st day. Repeat the 20-
   day simulation and compare the answer with that of part (c).
   Which policy would you recommend?

SOLUTION 2

The flow chart on the next page can assist in setting up the
simulations.

a) The mean number of stamps sold daily = (.10)(20) + (.15)(30)
   + (.20)(40) + (.25)(50) + (.20)(60) + (.10)(70) = 46.

b) The mean time until the machine is empty is:
   (Machine capacity)/(Mean number of stamps sold per day) =
   230/46 = 5 days.

Flow Chart of
Vending Machine Simulation

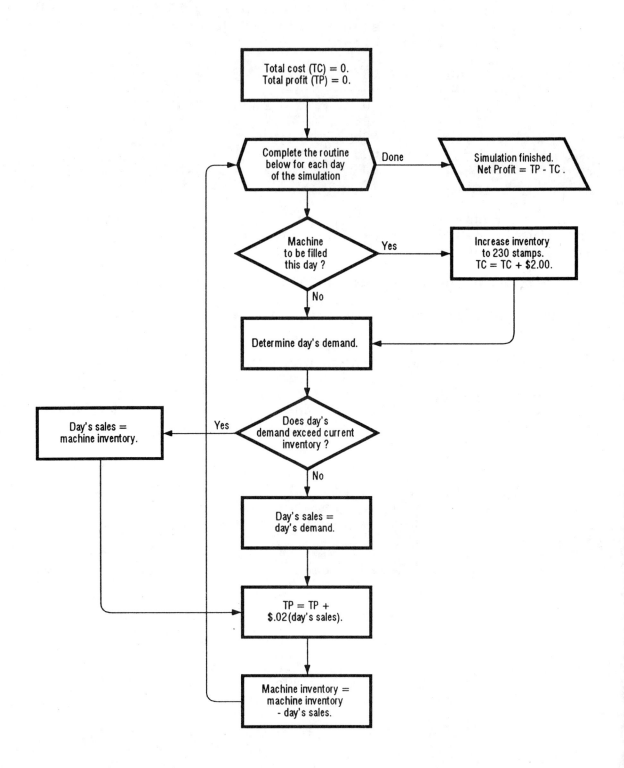

Assuming Shelly's fills the machine every fifth day,
determine a set of random numbers corresponding to each sales
level.

Number Sold Per Day	Range Of Numbers
20	00 - 09
30	10 - 24
40	25 - 44
50	45 - 69
60	70 - 89
70	90 - 99

Following the instructions of using the first two numbers in
column 3 of Appendix B generates the following simulation:

Day	Random Number	Demand	Number Of Stamps Left In Machine	Profit From Sale Of Stamps	Cost Of Refilling Machine	Daily Profit
1	71	60	170	1.20	2.00	- .80
2	95	70	100	1.40	--	1.40
3	83	60	40	1.20	--	1.20
4	44	40	0	.80	--	.80
5	34	40	0	0*	--	0
6	49	50	180	1.00	2.00	-1.00
7	88	60	120	1.20	--	1.20
8	56	50	70	1.00	--	1.00
9	05	20	50	.40	--	.40
10	39	40	10	.80	--	.80
11	75	60	170	1.20	2.00	- .80
12	12	30	140	.60	--	.60
13	03	20	120	.40	--	.40
14	59	50	70	1.00	--	1.00
15	29	40	30	.80	--	.80
16	77	60	170	1.20	2.00	- .80
17	76	60	110	1.20	--	1.20
18	57	50	60	1.00	--	1.00
19	15	30	30	.60	--	.60
20	53	50	0	.60**	--	.60

Total Profit = $9.60

*   0 since the machine was empty
** .60 since there were only 30 stamps left in the machine

Expected Profit per Day = (9.60)/20 = $.48.

d) In order to compare the two policies, the same set of input data should be generated. Thus the simulation below has the same input for daily demand as that of part (c). In this part, the machine is to be filled every fourth day.

Day	Random Number	Demand	Number Of Stamps Left In Machine	Profit From Sale Of Stamps	Cost Of Refilling Machine	Daily Profit
1	71	60	170	1.20	2.00	- .80
2	95	70	100	1.40	--	1.40
3	83	60	40	1.20	--	1.20
4	44	40	0	.80	--	.80
5	34	40	190	0	2.00	-1.20
6	49	50	140	1.00	--	1.00
7	88	60	80	1.20	--	1.20
8	56	50	30	1.00	--	1.00
9	05	20	210	.40	2.00	-1.60
10	39	40	170	.80	--	.80
11	75	60	110	1.20	--	1.20
12	12	30	80	.60	--	.60
13	03	20	210	.40	2.00	-1.60
14	59	50	160	1.00	--	1.00
15	29	40	120	.80	--	.80
16	77	60	60	1.20	--	1.20
17	76	60	170	1.20	2.00	- .80
18	57	50	120	1.00	--	1.00
19	15	30	90	.60	--	.60
20	53	50	40	.60	--	1.00

Total Profit = $8.80

Expected Daily Profit = $ .44

Based on the results of this simulation, Shelly's should fill the machine every fifth day rather than every fourth day.

PROBLEM 3

Wayne International Airport primarily serves domestic air traffic. Occasionally, however, a chartered plane from abroad will arrive with passengers bound for Wayne's two great amusement parks, Algorithmland and Giffith's Cherry Preserve.
   Whenever an international plane arrives at the airport the two customs inspectors on duty set up operations to process the passengers.
   Incoming passengers must first have their passports and visas checked. This is handled by one inspector. The time required to check a passenger's passports and visas can be described by the following probability distribution:

Time Required to Check a Passenger's Passport and Visa	Probability
20 seconds	.20
40 seconds	.40
60 seconds	.30
80 seconds	.10

After having their passports and visas checked, the passengers next proceed to the second customs official who does baggage inspections. Passengers form a single waiting line with the official inspecting baggage on a first come, first served basis.
   The time required for baggage inspection has the following probability distribution:

Time Required For Baggage Inspection	Probability
No Time	.25
1 minute	.60
2 minutes	.10
3 minutes	.05

a) If a chartered plane from abroad lands at Wayne Airport with 80 passengers, use simulation to determine how long it will take for the first 20 passengers to clear customs. (From Appendix B, use the first two digits in column 8 for passport control and the first two digits in column 9 for baggage inspection.)

b) What is the average length of time a customer waits before having his bags inspected after he clears passport control? How is this estimate biased?

SOLUTION 3

The problem is easiest to set up as a next-event simulation model. The random number mappings are:

Time Required to Check a Passenger's Passport and Visa	Probability	Random Numbers
20 seconds	.20	00 - 19
40 seconds	.40	20 - 59
60 seconds	.30	60 - 89
80 seconds	.10	90 - 99

Time Required For Baggage Inspection	Probability	Random Numbers
No Time	.25	00 - 24
1 minute	.60	25 - 84
2 minutes	.10	85 - 94
3 minutes	.05	95 - 99

For each passenger the following information must be recorded:
(1) When his service begins at the passport control inspection
(2) The length of time of this service
(3) When his service begins at the baggage inspection
(4) The length of time of this service

Note the following relationships:

(1) Time a passenger begins service by the passport inspector = (Time the previous passenger started passport service) + (Time of previous passenger's passport service)

(2) Time a passenger begins being served by the baggage inspector depends on whether or not the passenger must wait in line for this service. Thus,
   If passenger does not wait in line for baggage inspection:
   Time a passenger begins being served by the baggage inspector = (Time passenger completes service with the passport control inspector)
   If the passenger does wait in line for baggage inspection:
   Time a passenger begins being served by the baggage inspector = (Time previous passenger completes service with the baggage inspector)
(3) Time a customer completes service at the baggage inspector = (Time customer begins service with baggage inspector) + (Time required for baggage inspection).

The following table describes the simulation using the random number columns given in the problem statement. (Note service times are in minutes.)

| | Passport Control | | | | | Baggage Inspections | | |
Passenger Number	Time Begin	Random Number	Service Time	Time End	Time Begin	Random Number	Service Time	Time End
1	0:00	93	1:20	1:20	1:20	13	0:00	1:20
2	1:20	63	1:00	2:20	2:20	08	0:00	2:20
3	2:20	26	:40	3:00	3:00	60	1:00	4:00
4	3:00	16	:20	3:20	4:00	13	0:00	4:00
5	3:20	21	:40	4:00	4:00	68	1:00	5:00
6	4:00	26	:40	4:40	5:00	40	1:00	6:00
7	4:40	70	1:00	5:40	6:00	40	1:00	7:00
8	5:40	55	:40	6:20	7:00	27	1:00	8:00
9	6:20	72	1:00	7:20	8:00	23	0:00	8:00
10	7:20	89	1:00	8:20	8:20	64	1:00	9:20
11	8:20	49	:40	9:00	9:20	36	1:00	10:20
12	9:00	64	1:00	10:00	10:20	56	1:00	11:20
13	10:00	91	1:20	11:20	11:20	25	1:00	12:20
14	11:20	02	:20	11:40	12:20	88	2:00	14:20
15	11:40	52	:40	12:20	14:20	18	0:00	14:20
16	12:20	69	1:00	13:20	14:20	74	1:00	15:20
17	13:20	29	:40	14:00	15:20	75	1:00	16:20
18	14:00	96	1:20	15:20	16:20	29	1:00	17:20
19	15:20	95	1:20	16:40	17:20	80	1:00	18:20
20	16:40	84	1:00	17:40	18:20	25	1:00	19:20

For example, passenger 1 begins being served by the passport ontrol inspector immediately. His service time is 1:20 (80 seconds) at which time he goes immediately to the baggage inspector who waves him through without inspection.

Passenger 2 begins service with passport inspector 1:20 minutes (80 seconds) after arriving there (as this is when passenger 1 is finished) and requires 1:00 minute (60 seconds) for passport inspection. He is waved through baggage inspection as well.

This process continues in this manner for all 20 passengers.

a) Passenger 20 clears customs after 19 minutes 20 seconds.

b) For each passenger calculate his waiting time (in seconds):
(Baggage Inspection Begins) - (Passport Control Ends) =
0 + 0 + 0 + 40 + 0 + 20 + 20 + 40 + 40 + 0 + 20 + 20 + 0 +
40 + 120 + 60 + 80 + 60 + 40 + 40 = 640 total seconds.
This gives an average of 640/20 = 32 seconds per passenger.
This is a biased estimate because we assume that the
simulation began with the system empty. Thus, the results
tend to underestimate the average waiting time.

PROBLEM 4

Attendees at the National Management Science Society (NMSS)
Conference register by first standing in line to pay their fees.
They then proceed to a designated line based on the first letter
of their last name to collect their conference materials.

   At the conference, it is planned to have three different
parallel lines for the collection of materials: one each for
people whose last names begin with A-H, I-Q, and R-Z
respectively.

   During each minute of the morning registration period it is
anticipated that attendees will arrive to pay their fees
according to the following distribution:

Number of Arrivals	Probability
0	.30
1	.30
2	.30
3	.10

The time to pay one's fees is either one minute or two minutes
depending upon whether one uses a check or credit card. The
probability of a one-minute time is .60.

   After paying his fees, an attendee then goes to the correct
line for the conference materials. At this year's conference
35% of the attendees have last names beginning with A-H, 36%
with last names beginning with I-Q, and 29% with last names
beginning with R-Z. The time required to pick up conference
materials is fixed at 2 minutes.

a) Simulate the waiting line for the first 30 attendees during
   the morning registration. From Appendix B, use column 3 to
   generate the number of arrivals in any given minute, column 4
   to generate registration fee service time, and column 5 to
   generate the first letter of the last name. Assume
   registration begins at 8:00 AM.

b) What is the average size of the waiting line to pay fees (not
   including the person being served), and the average customer
   waiting time to pay fees based on this simulation?

c) What is the percentage of time each of the three individuals
   who distribute conference materials is working?

SOLUTION 4

a) For each minute, record the number of arrivals at the fee
   desk. Then for each arrival determine how long he must wait
   in line to pay fees, his service time to pay fees, which
   conference material line is joined, and his waiting and
   service time in that material line.

Random numbers are needed for the number of arrivals in a given minute to the fee line, the length of service time in the fee line, and first letter of the last name to determine to which conference material line the attendee will proceed. The random number mappings are:

Number of Arrivals	Probability	Random Numbers
0	.30	00 - 29
1	.30	30 - 59
2	.30	60 - 89
3	.10	90 - 99

Service Time To Pay Fees	Probability	Random Numbers
1 minute	.60	00 - 59
2 minutes	.40	60 - 99

First Letter Of Last Name	Probability	Random Numbers
A-H	.35	00 - 34
I-Q	.36	35 - 70
R-Z	.29	71 - 99

The simulation then flows chronologically through the events listed as headings on the simulation chart on the next page:
1. Time period begins with Q customers waiting to pay fees. (Q can be determined from the number of previous customers with end times in the fee pay line greater than this time period.)
2. Determine the number of arrivals in the period, #.
3. For each distinct arrival, I, determine begin, wait, and end times in the fee pay line.
4. For each distinct arrival, determine the last name and the begin, wait and end times in the conference material line.
5. Repeat until 30 customers have arrived.

b) The average length of the waiting line to pay fees is the average of the entries in the column Q over the 26 time intervals observed, including the 10 at the beginning of 8:26. This is 181/26 = 6.96.
   The average time a customer waits to pay his fees is the average of the entries in the Fee Pay Wait column over the 30 arrivals = 248/30 = 8.267 minutes.

c) To determine the percentage of time each of the three people who are distributing conference materials are working, take the total amount of time each works and divide by the total length of the simulation (= 42 minutes since 8:41 is the earliest the next arrival could want material service.)

$$
\begin{array}{llllll}
\text{A-H worker} & = & 20/42 & = & .476 & \text{or } 47.6\% \\
\text{I-Q worker} & = & 29/42 & = & .690 & \text{or } 69.0\% \\
\text{R-Z worker} & = & 8/42 & = & .190 & \text{or } 19.0\%
\end{array}
$$

| Arrivals | | | | Fee Pay | | | | | | Conference Materials | | | | |
Time	RN	#	Q	I	Wait	Begin	RN	Time	End	RN	Name	Wait	Begin	End
8:00	71	2	0	1	0	8:00	51	1	8:01	15	A-H	0	8:01	8:03
				2	1	8:01	79	2	8:03	08	A-H	0	8:03	8:05
8:01	95	3	1	3	2	8:03	09	1	8:04	19	A-H	1	8:05	8:07
				4	3	8:04	67	2	8:06	45	I-Q	0	8:06	8:08
				5	5	8:06	15	1	8:07	76	R-Z	0	8:07	8:09
8:02	83	2	3	6	5	8:07	58	1	8:08	42	I-Q	0	8:08	8:10
				7	6	8:08	04	1	8:09	38	I-Q	1	8:10	8:12
8:03	44	1	5	8	6	8:09	78	2	8:11	47	I-Q	1	8:12	8:14
8:04	34	1	5	9	7	8:11	30	1	8:12	82	R-Z	0	8:12	8:14
8:05	49	1	5	10	7	8:12	56	1	8:13	37	I-Q	1	8:14	8:16
8:06	88	2	6	11	7	8:13	75	2	8:15	49	I-Q	1	8:16	8:18
				12	9	8:15	75	2	8:17	43	I-Q	1	8:18	8:20
8:07	56	1	7	13	10	8:17	05	1	8:18	37	I-Q	2	8:20	8:22
8:08	05	0	7											
8:09	39	1	6	14	9	8:18	49	1	8:19	11	A-H	0	8:19	8:21
8:10	75	2	6	15	9	8:19	70	2	8:21	45	I-Q	1	8:22	8:24
				16	11	8:21	25	1	8:22	55	I-Q	2	8:24	8:26
8:11	12	0	8											
8:12	03	0	7											
8:13	59	1	6	17	9	8:22	26	1	8:23	89	R-Z	0	8:23	8:25
8:14	29	0	6											
8:15	77	2	6	18	8	8:23	10	1	8:24	09	A-H	0	8:24	8:26
				19	9	8:24	46	1	8:25	67	I-Q	1	8:26	8:28
8:16	76	2	7	20	9	8:25	16	1	8:26	84	R-Z	0	8:26	8:28
				21	10	8:26	64	2	8:28	51	I-Q	0	8:28	8:30
8:17	57	1	9	22	11	8:28	72	2	8:30	67	I-Q	0	8:30	8:32
8:18	15	0	9											
8:19	53	1	8	23	11	8:30	50	1	8:31	14	A-H	0	8:31	8:33
8:20	37	1	8	24	11	8:31	15	1	8:32	10	A-H	1	8:33	8:35
8:21	46	1	9	25	11	8:32	79	2	8:34	52	I-Q	0	8:34	8:36
8:22	85	2	9	26	12	8:34	22	1	8:35	03	A-H	0	8:35	8:37
				27	13	8:35	51	1	8:36	02	A-H	1	8:37	8:39
8:23	24	0	10											
8:24	53	1	9	28	12	8:36	01	1	8:37	09	A-H	2	8:39	8:41
8:25	72	2	9	29	12	8:37	47	1	8:38	13	A-H	3	8:41	8:43
				30	13	8:38	88	2	8:40	42	I-Q	0	8:40	8:42
8:26			10	Simulation Over										

| TOTALS | | | | | | | | | | | | | | |
| 26 | | | 181 | 248 | | | | 40 | 181 | | | | | |

In first 42 minutes (8:00-8:41) the number of minutes busy

A-H = 20
I-Q = 29
R-Z = 8

PROBLEM 5

Mark is a specialist at repairing large metal-cutting machines that use laser technology. His repair territory consists of the cities of Austin, San Antonio, and Houston. His day-to-day repair assignment locations can be modeled as a Markov process. The transition matrix is as follows:

		Next Day's Location		
		Austin	San Antonio	Houston
This Day's Location	Austin	.60	.15	.25
	San Antonio	.20	.75	.05
	Houston	.15	.05	.80

a) Show the random number assignments that can be used to simulate Mark's next day location when his current location is Austin, San Antonio, and Houston.

b) Assume Mark is currently in Houston. Simulate where Mark will be over the next 25 days. What percentage of time will Mark be in each of the three cities? (Use column 8 of Appendix B.)

c) Repeat the simulation in part b with Mark currently in Austin. (Use column 9 of Appendix B.) Compare the percentages with those found in part b.

SOLUTION 5

a)

Currently in Austin		Currently in San Antonio		Currently in Houston	
Next-Day Location	Random Numbers	Next-Day Location	Random Numbers	Next-Day Location	Random Numbers
Austin	00 - 59	Austin	00 - 19	Austin	00 - 14
San Ant.	60 - 74	San Ant.	20 - 94	San Ant.	15 - 19
Houston	75 - 99	Houston	95 - 99	Houston	20 - 99

b) Starting in Houston

Day	Random Number	Day's Location
1	93	Houston
2	63	Houston
3	26	Houston
4	16	San Ant.
5	21	San Ant.
6	26	San Ant.
7	70	San Ant.
8	55	San Ant.
9	72	San Ant.
10	89	San Ant.
11	49	San Ant.
12	64	San Ant.
13	91	San Ant.
14	02	Austin
15	52	Austin
16	69	San Ant.
17	29	San Ant.
18	96	Houston
19	95	Houston
20	84	Houston
21	61	Houston
22	09	Austin
23	06	Austin
24	00	Austin
25	63	San Ant.

```
Austin        =  5/25 = 20%
San Antonio = 13/25 = 52%
Houston       =  7/25 = 28%
```

c) Starting in Austin

Day	Random Number	Day's Location
1	13	Austin
2	08	Austin
3	60	San Ant.
4	13	Austin
5	68	San Ant.
6	40	San Ant.
7	40	San Ant.
8	27	San Ant.
9	23	San Ant.
10	64	San Ant.
11	36	San Ant.
12	56	San Ant.
13	25	San Ant.
14	88	San. Ant.
15	18	Austin
16	74	San Ant.
17	75	San Ant.
18	29	San Ant.
19	80	San Ant.
20	25	San Ant.
21	05	Austin
22	64	San Ant.
23	71	San Ant.
24	83	San Ant.
25	74	San Ant.

```
Austin        =  5/25 = 20%
San Antonio = 20/25 = 80%
Houston       =  0/25 =  0%
```

PROBLEM 6

Consider the following house renovation project.

Job and Description	Expected Completion Time (in days)
A - Remove old roof shingles	2
B - Plaster walls and ceilings	4
C - Lay new roof shingles	3
D - Paint exterior	4
E - Paint walls and ceilings	5
F - Hang new gutters	2
G - Install exterior lights	2
H - Lay wall-to-wall carpet	2

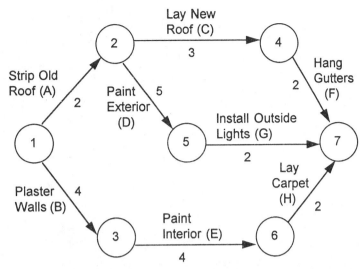

For each job the probabilities of being completed 1 day earlier than expected, on time, 1 day later than expected, and 2 days later than expected are .2, .5, .2, and .1, respectively.

a) Determine the critical path(s) and expected completion time of the project.

b) Do a five trial simulation using the last digit of column 4 of Appendix B for the random numbers to determine the average completion time of the project. Compare this result with your answer to part (a).

SOLUTION 6

a) A path in this context is a set of successive jobs that lead from the project network's starting node (node 1) to the finish node (node 7). There are three different paths in the network. They are A-C-F, A-D-G, and B-E-H. The critical (longest) path consists of jobs B-E-H.

The project's expected completion time is the sum of the expected completion times of the jobs on the critical path. Thus, the expected project completion time is 4+4+2=10 days.

b) The random number mappings are as follows. Note only single digit random numbers need be generated.

Job Completion Time	Probability	Random Numbers
Expected time minus 1 day	.2	0,1
Expected time	.5	2,3,4,5,6
Expected time plus 1 day	.2	7,8
Expected time plus 2 days	.1	9

The table on the following page describes the simulation. Note that due to the randomness of job times, a path other than B-E-H might actually be the critical path.

Job	RN	Job's Expected Time	Time Adjustment	Job's Actual Time	Critical Path and Project Completion Time
A	2	2	0	2	
B	5	4	0	4	
C	1	3	-1	2	
D	2	5	0	5	
E	0	4	-1	3	
F	7	2	+1	3	
G	8	2	+1	3	
H	1	2	-1	1	A–D–G = 10
A	7	2	+1	3	
B	5	4	0	4	
C	8	3	+1	4	
D	5	5	0	5	
E	5	4	0	4	
F	1	2	-1	1	
G	5	2	0	2	
H	0	2	-1	1	A–D–G = 10
A	8	2	+1	3	
B	8	4	+1	5	
C	2	3	0	3	
D	5	5	0	5	
E	6	4	0	4	
F	7	2	+1	3	
G	4	2	0	2	
H	4	2	0	2	B–E–H = 11
A	7	2	+1	3	
B	2	4	0	4	
C	3	3	0	3	
D	6	5	0	5	
E	7	4	+1	5	
F	6	2	0	2	
G	3	2	0	2	
H	4	2	0	2	A–D–G = 12
A	8	2	+1	3	
B	5	4	0	4	
C	1	3	-1	2	
D	2	5	0	5	
E	2	4	0	4	
F	5	2	0	2	
G	9	2	+2	4	
H	6	2	0	2	A–D–G = 12

The average project completion time is (10+10+11+12+12)/5 =
11 days. This a full day greater than the expected project
completion time. Note that the expected critical path was
only critical in one out of the five trials.

ANSWERED PROBLEMS

PROBLEM 7

Susan Winslow has two alternative routes to travel from her home
in Olport to her office in Lewisburg. She can travel on Freeway
5 to Freeway 57 or on Freeway 55 to Freeway 91. The time
distributions are as follows:

Freeway 5		Freeway 57		Freeway 55		Freeway 91	
Time	Relative Frequency	Time	Relative Frequency	Time	Relative Frequency	Time	Relative Frequency
5	.30	4	.10	6	.20	3	.30
6	.20	5	.20	7	.20	4	.35
7	.40	6	.35	8	.40	5	.20
8	.10	7	.20	9	.20	6	.15
		8	.15				

Do a five day simulation of each of the two combinations of
routes using columns 1, 2, 3, and 4 of Appendix B for the random
numbers. Based on this simulation, which routes should Susan
take if her objective is to minimize her total travel time.

PROBLEM 8

The Rumson Post Office serves a small rural town. In any one
minute interval during a Saturday morning either 0, 1, 2, or 3
customers arrive with the following probabilities: $P(0) = .40$;
$P(1) = .30$; $P(2) = .20$; $P(3) = .10$.
   The only clerk working on Saturday at the post office is Mrs.
Smith. Her service time per customer is also a random variable
with the following distribution of 1, 2, or 3 minutes per
service: $P(1) = .80$; $P(2) = .15$; $P(3) = .05$.
   If the system starts empty, simulate the waiting line over a
10 minute interval. Use Appendix B, column 1 to generate the
number of arrivals and column 2 to generate service times. What
is the average number of customers waiting in line for service?

PROBLEM 9

Consider the following PERT problem.

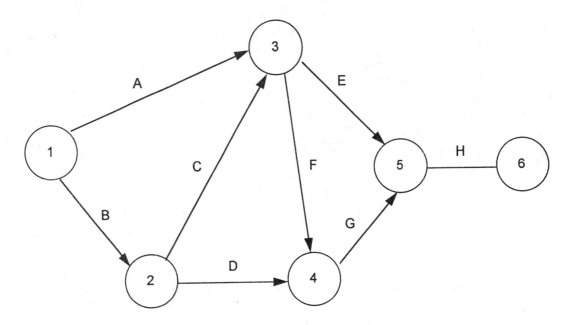

The expected completion time for each job is given below:

Job	Expected Completion Time in Weeks
A	7
B	4
C	3
D	6
E	5
F	3
G	3
H	4

a) Determine the critical path(s) and expected completion time of this project.

b) Suppose that each job has a 25% chance of being completed in a week less than its expected completion time and a 25% chance of being completed in a week more than its expected completion time.
   Do a five trial simulation using the last two digits of column 6 of Appendix B for the random numbers to determine the average completion time of this project. Compare this answer to part (a).

PROBLEM 10

Demand for mopeds at the Easy Rider Bike Shop is either 0, 1, 2, or 3 per day with the following probability distribution:

Demand	Probability
0	.15
1	.25
2	.35
3	.25

Each working day a moped remains in inventory costs Easy Rider $2 per moped. It costs Easy Rider $30 to process an order.
 The delivery time required to obtain new mopeds from the wholesaler is also random with the following distribution:

Delivery Time (in Working Days)	Probability
1	.20
2	.60
3	.20

Easy Rider has adopted the policy of offering customers an $8 per day discount for each working day they must wait for a moped if Easy Rider is out of stock.

a) Assume Easy Rider is open 200 days per year and delivery time is exactly two working days. Further, assume that although demand varies, it is actually constant at the level of average demand. What would be the optimal order policy?

b) Do a 20 day simulation using the answer you obtained in part (a) assuming a current inventory of 6 mopeds and that delivery time and demand follow the distributions given above. Use the first two digits in column 2 of Appendix B to generate demands and the first two digits of column 3 to generate lead times. What is the average inventory cost per day, where inventory holding costs are assessed on ending inventory?

PROBLEM 11

Miller's Carpets runs a store that carries a certain style of
carpet. Over the weeks Miller's has collected data concerning
the demand for the number of rolls of this brand of carpet:

Weekly Demand	Probability
0	.10
1	.20
2	.20
3	.20
4	.20
5	.10

Miller's policy has been to reorder 8 rolls whenever its
inventory reached 4 rolls or less at the end of the week.
Current inventory is 5 rolls. Reordering costs are $40 per
order and holding costs are $2 per roll per week. Stockout
costs are $10 per occurrence and these sales are lost.
   Lead time for an order has been observed to be:

Weeks	Probability
1	.40
2	.50
3	.10

a) Conduct an 8 week simulation of Miller's situation and
   determine the total cost for this period. Use column 4 of
   Appendix B for demand and column 6 for lead times.

b) Miller's has been offered a new policy. The wholesaler will
   automatically deliver 3 rolls to Miller's at the end of each
   week for a weekly service charge of $12. This eliminates
   reorder costs and lead times. Should Miller's accept this
   new policy or keep its current policy?

PROBLEM 12

Customers at Winkies Donuts can either eat their doughnut
purchase on the premises or carry it out. Winkies estimates
that 35% of its morning business customers enjoy their doughnuts
on the premises.
   Customers eating their doughnuts on the premises either buy
one or two doughnuts and nearly always order a beverage.
Winkies estimates the following profits and probabilities hold
for service times of the on-the-premises customers:

Service Times	Probability	Expected Profit
25 seconds	.15	$ .08
50 seconds	.60	$ .23
75 seconds	.25	$ .34

Carry-out customers typically purchase a couple of doughnuts or
a dozen. Winkies estimates the following profits and
probabilities hold for the service times of carry-out customers:

Service Times	Probability	Expected Profit
50 seconds	.30	$ .15
100 seconds	.70	$ .90

During any 25 second interval, either 0, 1, or 2 customers will
arrive at Winkies with the following probability distribution:

Customers	Probability
0	.75
1	.16
2	.09

Winkies has only one morning sales clerk on duty.

a) Conduct a 10 minute simulation of sales at Winkies. Using
   Appendix B, use column 1 for number of arrivals in 25
   seconds, column 2 for the eat-in/carry-out decision,
   column 3 for on-the-premises and carry-out service times.

b) What is the expected profit during this period?

c) What percentage of the time is the server busy?

d) What is the average number of customers at Winkies?

PROBLEM 13

Honest Archie's Appliance Company has decided to cease selling
microwave ovens. Archie has slashed prices on the three models
he has in stock -- Amana, Litton, and Tappan. He currently has
3 Amanas, 2 Littons, and 4 Tappans left in stock.
   Because of his low prices, Archie expects to have from one to
four customers come into his store each day inquiring about the
ovens. Archie believes the following daily probabilities hold:

Customers	Probability
1	.50
2	.30
3	.10
4	.10

For each inquiry, Archie believes the following probabilities
hold: P(not interested in any purchase) = .30; P(desires
Amana) = .30; P(desires Litton) = .25; P(desires Tappan) = .15.
   If a customer desires a particular brand of oven that Archie
is sold out of, Archie will try to sell the customer the brand
of oven in which his current stock is the largest. (If there is
a tie, he chooses the one that had the largest initial stock.)
Archie believes there is a 25% chance he will be successful in
convincing the person to switch to that brand and a 75% chance
of losing the sale.
   Do a simulation to determine the number of days it will take
Archie to sell out his stock of microwave ovens. Use column 7
of Appendix B for arriving customers, column 8 for oven
preference, and column 9 for brand switching.

PROBLEM 14

As the owner of a rent-a-car agency you have determined the
following statistics:

Number of Potential Rentals Daily	Probability	Length of Car Rental Per Rent	Probability
0	.10	1 day	.50
1	.15	2 days	.30
2	.20	3 days	.15
3	.30	4 days	.05
4	.25		

The gross profit is $40 per car per day rented. When there is
demand for a car when none is available there is a good will
loss of $80 and the rental is lost. Each day a car is unused
costs you $5 per car. Your firm initially has 4 cars.

a) Conduct a 10 day simulation of this business using column 1 of Appendix B for demand and column 2 for rental length.

b) If your firm can obtain another car for $200 for 10 days should you take the extra car?

PROBLEM 15

Scooper Dooper is a small ice cream parlor located next to the Lemonville exit of the Metropolitan Subway Line. Arriving customers to Scooper Dooper purchase either ice cream cones, malts, or sundaes. The following table gives the approximate service time required, expected profit, and the probability of each type of purchase:

Purchase	Probability	Service Time Required	Expected Profit
Ice Cream Cone	.75	30 seconds	$.12
Malt	.15	60 seconds	$.22
Sundae	.10	90 seconds	$.30

The store is small, holding a maximum of four customers. Customers who find the store full go elsewhere for their ice cream.
  Management estimates that during the lunch hour in each 30 second interval there will be either 0, 1, 2, or 3 arrivals with the following probability distribution:

Number of Arrivals	Probability
0	.30
1	.40
2	.20
3	.10

Simulate the operation of the Scooper Dooper ice cream parlor for a 15 minute period during the lunch hour. From Appendix B, use column 1 to generate the number of arrivals and column 2 to determine the type of purchase.

a) What is the expected profit earned during this period?

b) What percentage of the customers are lost due to a full store?

c) What is the average size of the waiting line?

PROBLEM 16

Three airlines compete on the route between New York and Los Angeles. Stanton Marketing has performed an analysis of first class business travelers to determine their airline choice.
Stanton has modeled this choice as a Markov process and has determined the following transition probabilities.

Next Airline

		A	B	C
	A	.50	.30	.20
Last Airline	B	.30	.45	.25
	C	.10	.35	.55

a) Show the random number assignments that can be used to simulate the first class business traveler's next airline when her last airline is A, B, and C.

b) Assume the traveler used airline C last. Simulate which airline the traveler will be using over her next 25 flights. What percentage of her flights are on each of the three airlines? (Use column 3 of Appendix B.)

TRUE/FALSE

17. Given the accuracy of computers, it is not necessary to validate a simulation program.

18. Using the next event simulation approach, the time between system updates is variable.

19. A random number mapping always maps a set of occurrences to numbers between 00 and 99.

20. Computer simulation requires a special purpose simulation language.

21. In comparing different policies using simulation, one should use the same set of random numbers whenever possible.

22. Flowcharts are useful in designing a simulation program.

23. In Monte Carlo simulation, outcomes are determined by choosing a random number and selecting the outcome corresponding to that number.

24. A computer simulator is a device which acts like a computer but is not a computer.

25. One is guaranteed an optimal solution to a problem using simulation.

26. A typical way to avoid start-up problems in simulation is to run the program for a specified time without recording any data corresponding to the simulation.

27. Probabilistic inputs to a Monte Carlo simulation must follow a discrete probability distribution.

28. If there are no probabilistic components in a problem, there is no reason to use computer simulation to solve it.

29. Simulation is a trial-and-error approach to problem solving.

30. If a computer simulator is correctly programmed, there will be no difference between the simulated and real distributions for a probabilistic component.

31. If a computer simulator is properly programmed, different random number sequences will not cause different output results.

CHAPTER

=====

14
Decision Analysis

KEY CONCEPTS

CONCEPT	ILLUSTRATED PROBLEMS	ANSWERED PROBLEMS
Payoff Tables	1,2,3	8-16
Nonprobabilistic Decision Criteria: Optimistic, Conservative, Minimax Regret Approaches	1,2	8,9,10,12,15
Probabilistic Decision Criteria: Expected Monetary Value, Expected Opportunity Loss	1-4	8-16
Decision Trees	1,3,4	10-16
Expected Value of Perfect Information	1,3	9,10,11, 13,14,16
Bayes' Rule: Revising Probabilities	3,4	11,13,14,16,19
Expected Value of Sample Information	3	11,13,14,16
Efficiency	3	11,13
Sensitivity Analysis	5	11,19
Decision Making Using Utility	6,7	17,18,19

REVIEW

1. A <u>decision</u> <u>problem</u> is characterized by decision alternatives, states of nature, and resulting payoffs.

2. The <u>decision</u> <u>alternatives</u> are the different possible strategies the decision maker can employ.

3. The <u>states</u> <u>of</u> <u>nature</u> refer to future events, not under the control of the decision maker, which may occur. States of nature should be defined so that they are mutually exclusive and collectively exhaustive.

4. For each decision alternative and state of nature, there is a resulting <u>payoff</u>. These are often represented in matrix form called a <u>payoff</u> <u>table</u>.

5. A decision is said to <u>dominate</u> another decision if the payoffs for every state of nature for one is at least equal to the corresponding payoffs for the other and is greater for at least one state of nature.

6. One way to solve a complex decision problem is by the use of a <u>decision</u> <u>tree</u>. This is a <u>chronological</u> <u>representation</u> of the decision problem.

7. Each decision tree has two types of nodes. <u>Round</u> <u>nodes</u> correspond to the states of nature while <u>square</u> <u>nodes</u> correspond to the decision alternatives. The branches leaving each round node represent the different states of nature while the branches leaving each square node represent the different decision alternatives.

8. At the end of each limb of a decision tree are the payoffs attained from the series of branches making up that limb. To solve the problem one "<u>folds</u> <u>back</u> <u>the</u> <u>tree</u>", working backwards from the ends of the branches towards the root node of the tree.

9. <u>Decision</u> <u>making</u> <u>under</u> <u>certainty</u> occurs when the decision maker knows with certainty which state of nature will occur.

10. If the decision maker does not know with certainty which state of nature will occur, then he is said to be doing <u>decision</u> <u>making</u> <u>under</u> <u>uncertainty</u>.

11. Three <u>commonly</u> <u>used</u> <u>criteria</u> for decision making under uncertainty when probability information regarding the likelihood of the states of nature is unavailable are: (1) the optimistic, (2) the conservative, and (3) the minimax regret approach.

12. The _optimistic approach_ would be used by an optimistic decision maker. The decision with the largest possible payoff is chosen. (If the payoff table was in terms of costs, the decision which had the lowest cost would be chosen.)

13. The _conservative approach_ would be used by a conservative decision maker. For each decision the minimum payoff is listed. Then the decision corresponding to the maximum of these minimum payoffs is selected. Hence, the minimum possible payoff is maximized. (If the payoff was in terms of costs, the maximum costs would be determined for each decision. The decision selected would be the one which had the minimum of these maximum costs.)

14. The _minimax regret approach_ requires the construction of a _regret table_ or an _opportunity loss table_. This is done by calculating for each state of nature the difference between each payoff and the largest payoff for that state of nature. Then, using this regret table, the maximum regret for each possible decision is listed. The decision chosen is the one corresponding to the minimum of the maximum regrets.

15. If probabilistic information regarding he states of nature is available, one may use the _expected value (EV)_ approach. Here the expected return for each decision is calculated by summing the products of the payoff under each state of nature and the probability of the respective state of nature occurring. The decision yielding the best expected return is chosen.

16. _Sensitivity analysis_ can be used to determine the probability range over which a decision will remain optimal. Such an analysis can provide a better perspective on management's original judgment regarding the state of nature probabilities.

17. Frequently information is available which can improve the probability estimates for the states of nature. The _expected value of perfect information (EVPI)_ is the _increase_ in the expected profit that would result if one knew with certainty which state of nature would occur. This quantity provides an upper bound on the expected value of any sample or survey information. EVPI can be calculated as follows:
    (1) determine the optimal return corresponding to each state of nature;
    (2) compute the expected value of these optimal returns;
    (3) Subtract the EV of the optimal decision from the amount determined in step (2).

18. Knowledge of sample or survey information can be used to revise the probability estimates for the states of nature. Prior to obtaining this information, the probability estimates for the states of nature are called <u>prior</u> <u>probabilities</u>. With knowledge of <u>conditional</u> <u>probabilities</u> for the outcomes or indicators of the sample or survey information, these prior probabilities can be revised by employing <u>Bayes'</u> <u>Theorem</u>. The outcomes of this analysis are called <u>posterior</u> <u>probabilities</u>.

19. <u>Posterior</u> <u>probabilities</u> are calculated as follows:
    (1) For each state of nature, multiply the prior probability by its conditional probability for the indicator -- this gives the <u>joint</u> <u>probabilities</u> for the states and indicator.
    (2) Sum these joint probabilities over all states -- this gives the <u>marginal</u> <u>probability</u> for the indicator.
    (3) For each state, divide its joint probability by the marginal probability for the indicator -- this gives the <u>posterior</u> <u>probability</u> distribution.

20. The <u>expected</u> <u>value</u> <u>of</u> <u>sample</u> <u>information</u> <u>(EVSI)</u> is the additional expected profit possible through knowledge of the sample or survey information. EVSI is calculated as follows:
    (1) determine the optimal decision and its expected return for the possible outcomes of the sample or survey using the posterior probabilities for the states of nature;
    (2) compute the expected value of these optimal returns;
    (3) Subtract the EV of the optimal decision obtained without using the sample information from the amount determined in step (2).

21. <u>Efficiency</u> of sample information is the ratio of EVSI to EVPI. As the EVPI provides an upper bound for the EVSI, efficiency is always a number between 0 and 1.

22. <u>Utility</u> is a measure of the total worth of a particular outcome, reflecting the decision maker's attitude towards a collection of factors. Some of these factors may be profit, loss, and risk. Utilities are used when the decision criteria must be based on more than just expected monetary values. While determining utility values is not an easy task, such an analysis should be performed in cases where payoffs can assume extremely high or extremely low values.

23. Once a utility function has been determined, the optimal decision can be chosen using the <u>expected</u> <u>utility</u> <u>approach</u>. Here, for each decision alternative, the utility corresponding to each state of nature is multiplied by the probability for that state of nature. The sum of these products for each decision alternative represents the expected utility for that alternative. The decision alternative with the highest expected utility is chosen.

24. Utility values are influenced by the attitude of the decision maker towards risk. A <u>risk</u> <u>avoider</u> will have a concave utility function when utility is measured on the vertical axis and monetary value is measured on the horizontal axis. Individuals purchasing insurance exhibit risk avoidance behavior.

25. <u>Risk</u> <u>takers</u>, such as gamblers, pay a premium to obtain risk. Their utility function is convex. This reflects the decision maker's increasing marginal value for money.

26. A <u>risk</u> <u>neutral</u> decision maker has a linear utility function. In this case, the expected value approach can be used.

27. Most individuals are risk avoiders for some amounts of money, risk neutral for other amounts of money, and risk takers for still other amounts of money. This explains why the same individual will both purchase insurance and also a lottery ticket.

ILLUSTRATED PROBLEMS

PROBLEM 1

Consider the following problem with three decision alternatives and three states of nature with the following payoff table representing profits:

		States of Nature		
		s_1	s_2	s_3
Decisions	d_1	4	4	-2
	d_2	0	3	-1
	d_3	1	5	-3

a) What is the optimal decision if the decision maker were conservative?

b) What is the optimal decision if the decision maker were optimistic?

c) What is the optimal decision using the minimax regret approach?

d) Use a decision tree to find the optimal decision if $P(s_1) = .20$, $P(s_2) = .50$, $P(s_3) = .30$.

e) Given the probabilities in (d) calculate the expected value of perfect information.

SOLUTION 1

a) A conservative decision maker would use the conservative approach. List the minimum payoff for each decision. Choose the decision with the maximum of these minimum payoffs.

Decision	Minimum Payoff	
d_1	-2	
d_2	-1	<==== maximum, choose d_2
d_3	-3	

b) An optimistic decision maker would use the optimisitic approach. All we really need to do is to choose the decision that has the largest single value in the payoff table. This largest value is 5, and hence the optimal decision is d_3.

c) For the minimax regret approach, first compute a regret table by subtracting each payoff in a column from the largest payoff in that column. In this example, in the first column subtract 4, 0, and 1 from 4; in the second column, subtract 4, 3, and 5 from 5; etc. The resulting regret table is:

	s_1	s_2	s_3
d_1	0	1	1
d_2	4	2	0
d_3	3	0	2

Then, for each decision list the maximum regret. Choose the decision with the minimum of these values:

Decision	Maximum Regret	
d_1	1	<===== minimum,
d_2	4	choose d_1
d_3	3	

d) The tree diagram looks as follows:

PAYOFFS

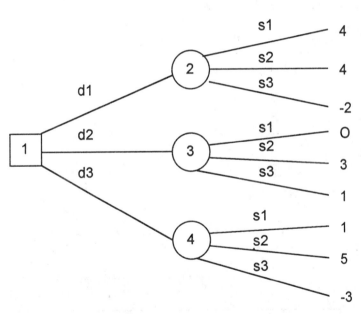

To calculate the expected values at nodes 2, 3, and 4, multiply the payoffs by the corresponding probabilities and then sum. The decision with the maximum expected value of 2.2, d_1, is then chosen.

EV(Node 2) = .20(4) + .50(4) + .30(-2) = 2.2 <==== maximum,
EV(Node 3) = .20(0) + .50(3) + .30(-1) = 1.2   choose d_1
EV(Node 4) = .20(1) + .50(5) + .30(-3) = 1.8

e) The EVPI is calculated by multiplying the maximum payoff for each state by the corresponding probability, summing these values, and then subtracting the expected value of the optimal decision from this sum. Thus, the EVPI = [.20(4) + .50(5) + .30(-1)] - 2.2 = .8

PROBLEM 2

Jim has been employed at Gold Key Realty at a salary of $2,000 per month during the past year. Because Jim is considered to be a top salesman, the manager of Gold Key is offering him one of three salary plans for the next year: (I) a 25% raise to $2,500 per month; (II) a base salary of $1,000 plus $600 per house sold; or, (III) a straight commission of $1,000 per house sold. Over the past year, Jim has sold up to 6 homes in a month.

a) Compute the monthly salary payoff table for Jim.

b) For this payoff table find Jim's optimal decision using: (1) the conservative approach, (2) minimax regret approach.

c) Suppose during the past year the following is Jim's distribution of home sales. If one assumes that this a typical distribution for Jim's monthly sales, which salary plan should Jim select?

Home Sales	Number of Months
0	1
1	2
2	1
3	2
4	1
5	3
6	2

SOLUTION 2

a) There are three decision alternatives (salary plans) and seven states of nature (the number of houses sold monthly).

	Number of Homes Sold						
	0	1	2	3	4	5	6
Plan I	2500	2500	2500	2500	2500	2500	2500
Plan II	1000	1600	2200	2800	3400	4000	4600
Plan III	0	1000	2000	3000	4000	5000	6000

b) (1) Conservative Approach

Decision	Minimum Payoff	
Plan I	2500	<==== choose Plan I
Plan II	1000	
Plan III	0	

(2) <u>Minimax</u> <u>Regret</u> <u>Approach</u>

Construct a regret table by subtracting all numbers in a column from the maximum number in the column:

Regret Table

	Number of Homes Sold						
	0	1	2	3	4	5	6
Plan I	0	0	0	500	1500	2500	3500
Plan II	1500	900	300	200	600	1000	1400
Plan III	2500	1500	500	0	0	0	0

Choose the decision with the minimum of the maximum regrets.

Decision	Maximum Regret	
Plan I	3500	
Plan II	1500	<==== minimum,
Plan III	2500	choose Plan II

c) Use the relative frequency method for determining the probabilities:

Homes Sold	Frequency	Probability
0	1	1/12
1	2	2/12
2	1	1/12
3	2	2/12
4	1	1/12
5	3	3/12
6	2	2/12

Use the expected value (EV) approach:

$$EV(\text{Plan I}) = 1/12(2500) + 2/12(2500) + 1/12(2500) \\ + 2/12(2500) + 1/12(2500) + 3/12(2500) \\ + 2/12(2500) \\ = 2500$$

$$EV(\text{Plan II}) = 1/12(1000) + 2/12(1600) + 1/12(2200) \\ + 2/12(2800) + 1/12(3400) + 3/12(4000) \\ + 2/12(4600) \\ = 3050$$

$$EV(\text{Plan III}) = 1/12(0) + 2/12(1000) + 1/12(2000) + 2/12(3000) \\ + 1/12(4000) + 3/12(5000) + 2/12(6000) \\ = 3417$$

Choose Plan III, the plan with the highest EV.

PROBLEM 3

Burger Prince Restaurant is contemplating opening a new restaurant on Main Street. It has three different models, each with a different seating capacity. Burger Prince estimates that the average number of customers per hour will be 80, 100, or 120. The payoff table for the three models is as follows:

| | Average Number of Customers Per Hour | | |
	$s_1 = 80$	$s_2 = 100$	$s_3 = 120$
Model A	$10,000	$15,000	$14,000
Model B	$ 8,000	$18,000	$12,000
Model C	$ 6,000	$16,000	$21,000

Burger Prince estimates the probability of 80 customers per hour is the same as the probability of 120 customers per hour and twice as much as the probability of 100 customers per hour.

a) What is the optimal decision using the expected value approach?

b) What is the expected value of perfect information?

c) Burger Prince must decide whether or not to purchase a marketing survey from Stanton Marketing for $1,000. The results of the survey are "favorable" or "unfavorable". The conditional probabilities are:

$P(\text{favorable} \mid 80 \text{ customers per hour}) = .2$

$P(\text{favorable} \mid 100 \text{ customers per hour}) = .5$

$P(\text{favorable} \mid 120 \text{ customers per hour}) = .9$

Should Burger Prince have the survey performed by Stanton Marketing?

d) What is the efficiency of the survey?

SOLUTION 3

a) (1) Determine the probabilities for 80, 100, and 120 customers:

$$P(80) + P(100) + P(120) = 1$$
$$P(80) = P(120)$$
$$P(80) = 2P(100).$$

This yields $P(80) = .4$, $P(100) = .2$, $P(120) = .4$.

(2) Calculate the expected value for each decision. The following decision tree can assist in this calculation. Here d_1, d_2, d_3 represent the decision alternatives of models A, B, C, and s_1, s_2, s_3 represent the states of nature of 80, 100, and 120.

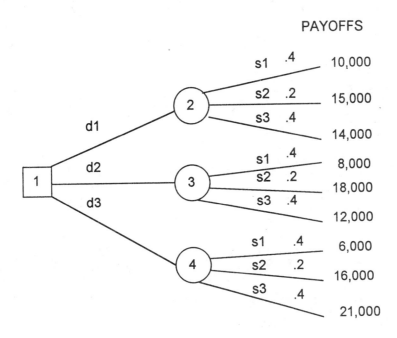

Calculating the expected value for each decision gives:

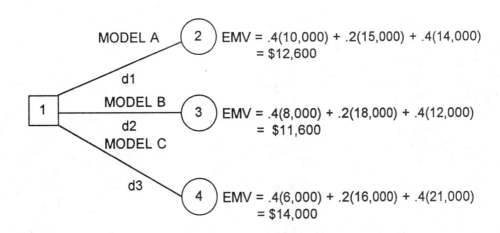

(3) Choose the model with largest EV -- Model C.

b) Calculate the expected value for the optimum payoff for each state of nature and subtract the EV of the optimal decision:
EVPI= .4(10,000) + .2(18,000) + .4(21,000) - 14,000 = $2,000.

c) Find the posterior probabilities:

FAVORABLE

State	Prior	Conditional	Joint	Posterior*
80	.4	.2	.08	.148
100	.2	.5	.10	.185
120	.4	.9	.36	.667
		Total	.54	1.000

UNFAVORABLE

State	Prior	Conditional	Joint	Posterior*
80	.4	.8	.32	.696
100	.2	.5	.10	.217
120	.4	.1	.04	.087
		Total	.46	1.000

Notes:
* Posterior probabilities = (Joint Probability)
                           /(Total of Joint Probabilities)

The decision tree for this problem is on the next page.

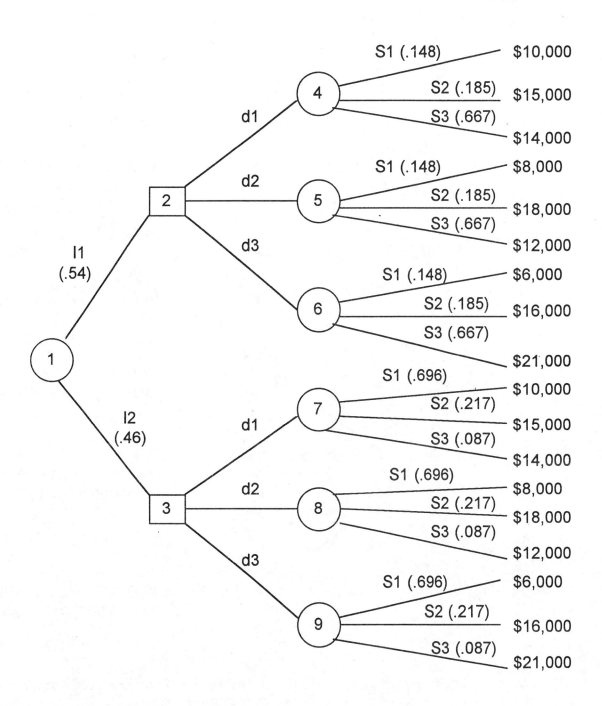

Calculate expected values

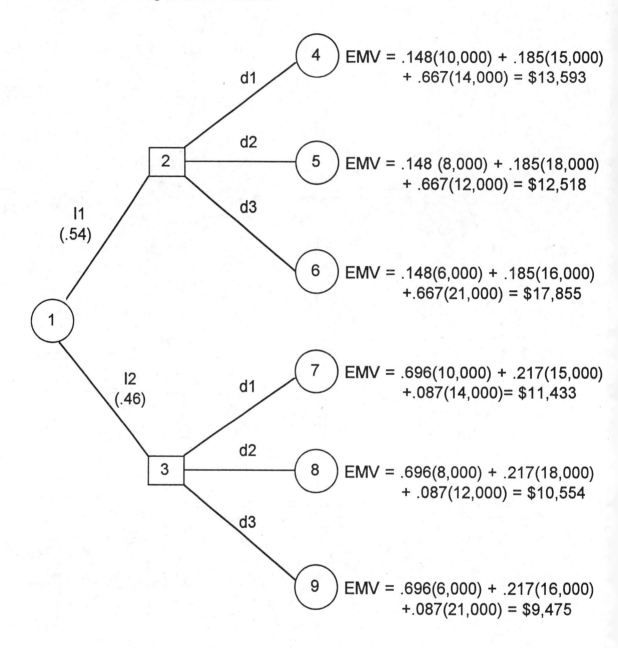

$$EMV = .148(10,000) + .185(15,000) + .667(14,000) = \$13,593$$

$$EMV = .148 (8,000) + .185(18,000) + .667(12,000) = \$12,518$$

$$EMV = .148(6,000) + .185(16,000) + .667(21,000) = \$17,855$$

$$EMV = .696(10,000) + .217(15,000) + .087(14,000) = \$11,433$$

$$EMV = .696(8,000) + .217(18,000) + .087(12,000) = \$10,554$$

$$EMV = .696(6,000) + .217(16,000) + .087(21,000) = \$9,475$$

Hence, if the outcome of the survey is "favorable" choose Model C. If it is unfavorable, choose model A.

$$EVSI = .54(\$17,855) + .46(\$11,433) - \$14,000 = \$900.88$$

Since this is less than the cost of the survey, the survey should not be purchased.

d) The efficiency = EVSI/EVPI = ($900.88)/($2000) = .4504.

PROBLEM 4

The past few years have seen a general decline in the economic conditions of the resort community of Pacific City. Certain town officials, as well as other interested parties from Las Vegas, believe that the legalization of casino gambling will greatly improve the city's future. They have succeeded in having a gambling referendum placed on the ballot in next month's special election.

One effect of the declining economic condition of Pacific City has been the bankruptcy last year of the St. Carlton Inn, the city's largest hotel. The St. Carlton is scheduled to be sold at a sealed bid auction next week. The terms of the auction call for an immediate 10% down payment by the highest bidder, with the remaining balance due in two months.

One party interested in bidding on the St. Carlton is Justin Thyme, a real estate promoter and publisher of Fantasy Magazine. Justin has learned from associates that there are at least three other parties interested in the property, including a syndicate from Chicago.

Justin has decided that if he submits a bid it will be for $5 million for the property. If he bids $5 million, he estimates that he has a 40% chance of winning the auction. He also estimates that if the gambling referendum passes, he can sell the property for $7.5 million. If the initiative fails, he will sacrifice his 10% deposit.

Justin believes, based on polls taken to date, that the gambling referendum has a 30% chance of passing. He is considering hiring the noted pollster, Harris Gallup, before the auction to give his opinion on the outcome of the referendum. Based on Gallup's past record, Justin estimates that the probability Gallup will correctly predict the outcome is .8. Gallup's fee is $100,000.

What should Justin do?

SOLUTION 4

To solve this problem, first construct a tree diagram with possible courses of actions and outcomes properly sequenced.

Justin's first decision is whether or not to hire Gallup. If he does, then he will either obtain a prediction from him that the referendum will pass or fail. At that point, or if he does not hire Gallup, he must decide whether or not to bid.

Following this, he will learn if his bid is a winning one. If it is, then he will next be concerned with whether the referendum passes or not. If it does, he sells his property for $7.5 million. If it does not pass, he sacrifices his $.5 million deposit.

The tree diagram is presented on the next page including returns and probabilities.

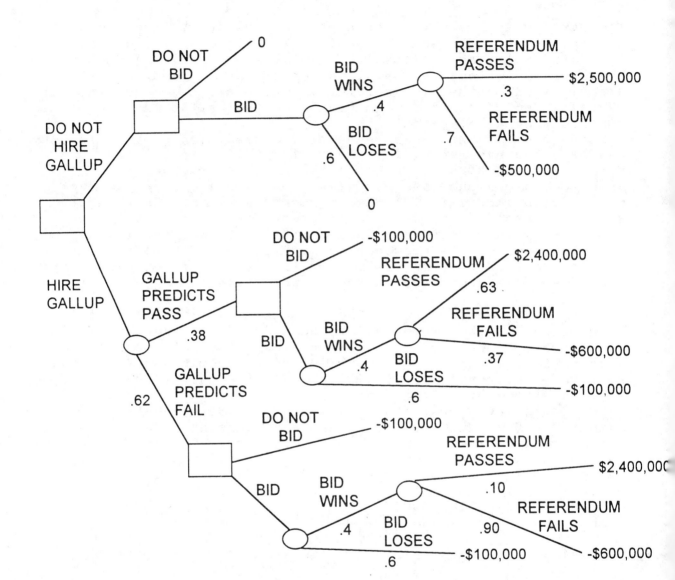

Beginning at the ends of the tree and working towards the root
gives the following expected returns:

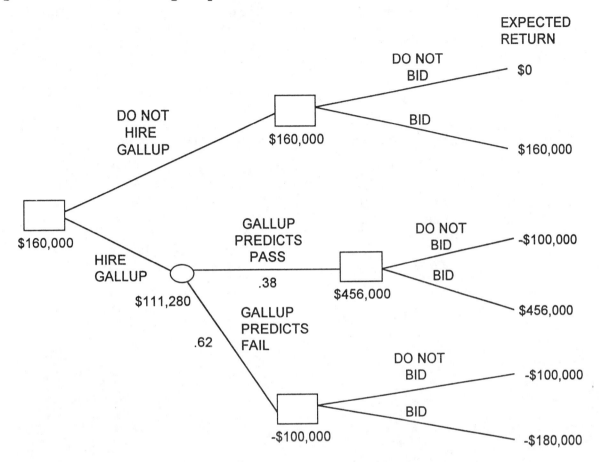

Therefore, if Justin does not hire Gallup, he should bid. If he
does hire Gallup, he should bid if Gallup predicts the
referendum will pass, and he should not bid if Gallup predicts
the referendum will fail.

The expected return if Justin hires Gallup is:

.38(456,000) + .62(-100,000) = $111,280

The expected return if Justin does not hire Gallup = $160,000.
Thus, his optimal strategy is not to hire Gallup and submit a
$5 million bid.

The probabilities for the Pass/Fail branches were obtained as
follows:

Indicator Information I_1 -- Gallup Predicts Pass

State	Prior	Conditional	Joint	Posterior
Referendum Passes	.30	.80	.24	.63
Referendum Fails	.70	.20	.14	.37
		Total	.38	1.00

Indicator Information I_2 -- Gallup Predicts Fail

State	Prior	Conditional	Joint	Posterior
Referendum Passes	.30	.20	.06	.10
Referendum Fails	.70	.80	.56	.90
		Total	.62	1.00

PROBLEM 5

East West Distributing is in the process of trying to determine
where they should schedule next year's production of a popular
line of kitchen utensils which they distribute. Manufacturers
in four different countries have submitted bids to East West.
However, a pending trade bill in Congress will greatly affect
the cost to East West due to proposed tariffs, favorable trading
status, etc.

   After careful analysis, East West has determined the following
cost breakdown for the four manufacturers (in $1,000's) based on
whether or not the trade bill passes:

	Bill Passes	Bill Fails
Country A	260	210
Country B	320	160
Country C	240	240
Country D	275	210

a) If East West estimates that there is a 40% chance of the bill
   passing, which country should they choose for manufacturing?

b) Over what range of values for the "bill passing" will the
   solution in part (a) remain optimal?

SOLUTION 5

a) Using the expected value approach, calculate the expected
   value for each country. Note that country D's costs are
   dominated by country A's costs (whether the bill passes or
   not, production is at least as expensive in country D as in
   country A) and therefore country D need not be considered.
   (Note that the probability that the bill will fail is 1 - .4
   = .6.)

$$EV(A) = .4(260) + .6(210) = 230$$
$$EV(B) = .4(320) + .6(160) = 224$$
$$EV(C) = .4(240) + .6(240) = 240$$

   East West should choose the country with the lowest expected
   cost: country B.

b) To determine the range for the probability of the bill
   passing over which country B will be optimal, compare
   choosing country B versus country A, and then compare
   choosing country B versus country C. Now let,

   p = the probability of the trade bill passing.

Country B would be preferred to country A as long as:

$$EV(B) \leq EV(A) \qquad or$$

$$p(320) + (1-p)160 \leq p(260) + (1-p)(210)$$

$$160p + 160 \leq 50p + 210$$

$$110p \leq 50$$

$$p \leq .455.$$

Similarly, Country B would be preferred to Country C as long as $EV(B) \leq EV(C)$. Using the same approach as above, this is equivalent to $p(320) + (1-p)160 \leq 240$. Solving, $p \leq .50$.

Thus as long as the probability of the bill passing is less than .455, then East West should choose Country B. The following graph illustrates the expected value of the decisions as a function of p:

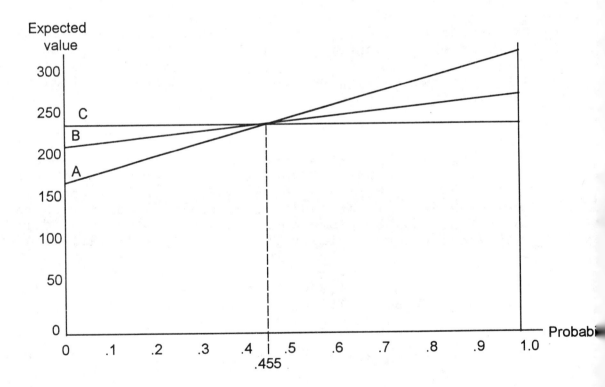

PROBLEM 6

Consider the following three state, four decision problem with the following payoff table (in $'s):

	s_1	s_2	s_3
d_1	+100,000	+40,000	-60,000
d_2	+ 50,000	+20,000	-30,000
d_3	+ 20,000	+20,000	-10,000
d_4	+ 40,000	+20,000	-60,000

The probabilities for the three states of nature are:
$P(s_1) = .1$, $P(s_2) = .3$, and $P(s_3) = .6$.

a) If the decision maker is risk neutral, what is the optimal decision?

b) Suppose two decision makers have the following utility values:

	Utility	
Amount	Decision Maker I	Decision Maker II
$100,000	100	100
$ 50,000	94	58
$ 40,000	90	50
$ 20,000	80	35
-$ 10,000	60	18
-$ 30,000	40	10
-$ 60,000	0	0

Graph the utility curves for the two decision makers.

c) Classify each of the two decision makers as either a risk avoider, a risk taker, or risk neutral.

d) Find the optimal decision for each of the decision makers.

SOLUTION 6

a) If the decision maker is risk neutral the expected value approach is applicable.

$EV(d_1)$ = .1(100,000) + .3(40,000) + .6(-60,000) = -$14,000
$EV(d_2)$ = .1(50,000) + .3(20,000) + .6(-30,000) = -$ 7,000
$EV(d_3)$ = .1(20,000) + .3(20,000) + .6(-10,000) = +$ 2,000

Note the EV for d_4 need not be calculated as decision d_4 is dominated by decision d_2.

The optimal decision is d_3.

b)

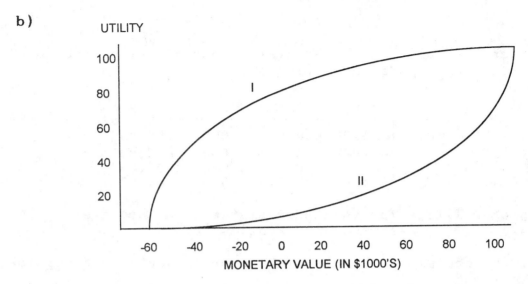

c) Decision Maker I has a concave utility function -- he is a risk avoider. Decision Maker II has a convex utility function -- he is a risk taker.

d) Note again that d_4 is dominated by d_2 and hence is not considered. For the remaining decisions, compute the expected utility for each decision maker using the probabilities given.

Utility Table I

	s_1	s_2	s_3	Expected Utility
d_1	100	90	0	37.0
d_2	94	80	40	57.4
d_3	80	80	60	68.0 <====
Probability	.1	.3	.6	

The largest expected utility is 68.0. Decision Maker I should make decision d_3.

Utility Table II

	s_1	s_2	s_3	Expected Utility
d_1	100	50	0	25.0 <====
d_2	58	35	10	22.3
d_3	35	35	18	24.8
Probability	.1	.3	.6	

The largest expected utility is 25.0. Decision Maker II should make decision d_1.

PROBLEM 7

In problem (6) suppose the probabilities for the three states of nature are changed to: $P(s_1) = .5$, $P(s_2) = .3$, and $P(s_3) = .2$.

a) Find the optimal decision for a risk neutral decision maker.

b) Find the optimal decision for Decision Makers I and II.

c) What is the value of this decision problem to Decision Maker I and Decision Maker II? What conclusion can you draw.

SOLUTION 7

a) Use the EV approach for a risk neutral decision maker:

$$EV(d_1) = .5(100,000) + .3(40,000) + .2(-60,000) = 50,000 \Longleftarrow$$
$$EV(d_2) = .5(\ 50,000) + .3(20,000) + .2(-30,000) = 25,000$$
$$EV(d_3) = .5(\ 20,000) + .3(20,000) + .2(-10,000) = 14,000$$

Hence, the risk neutral optimal decision is d_1.

b) Use the expected utility criterion for each decision maker:

Decision Maker I
$$EU(d_1) = .5(100) + .3(90) + .2(\ 0)\ = 77.0$$
$$EU(d_2) = .5(\ 94) + .3(80) + .2(40)\ = 79.0 \Longleftarrow$$
$$EU(d_3) = .5(\ 80) + .3(80) + .2(60)\ = 76.0$$

Hence, Decision Maker I's optimal decision is d_2.

Decision Maker II
$$EU(d_1) = .5(100) + .3(50) + .2(\ 0)\ = 65.0 \Longleftarrow$$
$$EU(d_2) = .5(\ 58) + .3(35) + .2(10)\ = 41.5$$
$$EU(d_3) = .5(\ 35) + .3(35) + .2(18)\ = 31.6$$

Hence, Decision Maker II's optimal decision is d_1.

c) To determine the value of the decision problem to a decision maker, find the amount that corresponds to the expected utility of the optimal decision.
   For Decision Maker I, the optimal expected utility is 79. He assigned a utility of 80 to +$20,000, and a utility of 60 to -$10,000. Linearly interpolating in this range 1 point is worth $30,000/20 = $1,500. Thus a utility of 79 is worth about $20,000 - $1,500 = $18,500.
   For Decision Maker II, the optimal expected utility is 65. He assigned a utility of 100 to 100,000, and a utility of 58 to $50,000. In this range, 1 point is worth $50,000/42 = $1190. Thus a utility of 65 is worth about $50,000 + 7($1190) = $58,330.
   Thus, the problem is worth more to Decision Maker II.

ANSWERED PROBLEMS

PROBLEM 8

Mark Investment Advisors has just completed an analysis on the returns of five utility stocks for next year. Mark hypothesizes that next year the economy will either be in a depression (s_1), a recession (s_2), an upward period (s_3), or a major expansionary period (s_4). The per dollar growth for the five stocks corresponding to each state of the economy are as follows:

	s_1	s_2	s_3	s_4
Stock A	-.40	-.20	+.10	+.60
Stock B	-.30	-.10	0	+.30
Stock C	-.10	0	+.05	+.30
Stock D	0	+.05	+.10	+.15
Stock E	+.05	+.15	-.10	-.20

a) If you had a chance to purchase shares of Stock B or Stock C, which would you purchase? Why?

b) Find the best stock to purchase undereach approach:
(1) optimistic; (2) minimax regret; (3) conservative.

c) Suppose Mark's financial outlook for next year is $P(s_1) = .2$; $P(s_2) = .4$; $P(s_3) = .2$; and $P(s_4) = .2$. Using the expected value approach, which stock would Mark recommend?

PROBLEM 9

Transrail is bidding on a project which it figures will cost $400,000 to perform. Using a 25% markup, it will charge $500,000, netting a profit of $100,000. However, it has been learned that another company, Rail Freight, is also considering bidding on the project. If Rail Freight does submit a bid, it figures to be a bid of about $470,000.
  Transrail really wants this project and is considering a bid with only a 15% markup to $460,000 to ensure winning regardless of whether or not Rail Freight submits a bid.

a) Prepare a profit payoff table from Transrail's point of view.

b) What decision would be made if Transrail was conservative?

c) If Rail Freight is known to submit bids on only 25% of the projects it considers, what decision should Transrail make?

d) Given the information in (c), how much would a corporate spy be worth to Transrail to find out if Rail Freight will bid?

PROBLEM 10

The Super Cola Company must decide whether or not to introduce a new diet soft drink. Management feels that if it does introduce the diet soda it will yield a profit of $1 million if sales are around 100 million, a profit of $200,000 if sales are around 50 million, or it will lose $2 million if sales are only around 1 million bottles. If Super Cola does not market the new diet soda, it will suffer a loss of $400,000.

a) Construct a payoff table for this problem.

b) Construct a regret table for this problem.

c) Should Super Cola introduce the soda if the company: (1) is conservative; (2) is optimistic; (3) wants to minimize its maximum disappointment?

d) An internal marketing research study has found P(100 million in sales) = 1/3; P(50 million in sales) = 1/2; P(1 million in sales) = 1/6. Should Super Cola introduce the new diet soda?

e) A consulting firm can perform a more thorough study for $275,000. Should management have this study performed?

PROBLEM 11

Super Cola is also considering the introduction of a root beer drink. The company feels that the probability that the product will be a success is .6. The payoff table is as follows:

	Success (s_1)	Failure (s_2)
Produce (d_1)	$250,000	-$300,000
Do Not Produce (d_2)	-$ 50,000	-$ 20,000

The company has a choice of two research firms to obtain additional information for this product. Stanton Marketing claims that it has market indicators, I_1 and I_2 for which $P(I_1|s_1) = .7$ and $P(I_1|s_2) = .4$. New World Marketing has indicators J_1 and J_2 for which $P(J_1|s_1) = .6$ and $P(J_1|s_2) = .3$.

a) What is the optimal decision if neither firm is used? Over what probability of success range is this decision optimal?

b) What is the EVPI?

[more questions on next page]

c) Find the EVSIs and efficiencies for Stanton and New World.

d) If both firms charge $5,000, which firm should be hired?

e) If Stanton charges $10,000 and New World charges $4,000, which firm should Super Cola hire? Why?

PROBLEM 12

Metropolitan Cablevision is investigating the installation of a cable TV system in town. The engineering department estimates the cost of the system (in present worth dollars) to be $700,000. The sales department has investigated four pricing plans. For each pricing plan the marketing division has estimated the revenue per household in present worth dollars to be:

Plan	Revenue Per Household
I	$15
II	$18
III	$20
IV	$24

The sales department estimates the number of household subscribers would be approximately either 10,000, 20,000, 30,000, 40,000, 50,000 or 60,000.

a) Construct a payoff table for this problem.

b) What is the company's optimal decision under (1) the optimistic approach; (2) the conservative approach; and (3) the minimax regret approach?

c) Suppose the sales department has determined that the number of subscribers will be a function of the pricing plan. The probability distributions for the pricing plans are given below. Use decision tree analysis to determine which pricing plan is optimal under the expected value approach.

Number of Subscribers	Probability Under Pricing Plan			
	I	II	III	IV
10,000	0	.05	.10	.20
20,000	.05	.10	.20	.25
30,000	.05	.20	.20	.25
40,000	.40	.30	.20	.15
50,000	.30	.20	.20	.10
60,000	.20	.15	.10	.05

PROBLEM 13

Dicom Corporation has developed a new high speed computer which
it intends to sell for $150,000. Dicom's salesmen have
scheduled demonstrations with four clients next month. For each
client, Dicom estimates there is a 40% chance of his purchasing
the computer.
  Because the company cannot completely shut down its assembly
line, it plans to make at least one computer next month but
could make as many as four. Production costs are $100,000 for
producing one computer, $190,000 for producing two, $260,000 for
producing three, and $310,000 for producing four.
  Any unsold computers produced will be sold at $60,000. Also,
if a client wants to purchase a computer, but all computers
produced have been sold, the company estimates it loses $20,000.

a) Determine a payoff table for this problem.

b) What is the optimal strategy using the expected monetary
   value criterion? (HINT: Use the binomial distribution to
   determine the probabilities for the states of nature.)

c) Dicom can have a survey performed to indicate the market
   impression of the new computer -- favorable or unfavorable.
   The following probabilities are believed to hold:

   P(favorable|0 sold) = .1   P(favorable|3 sold) = .9
   P(favorable|1 sold) = .2   P(favorable|4 sold) = 1.0
   P(favorable|2 sold) = .6

   How much should Dicom pay for this survey and what is its
   efficiency?

PROBLEM 14

Dollar Department Stores has just acquired the chain of
Wenthrope and Sons Custom Jewelers. Dollar has received an
offer from Harris Diamonds to purchase the Wenthrope store on
Grove Street for $120,000.
  Dollar has determined that the profit potential for this store
will depend on the economy. Probability estimates of the
store's future profitability are: P($80,000) = .2,
P($100,000) = .3, P($120,000) = .1, and P($140,000) = .4.

a) Should Dollar sell the store on Grove Street?

b) What is the EVPI?

c) Dollar can have an economic forecast performed, costing
   $10,000, that produces indicators I_1 and I_2, for which
   $P(I_1|80,000)$ = .1; $P(I_1|100,000)$ = .2; $P(I_1|120,000)$ = .6;
   $P(I_1|140,000)$ = .3. Should Dollar purchase the forecast?

PROBLEM 15

The firm of Cashman Engineering Associates will be leasing a new
office copier and is considering four leasing plans.

Plan	Monthly Lease	Unit Copy Cost
I	$100	$.02 for the first 10,000; $.016 thereafter
II	$200	$.012 for all copies
III	$150	first 5,000 free; $.022 thereafter
IV	$300	$.005 for all copies

The company has determined it will make either 12,600, 14,400,
16,200, 18,000, 19,800, 21,600 copies per month with
probabilities of .05, .10, .15, .25, .25, and .20 respectively.

a) Construct a monthly payoff table for Cashman in terms of costs

b) What is the optimal plan if the company uses the (1)
    optimistic approach or (2) the conservative approach?

c) What is the optimal plan using the expected value approach?

PROBLEM 16

An appliance dealer must decide how many (if any) new microwave
ovens to order for next month. The ovens cost $220 and sell for
$300. Because the oven company is coming out with a new product
line in two months, any ovens not sold next month will have to
be sold at the dealer's half price clearance sale.
Additionally, the appliance dealer feels he suffers a loss of
$25 for every oven demanded when he is out of stock. On the
basis of past months' sales data, the dealer estimates the
probabilities of monthly demand for 0, 1, 2, or 3 ovens to be
.3, .4, .2, and .1, respectively.
   The dealer is considering conducting a telephone survey on the
customers' attitudes towards microwave ovens. The results of
the survey will either be "favorable", "unfavorable" or "no
opinion". The dealer's probability estimates for the survey
results based on the number of units demanded are:

P(favorable|demand = 0) = .1   P(unfavorable|demand = 0) = .8
P(favorable|demand = 1) = .2   P(unfavorable|demand = 1) = .3
P(favorable|demand = 2) = .3   P(unfavorable|demand = 2) = .1
P(favorable|demand = 3) = .9   P(unfavorable|demand = 3) = .1

a) What is the appliance dealer's optimal decision without
    conducting the telephone survey?
b) What is the EVPI?
c) Based on the survey results what is the optimal decision
    strategy for the dealer?
d) What is the maximum amount he should pay for this survey?

PROBLEM 17

Burger Prince Restaurant is considering the purchase of a $100,000 fire insurance policy. The fire statistics indicate that in a given year the probability of property damage in a fire is as follows:

Fire Damage	Probability	Fire Damage	Probability
$ 0	.980	$ 50,000	.004
$ 10,000	.005	$ 75,000	.002
$ 25,000	.003	$100,000	.006

a) If Burger Prince was risk neutral, how much would they be willing to pay for fire insurance?

b) If Burger Prince has the utility values given below, approximately how much would they be willing to pay for fire insurance?

	Amount Of Loss ($'s)						
	100,000	75,000	50,000	25,000	10,000	5,000	0
Utility	0	30	60	85	95	99	100

PROBLEM 18

Dollar Department Stores has the opportunity of acquiring either 3, 5, or 10 leases from the bankrupt Granite Variety Store chain. Dollar estimates the profit potential of the leases depends on the state of the economy over the next five years. The payoff table is given below (payoffs are in $1,000,000's).

There are four possible states of the economy as modelled by Dollar Department Stores and its president estimates $P(s_1) = .4$, $P(s_2) = .3$, $P(s_3) = .1$, and $P(s_4) = .2$. The utility has also been estimated. Given the payoff and utility tables below which decision should Dollar make?

Payoff Table

		State Of The Economy Over The Next 5 Years			
		s_1	s_2	s_3	s_4
d_1	(buy 10 leases)	10	5	0	-20
d_2	(buy 5 leases)	5	0	-1	-10
d_3	(buy 3 leases)	2	1	0	- 1
d_4	(do not buy)	0	0	0	0

Utility Table

Payoff (in $ millions)	+10	+5	+2	0	-1	-10	-20
Utility	+10	+5	+2	0	-1	-20	-50

PROBLEM 19

Super Cola is considering the introduction of a new 8 oz. root
beer. The probability that the root beer will be a success is
believed to equal .6. The payoff table is as follows:

	Success (s_1)	Failure (s_2)
Produce	$250,000	-$300,000
Do Not Produce	-$ 50,000	-$ 20,000

Company management has determined the following utility values:

Amount	Utility
$250,000	100
-$ 20,000	60
-$ 50,000	55
-$300,000	0

a) Is the company a risk taker, risk averse, or risk neutral?

b) What is Super Cola's optimal decision? Over what range of
   the probability of success will this decision remain optimal?

c) Stanton Marketing has market indicators, I_1 and I_2 for which
   $P(I_1|s_1)$ = .7 and $P(I_1|s_2)$ =.4. New World Marketing has
   market indicators J_1 and J_2 for which $P(J_1|s_1)$ = .6 and
   $P(J_1|s_2)$ = .3. If both indicators are available for free,
   which one should be selected?

TRUE/FALSE

20. The expected value of sample information can never be less than the expected value of perfect information.

21. The expected value of perfect information must always be nonnegative.

22. The expected value of sample information is the difference between the expected value with perfect information and the expected value without perfect information.

23. Using the optimistic and conservative approaches will never give the same optimal decision.

24. The $P(I_k|s_j)$ must equal $P(s_j|I_k)$.

25. For each indicator, I_k, the joint probabilities must sum to 1.

26. Posterior probabilities are calculated by dividing each joint probability by the sum of the joint probabilities for that indicator.

27. The sum of $P(I_k|s_j)$ for all s_j is 1.0.

28. If one outcome is preferred to another, it will have a higher utility value.

29. When using the expected utility approach, a risk avoider and a risk taker will never choose the same decision.

30. If the expected value of sample information exceeds the cost of purchasing the sample information, one should not attempt to obtain the sample information.

31. The states of nature in a decision problem must be mutually exclusive and collectively exhaustive.

32. Maximizing the expected payoff and minimizing the expected opportunity loss result in the same recommended decision.

33. The expected value approach is more appropriate for a one-time decision than a repetitive decision.

34. $P(I_k|s_j)$ is a posterior probability.

CHAPTER

15

Multicriteria Decision Problems

KEY CONCEPTS

CONCEPT	ILLUSTRATED PROBLEMS	ANSWERED PROBLEMS
Goal Programming		
Formulations	1-3	8-10
Graphical Solution	1	8
Computer Solution	2	9
Analytic Hierarchy Process		
Pairwise Comparison Matrices	4-7	11-15
Priority Vectors	4-7	11-15
Overall Priorities	6,7	12-15
Consistency	4	12,13
Hierarchy Construction	7	13,14

REVIEW

1. <u>Goal</u> <u>programming</u> may be used to solve linear programs with multiple objectives. Each objective may be viewed as a "goal".

2. An approach to goal programming is to satisfy goals in a <u>priority</u> <u>sequence</u>. Second-priority goals are pursued without reducing the first-priority goals; third-priority goals are pursued without reducing first- or second-priority goals, etc.

3. In goal programming, d_i^+ and d_i^- are the amounts a targeted goal i is <u>overachieved</u> <u>or</u> <u>underachieved</u> respectively. Usually only one of d_i^+ or d_i^- is considered detrimental.

4. For each priority level, the objective function is to <u>minimize</u> <u>the</u> <u>(weighted)</u> <u>sum</u> <u>of</u> <u>the</u> <u>goal</u> <u>deviations</u>. Previous "optimal" achievements of goals are added to the constraint set so that they are not degraded while trying to achieve lesser priority goals. The goals themselves are added to the constraint set with d_i^+ and d_i^- acting as the surplus and slack variables.

5. <u>Infeasible</u> <u>linear</u> <u>programming</u> <u>problems</u> can be reformulated as goal programs so that some reasonable solution may be attained.

6. The <u>Analytic</u> <u>Hierarchy</u> <u>Process</u> <u>(AHP)</u>, is a procedure designed to quantify managerial judgments of the relative importance of each of several conflicting criteria used in the decision making process.

7. <u>Computer</u> <u>packages</u> can be used for evaluating AHPs. The AHP developed in this chapter is based on one such package, <u>EXPERT</u> <u>CHOICE</u>.

GOAL PROGRAMMING APPROACH

Assuming all of the objectives (goals) and functional constraints in the problem have been identified:

1. Decide the priority level of each goal.

2. If a priority level has more than one goal, for each goal i decide the weight, w_i, to be placed on the deviation(s), d_i^+ and/or d_i^-, from the goal.

3. Set up the initial linear program as follows:

(Assume d_1^+ and d_2^- are the detrimental deviations from first priority goals 1 and 2, respectively.)

$$\text{MIN } w_1 d_1^+ + w_2 d_2^-$$

$$\text{S.T.   Functional Constraints}$$
$$\text{Goal Constraints}$$

2. Solve this linear program. (Assume that the optimal value of the objective function is k.) If there is a lower priority level, go to step 3; otherwise, a final optimal solution has been reached.

3. Consider the next-lower priority level goals and formulate a new objective function based on these goals. Add a constraint requiring the achievement of the next-higher priority level goals to be maintained. The new linear program is:

(Assume d_3^+ and d_4^- are the detrimental deviations associated with the current priority level goals.)

$$\text{MIN } w_3 d_3^+ + w_4 d_4^-$$

$$\text{S.T.   Functional Constraints}$$
$$\text{Goal Constraints}$$
$$w_1 d_1^+ + w_2 d_2^- = k$$

Go to step 2. (Repeat steps 2 and 3 until all priority levels have been examined. Each time, solve a linear program with a lesser priority goal for the objective function and with the optimal achieved amounts of higher priority goals as added constraints.)

ANALYTIC HIERARCHY PROCESS

1. The first step is:
   (a) list an _overall_ _goal_ for the process;
   (b) list _criteria_ that make up the relevant factors
       that contribute to achieving the goal;
   (c) list the _(n)_ _possible_ _decision_ _alternatives_ for each
       of the individual criterion.

   *** For each criterion, perform steps 2 through 5. ***

2. Develop a _pairwise_ _comparison_ _matrix_ for a criterion by rating
   the relative importance between each pair of decision
   alternatives. The matrix lists the alternatives horizontally
   and vertically and has the numerical ratings comparing the
   horizontal (first) alternative with the vertical (second)
   alternative. Ratings are given as follows:

   Compared to the second alternative,
   the first alternative is: Numerical rating

extremely preferred	9
very strongly preferred	7
strongly preferred	5
moderately preferred	3
equally preferred	1

   Intermediate numeric ratings of 8, 6, 4, 2 can be assigned. A
   reciprocal rating (i.e. 1/9, 1/8, 1/7, etc.) is assigned when
   the second alternative is preferred to the first. The value of
   1 is always assigned when comparing an alternative with itself.

3. Develop the _normalized_ _matrix_ by dividing each number in a
   column of the pairwise comparison matrix by its column sum.

4. Develop the _priority_ _vector_ _for_ _the_ _criterion_ by averaging each
   row of the normalized matrix. These row averages form the
   priority _vector_ of alternative preferences with respect to the
   particular criterion. The values in this vector sum to 1.

5. The consistency of the subjective input in the pairwise
   comparison matrix can be measured by calculating a _consistency_
   ratio. (See details below.) A consistency ratio of less than
   .1 is good. For consistency ratios which are greater than .1,
   the subjective input should be re-evaluated.

6. After steps 2 through 5 has been performed for all criteria, the
   results of step 4 are summarized in a _priority_ _matrix_ by listing
   the decision alternatives horizontally and the criteria
   vertically. The column entries are the priority vectors for
   each criterion.

7. Develop a <u>criteria pairwise development matrix</u> in the same manner as that used to construct alternative pairwise comparison matrices by using subjective ratings (step 2). Similarly, normalize the matrix (step 3) and develop a <u>criteria priority vector</u> (step 4).

8. Develop an <u>overall priority vector</u> by multiplying the criteria priority vector (from step 7) by the priority matrix (from step 6).

Determining the Consistency Ratio

1. For each row of the pairwise comparison matrix, determine a weighted sum by summing the multiples of the entries by the priority of its corresponding (column) alternative.

2. For each row, divide its weighted sum by the priority of its corresponding (row) alternative.

3. Determine the average, λ_{max}, of the results of step 2.

4. Compute the <u>consistency index</u>, CI, of the n alternatives by:

$$CI = (\lambda_{max} - n)/(n - 1).$$

5. Determine the <u>random index</u>, RI, from the the following chart:

Number of Decision Alternatives, n	Random Index, RI
3	0.58
4	0.90
5	1.12
6	1.24
7	1.32
8	1.41

6. Determine the <u>consistency ratio</u>, CR as follows:

$$CR = CR/RI.$$

FLOW CHART OF
ANALYTIC HIERARCHY PROCESS

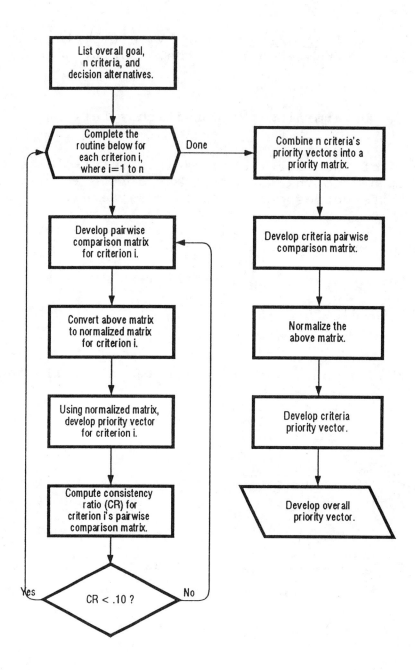

ILLUSTRATED PROBLEMS

> **NOTE:** Priorities and weights are not synonymous in
> goal programming. Think of priorities as absolute/
> firm/preemptive. No tradeoffs occur in the achieve-
> ment of goals with different priorities. However,
> tradeoffs can occur in the achievement of goals with
> the same priority and different weights.

PROBLEM 1

Conceptual Products is a computer company that produces the
CP286 and the CP386 computers. The computers use different
mother boards produced in abundant supply by the company, but
use the same cases and disk drives. The CP286 models use two
floppy disk drives and no hard disks whereas the CP386 models
use one floppy disk drive and one hard disk drive.

The disk drives and cases are bought from vendors. There are
1000 floppy disk drives, 500 hard disk drives, and 600 cases
available to Conceptual Products on a weekly basis. It takes
one hour to manufacture a CP286 and its profit is $200 and it
takes one and one-half hours to manufacture a CP386 and its
profit is $500.

The company has three goals which are given below.

    Priority 1: Meet a state contract of 200 CP286 machines
                weekly. (Goal 1)
    Priority 2: Make at least 500 total computers weekly. (Goal 2)
    Priority 3: Make at least $250,000 weekly. (Goal 3)
    Priority 4: Use no more than 400 man-hours per week. (Goal 4)

a) Formulate this problem as a goal program.

b) Solve graphically for the solution that best meets the goals
   of Conceptual Products as stated above.

c) Suppose Conceptual Products combined goals 3 and 4 into one
   priority level -- Priority 3. What would be the
   recommendation under the following conditions:
     (1) Each goal was equally desirable.
     (2) Each $1000 underachieved from its profit goal was three
         times as important as an extra man-hour.
     (3) Each $1000 underachieved from its profit goal was five
         times as important as an extra man-hour.

SOLUTION 1

a) Define Variables
X_1 = the number of CP286 computers produced weekly
X_2 = the number of CP386 computers produced weekly

Functional Constraints
Availability of floppy disk drives: $2X_1 + X_2 \leq 1000$

Availability of hard disk drives: $X_2 \leq 500$

Availability of cases: $X_1 + X_2 \leq 600$

Goals
Define: d_j^- as the amount the right hand side of goal j is
              deficient
          d_j^+ as the amount the right hand side of goal j is
              exceeded

(1) 200 CP286 computers weekly:
$$X_1 + d_1^- - d_1^+ = 200$$

(2) 500 total computers weekly:
$$X_1 + X_2 + d_2^- - d_2^+ = 500$$

(3) Profit in $1000's to be $250 (thousand):
$$.2X_1 + .5X_2 + d_3^- - d_3^+ = 250$$

(4) 400 total man-hours weekly:
$$X_1 + 1.5X_2 + d_4^- - d_4^+ = 400$$

Non-negativity
X_1, X_2, d_j^-, $d_j^+ \geq 0$ for all j

Objective Functions
Priority 1: Minimize the amount the state contract is not
            met: MIN d_1^-

Priority 2: Minimize the number under 500 computers produced
            weekly: MIN d_2^-

Priority 3: Minimize the amount under $250,000 earned weekly:
            MIN d_3^-

Priority 4: Minimize the man-hours over 400 used weekly:
             MIN d_4^+

Summary
Using the notation P_j to denote the priority level of the
objective functions, the problem becomes:

$$\text{MIN} \quad P_1(d_1^-) + P_2(d_2^-) + P_3(d_3^-) + P_4(d_4^+)$$

$$
\begin{array}{llll}
\text{S.T.} & 2X_1 & +X_2 & & & \leq 1000 \\
& & +X_2 & & & \leq 500 \\
& X_1 & +X_2 & & & \leq 600 \\
& X_1 & & +d_1^- -d_1^+ & & = 200 \\
& X_1 & +X_2 & +d_2^- -d_2^+ & & = 500 \\
& .2X_1 & +.5X_2 & & +d_3^- -d_3^+ & = 250 \\
& X_1 & +1.5X_2 & & +d_4^- -d_4^+ & = 400 \\
\end{array}
$$

$$X_1, \ X_2, \ d_1^-, \ d_1^+, \ d_2^-, \ d_2^+, \ d_3^-, \ d_3^+, \ d_4^-, \ d_4^+ \geq 0$$

b) To solve graphically, first graph the functional constraints as below. Then graph the first goal: $X_1 = 200$ and note that there is a set of points that exceeds $X_1 = 200$, i.e. where $d_1^- = 0$.

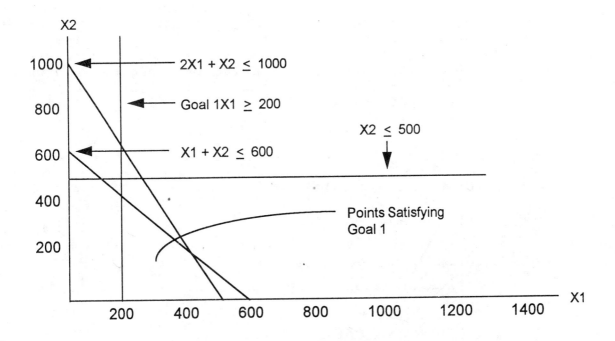

Now add goal 1 as $X_1 \geq 200$ and graph goal 2: $X_1 + X_2 = 500$ as below. Note there is still a set of points satisfying the first goal that also satisfies this second goal, i.e. where $d_2^- = 0$.

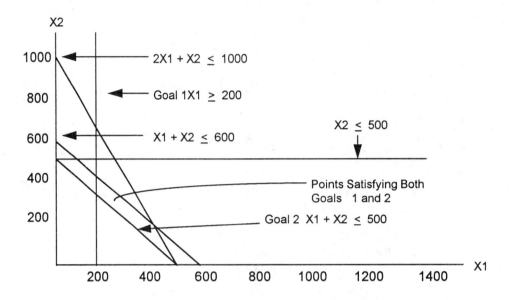

Now add goal 2 as: $X_1 + X_2 \geq 500$, and graph goal 3: $.2X_1 + .5X_2 = 250$. Note that no points satisfy the previous functional constraints and goals as well as this constraint. Thus to MIN d_3^-, this minimum value is achieved when we MAX $.2X1 + .5X2$. We note that this occurs at $X_1 = 200$, $X_2 = 400$, so that $.2X_1 + .5X_2 = 240$ or $d_3^- = 10$.

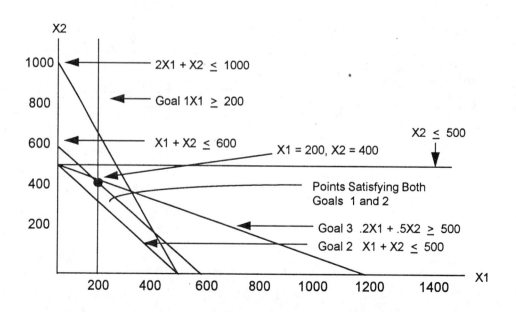

Since this is the only point the meets goal three with only a $10(thousand) deficiency, priority 4's objective becomes irrelevant. This is because if we add the constraint: $.2X_1 + .5X_2 = 240$, there is only one feasible point. This is our recommendation of $X_1 = 200$, $X_2 = 400$. Thus the recommendations is to make 200 CP286 computers and 400 CP386 computers weekly.

c) The first two priorities were met by a set of points and it was shown that there was no point that met the first two goals and goal 3. Similarly, by looking at the top graph on the previous page, it is seen that there are no points that meet the first two priorities and goal 4.

 Since both will not be achieved,

$$d_3^- = 250 - .2X_1 - .5X_2$$

$$d_4^+ = X_1 + 1.5X_2 - 400.$$

Case (1): MIN $d_3^- + d_4^+$ = MIN $.8X_1 + X_2 - 150$

Case (2): MIN $3d_3^- + d_4^+$ = MIN $.4X_1 + 350$

Case (3): MIN $5d_3^- + d_4^+$ = MIN $-X_2 + 850$

Ignoring the constant in each of the above, it can be seen in the next three graphs that Case (i) is minimized at $X_1 = 500$, $X_2 = 0$; Case (ii) is minimized by all points on the line $X_1 = 200$ between $X_2 = 300$ and $X_2 = 400$; and, Case (iii) is minimized where X_2 takes on its maximum value, i.e. at $X_1 = 200$, $X_2 = 400$.

CASE (1)

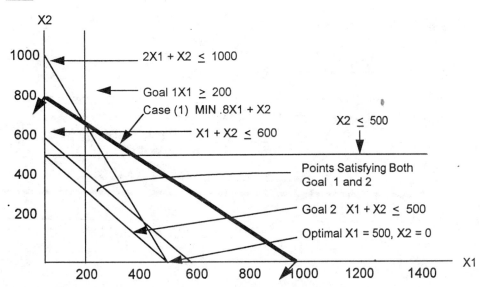

CASE (2)

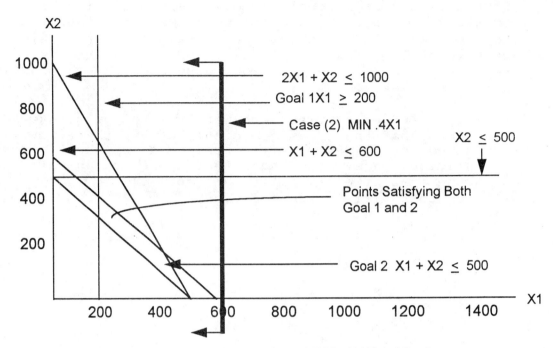

Line between (200, 300) and (200, 400) is optimal

CASE (3)

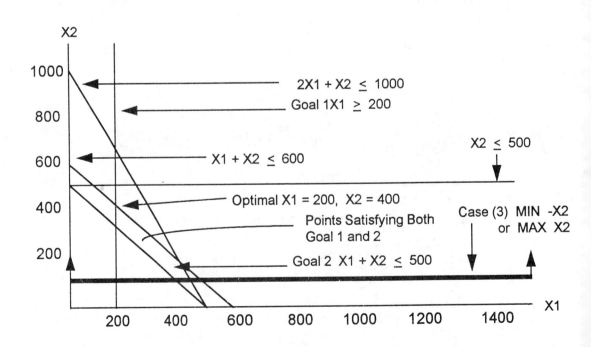

PROBLEM 2

Suppose in problem 1, Conceptual Products made a third computer, the CP486 which requires two floppy disks and a hard disk. It takes two hours to manufacture and the profit is $900. Use a computer program such as the Management Scientist to solve the goal program of Case (3) in part (c) of problem 1.

SOLUTION 2

The goal programming formulation is now:

$$\text{MIN } P_1(d_1^-) + P_2(d_2^-) + P_3(5d_3^-) + P_3(d_4^+)$$

$$
\begin{array}{lll}
\text{S.T.} \quad 2X_1 \ +X_2 \ +X_3 & \leq 1000 & \text{(floppy disks)} \\
X_2 \ +X_3 & \leq 500 & \text{(hard disks)} \\
X_1 \ +X_2 \ +X_3 & \leq 600 & \text{(cases)}
\end{array}
$$

Priority 1: $X_1 \qquad\qquad + d_1^- \ -d_1^+ = 200$ (Goal 1: contract)

Priority 2: $X_1 \ +X_2 \ +X_3 +d_2^- \ -d_2^+ = 500$ (Goal 2: total)

Priority 3: $.2X_1 +.5X_2 +.9X_3 +d_3^- \ -d_3^+ = 250$ (Goal 3: profit)
$\ X_1 +1.5X_2 + 2X_3 +d_4^- \ -d_4^+ = 400$ (Goal 4: man-hours)

$$X_j, \ d_j^-, \ d_j^+ \geq 0 \quad \text{for all } j$$

Priority 1 Program

The following was input into the MANAGEMENT SCIENTIST:

```
    MIN D1MINUS

    S.T.  2X1 +   X2 +   X3                              <  1000

               X2 +   X3                                 <   500

         X1 +   X2 +   X3                                <   600

         X1                    + D1MINUS - D1PLUS =  200

         X1 +   X2 +   X3 + D2MINUS - D2PLUS =  500

        .2X1 + .5X2 + .9X3 + D3MINUS - D3PLUS =  250

         X1 + 1.5X2 +  2X3 + D4MINUS - D4PLUS =  400
```

The following output was attained:

OBJECTIVE FUNCTION VALUE =   0.000

VARIABLE	VALUE	REDUCED COSTS
X1	200.000	0.000
X2	0.000	0.000
X3	233.333	0.000
D1MINUS	0.000	1.000
D1PLUS	0.000	0.000
D2MINUS	66.667	0.000
D2PLUS	0.000	0.000
D3MINUS	0.000	0.000
D3PLUS	0.000	0.000
D4MINUS	0.000	0.000
D4PLUS	266.667	0.000

Thus the priority 1 objective is met since the value of the
objective function, D1MINUS = 0. For the priority 2 problem,
add to the constraints on the previous page a constraint
requiring the priority 1 objective to be maintained at 0:
D1MINUS = 0, _and_ change the objective to the priority 2
objective MIN D2MINUS.

The following output is generated:

OBJECTIVE FUNCTION VALUE =   0.000

VARIABLE	VALUE	REDUCED COSTS
X1	285.714	0.000
X2	0.000	0.000
X3	214.286	0.000
D1MINUS	0.000	0.000
D1PLUS	85.714	0.000
D2MINUS	0.000	1.000
D2PLUS	0.000	0.000
D3MINUS	0.000	0.000
D3PLUS	0.000	0.000
D4MINUS	0.000	0.000
D4PLUS	314.286	0.000

Thus the priority 2 objective is met since the value of the
objective function, D2MINUS = 0. For the priority 3 problem,
add to the previous constraints, a constraint requiring that the
priority 2 objective to be maintained at 0: D2MINUS = 0, _and_
change the objective to the priority 3 objective:

        MIN 5 D3MINUS + D4PLUS.

The following output is generated:

OBJECTIVE FUNCTION VALUE =   314.286

VARIABLE	VALUE	REDUCED COSTS
X1	285.714	0.000
X2	0.000	0.071
X3	214.286	0.000
D1MINUS	0.000	0.000
D1PLUS	85.714	0.000
D2MINUS	0.000	0.000
D2PLUS	0.000	0.714
D3MINUS	0.000	3.571
D3PLUS	0.000	1.429
D4MINUS	0.000	1.000
D4PLUS	314.286	0.000

Thus the optimal recommendation is to produce 285.714286 CP286
computers weekly and 214.285714 CP486 computers weekly. All
goals will be met except goal 4. 314.285714 extra man-hours or
a total of 714.285714 man-hours will be used.

PROBLEM 3

The campaign headquarters of Jerry Black, a candidate for the Board of Supervisors, has 100 volunteers. With one week to go in the election, there are three major strategies remaining: media advertising, door-to-door canvassing, and telephone campaigning. It is estimated that each phone call will take approximately four minutes and each door-to-door personal contact will average seven minutes. These times include time between contacts for breaks, transportation, dialing, etc. Volunteers who work on advertising will not be able to handle any other duties. Each ad will utilize the talents of three workers for the entire week.

Volunteers are expected to work 12 hours per day during the final seven days of the campaign. At a minimum, Jerry Black feels he needs 30,000 phone contacts, 20,000 personal contacts, and three advertisements during the last week. However, he would like to see 50,000 phone contacts and 50,000 personal contacts made and five advertisements developed. It is felt that advertising is 50 times as important as personal contacts which in turn is twice as important as phone contacts.

Formulate this problem as a goal program with a single weighted priority to determine how the work should be distributed during the final week of the campaign.

SOLUTION 3

Define variables

X_1 = number of volunteers doing phone work during the week
X_2 = number of volunteers making personal contacts during week
X_3 = number of volunteers preparing advertising during the week

Define goals

1) 50,000 phone contacts:
  d_1^+ and d_1^- = the amount this quantity is overachieved and underachieved, respectively
2) 50,000 personal contacts:
  d_2^+ and d_2^- = the amount this quantity is overachieved and underachieved, respectively
3) 5 advertisements:
  d_3^+ and d_3^- = the amount this quantity is overachieved and underachieved respectively

Define objective

It would not hurt Jerry Black if his goals were exceeded, however since the importance of his goals are in the ratio 1:2:100, the goal programming objective function would be:

$$\text{MIN} \quad d_1^- + 2d_2^- + 100d_3^-$$

Define Constraints

There are (7 days)x(12 hours per day)x(60 minutes per hour) = 5040 minutes per worker. Thus a phone worker could make 5040/4 = 1260 phone calls in the week. And a door-to-door canvasser could make 5040/7 = 720 personal contacts during the week.

Linear Programming Constraints

1) At least 30,000 phone contacts: $1260 X_1 \geq 30,000$

2) At least 20,000 personal contacts: $720 X_2 \geq 20,000$

3) At least 3 advertisements: $1/3 X_3 \geq 3$

4) 100 volunteers: $X_1 + X_2 + X_3 = 100$

Goal Constraints

5) Make 50,000 phone contacts: $1260X_1 - d_1^+ + d_1^- = 50,000$

6) Make 50,000 personal contacts: $720X_2 - d_2^+ + d_2^- = 50,000$

7) Design 5 advertisements: $(1/3) X_3 - d_3^+ + d_3^- = 5$

Non-negativity of Variables

$$X_1, X_2, X_3, d_1^+, d_1^-, d_2^+, d_2^-, d_3^+, d_3^- \geq 0$$

PROBLEM 4

Designer Gill Glass must decide which of three manufacturers will develop his "signature" toothbrushes. Three factors seem important to Gill: (1) his costs; (2) reliability of the product; and, (3) delivery time of the orders.

The three manufacturers are Cornell Industries, Brush Pik, and Picobuy. Cornell Industries will sell toothbrushes to Gill Glass for $100 per gross, Brush Pik for $80 per gross, and Picobuy for $144 per gross. Gill has decided that in terms of price, Brush Pik is moderately preferred to Cornell and very strongly preferred to Picobuy. In turn Cornell is strongly to very strongly preferred to Picobuy.

a) Form the pairwise comparison matrix for cost.

b) Calculate the normalized matrix for cost.

c) Determine the priority vector for cost.

d) Are Gill Glass's responses to cost consistent? Explain.

SOLUTION 4

a) Since Brush Pik is moderately preferred to Cornell, Cornell's entry in the Brush Pik row is 3 and Brush Pik's entry in the Cornell row is 1/3.

Since Brush Pik is very strongly preferred to Picobuy, Picobuy's entry in the Brush Pik row is 7 and Brush Pik's entry in the Picobuy row is 1/7.

Since Cornell is strongly to very strongly preferred to Picobuy, Picobuy's entry in the Cornell row is 6 and Cornell's entry in the Picobuy row is 1/6.

All diagonal entries are 1. Hence:

Pairwise comparison matrix for cost

	Cornell	Brush Pik	Picobuy
Cornell	1	1/3	6
Brush Pik	3	1	7
Picobuy	1/6	1/7	1

b) To determine normalized matrix, divide each entry in the matrix by its corresponding column sum. For Cornell the column sum = 1 + 3 + 1/6 = 25/6. For Brush Pik the column sum is 1/3 + 1 + 1/7 = 31/21. For Picobuy the column sum is 6 + 7 + 1 = 14. This gives:

Normalized matrix for cost

	Cornell	Brush Pik	Picobuy
Cornell	6/25	7/31	6/14
Brush Pik	18/25	21/31	7/14
Picobuy	1/25	3/31	1/14

c) The priority vector is determined by averaging the row entries in the normalized matrix. Converting to decimals we get:

Priority vector for cost

$$
\begin{array}{lll}
\text{Cornell:} & (\ 6/25\ +\ \ 7/31\ +\ 6/14)/3\ = & .298 \\
\text{Brush Pik:} & (18/25\ +\ 21/31\ +\ 7/14)/3\ = & .632 \\
\text{Picobuy:} & (\ 1/25\ +\ \ 3/31\ +\ 1/14)/3\ = & .069
\end{array}
$$

d) To check consistency,

(1) Multiply each column of the pairwise comparison matrix by its priority:

$$
.298 \begin{bmatrix} 1 \\ 3 \\ 1/6 \end{bmatrix} + .632 \begin{bmatrix} 1/3 \\ 1 \\ 1/7 \end{bmatrix} + .069 \begin{bmatrix} 6 \\ 7 \\ 1 \end{bmatrix} = \begin{bmatrix} .923 \\ 2.009 \\ .209 \end{bmatrix}
$$

(2) Divide these number by their priorities to get:

$$
\begin{array}{lll}
.923/.298 & = & 3.097 \\
2.009/.632 & = & 3.179 \\
.209/.069 & = & 3.029
\end{array}
$$

(3) Average the above results to get λ_{max}.

$$\lambda_{max} = (3.097 + 3.179 + 3.029)/3 = 3.102$$

(4) Compute the consistence index, CI, for two terms by:

$$CI = (\lambda_{max} - n)/(n - 1) = (3.102 - 3)/2 = .051.$$

(5) Compute the consistency ratio, CR, by CI/RI, where RI = .58 for 3 factors:

$$CR = CI/RI = .051/.58 = .088$$

Since the consistency ratio, CR, is less than .10, this is well within the acceptable range for consistency.

PROBLEM 5

Referring to problem (4), Gill Glass has determined that for reliability, Cornell is very strongly preferable to Brush Pik and equally to moderately preferable to Picobuy. Also, Picobuy is strongly preferable to Brush Pik.
   Regarding delivery time, Cornell is equally preferred with Picobuy and both very strongly to extremely preferable to Brush Pik.

a) Construct pairwise comparison matrices for reliability and for delivery time.

b) Construct priority vectors for reliability and delivery time.

SOLUTION 5

a) Pairwise comparison matrix for reliability

	Cornell	Brush Pik	Picobuy
Cornell	1	7	2
Brush Pik	1/7	1	5
Picobuy	1/2	1/5	1

Pairwise comparison matrix for delivery time

	Cornell	Brush Pik	Picobuy
Cornell	1	8	1
Brush Pik	1/8	1	1/8
Picobuy	1	8	1

b) For reliability the column sums are 23/14, 41/5, and 8. Dividing each entry by its corresponding column sum, we get:

Normalized matrix for reliability

	Cornell	Brush Pik	Picobuy
Cornell	14/23	35/41	2/8
Brush Pik	2/23	5/41	5/8
Picobuy	7/23	1/41	1/8

Priority vector for reliability

        Cornell: (14/23 + 35/41 + 2/8)/3   = ⎡ .571 ⎤
     Brush Pik: (2/23 +   5/41 + 5/8)/3   = ⎢ .278 ⎥
      Picobuy: (7/23 +   1/41 + 1/8)/3   = ⎣ .151 ⎦

For delivery time the column sums are 17/8, 17, and 17/8
respectively. Dividing each entry by its corresponding
column sum gives:

Normalized matrix for delivery time

	Cornell	Brush Pik	Picobuy
Cornell	8/17	8/17	8/17
Brush Pik	1/17	1/17	1/17
Picobuy	8/17	8/17	8/17

Priority vector for delivery time

        Cornell: (8/17 + 8/17 + 8/17)/3   = ⎡ .471 ⎤
     Brush Pik: (1/17 + 1/17 + 1/17)/3   = ⎢ .059 ⎥
      Picobuy: (8/17 + 8/17 + 8/17)/3   = ⎣ .471 ⎦

PROBLEM 6

The accounting department at Gill Glass (problems (4) and (5)) has determined that in terms of criteria, cost is extremely preferred to delivery time and very strongly preferred to reliability, and that reliability is very strongly preferred to delivery time.

a) Construct a pairwise comparison matrix for the criteria.

b) Construct a normalized pairwise matrix for the criteria.

c) Determine a priority vector for the criteria.

d) Determine an overall priority vector for the decision alternatives based on the criteria of the accounting dept.

SOLUTION 6

a) Pairwise comparison matrix for criteria

	Cost	Reliability	Delivery
Cost	1	7	9
Reliability	1/7	1	7
Delivery	1/9	1/7	1

b) The column sums are 79/63, 57/7, and 17 respectively. Dividing each entry by its corresponding column sum gives:

Normalized matrix for criteria

	Cost	Reliability	Delivery
Cost	63/79	49/57	9/17
Reliability	9/79	7/57	7/17
Delivery	7/79	1/57	1/17

c) Average the rows of the normalized matrix to get:

Priority vector for criteria

$$
\begin{array}{lll}
\text{Cost:} & (73/79 + 49/57 + 9/17)/3 & = \\
\text{Reliability:} & (\ 9/79 + \ 7/57 + 7/17)/3 & = \\
\text{Delivery time:} & (\ 7/79 + \ 1/57 + 1/17)/3 & =
\end{array}
\begin{bmatrix} .729 \\ .216 \\ .055 \end{bmatrix}
$$

d) The overall priorities are determined by multiplying the priority vector of the criteria by the priorities for each decision alternative for each objective:

```
Priority Vector
for criteria -> [ .729         .216         .055 ]
                   Cost     Reliability   Delivery
```

	Cost	Reliability	Delivery
Cornell	.298	.571	.471
Brush Pik	.632	.278	.059
Picobuy	.069	.151	.471

(Priority Matrix)

Thus the overall priority vector is:

Cornell: $(.729)(.298) + (.216)(.571) + (.055)(.471) = \begin{bmatrix} .366 \\ .524 \\ .109 \end{bmatrix}$
Brush Pik:$(.729)(.632) + (.216)(.278) + (.055)(.059) = $
Picobuy: $(.729)(.069) + (.216)(.151) + (.055)(.471) = $

Thus, Brush Pik appears to be the overall recommendation.

PROBLEM 7

A student has one quantitative elective left to select to
complete his graduation requirements. The two quantitative
electives that are available are an advanced management science
class (MS) and an advanced statistics class (STAT). Two factors
which are important to the student in his selection process are
relevance (R) and difficulty (D). The student formulated the
following pairwise consistency matrices:

Criteria	R	D		Relevance	MS	STAT		Difficulty	MS	STAT
R	1	1/3		MS	1	1/3		MS	1	5
D	3	1		STAT	3	1		STAT	1/5	1

a) Draw the hierarchy for this decision problem.

b) Compute the priorities for each of the pairwise comparison
   matrices.

c) Determine an overall priority for the course selection
   process.

SOLUTION 7

a) First, list the overall goal: Select the best course.
   Then, list the evaluation criteria: Relevance, Difficulty.
   Last, list the alternatives: Management Science, Statistics.

b) Priority Vectors:

Relevance

The column sums are 4 and 4/3 respectively. Dividing the
entries by the column sums yields the following normalized
matrix:

	MS	STAT
MS	1/4	1/4
STAT	3/4	3/4

Averaging the rows gives the following priority vector for
relevance:

$$\text{MS} \begin{bmatrix} 1/4 \\ 3/4 \end{bmatrix}$$
$$\text{STAT}$$

<u>Difficulty</u>

The column sums are 6/5 and 6 respectively. Dividing the
entries by the column sums yields the following <u>normalized</u>
<u>matrix</u>:

	MS	STAT
MS	5/6	5/6
STAT	1/6	1/6

Averaging the rows gives the following <u>priority</u> <u>vector</u> for
difficulty:

$$\begin{array}{c} \text{MS} \\ \text{STAT} \end{array} \left[\begin{array}{c} 5/6 \\ 1/6 \end{array} \right]$$

<u>Criteria</u>

The column sums are 4 and 4/3 respectively. Dividing the
entries by the column sums yields the following <u>normalized</u>
<u>matrix</u>:

	Rel.	Dif.
Rel.	1	1/3
Dif.	3	1

Averaging the rows gives the following <u>priority</u> <u>vector</u> <u>for</u>
<u>criteria</u>:

$$\begin{array}{c} \text{Relevance} \\ \text{Difficulty} \end{array} \left[\begin{array}{c} 1/4 \\ 3/4 \end{array} \right]$$

c) Determine the overall priorities for MS and STAT by
multiplying their relevance and difficulty vectors by their
priority:

Priority vector
for criteria -->   [1/4   3/4]   <u>Overall</u>
                           Rel.   Dif.   <u>Priority</u>
                           Vector   Vector   <u>Vector</u>

	Rel. Vector	Dif. Vector	Overall Priority Vector
MS	1/4	5/6	11/16
STAT	3/4	1/6	5/16

(Priority Matrix)

ANSWERED PROBLEMS

PROBLEM 8

Alfax Industries is trying to promote a new product which it recently developed. It wishes to restrict advertising to television and radio ads. Television ads cost $50,000 each to produce and radio ads $15,000 each. Each television ad will require the use of three Alfax marketing employees and each radio ad will require one. There are 24 persons in the marketing department. Management requires a minimum of six total ads monthly.
   Alfax has set the following goals for the production of ads:
   (1) Do not exceed a monthly advertising budget of $250,000.
   (2) Do not use more than 50% of its marketing personnel on this project.
   (3) Produce at least 4 television ads monthly.
   (4) Produce at least 4 radio ads monthly.

a) Using the goals as simple constraints, formulate the constraint set for this problem and show it is infeasible.

b) Solve the above goal program graphically with four levels of priority.

c) Suppose goals (3) and (4) were within the same priority level but with the goal of producing at least 4 television ads monthly deemed twice as important as making 4 radio ads. Resolve this problem with three levels of priority.

PROBLEM 9

Barry College has received a $200,000 donation for its scholarship fund to be used for $3000 athletic scholarships, $2500 minority scholarships and $2000 women's scholarships. The donor, an avid sports fan, has stipulated at least 20 athletic scholarships must be awarded.
   The Board of Trustees of Barry College has three levels of priority for awarding the scholarships:
   (1) It would like at least 80 total scholarships.
   (2) It would like no more than 25% of the scholarships to be athletic scholarships.
   (3) It would like at least 25 athletic scholarships, 40 minority scholarships, and 30 women's scholarships. (Meeting the target for minorities is viewed as three times as important as meeting the target for athletes or women.)

Formulate a goal program for Barry College and solve by a computer package such as the Management Scientist.

PROBLEM 10

Universal Electric (UE) has facilities all over the United
States. Currently UE has 150,000 employees, 5,000 of which are
in management positions. The government contends that UE is
delinquent in its Affirmative Action policies and will take
action if UE does not rectify the situation.

Although UE currently has 12,000 minority employees (8% of its
total), only 50 are in management positions (or 1% of the
management positions). UE has submitted a plan to the federal
government which expresses that UE has a target of 20% minority
employees by the end of the year. In negotiating with various
minority groups, UE has promised that by the end of the year, at
least 10% of its management positions will be held by
minorities.

Attrition rates of all employees (both management and otherwise) are 8% for non-minorities, 4% for minorities. Because of
a good year, UE will create 6,000 new positions, 200 of which
will be in management. However, the mandate from the top is
that it would be unwise from a community relations point of
view, if more than 2/3 of the new employee positions and more
than 2/3 of the promotions to management positions be
minorities.

Assume all management positions will be filled in-house and
hence all hiring will be for non-management positions. Further
assume violations of the company mandate have the same weight as
not meeting the goal of 10% minority management positions.
However, not meeting federal standards is considered three times
more serious. Formulate this problem as a goal programming
problem with a single weighted priority.

PROBLEM 11

Consider a beauty pageant in which there are three finalists. They are to be judged on (1) evening gown; (2) swim suit; and, (3) answering a corny question posed by an equally corny MC. The three finalists are Miss Northern State, Miss Central State, and Miss Southern State.

It is known that Judge Jones believes that swim suit is strongly more important than evening gown appearance and extremely more important than answering the question. Further, he feels that the evening gown appearance is very strongly more important than answering the question.

In the evening gown competition, Miss Central State performed very strongly compared to Miss Southern State and strongly compared to Miss Northern State. Miss Northern State compared equally to moderately more strongly than Miss Southern State.

In the swim suit competition, Miss Southern State was extremely preferred to both Miss Northern State or Miss Central State and Miss Northern State was moderately preferred to Miss Central State.

In the question competition, Miss Northern State was extremely preferred to Miss Southern State and strongly preferred to Miss Central State. Miss Central State was moderately preferred to Miss Southern State.

Judge Jones has 100 points to distribute among the three finalists. Using his observations and preferences, how should he divide his 100 points between the three finalists?

PROBLEM 12

The Drezners have a choice of three neighborhood supermarkets:
Gamma Delta, Bill's, and Hewes. Five factors are important to
the Drezners: (1) Location; (2) Overall Prices; (3)
Cleanliness; (4) Ease of Parking; and, (5) Selection/Quality.
The pairwise comparison matrices have been determined below:

Location:

	GD	B	H
GD	1	1/2	4
B	2	1	3
H	1/4	1/3	1

Overall Prices:

	GD	B	H
GD	1	3	3
B	1/3	1	2
H	1/3	1/2	1

Cleanliness:

	GD	B	H
GD	1	1/3	1/4
B	3	1	1/2
H	4	2	1

Ease of Parking:

	GD	B	H
GD	1	1/4	1/5
B	4	1	4
H	5	1/4	1

Selection/Quality:

	GD	B	H
GD	1	1/5	1/3
B	5	1	7
H	3	1/7	1

a) Determine the priority vector for each of the criteria.

b) If all five criteria were equally important, what would be the overall supermarket priority vector.

Now assume the Drezners feel that:
  (1) Location and ease of parking have equal priority.
  (2) Overall price is moderately more important than cleanliness or selection, and is very strongly more important than location or ease of parking.
  (3) Cleanliness is strongly more important than ease of parking, very strongly more important than location, and moderately more important than selection.
  (4) Selection/quality are moderately more important than location and very strongly more important than parking.

c) Given these preferences, construct a criteria pairwise comparison matrix.

d) Calculate the consistency ratio for the criteria and comment.

e) Determine the overall priority vector for the Drezners.

PROBLEM 13

Abraham L. Ford is a lifelong Republican who has a dilemma in the upcoming election. In general, Mr. Ford very strongly prefers Republicans over Democrats and strongly prefers Republicans over Independents. He moderately favors Independents over Democrats.

However, in the upcoming election, on the issues he strongly to very strongly favors Democrat Fritz Carter over Republican Ron Nixon and strongly favors Fritz Carter over Independent George Anderson. He moderately favors Anderson over Nixon. He has decided that issues are moderately to strongly more important to him than party.

a) Determine the hierarchy for this problem.

b) Determine the pairwise comparison matrix for each alternative.

c) Determine the priority vector for the alternatives for each criterion.

d) Determine the consistency ratio for the issues criterion.

e) Determine a priority vector for the criteria.

f) Determine Mr. Ford's overall priority vector for the candidates.

PROBLEM 14

Terry's Trucking is trying to determine which database package to purchase for its microcomputer. It has narrowed its choices to BASE 8 and DATA RECORD. BASE 8 is very strongly to extremely preferred in price, but DATA RECORD is strongly to very strongly preferred for ease of use.

a) Determine the hierarchy for Terry's Trucking's decision.

b) Construct the pairwise comparison matrix for each criterion.

c) Determine the priority vector for the alternatives for each criterion.

d) Determine the overall priority vector if:
   (1) price is extremely preferred to ease of use; or if
   (2) ease of use is extremely preferred to price; or if
   (3) price and ease of use are equally preferred.

e) Approximately what relation between price and ease of use would give BASE 8 and DATA RECORD equal priority in an overall priority vector.

PROBLEM 15

Consider the following military application regarding the so called "star wars" or "strategic defense initiative". The overall goal is to maintain peace.
  The criteria are: (1) strong defense; (2) international image; (3) U.S. - Soviet relations.
  The decision alternatives are: (1) continue with "star wars" development; (2) scale down "star wars" development; (3) abandon "star wars" development.

a) Make up your own preferences and feelings regarding the criteria and alternatives. Determine an overall priority vector of the alternatives.

b) Comment on a possible limitation of this model with regard to the scale used for the pairwise comparison matrices.

TRUE/FALSE

16. A goal programming problem will always have more than one priority level.

17. The number of linear programs that must be sequentially solved to develop the solution to a goal program is determined by the number of goals in the objective function.

18. For each goal in a goal program, two variables are added: one for underachieving the goal and one for overachieving the goal.

19. It is not possible to have two penalties for the same goal, one for underachieving the goal and another for overachieving it.

20. For a particular goal program, the Phase 1 objective function was Minimize d_1^+. The objective was not satisfied but underachieved by an amount of 50. Any solution to the Phase 2 problem of Minimize d_2^- must have $d_1^+ = 50$.

21. In the process of satisfying second-priority goals, improvement in the satisfaction of first-priority goals sometimes occurs.

22. Trade-offs among goals at the same priority level will not occur unless the goals have the same relative weight.

23. In the analytic hierarchy process, if the entry in row A for decision B is 2, the entry in row B for decision A is 1/2.

24. In the analytic hierarchy process, a consistency ratio of .99 is extremely good.

25. If the consistency index is .90, the consistency ratio is .90.

26. The analytic hierarchy process utilizes pairwise comparisons to establish priority measures for both the criteria and the decision alternatives.

27. The criteria priority vector for gum is: Price: .3, Taste: .7. For Price, BRAND A's priority is .8 and BRAND B's is .2. For Taste, BRAND A's priority is .4 and BRAND B's is .6. Overall BRAND A has a higher priority than BRAND B.

28. On the 1-to-9 pairwise comparison scale, a numerical rating of 9 means extremely preferred and 5 means equally preferred.

29. In the analylic hierarchy process, the hierarchy from top to bottom is overall goal, decision alternatives, and criteria.

30. A consistency ratio measures the consistency of a decision alternative's relative rank from one criterion to another.

CHAPTER

16
Forecasting

KEY CONCEPTS

CONCEPT	ILLUSTRATED PROBLEMS	ANSWERED PROBLEMS
Moving Average	1	8
Weighted Moving Average	2	5
Exponential Smoothing	1	5,6
Linear Trend Projection	2	9,11
Multiplicative Time Series Model	3,4	7,10,12
Mean Squared Error	1	5,6,8

REVIEW

1. A time series is a set of observations measured at successive points in time or over successive periods of time. A time series is analyzed so that one may determine good forecasts or predictions of future values for the time series.

2. While a time series may consist of numerous components, a usual assumption is that four separate components combine to affect the values of a time series. These four components are: (1) a trend component; (2) a cyclical component; (3) a seasonal component; and, (4) irregular components.

3. The trend component accounts for the gradual shifting of the time series over a long period of time.

4. Any regular pattern of sequences of values above and below the trend line is attributable to the cyclical component of the series.

5. The seasonal component of the series accounts for regular patterns of variability within certain time periods, such as over a year.

6. The irregular component of the series is caused by short-term, unanticipated and non-recurring factors that affect the values of the time series. One cannot attempt to predict its impact on the time series in advance.

7. In cases in which the time series is fairly stable and has no significant trend, seasonal, or cyclical effects, one can use smoothing methods to average out the irregular components of the time series.

8. The moving average smoothing method consists of computing an average of the most recent n data values for the series and using this average for forecasting the value of the time series for the next period.

9. The centered moving average method consists of computing an average of n periods' data and associating it with the midpoint of the periods. For example, the average for periods 5, 6, and 7 is associated with period 6. This methodology is useful in the process of computing season indexes.

10. In the weighted moving average smoothing method for computing the average of the most recent n periods, the more recent observations are typically given more weight than older observations. (For convenience, the weights usually sum to 1.)

11. One difficulty of both the moving average and the weighted moving average methods is that n historical data points must be stored in order to compute the forecast for the next period. In _exponential_ _smoothing_ only two pieces of information are needed to compute the forecast: (1) the forecasted value for the current period, and (2) the actual value for the current period.

12. Using _exponential_ _smoothing_, the forecast is calculated by:
    a[the actual value for the current period] +
    $(1-a)$[the forecasted value for the current period],
    where the _smoothing_ _constant_, a, is a number between 0 and 1.

13. Another way to view _exponential_ _smoothing_ is that the forecast for the next period is equal to the forecast for the current period plus a proportion (a) of the forecast error in the current period.

14. It is essential that forecasts be as accurate as possible. One measure of _forecast_ _accuracy_ is known as the _mean_ _squared_ _error_. In this measure the average of the squared forecast errors for the historical data is calculated. The forecasting method or parameter(s) which minimize this mean squared error is then selected.

15. An alternative measure for the performance of a forecasting technique is the _mean_ _absolute_ _deviation_. In this measure, the mean of the absolute values of all forecast errors is calculated, and the forecasting method or parameter(s) which minimize this measure is selected. The mean absolute deviation measure is less sensitive to individual large forecast errors than the mean squared error measure.

16. If a time series exhibits a linear trend, the _method_ _of_ _least_ _squares_ may be used to determine a trend line (projection) for future forecasts. This statistical technique, also used in regression analysis, determines the unique trend line forecast which minimizes the mean square error between the trend line forecasts and the actual observed values for the time series.

17. Using the method of least squares, the formula for the _trend_ _projection_ is: $T_t = b_0 + b_1 t$.

    Here, T_t = the trend forecast for time period t
          b_1 = the slope of the trend line
          b_0 = the trend line projection for time 0

    The formulas for b_1 and b_0 are:

$$b_1 = \frac{n\Sigma t Y_t - \Sigma t \Sigma Y_t}{n\Sigma t^2 - (\Sigma t)^2} \qquad b_0 = \bar{Y} - b_1 \bar{t}$$

Here,

Y_t = the observed value of the time series at time period t

$\bar{Y}$ = the average of the observed values for Y_t

$\bar{t}$ = the average time period for the n observations

18. In the case of <u>nonlinear</u> <u>trend</u>, a more advanced statistical technique might possibly be used to develop the forecasting curve.

19. The <u>multiplicative</u> <u>time</u> <u>series</u> <u>model</u> assumes that the actual time series value, Y_t, is equal to the product of the four time series components: (1) trend (T_t); (2) cyclical (C_t); (3) seasonal (S_t); and (4) irregular (I_t). Thus, $Y_t = T_t C_t S_t I_t$.

20. In situations in which no historical data is available or when historical data will not give an accurate picture of the future, <u>nonquantitative</u> <u>techniques</u> for forecasting may be used.

21. An example of a nonquantitative forecasting technique is the <u>delphi</u> <u>approach</u>. A panel of experts, each of whom is physically separated from the others and is anonymous, is asked to respond to a sequential series of questionnaires. After each questionnaire, the responses are tabulated and the information and opinions of the entire group are made known to each of the other panel members so that they may revise their previous forecast response. The process continues until some degree of consensus is achieved.

22. Another nonquantitative approach, <u>scenario</u> <u>writing</u>, consists of developing a conceptual scenario of the future based on a well defined set of assumptions. After several different scenarios have been developed, the decision maker determines which is most likely to occur in the future and makes decisions accordingly.

23. <u>Subjective</u> or <u>interactive</u> <u>qualitative</u> <u>approaches</u>, commonly known as "brainstorming sessions" are another way to perform a nonquantitative forecast. It is important in such sessions that any ideas or opinions be permitted to be presented without regard to its relevancy and without fear of criticism.

MULTIPLICATIVE TIME SERIES PROCEDURE

1. Calculate the centered moving averages (CMAs).
   The centered moving average represents the combined trend and
   cyclical components of the series. Calculate n-period moving
   averages (where n is the number of seasons, i.e. quarterly data
   would have four seasons whereas monthly data would have twelve
   seasons.)

2. Center the CMAs on integer-valued periods.
   Associate each moving average with the middle period of the n
   data points comprising the average. When n is an even number
   there is no distinct middle period. In this case, taking the
   average of two successive moving averages (one centered just
   above the period and one centered just below the period) gives
   the moving average associated with that period.

3. Determine the seasonal and irregular factors $(S_t I_t)$.
   For each centered moving average found in step 2, divide this
   value into the observed value, Y_t. This quotient represents the
   seasonal and irregular factors.

4. Determine the average seasonal factors.
   For each season, average the corresponding quotients found in
   step 3 to smooth out the irregular component and isolate the
   seasonal factors.

5. Scale the seasonal factors (S_t).
   To ensure that the seasonal factors average to 1, adjust the
   seasonal factors by dividing each by the average seasonal factor
   value.

6. Determine the deseasonalized data.
   Divide each data value, Y_t, by its seasonal factor.

7. Determine a trend line of the deseasonalized data.
   Use the method of least squares on this data set to identify the
   trend line for the data.

8. Determine the deseasonalized predictions.
   Determine the trend forecast(s) associated with the future
   period(s) by using the trend line equation found in step 7.

9. Take into account the seasonality.
   Multiply each deseasonalized prediction by the appropriate
   seasonal factor.

FLOW CHART OF
MULTIPLICATIVE TIME SERIES PROCEDURE

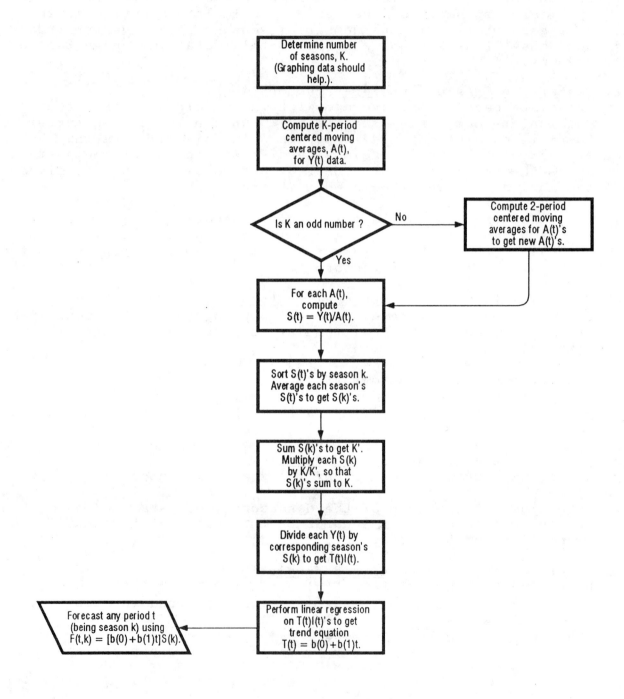

ILLUSTRATED PROBLEMS

PROBLEM 1

During the past ten weeks, sales of cases of Comfort brand headache medicine at Robert's Drugs have been as follows:

Week	Sales	Week	Sales
1	110	6	120
2	115	7	130
3	125	8	115
4	120	9	110
5	125	10	130

a) If Robert's uses exponential smoothing to forecast sales, which value for the smoothing constant a, $a = .1$ or $a = .8$, gives better forecasts?

b) Using your value for a in part (a) that gave better forecasts, forecast the sales for week 11.

c) Forecast sales in week 11 using a three week moving average.

SOLUTION 1

a) To evaluate the two smoothing constants, determine how the forecasted values would compare with the actual historical values in each case. Let

Y_t = actual sales in week t

F_t = forecasted sales in week t

For $a = .1$, $1 - a = .9$

$F_1 = Y_1 = 110.$ For other weeks,

$F_{t+1} = .1Y_t + .9F_t$

$$
\begin{aligned}
F_1 &&&&&&= 110 \\
F_2 &= .1Y_1 + .9F_1 &=& .1(110) + .9(110) &=& 110 \\
F_3 &= .1Y_2 + .9F_2 &=& .1(115) + .9(110) &=& 110.5 \\
F_4 &= .1Y_3 + .9F_3 &=& .1(125) + .9(110.5) &=& 111.95 \\
F_5 &= .1Y_4 + .9F_4 &=& .1(120) + .9(111.95) &=& 112.76 \\
F_6 &= .1Y_5 + .9F_5 &=& .1(125) + .9(112.76) &=& 113.98 \\
F_7 &= .1Y_6 + .9F_6 &=& .1(120) + .9(113.98) &=& 114.58 \\
F_8 &= .1Y_7 + .9F_7 &=& .1(130) + .9(114.58) &=& 116.12 \\
F_9 &= .1Y_8 + .9F_8 &=& .1(115) + .9(116.12) &=& 116.01 \\
F_{10} &= .1Y_9 + .9F_9 &=& .1(110) + .9(116.01) &=& 115.41
\end{aligned}
$$

For $a = .8$, $1 - a = .2$

$$F_1 = 110$$
$$F_2 = .8(110) + .2(110) = 110$$
$$F_3 = .8(115) + .2(110) = 114$$
$$F_4 = .8(125) + .2(114) = 122.80$$
$$F_5 = .8(120) + .2(122.80) = 120.56$$
$$F_6 = .8(125) + .2(120.56) = 124.11$$
$$F_7 = .8(120) + .2(124.11) = 120.82$$
$$F_8 = .8(130) + .2(120.82) = 128.16$$
$$F_9 = .8(115) + .2(128.16) = 117.63$$
$$F_{10} = .8(110) + .2(117.63) = 111.53.$$

In order to determine which smoothing constant gives the better performance, calculate, for each, the mean squared error for the nine weeks of forecasts, weeks 2 through 10 by:

$$[(Y_2 - F_2)^2 + (Y_3 - F_3)^2 + (Y_4 - F_4)^2 + \ldots + (Y_{10} - F_{10})^2] / 9$$

Week	Y_t	$a = .1$		$a = .8$	
		F_t	$(Y_t - F_t)^2$	F_t	$(Y_t - F_t)^2$
1	110				
2	115	110.00	25.00	110.00	25.00
3	125	110.50	210.25	114.00	121.00
4	120	111.95	64.80	122.80	7.84
5	125	112.76	149.94	120.56	19.71
6	120	113.98	36.25	124.11	16.91
7	130	114.58	237.73	120.82	84.23
8	115	116.12	1.26	128.16	173.30
9	110	116.01	36.12	117.63	58.26
10	130	115.41	212.87	111.53	341.27
		Sum	974.22	Sum	847.52
MSE		Sum/9	108.25	Sum/9	94.17

Hence, based on the mean squared error criterion, using $a = .8$ gives a slightly better forecast than using $a = .1$.

b) If $a = .8$, then the forecast for week 11 will be
   $.8Y_{10} + .2F_{10} = .8(130) + .2(111.53) = 126.31$.

c) Using a three week moving average, the forecast for week 11 will be the average of the preceding three weeks: weeks 8, 9, and 10.

   $$F_{11} = (115 + 110 + 130)/3 = 118.33$$

PROBLEM 2

The number of plumbing repair jobs performed by Auger's Plumbing Service in each of the last nine months are listed below.

Month	Jobs	Month	Jobs	Month	Jobs
March	353	June	374	September	399
April	387	July	396	October	412
May	342	August	409	November	408

a) Assuming a linear trend function, forecast the number of repair jobs Auger's will perform in December using the squares method.

b) What is your forecast for December using a three-period weighted moving average with weights of .6, .3, and .1? How does it compare with your forecast from part (a)?

SOLUTION 2

> **NOTE:** The method of least squares requires time periods to be numbered. If your periods are labeled with words (e.g. February or Thursday) or the number labels are large (e.g. 1983), simply assign the first period in your data set the number 1, etc. Determine the number of the time period you want to forecast accordingly. For example, if 1983 is period 1, then 1998 is period 16.

a) The trend line is $T_t = b_0 + b_1 t$.
The least squares method gives:

t	Y_t	tY_t	t^2
(Mar.) 1	353	353	1
(Apr.) 2	387	774	4
(May) 3	342	1026	9
(June) 4	374	1496	16
(July) 5	396	1980	25
(Aug.) 6	409	2454	36
(Sep.) 7	399	2793	49
(Oct.) 8	412	3296	64
(Nov.) 9	408	3672	81
Sum 45	3480	17844	285

Thus, $\bar{t} = 5$ $\bar{Y} = 386.667$

$$b_1 = \frac{n\Sigma tY_t - \Sigma t\Sigma Y_t}{n\Sigma t^2 - (\Sigma t)^2} = \frac{(9)(17844) - (45)(3480)}{(9)(285) - (45)^2} = 7.4$$

$$b_0 = \overline{Y} - b_1\overline{t} = 386.667 - 7.4(5) = 349.667$$

$$T_{10} = 349.667 + (7.4)(10) = 423.667$$

b) Using a three-month weighted moving average, the forecast for December will be the weighted average of the preceding three months: September, October, and November.

$$F_{10} = .1Y_{Sep.} + .3Y_{Oct.} + .6Y_{Nov.}$$

$$= .1(399) + .3(412) + .6(408) = 408.3$$

Due to the positive trend component in the time series, the least squares method produced a forecast that is more in tune with the trend that exists. The weighted moving average, even with heavy weight (.6) placed on the current period, produced a forecast that is lagging behind the changing data.

PROBLEM 3

Quarterly revenues (in $1,000,000's) for a national restaurant chain for a five year period were as follows:

Quarter	Year 1	2	3	4	5
1	33	42	54	70	85
2	36	40	53	67	82
3	35	42	54	70	87
4	38	47	62	77	99

Forecast the revenues for the next four quarters.

SOLUTION 3

Assume the data values are a multiplicative function of the data's trend, cyclical, seasonal, and irregular factors, i.e.

$$Y_t = T_t * C_t * S_t * I_t$$

Step 1: Calculate the centered moving averages (CMAs).
First, use a moving average over the four quarters to mask the effects of the seasonal and irregular factors. For each four quarter period, calculate the moving average and associate it with the "middle period". For example, the first moving average is: $(33+36+35+38)/4 = 35.5$. The second equals $= 37.75$, etc.

Step 2: Center the CMAs on integer-valued periods.
Because the number of quarters is even, there is no integer
valued "middle period" (the middle of the first four quarters
would be quarter 2.5 in year 1).

In order to have the moving average "centered" at a particular
quarter, average the half-period moving average preceding this
quarter and the half-period moving average succeeding this
quarter. For example, the moving average of quarter 2.5 is 35.5
and the moving average of quarter 3.5 is 37.75. Thus the
centered moving average for quarter 3 is (35.5 + 37.75)/2 =
36.625.

Year	Quarter	Revenues	Four Quarter Moving Average	Centered Moving Average
1	1	33		
	2	36		
	(2.5)		35.50	
	3	35		36.625
	(3.5)		37.75	
	4	38		38.250
	(4.5)		38.75	
2	1	42		39.625
	(1.5)		40.50	
	2	40		41.625
	(2.5)		42.75	
	3	42		44.250
	(3.5)		45.75	
	4	47		47.375
	(4.5)		49.00	
3	1	54		50.500
	(1.5)		52.00	
	2	53		53.875
	(2.5)		55.75	
	3	54		57.750
	(3.5)		59.75	
	4	62		61.500
	(4.5)		63.25	
4	1	70		65.250
	(1.5)		67.25	
	2	67		69.125
	(2.5)		71.00	
	3	70		72.875
	(3.5)		74.75	
	4	77		76.625
	.(4.5)		78.50	
5	1	85		80.625
	(1.5)		82.75	
	2	82		85.500
	(2.5)		88.25	
	3	87		
	4	99		

Step 3: Determine the seasonal and irregular factors (S_tI_t).
The centered moving averages represent the combine effects of
the trend and cyclical factors (T_tC_t). Since $Y_t = T_tC_tS_tI_t$,
$S_tI_t = Y_t/(T_tC_t) = Y_t/$(centered moving average for period t).
Hence, dividing each data point by its centered moving average
gives an estimate of S_tI_t.
   For example for period 3 (year 1, quarter 3), the data point,
$Y_3 = 35$, and its centered moving average $T_3C_3 = 36.625$. Thus,
for this period, $S_3I_3 = 35/36.625 = .956$
   Continue this procedure for determining S_tI_t for all periods:

Year	Quarter	Revenues (Y_t)	Average (T_tC_t)	S_tI_t
1	3	35	36.625	.956
	4	38	38.250	.993
2	1	42	39.625	1.060
	2	40	41.625	.961
	3	42	44.250	.949
	4	47	47.375	.992
3	1	54	50.500	1.069
	2	53	53.875	.984
	3	54	57.750	.935
	4	62	61.500	1.008
4	1	70	65.250	1.073
	2	67	69.125	.969
	3	70	72.875	.961
	4	77	76.625	1.005
5	1	85	80.625	1.054
	2	82	85.500	.959

Step 4: Determine the average seasonal factors.
To eliminate the irregular effects, take the average of the S_tI_t
over the four years. That is, to find the average of S_tI_t for
quarter 1, average the quarter 1 values for years 2, 3, 4 and 5.
Do the same for quarter 2. For quarters 3 and 4, the average
would be over years 1, 2, 3, and 4. This gives:

S_1 = (1.060 + 1.069 + 1.073 + 1.054) / 4 = 1.064
S_2 = (.961 + .984 + .969 + .959) / 4 = .968
S_3 = (.956 + .949 + .935 + .961) / 4 = .950
S_4 = (.993 + .992 + 1.008 + 1.005) / 4 = 1.000

Step 5: Scale the seasonal factors (S_t).
Each seasonal average must be adjusted by the average of the
seasonal factors, (1.064 + .968 + .950 + 1.000) / 4 = .9955,
giving:

S_1 = 1.064/.9955 = 1.069
S_2 = .968/.9955 = .973
S_3 = .950/.9955 = .954
S_4 = 1.000/.9955 = 1.004

Step 6: Determine the deseasonalized data.
The seasonal factors (S_t) can now be removed from the data by
dividing each data point by its seasonal factor. This gives
deseasonalized data which will only be a function of trend,
cyclical and irregular factors. The deseasonalized data will
be:

Year	Quarter	Y_t	Deseasonalized (Y_t/S_t)
1	1	33	33/1.069 = 30.87
	2	36	36/ .973 = 37.00
	3	35	35/ .954 = 36.69
	4	38	38/1.004 = 37.84
2	1	42	42/1.069 = 39.29
	2	40	40/ .973 = 41.11
	3	42	42/ .954 = 44.03
	4	47	47/1.004 = 46.44
3	1	54	54/1.069 = 50.51
	2	53	53/ .973 = 54.47
	3	54	54/ .954 = 56.60
	4	62	62/1.004 = 61.75
4	1	70	70/1.069 = 65.48
	2	67	67/ .973 = 68.86
	3	70	70/ .954 = 73.38
	4	77	77/1.004 = 76.69
5	1	85	85/1.069 = 79.51
	2	82	82/ .973 = 84.28
	3	87	87/ .954 = 91.19
	4	99	99/1.004 = 98.61

Step 7: Determine a trend line of the deseasonalized data.
Now, labeling the periods t = 1 through t = 20, use the
regression trend analysis (see problem 2) to determine the
following trend line describing the seasonally adjusted data
over the 20 quarters:

$$T_t = 23.436 + 3.361t$$

Step 8: Determine the deseasonalized predictions.
Use this trend line to determine the trend predictions for the
four quarters of year 6.

Step 9: Take into account the seasonality.
Then adjust these quarterly predictions by multiplying each by
its seasonal adjustment factor.

Quarter	Period t	Trend Prediction (T_t=23.436+3.361t)	Seasonally Adjusted Forecast (T_tS_t)
1	21	94.02	(94.02)(1.069) = 100.50
2	22	97.38	(97.38)(.973) = 94.72
3	23	100.74	(100.74)(.954) = 96.15
4	24	104.10	(104.10)(1.004) = 104.53

PROBLEM 4

Business at Terry's Tie Shop can be viewed as falling into three distinct seasons: (1) Christmas (November-December); (2) Father's Day (late May - mid-June); and (3) all other times. Average weekly sales (in $'s) during each of these three seasons during the past four years has been as follows:

Season	Year			
	1	2	3	4
1	1856	1995	2241	2280
2	2012	2168	2306	2408
3	985	1072	1105	1120

Determine a forecast for the average weekly sales in year 5 for each of the three seasons.

SOLUTION 4

The table on the next page summarizes the computations in steps 1-6.

Step 1: Calculate the centered moving averages.
There are three distinct seasons in each year. Hence, take a three season moving average to eliminate seasonal and irregular factors. For example the first moving average is:

(1856 + 2012 + 985)/3 =1617.67.

Step 2: Center the CMAs on integer-valued periods.
The first moving average computed in step 1 (1617.67) will be centered on season 2 of year 1. Note that the moving averages from step 1 center themselves on integer-valued periods because n is an odd number.

Step 3: Determine the seasonal and irregular factors $(S_t I_t)$ by isolating the trend and cyclical components. For each period t, this is given by Y_t/(Moving Average for period t).

Step 4: Determine the average seasonal factors by averaging the all $S_t I_t$ values corresponding to that season:

Season 1: (1.163 + 1.196 + 1.181) / 3   = 1.180
Season 2: (1.244 + 1.242 + 1.224 + 1.244) / 4 = 1.238
Season 3: (.592 + .587 + .582) / 3   = .587

Step 5: Scale the seasonal factors (S_t) by dividing each
seasonal factor by the average of the seasonal factors. Then
average the seasonal factors = $(1.180 + 1.238 + .587)/3 = 1.002$.

Season 1:   1.180/1.002   =   1.178
Season 2:   1.238/1.002   =   1.236
Season 3:   .587/1.002   =   .586

Step 6: Determine the deseasonalized data by dividing the data
point values, Y_t, by S_t.

Year	Season	Dollar Sales (Y_t)	Moving Average	$S_t I_t$	Scaled S_t	Y_t/S_t
1	1	1856			1.178	1576
	2	2012	1617.67	1.244	1.236	1628
	3	985	1664.00	.592	.586	1681
2	1	1995	1716.00	1.163	1.178	1694
	2	2168	1745.00	1.242	1.236	1754
	3	1072	1827.00	.587	.586	1829
3	1	2241	1873.00	1.196	1.178	1902
	2	2306	1884.00	1.224	1.236	1866
	3	1105	1897.00	.582	.586	1886
4	1	2280	1931.00	1.181	1.178	1935
	2	2408	1936.00	1.244	1.236	1948
	3	1120			.586	1911

Step 7: Determine a trend line of the deseasonalized data by
linear regression. Using the method illustrated in problem 2.
For t = 1, 2, ..., 12, this gives:

$T_t = 1580.11 + 33.96t$.

Step 8: Determine the deseasonalized predictions for the next
three quarters (13, 14, 15) by substituting t = 13, 14, and 15
respectively into the above equation:

T_{13} =   1580.11 + (33.96)(13)   =   2022
T_{14} =   1580.11 + (33.96)(14)   =   2056
T_{15} =   1580.11 + (33.96)(15)   =   2090

Step 9: Take into account the seasonality by multiplying each
deseasonalized prediction by its seasonal factor to give the
following forecasts for year 5:

Season 1:   (1.178)(2022)   =   2382
Season 2:   (1.236)(2056)   =   2541
Season 3:   (.586)(2090)   =   1225

ANSWERED PROBLEMS

PROBLEM 5

The monthly electricity bill at the Chez Paul Restaurant over the past 12 months has been as follows:

Month	Amount	Month	Amount
JAN	$271.90	JUL	$330.70
FEB	305.70	AUG	300.10
MAR	306.40	SEP	275.50
APR	297.30	OCT	301.30
MAY	315.30	NOV	279.40
JUN	297.20	DEC	306.60

Paul is considering using exponential smoothing with $a = .5$ or a four period weighted moving average with weights of .4, .3, .2, and .1 to forecast future electricity costs.

a) Which forecasting technique will give the smallest mean square error?

b) Give next January's forecast for each method.

PROBLEM 6

Sales (in thousands) of the new Thorton Model 506 convection oven over the eight week period since its introduction have been as follows:

Week	Sales
1	18.6
2	21.4
3	25.2
4	22.4
5	24.6
6	19.2
7	21.7
8	23.8

a) Which exponential smoothing model provides better forecasts, one using $a = .6$ or $a = .2$? Compare them using mean squared error.

b) Using the two forecast models in part (a), what are the forecasts for week 9?

PROBLEM 7

Forecast the sales of Jami Michelle skin cream for year 6 given the following quarterly sales (in thousands) over the past five years:

Quarter	Year				
	1	2	3	4	5
1	34	38	43	47	49
2	27	33	37	39	45
3	49	51	60	68	72
4	27	28	29	32	40

PROBLEM 8

Weekly sales of the Weber La Guillotine food processor for the past ten weeks have been:

Week	Sales	Week	Sales
1	980	6	990
2	1040	7	1030
3	1120	8	1260
4	1050	9	1240
5	960	10	1100

a) Determine whether a three period simple moving average model or a four period simple moving average model gives a better forecast for this problem. Evaluate on the basis of minimizing the mean square error.

b) For each model, forecast sales for week 11.

PROBLEM 9

Four months ago, the Bank Drug Company introduced Jeffrey William brand designer bandages. Advertised using the slogan, "What the best dressed cuts are wearing", weekly sales for this period (in 1000's) have been as follows:

Week	Sales	Week	Sales
1	12.8	9	19.9
2	14.6	10	23.6
3	15.2	11	24.2
4	16.1	12	23.8
5	15.8	13	25.1
6	17.2	14	24.7
7	20.6	15	26.5
8	18.5	16	28.9

a) Plot a graph of sales vs. weeks. Does linear trend appear reasonable?

b) Assuming linear trend, forecast sales for weeks 17, 18, 19, and 20.

PROBLEM 10

The number of haircuts performed each day at KwikKuts in the last four weeks are lissted below:

Week	Monday	Tuesday	Workday Wednesday	Thursday	Friday
1	122	122	103	133	98
2	127	130	106	137	97
3	126	131	111	151	104
4	135	135	110	146	107

a) Plot the sales data. Do you see both trend and seasonality components in the data?

b) Forecast the number of haircuts to be performed in each workday of week 6.

PROBLEM 11

At a local car dealership the following is a record of sales for the past 12 months:

MONTH	SALES	MONTH	SALES
JAN	36	JUL	25
FEB	34	AUG	22
MAR	28	SEP	26
APR	30	OCT	22
MAY	27	NOV	21
JUN	24	DEC	19

a) Using the method of least squares, determine a trend line for forecasting future sales.

b) Using your model in part (a), determine how long it will be before zero sales are forecasted.

c) Consider your answer to part (b). What will be the forecasted sales for the month after that? Does this make sense? Comment on the validity of the model. What assumption about the model appears to be in error?

PROBLEM 12

A 24-hour coffee/donut shop makes donuts every eight hours. The
manager must forecast donut demand so that the bakers have the
fresh ingredients they need. Listed below is the actual number
of glazed donuts (in dozens) sold in each of the preceding 13
eight-hour shifts.

Date	Shift	Demand (dozens)
June 3	Day	59
	Evening	47
June 4	Night	35
	Day	64
	Evening	43
June 5	Night	39
	Day	62
	Evening	46
June 6	Night	42
	Day	64
	Evening	50
June 7	Night	40
	Day	69

Forecast the demand for glazed donuts for the three shifts of
June 8 and the three shifts of June 9.

TRUE/FALSE

13. If a time series has a trend component, then one should not use a moving average to forecast.

14. In forecasting with trend and seasonal components using a multiplicative model, one computes moving averages in order to isolate the combined seasonal and irregular components.

15. If the random variability in a time series is great, a high α value should be used to exponentially smooth out the fluctuations.

16. In exponential smoothing, one typically chooses the smoothing constant as that value which minimizes the mean squared error.

17. Forecasting errors are always less using exponential smoothing than a weighted moving average.

18. A forecaster would choose trend projection using the least squares method over exponential smoothing if the data exhibited a trend component.

19. To forecast using the multiplicative model, one must adjust the trend component by the seasonal factor.

20. In a weighted moving average, the most recent occurrence is typically given the least weight.

21. In using the Delphi technique, one attempts to obtain a group consensus.

22. One advantage of exponential smoothing over moving averages is that fewer data points are used in the forecast.

23. An α equal to 0.2 will cause an exponential smoothing forecast to react more quickly to a sudden drop in demand than will an α equal to 0.4.

24. Exponential smoothing with α = .2 and a moving average with n = 5 put the same weight on the actual value for the current period.

25. The sum of the seasonal indexes should be adjusted, if necessary, to equal 1.

26. With fewer periods in a moving average, it will take longer to adjust to a new level of demand.

27. A causal forecasting method is most effective when demand data exhibit fluctuations caused by seasonal influences.

CHAPTER

17

Markov Processes

KEY CONCEPTS

CONCEPT	ILLUSTRATED PROBLEMS	ANSWERED PROBLEMS
Transition Probabilities	1-4	5-13
Probabilities at Stage n	1,2,3	8,10,11,12,13
Steady State Probabilities	1,2	6,7,8,9,12
Fundamental Matrix	3,4	5,10,11,13
Markov Chain Applications	1-4	5-13

REVIEW

1. <u>Markov process</u> models are useful in studying the evolution of systems over <u>repeated trials</u> or <u>sequential time periods</u> or <u>stages</u>.

2. <u>Transition probabilities</u> govern the manner in which the <u>state</u> of the system changes from one stage to the next. These are often represented in a <u>transition matrix</u>.

3. A system has a finite <u>Markov chain</u> with <u>stationary transition probabilities</u> if:
   1) there are a finite number of states,
   2) the transition probabilities remain constant from stage to stage, and
   3) the probability of the process being in a particular state at stage n+1 is completely determined by the state of the process at stage n (and not the state at stage n-1). This is referred to as the <u>memory-less property</u>.

4. The <u>state probabilities</u> at any stage of the process can be recursively calculated by multiplying the initial state probabilities by the state of the process at stage n.

5. The probability of the system being in a particular state after a large number of stages is called a <u>steady-state probability</u>. <u>Steady-state probabilities</u> are independent of the initial state of the system.

6. <u>Steady state probabilities</u> can be found by solving the system of equations $\Pi P = \Pi$ together with the condition for probabilities that $\Sigma \pi_i = 1$. Here the matrix P is the transition probability matrix and the vector, Π, is the vector of steady state probabilities.

7. An <u>absorbing state</u> is one in which the probability that the process remains in that state once it enters the state is 1.

8. If a Markov chain has both absorbing and nonabsorbing states, the states may be rearranged so that the transition matrix can be written as the following composition of <u>four submatrices</u>: I, 0, R, and Q:

$$\left[\begin{array}{c|c} I & 0 \\ \hline R & Q \end{array} \right]$$

where:
  I = an identity matrix indicating one always remains in
      an absorbing state once it is reached,
  0 = a zero matrix representing 0 probability of
      transitioning from the absorbing states to the
      nonabsorbing states,
  R = the transition probabilities from the nonabsorbing states
      to the absorbing states, and
  Q = the transition probabilities between the nonabsorbing
      states.

9. The <u>fundamental</u> <u>matrix</u>, N, is the inverse of the difference
   between the identity matrix and the Q matrix, i.e.

$$N = (I - Q)^{-1}$$

10. The <u>NR</u> <u>matrix</u>, the product of the fundamental matrix and the R
    matrix, gives the probabilities of eventually moving from each
    nonabsorbing state to each absorbing state. Multiplying any
    vector of initial nonabsorbing state probabilities by NR gives
    the vector of probabilities for the process eventually reaching
    each of the absorbing states. Such computations enable
    economic analyses of systems and policies.

ILLUSTRATED PROBLEMS

PROBLEM 1

Henry, a persistent salesman, calls North's Hardware Store once a week hoping to speak with the store's buying agent, Shirley. If Shirley does not accept Henry's call this week, the probability she will do the same next week is .35. On the other hand, if she accepts Henry's call this week, the probability she will not do so next week is .20.

a) Construct the transition matrix for this problem.

b) How many times per year can Henry expect to talk to Shirley?

c) What is the probability Shirley will accept Henry's next two calls if she does not accept his call this week?

d) What is the probability of Shirley accepting exactly one of Henry's next two calls if she accepts his call this week?

SOLUTION 1

a) The transition matrix is:

		Next Week's Call	
		Refuses	Accepts
This Week's Call	Refuses	.35	.65
	Accepts	.20	.80

b) To find the expected number of accepted calls per year, find the long-run proportion (probability) of a call being accepted and multiply it by 52 weeks.

Let π_1 = the long run proportion of refused calls
π_2 = the long run proportion of accepted calls

Then,

$$[\pi_1 \quad \pi_2] \begin{bmatrix} .35 & .65 \\ .20 & .80 \end{bmatrix} = [\pi_1 \quad \pi_2]$$

Thus,
$$.35\pi_1 + .20\pi_2 = \pi_1 \qquad (1)$$
$$.65\pi_1 + .80\pi_2 = \pi_2 \qquad (2)$$
and,
$$\pi_1 + \pi_2 = 1 \qquad (3)$$

Solving using equations (2) and (3), (equation 1 is redundant), substitute $\pi_1 = 1 - \pi_2$ into (2) to give:

$$.65(1 - \pi_2) + .80\pi_2 = \pi_2$$

This gives $\pi_2 = .76471$. Substituting back into (3) gives $\pi_1 = .23529$.

Thus the expected number of accepted calls per year is $(.76471)(52) = 39.76$ or about 40.

c) The tree diagram for this problem is:

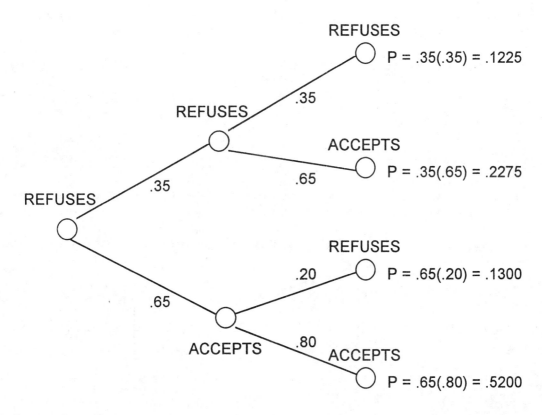

Hence, the probability the next two calls are accepted given that this week's call is refused is $.65(.80) = .52$.

d) The probability of exactly one of the next two calls being accepted if this week's call is accepted can be found by adding the probabilities of (accept next week and refuse the following week) and (refuse next week and accept the following week) = $.13 + .16 = .29$.

PROBLEM 2

   Joe Ferris, a stock trader at the brokerage firm of Smith,
   Jones, Johnson, and Thomas, Inc. has noticed that price changes
   in the shares of Dollar Department Stores at each trade are
   dependent upon the previous trade's price change. His
   observations can be summarized by the following transition
   matrix.

	Next Price Change		
	+1/8	0	-1/8
Current Price Change +1/8	.7	.2	.1
0	.3	.4	.3
-1/8	.2	.1	.7

   a) What is the long-run average change in the value of a share
       of Dollar Department Stores' stock per trade?

   b) If the shares of Dollar Department Stores are currently
       traded at $18 and the last trade was at 17 7/8, what is the
       probability the shares will sell at 18 in two trades?

SOLUTION 2

   a) Let,
       p_1 = the long-run probability of a +1/8 stock price change
       p_2 = the long-run probability of a 0 stock price change
       p_3 = the long-run probability of a -1/8 stock price change

   To determine the long-run (steady state) probabilities,
   solve:

$$[\pi_1 \quad \pi_2 \quad \pi_3] \begin{bmatrix} .7 & .2 & .1 \\ .3 & .4 & .3 \\ .2 & .1 & .7 \end{bmatrix} = [\pi_1 \quad \pi_2 \quad \pi_3]$$

   This gives the following set of equations:

$$.7\pi_1 + .3\pi_2 + .2\pi_3 = \pi_1 \quad (1)$$
$$.2\pi_1 + .4\pi_2 + .1\pi_3 = \pi_2 \quad (2)$$
$$.1\pi_1 + .3\pi_2 + .7\pi_3 = \pi_3 \quad (3)$$

   and,

$$\pi_1 + \pi_2 + \pi_3 = 1 \quad (4)$$

Note, that any one of (1), (2) or (3) can be considered
redundant. Delete (1) and solve (2), (3), and (4). From (4)
substitute $\pi_1 = 1 - \pi_2 - \pi_3$. This leaves the following two
equations in two unknowns:

$$.2(1 - \pi_2 - \pi_3) + .4\pi_2 + .1\pi_3 = \pi_2$$

and
$$.1(1 - \pi_2 - \pi_3) + .3\pi_2 + .7\pi_3 = \pi_3$$

or

$$.8\pi_2 + .1\pi_3 = .2$$

and
$$-.2\pi_2 + .4\pi_3 = .1$$

Solving these two gives $\pi_2 = 7/34$ and $\pi_3 = 12/34$.
Substituting into (4) gives $\pi_1 = 15/34$. Hence, the long run
average change per trade is:

$$(15/34)(1/8) + (7/34)(0) + (12/34)(-1/8) = \$.011.$$

b) The fact that the last trade was 17 7/8 means that the last
price change was +1/8. The tree diagram for the problem is:

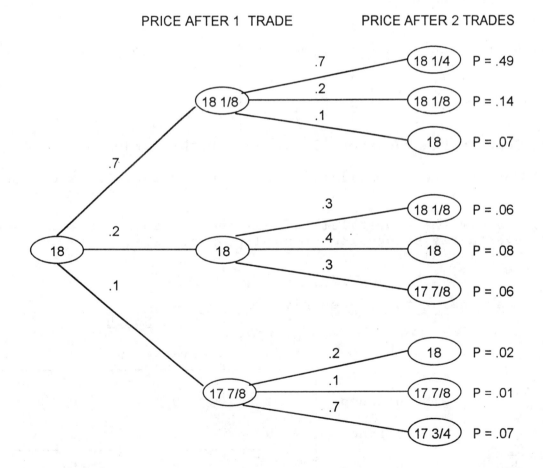

PRICE AFTER 1 TRADE   PRICE AFTER 2 TRADES

The probability that the stock will sell at 18 after 2 trades
is .07 + .08 + .02 = .17.

PROBLEM 3

Joe Isley, the owner of Big I HiFi, believes that the store's inventory can be modelled as a Markov process. If items are either classified as in stock, out of stock, discontinued from stock or put on clearance sale, then the following transition matrix has been estimated:

| | | Next Month | | | |
		In Stock	Out of Stock	Discontinued from Stock	Put On Clearance Sale
	In Stock	.67	.20	.05	.08
THIS MONTH	Out of Stock	.48	.42	.10	0
	Discontinued	0	0	1	0
	Clearance Sale	0	0	0	1

a) Rewrite the transition matrix for the problem in the form:

$$\begin{bmatrix} I & \vdots & 0 \\ \hline R & \vdots & Q \end{bmatrix}$$

b) Compute the fundamental matrix for this problem.

c) What is the probability of an item currently in stock being out of stock in two months?

d) What is the probability of an item currently out of stock eventually being discontinued from stock?

SOLUTION 3

a) Rearranging the states gives:

| | | Next Month | | | |
		Discontinued	Clearance	In Stock	Out Of Stock
	Discontinued	1	0	0	0
	Clearance	0	1	0	0
This Month	In Stock	.05	.08	.67	.20
	Out of Stock	.10	0	.48	.42

Note, $R = \begin{bmatrix} .05 & .08 \\ .10 & 0 \end{bmatrix}$ and $Q = \begin{bmatrix} .67 & .20 \\ .48 & .42 \end{bmatrix}$

b)
$N = (I - Q)^{-1} = \begin{bmatrix} .33 & -.20 \\ -.48 & .58 \end{bmatrix}^{-1}$

To compute $(I - Q)^{-1}$, first calculate its determinant,

$d = a_{11}a_{22} - a_{21}a_{12} = (.33)(.58) - (-.48)(-.20) = .0954$

Then, $N = \begin{bmatrix} (.58/.0954) & (.20/.0954) \\ (.48/.0954) & (.33/.0954) \end{bmatrix} = \begin{bmatrix} 6.08 & 2.10 \\ 5.03 & 3.46 \end{bmatrix}$

c) The tree diagram is:

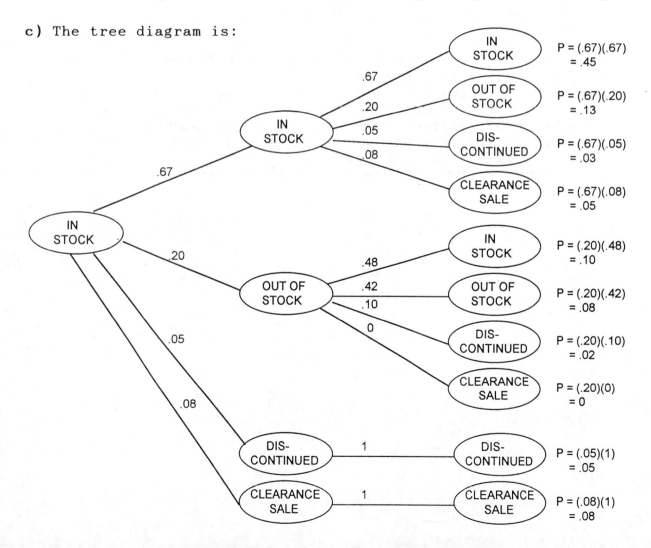

Therefore, the probability of an item currently in stock being out of stock in two months is .13 + .08 = .21.

d) The probability of eventually moving into each of the absorbing states from the nonabsorbing states is given by:

$$
NR = \begin{bmatrix} 6.08 & 2.10 \\ 5.03 & 3.46 \end{bmatrix} = \begin{bmatrix} .05 & .08 \\ .10 & 0 \end{bmatrix}
$$

$$
= \begin{array}{c} \text{In Stock} \\ \text{Out Of Stock} \end{array} \begin{matrix} \text{Discontinued} & \text{Clearance Sale} \\ \begin{bmatrix} .51 & .49 \\ .60 & .40 \end{bmatrix} \end{matrix}
$$

Hence, the probability of an item currently out of stock eventually being discontinued is .60.

NOTE: If there is more than one absorbing state, then a steady-state condition independent of initial state conditions does not exist. For example, in the above problem we cannot state what percentage of all inventory items eventually are discontinued or what percentage are put on clearance.

PROBLEM 4

The vice president of personnel at Jetair Aerospace has noticed that yearly shifts in personnel can be modelled by a Markov process. The transition matrix is:

| | | Next Year | | | |
	Same Position	Promotion	Retire	Quit	Fired
Same Position	.55	.10	.05	.20	.10
Promotion	.70	.20	0	.10	0
Current Year — Retire	0	0	1	0	0
Quit	0	0	0	1	0
Fired	0	0	0	0	1

a) Write the transition matrix in the following form:

$$\begin{bmatrix} I & \vdots & 0 \\ ---- & \vdots & ---- \\ R & \vdots & Q \end{bmatrix}$$

b) Compute the fundamental matrix for this problem.

c) What is the probability of an employee who was just promoted eventually retiring? Quitting? Being fired?

SOLUTION 4

a) Since the identity matrix must be in the upper right corner, rewrite the transition matrix as follows:

| | | Next Year | | | |
	Retire	Quit	Fired	Same	Promotion
Retire	1	0	0	0	0
Quit	0	1	0	0	0
Current Year — Fired	0	0	1	0	0
Same	.05	.20	.10	.55	.10
Promotion	0	.10	0	.70	.20

Note,

$$Q = \begin{bmatrix} .55 & .10 \\ .70 & .20 \end{bmatrix} \qquad R = \begin{bmatrix} .05 & .20 & .10 \\ 0 & .10 & 0 \end{bmatrix}$$

b)

$$N = (I - Q)^{-1} = \begin{bmatrix} 1 & 0 \\ 0 & 1 \end{bmatrix} - \begin{bmatrix} .55 & .10 \\ .70 & .20 \end{bmatrix}^{-1}$$

$$= \begin{bmatrix} .45 & -.10 \\ -.70 & .80 \end{bmatrix}^{-1}$$

The determinant, $d = a_{11}a_{22} - a_{21}a_{12}$

$$= (.45)(.80) - (-.70)(-.10) = .29$$

Thus,
$$N = \begin{bmatrix} .80/.29 & .10/.29 \\ .70/.29 & .45/.29 \end{bmatrix} = \begin{bmatrix} 2.76 & .34 \\ 2.41 & 1.55 \end{bmatrix}$$

c) The probabilities of eventually moving to the absorbing states from the nonabsorbing states are given by:

$$NR = \begin{bmatrix} 2.76 & .34 \\ 2.41 & 1.55 \end{bmatrix} = \begin{bmatrix} .05 & .20 & .10 \\ 0 & .10 & 0 \end{bmatrix}$$

$$= \begin{matrix} & \text{Retire} \quad \text{Quit} \quad \text{Fired} \\ \begin{matrix} \text{Same} \\ \text{Promotion} \end{matrix} & \begin{bmatrix} .14 & .59 & .28 \\ .12 & .64 & .24 \end{bmatrix} \end{matrix}$$

The probability of someone just being promoted eventually being in one of the absorbing states is given by the bottom row of this probability matrix. The answers are therefore:

Eventually Retiring   =   .12
Eventually Quitting   =   .64
Eventually Being Fired   =   .24

ANSWERED PROBLEMS

PROBLEM 5

Rent-To-Keep rents household furnishings by the month. At the
end of a rental month a customer can: a) rent the item for
another month, b) buy the item, or c) return the item. The
matrix below describes the month-to-month transition
probabilities for 32-inch stereo televisions the shop stocks.

		Next Month		
		Rent	Buy	Return
	Rent	.72	.10	.18
This Month	Buy	0	1	0
	Return	0	0	1

What is the probability that a customer who has rented a
television this month will eventually buy it?

PROBLEM 6

The evening television news broadcast that individuals view on
one evening is influenced by which broadcast they viewed
previosly. An executive at the C network has determined the
following transition probability matrix describing this
phenomenon.

		Next Network News Watched		
		A	C	N
Current Network News Watched	A	.80	.12	.08
	C	.08	.85	.07
	N	.08	.09	.83

a) Which network has the most loyal viewers?

b) What are the three networks' long-run market shares?

c) Suppose each of the three networks earns $1,250 in daily
   profit from advertising revenue for each 1,000,000 viewers it
   has. If on the average 40,000,000 people watch the evening
   television news, compute the long run average daily profit
   each network generates from its evening news broadcast.

PROBLEM 7

On any particular day an individual can take one of two routes to work. Route A has a 25% chance of being congested, whereas route B has a 40% chance of being congested.

The probability of the individual taking a particular route depends on his previous day's experience. If one day he takes route A and it is not congested, he will take route A again the next day with probability .8. If it is congested, he will take route B the next day with probability .7.

On the other hand, if on a day he takes route B and it is not congested, he will take route B again the next day with probability .9. Similarly if route B is congested, he will take route A the next day with probability .6.

a) Construct the transition matrix for this problem. (HINT: there are 4 states corresponding to the route taken and the congestion. The transition probabilities are products of the independent probabilities of congestion and next day choice.)

b) What is the long-run proportion of time that route A is taken?

PROBLEM 8

Mark is a specialist at repairing large metal-cutting machines that use laser technology. His repair territory consists of the cities of Austin, San Antonio, and Houston. His day-to-day repair assignment locations can be modeled as a Markov process. The transition matrix is as follows:

		Next Day's Location		
		Austin	San Antonio	Houston
This Day's Location	Austin	.35	.35	.30
	San Antonio	.25	.50	.25
	Houston	.10	.20	.70

a) Determine the probability of Mark working the next three days in Houston (where his girlfriend lives) if today he is working in Austin.

b) Find the long-run proportions of time Mark will work in each of the three cities.

PROBLEM 9

There are currently only two fast food restaurants in the Main Street area, Burger Prince and Feisty Fowl. The probability of a customer eating at one restaurant is dependent upon which restaurant he ate at previously. The probabilities can be summarized by the following transition matrix.

<u>Next</u> <u>Restaurant</u>

		Burger Prince	Feisty Fowl
	Burger Prince	.7	.3
Last Restaurant	Feisty Fowl	.4	.6

Colonel Mustard's Hot Dogs is planning to open a new restaurant next to Burger Prince. Burger Prince's management estimates the new restaurant will result in the transition matrix below. By how much will the long-run market share of Burger Prince and Feisty Fowl change with the opening of Colonel Mustard's.

<u>Next</u> <u>Restaurant</u>

		Burger Prince	Feisty Fowl	Colonel Mustard's
	Burger Prince	.5	.3	.2
Last Restaurant	Feisty Fowl	.3	.5	.2
	Col. Mustard's	.3	.3	.4

PROBLEM 10

Precision Craft, Inc. manufactures ornate pedestal sinks. On
any day, the status of a given sink is either: a) somewhere in
the normal manufacturing process, b) being reworked because of a
detected flaw, c) finished successfully, or d) scrapped because
a flaw could not be corrected. The transition matrix is:

Tomorrow's Status

		In-Process	Rework	Finished	Scrapped
	In-Process	.30	.15	.50	.05
	Rework	.40	.10	.30	.20
Today's Status	Finished	0	0	1	0
	Scrapped	0	0	0	1

a) What is the probability of a sink eventually being finished
if it is currently in process?

b) What is the probability of a sink eventually being scrapped
if it is currently in rework?

c) What is the probability that a sink currently in rework will
have a "finished" status either tomorrow or the next day?
(HINT: there are three ways this can happen.)

PROBLEM 11

Southside College has modeled its student loan program as a
Markov process. Each year a student with a prior loan either
borrows again, defers repayment for a year, makes payments,
pays the loan balance in full, or defaults on repayment. The
transition matrix is as follows:

Next Year

		Borrowing	Deferring	Paying	Paid-Off	Default
	Borrowing	.60	.30	0	.10	0
	Deferring	.15	0	.65	.10	.10
This Year	Paying	0	0	.75	.15	.10
	Paid-Off	0	0	0	1	0
	Defaulted	0	0	0	0	1

a) If currently a student is making payments on his/her loan,
   what is the probability the loan will be paid in full
   eventually?

b) Is the probability of eventually defaulting greater for a
   student who is currently borrowing more or a student who is
   making payments?

c) What is the probability a student who is borrowing this year
   will repay the loan balance in full in two years or less?

PROBLEM 12

Three airlines compete on the route between New York and Los
Angeles. Stanton Marketing has performed an analysis of first
class business travelers to determine their airline choice.
    Stanton has modeled this choice as a Markov process and has
determined the following transition probabilities.

Next Airline

		A	B	C
	A	.50	.30	.20
Last Airline	B	.30	.45	.25
	C	.10	.35	.55

a) Determine the long-run share for each of the three airlines.

b) Determine the probability of a passenger flying on three
   different airlines on his next three flights if his next
   flight is on:
   (1) A
   (2) B
   (3) C

c) The weekly profit of each airline is estimated to be
   $(y - .28)$ millions of dollars, where y is the airline's
   market share of the New York - Los Angeles traffic. The
   management of airline A is contemplating an advertising
   campaign which it believes will result in new business.
   Stanton Marketing has projected that such an advertising
   campaign will result in the following transition probability
   matrix.

Next Airline

		A	B	C
	A	.50	.25	.25
Last Airline	B	.35	.45	.20
	C	.15	.30	.55

What is the maximum amount that management should spend per
week on this advertising campaign?

PROBLEM 13

A recent study done by an economist for the Small Business
Administration investigated failures of small business.
Failures were either classified as due to poor financing, poor
management, or a poor product. The failure rates differed for
new businesses (under one year old) versus established
businesses (over one year old.)
   As the result of the economists study, the following
probabilities were determined. For new businesses the
probability of failure due to financing was .15, due to
management .20, and due to product .05. The corresponding
probabilities for established businesses were .10, .06, and .03
respectively.

a) Determine a five-state Markov Chain transition matrix with
   states for new, established, and each of the three failure
   states. Write it in the form:

$$
\begin{bmatrix}
I & | & 0 \\
--- & | & --- \\
R & | & Q
\end{bmatrix}
$$

b) Determine the probability that a new business will survive
   during the next three years.

c) What proportion of new businesses eventually fail due to:
   (1)   poor financing?
   (2)   poor management?
   (3)   poor product?

TRUE/FALSE

14. The sum of the probabilities in a transition matrix equals the number of rows in the matrix.

15. All Markov chains have steady-state probabilities.

16. If the initial state probability distribution equals the Markov chain's steady-state probability distribution then all states will have this probability distribution.

17. The steady-state probability distribution is a function of the initial state probability distribution.

18. All Markov chain transition matrices have the same number of rows as columns.

19. The fundamental matrix is used to calculate the probability of the process moving into each absorbing state.

20. A state, i, is an absorbing state if, when i=j, p_{ij} = 1.

21. A Markov chain cannot consist of all absorbing states.

22. If a Markov chain has at least one absorbing state, steady-state probabilities cannot be calculated.

23. In a Markov chain, p_{ij} must equal p_{ji}.

24. Transition probabilities are joint probabilities.

25. The sum of the "from" probabilities in any "to" column in a transition matrix must equal 1.

26. The probability p_{ij}, when i=j, is a steady-state probability.

27. The "memory-less" property of first-order Markov processes refers to not needing to know the state of the system prior to the current state in order to predict the future state.

28. State j is an absorbing state if p_{ij} = 1.

18

Dynamic Programming

KEY CONCEPTS

CONCEPT	ILLUSTRATED PROBLEMS	ANSWERED PROBLEMS
Formulations Using Dynamic Programming	2,3,4	5,6,8,9,10,11,12
Shortest Route Problems	1	7,10
Knapsack Problems	3	5,8,9
Inventory Control Problems	4	6,11,12

REVIEW

1. <u>Dynamic programming</u> is an approach to problem solving which permits decomposing of the original problem into a series of several smaller subproblems.

2. To successfully apply dynamic programming, the original problem must be viewed as a <u>multistage decision problem</u>. Defining the <u>stages</u> is sometimes obvious, but at other times this requires subtle reasoning.

3. Generally, a dynamic programming problem is solved by starting at the final stage and working backwards to the initial stage. This is called <u>backwards recursion.</u>

4. At each stage, n, of the dynamic program, there is a <u>state variable</u>, x_n, and an optimal <u>decision variable</u>, d_n. One way to identify the data needed to be included in the state variable is to imagine being called in as a consultant to help solve the problem at a particular stage. The information one would have to know to finish solving the problem is the state information.

5. For each value of x_n and d_n at stage n, there is a <u>return function</u> value, $r_n(x_n, d_n)$.

6. The output of the process at stage n is x_{n-1}, the state variable for stage n-1. It is calculated by a <u>stage transformation function</u>, $t_n(x_n, d_n)$.

7. The <u>optimal value function</u>, $f_n(x_n)$, is the cumulative return starting at stage n in state x_n and proceeding to stage 1 under an optimal policy (strategy).

8. The power of dynamic programming is that one need solve only a small portion of all subproblems. This is due to Bellman's <u>principle of optimality.</u> It states that regardless of what decisions were made at previous stages, if the decision to be made at stage n is to be part of an overall optimal solution, then the decision made at stage n must be optimal for all remaining stages.

9. The following <u>recursion relation</u> can be used to operationalize the principle of optimality:

$$f_n(x_n) = \max_{d_n} \{r_n(x_n, d_n) + f_{n-1}(t_n(x_n, d_n))\}$$

10. A problem is solved beginning at stage 0 with the <u>boundary condition</u> $f_0(x_0) = 0$, and working backwards to the last stage, N.

11. Three classes of problems which conveniently lend themselves to dynamic programming are: (1) the <u>shortest route problem</u>, (2) the <u>knapsack or cargo loading problem</u>, and, (3) <u>production and inventory control problems</u>.

12. In solving a <u>shortest route problem</u> using dynamic programming, one should consider the network as a series of stages with a unique subset of nodes corresponding to each stage. The state variables correspond to the different nodes at each stage.

13. The <u>knapsack problem</u> seeks to determine the optimal number of each of N items (which must not be fractional) to select in order to maximize profit subject to an overall capacity constraint. In solving a knapsack problem using dynamic programming, the stages correspond to the different items being placed into a knapsack. The state variables correspond to the capacity available at the stage.

14. In <u>production and inventory control problems</u>, the stages correspond to time periods and the state variables generally will refer to the amounts of inventory on hand at the beginning of each stage.

ILLUSTRATED PROBLEMS

PROBLEM 1

Use dynamic programming to determine the shortest path(s) from node 1 to node 15 assuming travel is only permitted from left to right in the network.

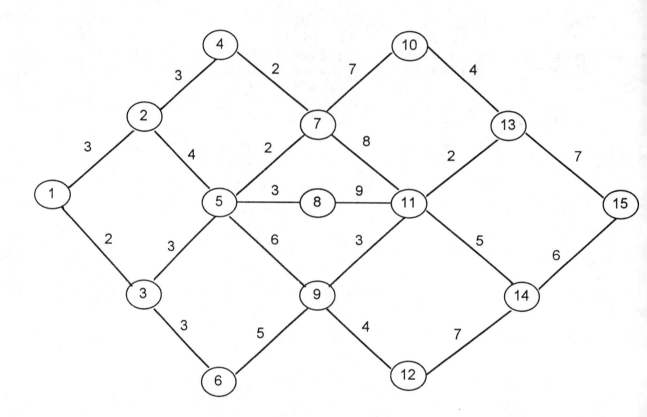

SOLUTION 1

This problem can be viewed as a six stage decision problem. Working backwards through the network, let stage 1 correspond to nodes 13 and 14; stage 2 correspond to nodes 10, 11, and 12; stage 3 correspond to nodes 7, 8, and 9; stage 4 correspond to nodes 4, 5, and 6; stage 5 correspond to nodes 2 and 3; and stage 6 correspond to node 1.

At each stage a decision will be made as to how to move from the particular state to the final state (node 15) in the shortest possible distance.

Stage 1

At stage 1 there are two states: nodes 13 and 14.   Because there
is no choice of how to reach node 15 from either of these nodes,
each decision is automatic.   This is summarized as:

Input Nodes	Arc Decision	Shortest Distance
13	13-15	7
14	14-15	6

In the table, column 1 gives the particular states of this
stage, column 2 gives the optimal arc decision, and column 3
gives the shortest distance to reach the final node.   The
information in this third column is used at the next stage and
the information in the second column is used to determine the
optimal strategy.

Stage 2

At stage 2 there are three states: nodes 10, 11, and 12.   From
nodes 10 and 12 there is no decision required to determine the
shortest path.   However a decision must be made at node 11.
From node 11 there are two possibilities: travel on arc 11-13
to node 13 or on arc 11-14 to node 14.   The distance of arc 11-
13 is 2 and from the table at stage 1, the distance from node 13
to node 15 is 7 (column 3) for a total of 9.   Similarly the
distance of arc 11-14 is 5 and the distance from node 14 to node
15 is 6 for a total of 11.   Since 9 is less than 11, the optimal
decision if one were at node 11 is travel on arc 11-13 to reach
node 13.   These analyses can be summarized as:

Input Nodes	Arc Decision	Output Nodes	Shortest Distance To Node 15
10	10-13	13	11
11	11-13	13	9
12	12-14	14	13

Note that a new column has been added to the table to list the
output node.   For this problem this information is redundant
since it can be determined by the arc decision.   In many
problems, however, the output node cannot be determined from the
arc decision easily and therefore should be listed.

Stage 3

At stage 3 a decision must be made at nodes 7 and 9 regarding the best route. From node 7 one could either move to node 10 or node 11. The distance from node 7 to node 10 is 7 and from stage 2, the distance from node 7 to 15 (column 4) is 11 for a total of 18. Similarly, the total distance from node 7, taking the 7-11 arc, can be determined to be 17. Hence, the best decision from node 7 is to travel 7-11. The complete results for stage 3 are summarized by:

Input Nodes	Arc Decision	Output Nodes	Shortest Distance To Node 15
7	7-11	11	17
8	8-11	11	18
9	9-11	11	12

Writing the shortest distance to node 15 above each node calculated thus far gives:

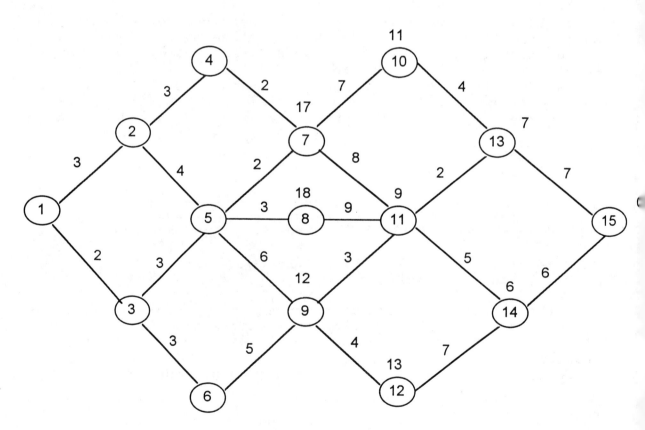

Stage 4

At stage 4, there are three possible arcs to travel on from node 5. The best decision is found in a similar manner to previous stages by calculating the minimum of (the arc distance from 5) + (the shortest distance to node 15 from the resulting node). This equals minimum of {(2 + 17), (3 + 18), (6 + 12)} = 18 by travelling on the arc 5-9. Note there are no comparisons for nodes 4 and 6.

Summarizing the results for stage 4,

Input Nodes	Arc Decision	Output Nodes	Shortest Distance To Node 15
4	4-7	7	19
5	5-9	9	18
6	6-9	9	17

Stage 5

At stage 5 decisions must be made at both nodes 2 and 3.
Node 2: Min {(3 + (distance from node 4)), (4 + (distance from node 5))} = Min {(3 + 19), (4 + 18)}. Both give 22. Similarly, for node 3: Min {(3 + 18), (3 + 17)} = 20.

Summarizing,

Input Nodes	Arc Decision	Output Nodes	Shortest Distance To Node 15
2	2-4 or 2-5	2 or 5	22
3	3-6	6	20

Stage 6

At stage 6 a decision must be made to travel on 1-2 or 1-3. Choose the minimum {(3 + 22), (2 + 20)} = 22. Hence, the minimum distance from node 1 to node 15 is 22.

Input Nodes	Arc Decision	Output Nodes	Shortest Distance To Node 15
1	1-3	3	22

Working forwards through the network (backwards through the stages) the best route is 1-3 (stage 6), then 3-6 (stage 5), then 6-9 (stage 4), then 9-11 (stage 3), then 11-13 (stage 2) and finally 13-15 (stage 1) or 1-3-6-9-11-13-15. The final network, including the shortest distance to node 15 at each node is given on the next page.

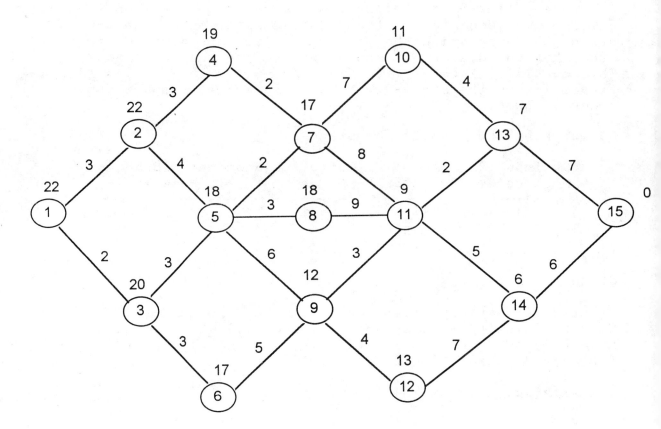

PROBLEM 2

Dollar Department Stores has four operating divisions: Dollar
Stores, Wenthrope Jewelry, Fidelity Insurance, and the newly
acquired Burger Prince Restaurants. Dollar management is
currently planning its yearly budget and has decided to allocate
$20,000,000 to the four divisions.

The four division vice presidents have prepared various
requests for funds together with the estimated future
discounted, after tax profitability to Dollar. These amounts
(in $1,000,000's) are summarized in the table below. Note that
the maximum requests from the divisions vary. If each division
must receive at least $3,000,000 in funds, how should the money
be allocated to each division to maximize Dollar's total future
discounted, after tax profitability?

| | Future Discounted After-Tax Profitability of Requests | | | |
Request	Dollar Stores	Wenthrope Jewelry	Fidelity Insurance	Burger Prince Restaurants
3	5	7	2	7
4	7	10	5	10
5	8	13	10	15
6	11	15	14	19
7	13	18	17	23
8	14	22	20	25
9	16	--	23	29
10	18	--	26	--
11	--	--	28	--

SOLUTION 2

Stage 1

At stage 1, we consider allocating to Dollar stores only.
Letting x_1 = the amount allocated to stage 1, and $f_1(x_1)$ be the
maximum return of allocating to stages 1 to 1, and d_1* be the
optimal allocation to stage 1 we have:

x_1	$f_1(x_1)$	d_1*
0-2	$-\infty$	---
3	5	3
4	7	4
5	8	5
6	11	6
7	13	7
8	14	8
9	16	9
10-20	18	10

Stage 2

At stage 2 consider allocation to both Wenthrope Jewelry and Dollar Stores;

$ avail. x_2	d_2 to Wenthrope						d_2*	$f_2(x_2)$	$x_2 - d_2$* $= x_1$
	3	4	5	6	7	8			
0-5								$-\infty$	
	(12)	$-\infty$	$-\infty$	$-\infty$			3	12	3
7	14	(15)	$-\infty$	$-\infty$	$-\infty$		4	15	3
8	15	17	(18)	$-\infty$	$-\infty$	$-\infty$	5	18	3
9	18	18	(20)	(20)	$-\infty$	$-\infty$	5,6	20	4,3
10	20	21	21	22	(23)	$-\infty$	7	23	3
11	21	23	24	23	25	(27)	8	27	3
12	23	24	26	26	26	(29)	8	29	4
13	25	26	27	28	29	(30)	8	30	5
14	25	28	29	29	31	(33)	8	33	6
15	25	28	31	31	32	(35)	8	35	7
16	25	28	31	33	34	(36)	8	36	8
17	25	28	31	33	36	(38)	8	38	9
18-20	25	28	31	33	36	(40)	8	40	10

(Sample Calculation: With x_2 = \$11, if d_2 = \$7 is allocated to Wenthrope there is a return of 18. This leaves (11-7) = \$4 to be allocated to stage 1. Look at chart for stage 1. This value is a return of 7, for a total of 7 + 18 = 25, which is the corresponding number in the x_2 = 11 row, d_2 = 7 column.)

Stage 3

At this stage consider allocation of funds to Fidelity Insurance, Wenthrope Jewelry, and Dollar Stores.

$ avail. x_3	d_3 to Fidelity Insurance									d_3*	$f_3(x_3)$	$x_3 - d_3$* $= x_2$
	3	4	5	6	7	8	9	10	11			
0-8											$-\infty$	
9	(14)	$-\infty$	$-\infty$	$-\infty$	$-\infty$	$-\infty$	$-\infty$	$-\infty$	$-\infty$	3	14	6
10	(17)	(17)	$-\infty$	$-\infty$	$-\infty$	$-\infty$	$-\infty$	$-\infty$	$-\infty$	3,4	17	7,6
11	20	20	(22)	$-\infty$	$-\infty$	$-\infty$	$-\infty$	$-\infty$	$-\infty$	5	22	6
12	22	23	25	(26)	$-\infty$	$-\infty$	$-\infty$	$-\infty$	$-\infty$	6	26	6
13	25	25	28	(29)	(29)	$-\infty$	$-\infty$	$-\infty$	$-\infty$	6,7	29	7,6
14	29	28	30	(32)	(32)	(32)	$-\infty$	$-\infty$	$-\infty$	6,7,8	32	8,7,6
15	31	32	33	34	(35)	(35)	(35)	$-\infty$	$-\infty$	7,8,9	35	8,7,6
16	32	34	37	37	37	(38)	(38)	(38)	$-\infty$	8,9,10	38	8,7,6
17	35	35	39	(41)	40	40	(41)	(41)	40	6,9,10	41	11,8,7
18	37	38	40	43	(44)	43	43	(44)	43	7,10	44	11,8
19	38	40	43	44	46	(47)	46	46	46	8	47	11
20	40	41	45	47	47	49	(50)	49	48	9	50	11

Stage 4

At stage 4 consider allocating funds to all four divisions. However, we know that we only have to consider allocating x_4 = $20.

$\$$ avail. x_4	$\$d_4$ to Burger Prince							d_4*	$f_4(x_4)$	x_4-d_4* $= x_3$
	3	4	5	6	7	8	9			
20	48	48	50	51	⑤②	51	51	7	52	13

The optimal discounted after tax profitability is $52,000,000. To see how this is determined, retrace the decisions through the various stages.

The optimal allocation for stage 4 is d_4* = 7, leaving x_3 = 13 for stages 1 to 3.

The optimal allocation at stage 3 of 13 is d_3* = 6 or d_3* = 7. This leaves x_2 = 7 or 6 respectively for stages 1 to 2.

The optimal allocation at stage 2 of 7 is d_2* = 4 and of 6 is d_2* = 3. In either case this leaves 3 for stage 1.

Thus the following are optimal allocations:

	Give	Return		Give	Return
Burger Prince	7	23		7	23
Fidelity Insurance	6	14	or	7	17
Wenthrope Jewelry	4	10		3	7
Dollar Stores	3	5		3	5
Total		52			52

PROBLEM 3

The Dreyfus Advertising Agency is currently handling the Super-Cola account. Super-Cola has earmarked $15,000 for next month's advertising of Burple powdered soft drink.

Dreyfus has determined a value, in terms of long term profit, for each form of advertising. Also, Super-Cola has placed restrictions on the maximum number of times a particular advertising medium can be used. This is summarized below:

Medium	Cost Per Use	Value Per Use	Maximum # of Uses
TV	$ 7,000	11	2
Radio	$ 2,000	5	3
Newspaper	$ 1,000	2	6
Burple Challenge	$12,000	18	1
Magazine	$ 4,000	9	2

How should Dreyfus spend the $15,000 to maximize the total value rating?

SOLUTION 3

This problem is a knapsack problem. The different advertising media correspond to the items going into the knapsack. As there are five different media, the problem will have five stages.

At stage 1, determine the number of TV ads to buy, at stage 2, determine the number of radio ads to buy, etc.

d_n = the number of times advertising medium n is used
x_n = the number of advertising dollars (in $1,000's) remaining at stage n to allocate to media 1 through n

The stage transformation functions for this problem give the amount of money remaining to allocate the previous stages after a certain number of ads of type n are selected at stage n. Specifically,

$$\text{Stage 5:} \quad x_4 = t_5(x_5, d_5) = x_5 - 4d_5$$
$$\text{Stage 4:} \quad x_3 = t_4(x_4, d_4) = x_4 - 12d_4$$
$$\text{Stage 3:} \quad x_2 = t_3(x_3, d_3) = x_3 - d_3$$
$$\text{Stage 2:} \quad x_1 = t_2(x_2, d_2) = x_2 - 2d_2$$
$$\text{Stage 1:} \quad x_0 = t_1(x_1, d_1) = x_1 - 7d_1$$

The return function at each stage gives the return for only allocating d_n ads to media n. Specifically,

$$\text{Stage 5:} \quad r_5(x_5, d_5) = 9d_5$$
$$\text{Stage 4:} \quad r_4(x_4, d_4) = 18d_4$$
$$\text{Stage 3:} \quad r_3(x_3, d_3) = 2d_3$$
$$\text{Stage 2:} \quad r_2(x_2, d_2) = 5d_2$$
$$\text{Stage 1:} \quad r_1(x_1, d_1) = 11d_1$$

Stage 1

At stage 1, compute the value associated with allocating up to
$15,000 to TV commercials (in units of $1,000's). For each
amount (value of x_1) compute the optimal allocation, d_1*, and
the resulting return from this action, $f_1(x_1)$. These are
summarized below.

x_1	d_1*	$f_1(x_1)$
0-6	0	0
7-13	1	11
14-15	2	22

Stage 2

At stage 2, determine how many radio commercials to purchase.
The input at stage 2, x_2, will be the number of thousand of
dollars available to be spent on both radio (stage 2) AND TV
(stage 1). Again this amount may be any amount between $0 and
$15,000.

The decision, d_2*, will be the optimal number of radio ads to
purchase. Since there is an upper limit of 3 radio ads, d_2 can
only be 0, 1, 2, or 3. For each possible value of d_2,
calculate:

$$r_2(x_2,d_2) + f_1(x_1) = 5d_2 + f_1(x_2-2d_2)$$

The value of d_2 that maximizes this function is designated as
d_2* and the corresponding value of the function is designated as
$f_2(x_2)$. The values of this function and the analysis for d_2*
and $f_2(x_2)$ are summarized below:

x_2	d_2 0	1	2	3	d_2*	$f_2(x_2)$	$x_2 - 2d_2* = x_1$
0	0				0	0	0
1	0				0	0	1
2	0	5			1	5	0
3	0	5			1	5	1
4	0	5	10		2	10	0
5	0	5	10		2	10	1
6	0	5	10	15	3	15	0
7	11	5	10	15	3	15	1
8	11	5	10	15	3	15	2
9	11	16	10	15	1	16	7
10	11	16	10	15	1	16	8
11	11	16	21	15	2	21	7
12	11	16	21	15	2	21	8
13	11	16	21	26	3	26	7
14	22	16	21	26	3	26	8
15	22	16	21	26	3	26	9

A sample calculation for the previous table for row $x_2 = 14$, column $d_2 = 1$: The return from $d_2 = 1$ is $r_2(x_2,d_2) = 5d_2 = 5(1)$ = 5. This leaves $x_1 = t_2(x_2,d_2) = x_2 - 2d_2 = 14 - 2 = 12$ to be allocated to the previous stages. The optimal value from the previous chart of $f_1(12) = 11$. Adding these two numbers (5 and 11) together gives the entry of 16 for this row and column.

Stage 3

At stage 3 the recurrence relation is:

$$f_3(x_3) = \underset{d_3 \le 6}{\text{MAX}} \{2d_3 + f_2(x_3-d_3)\}$$

The resulting table is:

x_3	d_3 0	1	2	3	4	5	6	d_3*	$f_3(x_3)$	$x_3 - d_3$* $= x_2$
0	0							0	0	0
1	0	2						1	2	0
2	5	2	4					0	5	2
3	5	7	4	6				1	7	2
4	10	7	9	6	8			0	10	4
5	10	12	9	11	8	10		1	12	4
6	15	12	14	11	13	10	12	0	15	6
7	15	17	14	16	13	15	12	1	17	6
8	15	17	19	16	18	15	17	2	19	6
9	16	17	19	21	18	20	17	3	21	6
10	16	18	19	21	23	20	22	4	23	6
11	21	18	20	21	23	25	22	5	25	6
12	21	23	20	22	23	25	27	6	27	6
13	26	23	25	22	24	25	27	6	27	7
14	26	28	25	27	24	26	27	1	28	13
15	26	28	30	27	29	26	28	2	30	13

A sample calculation for the previous table for row $x_3 = 14$, column $d_3 = 3$: The return from $d_3 = 3$ is $r_3(x_3,d_3) = 2d_3 = 2(3)$ = 6. This leaves $x_2 = t_3(x_3,d_3) = x_3 - d_3 = 14 - 3 = 11$ to be allocated to the previous stages. The optimal value from the previous chart of $f_2(11) = 21$. Adding these two numbers (6 and 21) together gives the entry of 27 for this row and column.

Stage 4

The recurrence relation for this stage is:

$$f_4(x_4) = \underset{d_4 \le 1}{\text{MAX}} \{18d_4 + f_3(x_4-12d_4)\}$$

The resulting table is as follows:

x_4	d_4 0	1	d_4*	$f_4(x_4)$	x_4-12d_4* $= x_3$
0	(0)		0	0	0
1	(2)		0	2	1
2	(5)		0	5	2
3	(7)		0	7	3
4	(10)		0	10	4
5	(12)		0	12	5
6	(15)		0	15	6
7	(17)		0	17	7
8	(19)		0	19	8
9	(21)		0	21	9
10	(23)		0	23	10
11	(25)		0	25	11
12	(27)	18	0	27	12
13	(27)	20	0	27	13
14	(28)	23	0	28	14
15	(30)	25	0	30	15

A sample calculation for the previous table for row $x_4 = 14$,
column $d_4 = 1$: The return from $d_4 = 1$ is $r_4(x_4,d_4) = 18d_4 = 18$.
This leaves $x_3 = t_4(x_4,d_4) = x_4 - 12d_4 = 14 - 12 = 2$ to be
allocated to the previous stages.   The optimal value from the
previous chart of $f_3(2) = 5$.   Adding these two numbers (18 and
5) together gives the entry of 23 for this row and column.

Stage 5

The recurrence relation for this stage is:

$$f_5(x_5) = \underset{d_5 \leq 2}{\text{MAX}} \{9d_5 + f_4(x_5-4d_5)\}$$

At this stage the only calculation needed is for $x_5 = 15$ as
Dreyfus wants to spend the entire \$15,000.   The resulting table
is:

x_5	d_5 0	1	2	d_5*	$f_5(x_5)$	x_5-4d_5* $= x_4$
15	30	34	(35)	2	35	7

The optimal value is 35.   Working back through the network,
select 2 magazine ads (stage 5), leaving 7 for stage 4 giving
0 Burple Challenges, leaving 7 for stage 3 giving 1 newspaper
ad, leaving 6 for stage 2 giving 3 radio ads, leaving 0 for TV.

PROBLEM 4

Dicom Corporation wishes to determine a production schedule for its new Model 44/12 virtual memory computer. Because of differences in parts availability and spare production capacity, the cost of producing the machines will vary from month to month.

The following table gives these costs together with the sales demand over the next 5 months as well as the maximum possible production level per month.

Month	Cost of Production Per Machine (in $100,000's)	Maximum Production Level for Month	Sales Demand (in Units)
July	42	5	3
August	32	4	2
September	18	3	1
October	26	4	5
November	45	5	3

The holding cost for each unsold machine still in inventory at the end of the month is $500,000. Corporate policy dictates that the maximum number of machines allowed in inventory at the end of any month is 8.

Determine an optimal 5 month production schedule for the Dicom Model 44/12.

SOLUTION 4

This is an $N = 5$ period dynamic programming problem with each period corresponding to one month. Working backwards, let stage one correspond to November, stage 2 to October, etc. The following data can be inferred from above:

Month (n)	Demand D_n	Production Capacity P_n	Storage Capacity W_n	Production Cost Per Unit C_n	Holding Cost Per unit H_n
1	3	5	8	45	5
2	5	4	8	26	5
3	1	3	8	18	5
4	2	4	8	32	5
5	3	5	8	42	5

(Costs are in $100,000's)

If, at some month between July and November, a consultant was called in to solve this problem, besides the above data he would have to know how many computers were currently in inventory.

Hence, define the state variable x_n = the number of computers in inventory at the beginning of month n. Since the computer is new, there will be no inventory at the start of July ($x_5 = 0$).

Also define d_n = the production quantity for month n. Then the stage transformations for months 0 through 4 can be defined by: (Previous month's inventory) + (production this month) − (demand this month), or

$$x_{n-1} = x_n + d_n - D_n$$

The return (cost) at each stage, $r_n(x_n, d_n)$, is the sum of the production and holding costs for the month. The production cost is the production cost per unit multiplied by the number of units produced (d_n). The holding cost is the ending inventory for the month multiplied by the holding cost per unit.

Hence,

$$r_n(x_n, d_n) = C_n d_n + H_n(x_n + d_n - D_n)$$

This gives:

$$r_1(x_1, d_1) = 50d_1 + 5x_1 - 15$$
$$r_2(x_2, d_2) = 31d_2 + 5x_2 - 25$$
$$r_3(x_3, d_3) = 23d_3 + 5x_3 - 5$$
$$r_4(x_4, d_4) = 37d_4 + 5x_4 - 10$$
$$r_5(x_5, d_5) = 47d_5 + 5x_5 - 15$$

There are, however, certain restrictions on x_n and d_n:

1) Since backordering is not allowed, we must be able to meet the sales demand. That is, for month n:

$$x_n + d_n \geq D_n. \qquad (1)$$

2) Because there is a maximum storage of W_n at each stage n, the total inventory at the end of any month cannot exceed W_n. Hence, for each month it must be true that $x_n + d_n - D_n \leq W_n$, or

$$x_n + d_n \leq W_n + D_n. \qquad (2)$$

3) The amount produced in any given month cannot exceed the production capacity for that month, or

$$d_n \leq P_n . \qquad (3)$$

Define the optimal value function, $f_n(x_n)$ to be the optimal return (minimal cost) for stages 1 through n given one starts stage n with x_n computers in inventory. Then,

$$f_n(x_n) = \underset{d_n}{\text{MIN}} \{r_n(x_n, d_n) + f_{n-1}(x_{n-1})\}$$

where the d_n is constrained by restrictions (1), (2), and (3).

Stage 1

Starting at stage 1 (November), since $f_0(x_0) = 0$ is a boundary condition, then,

$$f_1(x_1) = \underset{d_1}{\text{MIN}}\ r_1(x_1, d_1)$$

Using the expression for $r_1(x_1, d_1)$ and restrictions (1), (2), and (3),

$$f_1(x_1) = \text{MIN}\ \ 5x_1 + 50d_1 - 15$$

$$\text{s.t.}\quad x_1 + d_1 \geq 3 \qquad (1)$$

$$x_1 + d_1 \leq 11 \qquad (2)$$

$$d_1 \leq 5 \qquad (3)$$

$$\text{and,}\quad d_1 \geq 0$$

Thus the restrictions are that $0 \leq d_1 \leq 5$, and from (2), $x_1 \leq 11$. Tabulating the values for $50d_1 + 5x_1 - 15$ for feasible values gives:

x_1	0	1	2	d_1 3	4	5	d_1*	$f_1(x_1)$
0				(135)	185	235	3	135
1			(90)	140	190	240	2	90
2		(45)	95	145	195	245	1	45
3	(0)	50	100	150	200	250	0	0

Note that although one might wish to consider all possibilities for x_1 up to 11, this is unnecessary. Having $x_1 > 3$ would result in Dicom having computers in inventory at the end of November. This is undesirable in this problem and will actually cause an increase in costs.

Stage 2

At stage 2 the recurrence relation is:

$$f_2(x_2) = \underset{d_2}{\text{MIN}}\ \ 5x_2 + 31d_2 - 25 + f_1(x_1)$$

Given the restrictions, the subproblem is:

$$f_2(x_2) = \text{MIN} \quad 5x_2 + 31d_2 - 25 + f_1(x_2 + d_2 - 5)$$

$$\text{s.t.} \quad x_2 + \quad d_2 \geq \quad 5 \quad (1)$$

$$x_2 + \quad d_2 \leq \quad 13 \quad (2)$$

$$d_2 \leq \quad 4 \quad (3)$$

$$\text{and} \quad d_2 \geq \quad 0$$

The table for the values of $5x_2 + 31d_2 - 25 + f_1(x_1)$ is:

x_2	d_2 0	1	2	3	4	d_2*	$f_2(x_2)$	$x_2 + d_2* - 5 = x_1$
1					(239)	4	239	0
2				213	(199)	4	199	1
3			187	173	(159)	4	159	2
4		161	147	133	(119)	4	119	3
5	135	121	107	(93)		3	93	3
6	95	81	(67)			2	67	3
7	55	(41)				1	41	3
8	(15)					0	15	3

Note that $x_2 = 0$ is infeasible and therefore there is no row corresponding to $x_2 = 0$.

Stage 3

The recurrence relation for stage 3 is:

$$f_3(x_3) = \text{MIN} \quad 5x_3 + 23d_3 - 5 + f_2(x_3 + d_3 - 1)$$

$$\text{s.t.} \quad x_3 + \quad d_3 \geq \quad 1 \quad (1)$$

$$x_3 + \quad d_3 \leq \quad 9 \quad (2)$$

$$d_3 \leq \quad 3 \quad (3)$$

$$\text{and} \quad d_3 \geq \quad 0$$

The table for the values of $5x_3 + 23d_3 - 5 + f_2(x_3 + d_3 - 1)$ is:

x_3	d_3 0	1	2	3	d_3*	$f_3(x_3)$	x_3+d_3*-1 $= x_2$
0			280	263	3	263	2
1		263	245	228	3	228	3
2	244	227	210	193	3	193	4
3	209	192	175	172	3	172	5
4	174	157	154	151	3	151	6
5	139	136	133	130	3	130	7
6	118	115	112	109	3	109	8
7	97	94	91		1	91	8
8	76	73			1	73	8

Stage 4

The recurrence relation for stage 4 is:

$$f_4(x_4) = MIN \quad 5x_4 + 37d_4 - 10 + f_3(x_4 + d_4 - 2)$$

$$\text{s.t.} \quad x_4 + d_4 \geq 2 \qquad (1)$$

$$x_4 + d_4 \leq 10 \qquad (2)$$

$$d_4 \leq 4 \qquad (3)$$

$$\text{and} \quad d_4 \geq 0$$

The table for the values of $5x_4 + 37d_4 - 10 + f_3(x_4 + d_4 - 2)$ is:

x_4	d_4 0	1	2	3	4	d_4*	$f_4(x_4)$	x_4+d_4*-2 $= x_3$
0			327	329	331	2	327	0
1		295	297	299	315	1	295	0
2	263	265	267	283	299	0	263	0
3	233	235	251	267	283	0	233	1
4	203	219	235	251	267	0	203	2
5	187	203	219	235	254	0	187	3
6	171	187	203	220	241	0	171	4
7	155	171	190	209		0	155	5
8	139	158	177			0	139	6

Stage 5

The recurrence relation for stage 5 is:

$$f_5(x_5) = \text{MIN} \quad 5x_5 + 47d_5 - 15 + f_4(x_5 + d_5 - 3)$$

$$\text{s.t.} \quad x_5 + d_5 \geq 3 \qquad (1)$$

$$x_5 + d_5 \leq 11 \qquad (2)$$

$$d_5 \leq 5 \qquad (3)$$

$$\text{and} \quad d_5 \geq 0$$

Since July starts with $x_5 = 0$ inventory on hand, compute the table for $5x_5 + 47d_5 - 15 + f_4(x_5 + d_5 - 3)$ only for $x_5 = 0$.

x_5	0	1	2	d_5 3	4	5	d_5*	$f_5(x_5)$	x_5+d_5*-3 $= x_4$
0				(453)	468	483	3	453	0

Working backwards through the tables, one can determine the optimal solution that gives the minimum cost of $453 \times 100,000 = \$43,500,000$.

Stage	Month	Produce (d_n*)	Inventory On-Hand Beginning Next Month x_{n-1}
5	July	3	0
4	August	2	0
3	September	3	2
2	October	4	1
1	November	2	0

ANSWERED PROBLEMS

PROBLEM 5

Ajax Sound is in the business of fabricating phonograph connection wire. They purchase 30 foot spools of wire from National Electric at $3.00 per spool and cut the wire into various lengths.

Each length of wire is fitted with phono connector jacks at both ends and then packaged. The phono connector jacks cost $.40 per pair (one pair is used in each package of wire). Packaging and labor together cost $.20 per package.

Because of Ajax's superior marketing skills they are in the enviable position of being able to sell all the phonograph connection wire they produce. They are currently contemplating offering four different sized packages of wire:

Size	Wholesale Package Price
5'	$1.30
8'	$1.80
12'	$2.50
16'	$3.30

If unused wire from a spool can be sold for scrap at $.03 per foot, how many packages of each size wire should Ajax make from a 30-foot spool?

PROBLEM 6

Unidyde Corporation is currently planning the production of red dye number 56 for the next four months. Production and handling costs, as well as production and storage capacity, vary from month to month. This data is given in the table below.

Production and holding costs are in ($1,000's per batch) and production levels and storage capacities are in batches. Holding costs are based on inventory on hand at the end of the month. The number of orders for batches the sales department has received over the four month period are also given.

Month	Produc-tion Cost	Maximum Production	Holding Cost	Storage Capacity	Orders Received
Febr.	11	3	3	4	2
March	15	4	2	3	4
April	16	3	2	5	2
May	9	2	1	2	3

Unidyne does not wish to have any inventory of the dye at the end of May. Its current inventory is 2 batches.

Determine a production schedule for the next four months.

PROBLEM 7

Given the following shortest path problem in which travel is only permitted from left to right. Use dynamic programming to determine the shortest path from node 1 to:

a) Node 15.

b) Node 14.

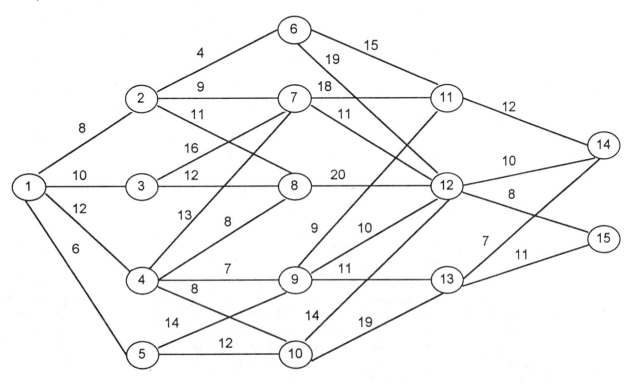

PROBLEM 8

Marvelous Marvin is planning his annual "Almost Everything Must Go" inventory clearance sale. Marvin has decided to allocate 18 shelf feet to the cooking section. He is considering offering up to five items for sale in this category:

Item	Shelf Feet Required	Expected Profit
A	1	$ 10
B	2	$ 25
C	3	$ 40
D	5	$ 70
E	7	$100

If Marvin wants at least one item A and one item B on sale, what stock should he have on sale and what is the total expected profit?

PROBLEM 9

Mission Bay Development Corporation is engaged in developing an exclusive 25 acre parcel of property. They have received bids from five builders to purchase construction lots. Because of the different nature of the builders, they desire different sized lots. The data is as follows:

Builder	Lot Size Requested	Offered Price Per Lot	Maximum Number Of Lots Desired
1	3 acre	$ 50,000	6
2	1 acre	$ 15,000	5
3	6 acre	$105,000	8
4	20 acre	$350,000	1
5	5 acre	$ 91,000	2

How should Mission Bay sell their land to maximize total sales revenue?

PROBLEM 10

Universal Telephone and Television has $6,000,000 earmarked for investment among three divisions which are having earnings difficulties. The three divisions are Bolivia Telephone Company, Camden Insurance Corporation, and Host Baking Company.
   The company is considering either giving Bolivia Telephone 0, 2, 4, or 6 million dollars or selling it for 2 million dollars. It is also considering giving Camden Insurance either 0, 2, 4, or 6 million dollars but it is not contemplating selling this division. Finally, it is considering either giving Host Baking 0, 4, or 6 million dollars or selling it for 4 million dollars.
   The table below gives estimates of the long term present value return of each action. All figures are in $1,000,000's.

Action	Bolivia Telephone	Camden Insurance	Host Baking
Sell	$ 2	---	$ 4
Give $0	$-1	$ 1	$ 3
Give $2	$ 4	$ 5	---
Give $4	$ 7	$ 8	$ 5
Give $6	$10	$12	$ 8

By careful modelling of the problem, it can be shown that the network on the next page corresponds to this investment problem. The arc distances are the long term results associated with each investment alternative.
   Use dynamic programming to find the longest path(s) through this network and determine how Universal Telephone and Television should disperse the $6,000,000.

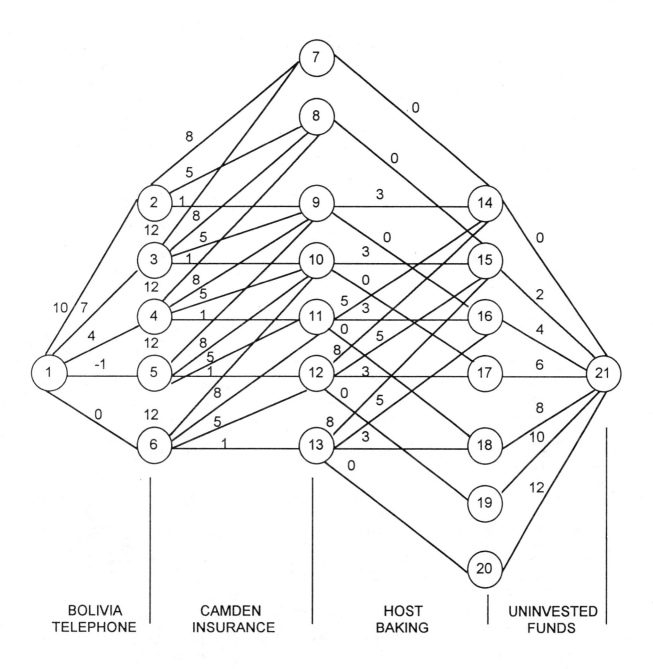

BOLIVIA
TELEPHONE

CAMDEN
INSURANCE

HOST
BAKING

UNINVESTED
FUNDS

PROBLEM 11

Franklin Plate Company is in the business of manufacturing commemorative plates for holidays. The company is currently planning its production schedule for this year's Thanksgiving plate.

Discussions with the sales manager have indicated that sales of the plate will run from August through November. The production manager has determined the manufacturing cost per plate for each of these months as well as the sales demand (in 1000's) and manufacturing capacity (in 1000's). The data is as follows:

Month	Demand	Manufacturing Cost Per Plate	Maximum Production
August	2	2	6
September	4	3	6
October	6	3	4
November	3	4	3

It is also known that the maximum inventory level possible at the end of any month is 5,000 plates. The storage cost per plate for each plate in inventory at the end of the month is $.50.

Franklin has no inventory on hand at the beginning of August and wishes to have no inventory left after November. Use dynamic programming to determine an optimal production schedule.

PROBLEM 12

Walt's Custom Boats manufactures luxury yachts. Walt is phasing out production of his 42-foot Sportfisher which he plans to replace with a 44-foot Sportfisher. Walt currently has orders for the next four months for the 42-foot model after which he will cease production. The following data (with costs in $1,000's) is given for the next four months:

Mon.	Production Cost Per Boat	Maximum Production Level	Holding Cost Per Boat In Inventory At End Of Month	Maximum Storage Capacity	# Boats To Be Delivered In Month
May	25	4	1	6	1
June	27	3	1	5	3
July	30	2	2	3	3
Aug.	29	3	1	4	4

If Walt's current inventory of 42-foot Sportfishers is 1 boat, how should Walt schedule production of the 42-foot Sportfisher over the next four months to minimize the total production and inventory holding costs?

TRUE/FALSE

13. In order to use dynamic programming one must be able to view the problem as a multistage decision problem.

14. The stage transformation function identifies which state one reaches at the next stage for a given decision.

15. At each stage of a dynamic programming problem one must solve a separate subproblem.

16. The stages of a dynamic programming problem must all have the same number of states.

17. In a knapsack problem, the stages can correspond to the different types of items.

18. The subscripts used in dynamic programming notation refer to states.

19. In a knapsack problem, if one adds another item, one must completely resolve the problem in order to find a new optimal solution.

20. In a production and inventory control problem, the states can correspond to the amount of inventory on hand at the beginning of each period.

21. In a dynamic programming problem the number of stages must equal the number of states.

22. The stage transformation function is a function of all previous decisions.

23. The principle of optimality states that regardless of which decisions were made at previous stages, if the decision made at stage n is to be part of an overall optimal solution, then the decision must be optimal for all remaining stages.

24. Stage 1 in a dynamic programming problem involves finding the best choice for the final decision to actually be made.

25. Using dynamic programming, total enumeration of all possible solutions to a problem is performed.

26. Dynamic programming, like linear programming, is a specific technique that can be applied in a consistent manner to a wide variety of problems.

27. Finding the optimal solution at each stage of a dynamic programming problem will lead to an optimal solution to the total problem.

CHAPTER

19

Calculus–Based Solution Procedures

KEY CONCEPTS

CONCEPT	ILLUSTRATED PROBLEMS	ANSWERED PROBLEMS
Unconstrained Optimization With One Variable	1,4	6,7,8,12
Optimizing a Function of One Variable Over an Interval	1	6
Unconstrained Optimization With More Than One Variable	2	11
Constrained Optimization With More Than One Variable/LaGrange Multipliers	2,3,5	9,10,11

REVIEW

1. <u>Calculus</u> <u>based</u> <u>solution</u> <u>procedures</u> are frequently required to solve problems with <u>non-linear</u> <u>functions</u>.

2. For a problem with one variable and no constraints, sufficient conditions for a point x* to be a <u>local</u> <u>maximum</u> <u>(minimum)</u> are:

$$(1) \quad \frac{df}{dx} = 0$$

$$(2) \quad \frac{d^2f}{dx^2} < 0 \quad \text{for a maximum} \quad (> 0 \quad \text{for a minimum})$$

3. To find a <u>global</u> <u>maximum</u> <u>(minimum)</u> for a problem with one variable over an interval from a to b, select the point with the highest (lowest) objective function values among all local maxima (minima) and each end point (a and b).

4. For <u>unconstrained</u> <u>functions</u> <u>in</u> <u>more</u> <u>than</u> <u>one</u> <u>variable</u>, a necessary condition for a point, x*, to be a local maximum or minimum is that all partial derivatives with respect to each variable evaluated at x* must be 0.

5. Sufficient conditions for (x_1^*, x_2^*) to be a local maximum (minimum) for an <u>unconstrained</u> <u>function</u> <u>in</u> <u>two</u> <u>variables</u> are that at (x_1^*, x_2^*):

$$(1) \quad \frac{df}{dx_1} = 0; \qquad \frac{df}{dx_2} = 0$$

$$(2) \quad \frac{d^2f}{dx_1^2} < 0 \quad \text{for a maximum} \quad (> 0 \quad \text{for a minimum})$$

$$(3) \quad \left[\frac{d^2f}{dx_1^2}\right]\left[\frac{d^2f}{dx_2^2}\right] - \left[\frac{d^2f}{dx_1\,dx_2}\right]^2 > 0$$

6. A <u>Lagrangian</u> <u>function</u> for an objective function, $f(x_1,x_2)$ with one equality constraint of the form $g(x_1,x_2) = b$ is given by: $L(x_1,x_2,\lambda) = f(x_1,x_2) + \lambda(g(x_1,x_2) - b)$. Sufficient conditions for (x_1*,x_2*) to be optimal are the same as in (5) with the function $L(x_1,x_2,\lambda)$ replacing $f(x_1,x_2)$ along with $df/d\lambda = 0$. Note these functions are evaluated with $\lambda = \lambda*$.

7. The interpretation of a <u>Lagrange</u> <u>multiplier</u>, λ, is similar to that of a shadow or dual price in linear programming. It gives the instantaneous amount the objective function will <u>decrease</u> per unit increase in the right hand side value of the constraint, but its value changes immediately with changes to the right hand side.

8. A <u>problem</u> <u>with</u> <u>one</u> <u>inequality</u> <u>constraint</u> may be solved as follows:

   (a) Ignore the inequality constraint and solve as in (5). If the constraint is satisfied by the solution, STOP. (this is optimal) Otherwise, then go to (b).

   (b) Note all local maxima (or minima) satisfying the inequality constraint.

   (c) Solve the problem as if the constraint were an equality using the Lagrangian method in (6) above.

   (d) The optimal solution is that solution in (b) or (c) that gives the best objective function value.

9. <u>Computer</u> <u>programs</u> exist for solving many non-linear models, but they are much more complex and more difficult to use than linear programming packages. They typically are written for specific non-linear models and may, in fact, give local optima rather than global optima solutions.

10. Frequently, in an effort to avoid the problems associated with non-linearity, <u>approximate</u> <u>linear</u> <u>models</u> are used unless the results prove unacceptable.

ILLUSTRATED PROBLEMS

PROBLEM 1

Given the function: $f(x) = 3x^4 - 4x^3 - 12x^2$

a) Find all local maxima and minima for the function.

b) What is the global maxima for the function?

c) What is the global minimum for the function?

d) What is the global maximum if x is constrained to be in the interval: $-2 \leq x \leq 4$?

SOLUTION 1

a) A necessary condition for a point to be a local maximum or minimum is that df/dx = 0. Now,

$$df/dx = 12x^3 - 12x^2 - 24x.$$

Setting this to 0 and factoring gives: $12x(x-2)(x+1) = 0$.
Thus the local optima are the values of x that make the terms above equal 0. These are x = -1, x = 0, and x = 2.
   To see which are local maxima and which are local minima, determine the second derivative at these values.

$$d^2f/dx^2 = 36x^2 - 24x - 24$$

Evaluated at x = -1 gives $36(-1)^2 - 24(-1) - 24 = 36$.
   Since this is positive, x = -1 is a local minima.
Evaluated at x = 0 gives $36(0)^2 - 24(0) - 24 = -24$.
   Since this is negative, x = 0 is a local maxima.
Evaluated at x = 2 gives $36(2)^2 - 24(2) - 24 = 72$.
   Since this is positive, x = 2 is a local minima.

b) Note that the global minimum can occur at a local minimum or at x = $-\infty$ or x = $+\infty$. But f($-\infty$) and f($+\infty$) = ∞. Thus either x = -1 or x = 2 is the global minimum. Substituting these values into f(x):
   $f(-1) = 3(-1)^4 - 4(-1)^3 - 12(-1)^2 = -5$, and
   $f(2) = 3(2)^4 - 4(2)^3 - 12(2)^2 = -32$.
Thus x = 2 is the global minimum.

c) As pointed out above x = $-\infty$ or x = $+\infty$ gives the global maximum.

d) The global maximum can occur at the local maximum or at an end point. Substituting x = -2, 0, and 4 into f(x) gives $f(-2) = 32$, $f(0) = 0$, and $f(4) = 320$. x = 4 is the global maximum.

PROBLEM 2

Given the following problem:

$$\text{MAX} \quad f(x_1, x_2) = -4x_1^2 - 3x_2^2 + 2x_1x_2 + 12x_1 + 30x_2$$

a) Solve for the optimal solution. Give the optimal value of the function and verify it is a maximum.

b) Solve for the optimal solution if $4x_1 + 3x_2 \leq 36$.

c) Solve for the optimal solution if $4x_1 + 3x_2 \leq 24$.

SOLUTION 2

a)
$$\frac{df}{dx_1} = -8x_1 + 2x_2 + 12 = 0 \tag{1}$$

$$\frac{df}{dx_2} = 2x_1 - 6x_2 + 30 = 0 \tag{2}$$

From (1), $x_2 = 4x_1 - 6$. Substituting this into (2) gives:

$2x_1 - 6(4x_1 - 6) + 30 = -22x_1 + 66 = 0$. This yields $x_1 = 3$.

Substituting this into the above expression for x_2 gives:

$x_2 = 4x_1 - 6 = 4(3) - 6 = 6$.

To show this is a maximum:

$$\frac{d^2f}{dx_1^2} = -8 \quad \text{which is} < 0.$$

$$\left[\frac{d^2f}{dx_1^2}\right]\left[\frac{d^2f}{dx_2^2}\right] - \left[\frac{d^2f}{dx_1dx_2}\right]^2 = (-8)(-6) - (2)^2 = 44 > 0$$

This satisfies the conditions for a maximum.

b) First try the solution in the constraint:

$$4x_1 + 3x_2 = 4(3) + 3(6) = 30 < 36.$$

Since the constraint is satisfied, the solution is optimal.

c) Since the optimal solution to (a) does not satisfy this constraint now, solve using the Lagrangian method with the constraint holding as an equality. To form the Lagrangian, subtract λ times the constraint from the objective function:

$$L(x_1,x_2,\lambda) = -4x_1^2 - 3x_2^2 + 2x_1x_2 + 12x_1 + 30x_2 + \lambda(4x_1 + 3x_2 - 24)$$

$$\frac{dL}{dx_1} = -8x_1 + 2x_2 + 12 + 4\lambda = 0 \qquad (1)$$

$$\frac{dL}{dx_2} = -6x_2 + 2x_1 + 30 + 3\lambda = 0 \qquad (2)$$

$$\frac{dL}{d\lambda} = 4x_1 + 3x_2 - 24 = 0 \qquad (3)$$

From (3), $x_1 = -3/4\ x_2 + 6$. Substituting into (1) and (2) gives:

$$-8(-3/4\ x_2 + 6) + 2x_2 + 12 + 4\lambda = 0 \qquad (4)$$

and, $\quad -6x_2 + 2(-3/4\ x_2 + 6) + 30 + 3\lambda = 0 \qquad (5)$

Simplifying, (4) and (5) become:

$$8x_2 + 4\lambda = 36 \qquad (6)$$
$$15/2\ x_2 - 3\lambda = 24 \qquad (7)$$

Solving the two equations (6) and (7) in two unknowns gives:

$$x_2 = 46/9; \quad \lambda = -11/9$$

Substituting into (3) gives $x_1 = 13/6$.

To show that $x_1 = 13/6$, $x_2 = 46/9$ is a maximum, look at the second partial derivatives of the Lagrangian:

$$\frac{d^2L}{dx_1^2} = -8 < 0$$

$$\left[\frac{d^2L}{dx_1^2}\right]\left[\frac{d^2L}{dx_2^2}\right] - \left[\frac{d^2L}{dx_1dx_2}\right]^2 = (-8)(-6) - (2)^2 = 44 > 0$$

Thus this is a maximum.

PROBLEM 3

Given the following problem:

$$\text{MAX} \quad -x_1^2 - 2x_2^2 - x_1x_2 + 8x_1 + 10x_2$$

$$\text{s.t.} \quad x_1 + 2x_2 = 4$$

a) Using the Lagrangian, solve for the optimal solution.

b) Using the result to (a) determine the value of an extra unit of the resource of the constraint.

c) Solve for the optimal solution if the constraint were:
$x_1 + 2x_2 \geq 4$.

d) Solve for the optimal solution if the constraint were:
$x_1 + 2x_2 \leq 4$.

SOLUTION 3

a) First rewrite the constraint as: $x_1 + 2x_2 - 4 = 0$. Then form the Lagrangian by multiplying this constraint by λ and adding it to the objective function:

$$L(x_1,x_2,\lambda) = -x_1^2 - 2x_2^2 - x_1x_2 + 8x_1 + 10x_2 + \lambda(x_1 + 2x_2 - 4)$$

Taking the partial derivatives with respect to x_1, x_2, and and setting them equal to 0 gives:

$$dL/dx_1 = -2x_1 - x_2 + 8 + \lambda = 0 \qquad (1)$$

$$dL/dx_2 = -4x_2 - x_1 + 10 + 2\lambda = 0 \qquad (2)$$

$$dL/d\lambda = x_1 + 2x_2 - 4 = 0 \qquad (3)$$

To solve, note that from the last equation: $x_1 = -2x_2 + 4$. Substituting in the first equation gives:

$$-2(-2x_2 + 4) - x_2 + 8 + \lambda = 0 \text{ or } 3x_2 + \lambda = 0. \quad \text{So, } \lambda = -3x_2$$

Substituting these values for x_1 and λ into (2) gives:

$$-4x_2 - (-2x_2 + 4) + 10 + 2(-3x_2) = 0 \quad =====> \quad x_2 = 3/4$$

Substituting in the expression for λ gives:

$$\lambda = -3x_2 \qquad\qquad =====> \quad \lambda = -9/4$$

Finally, substituting these into the expression for x_1 gives:

$$x_1 = -2x_2 + 4 \qquad\qquad =====> \quad x_1 = 5/2.$$

To show this solution is a local maximum, show that

$$\frac{d^2L}{dX_1^{\;2}} < 0 \quad\text{and}\quad \left[\frac{d^2L}{dx_1^{\;2}}\right]\left[\frac{d^2L}{dx_2^{\;2}}\right] - \left[\frac{d^2L}{dx_1 dx_2}\right]^2 > 0$$

For this problem,

$$\frac{d^2L}{dX_1^{\;2}} = -2 \quad\text{and}\quad \left[\frac{d^2L}{dx_1^{\;2}}\right]\left[\frac{d^2L}{dx_2^{\;2}}\right] - \left[\frac{d^2L}{dx_1 dx_2}\right]^2 = (-2)(-4)-(-1)^2 = 7$$

b) The value of the extra unit of the resource is the negative of the value of the Lagrange multiplier or $2.25.

c) Find the unconstrained maximum using partial derivatives:

$$\frac{df}{dx_1} = -2x_1 - x_2 + 8 = 0; \qquad \frac{df}{dx_2} = -4x_2 - x_1 + 10 = 0$$

Solving these two equations for x_1 and x_2 gives $x_1 = 22/7$, $x_2 = 12/7$. Now test to see if this is a local maxima:

$$\frac{d^2f}{dX_1^{\;2}} = -2 \quad\text{which is} < 0.$$

$$\left[\frac{d^2f}{dx_1^{\;2}}\right]\left[\frac{d^2f}{dx_2^{\;2}}\right] - \left[\frac{d^2f}{dx_1 dx_2}\right]^2 = (-2)(-4) - (-1)^2 = 7 > 0$$

This satisfies the conditions for a local maxima. Furthermore, substituting the values for x_1 and x_2 into the constraint gives:

$$x_1 + 2x_2 = (22/7) + 2(12/7) = 46/7 \text{ which is} > 4.$$

Since the constraint is satisfied by this solution, it is optimal.

d) This constraint is not satisfied by the local maxima found in (c). Thus the Lagrangian would be formed and partial derivatives taken with respect to x_1, x_2 and g and set to 0. This was done in part (a). Since there are no other local maxima, the solution found in part (a) is optimal here: $x_1 = 5/2$, $x_2 = 3/4$.

PROBLEM 4

A shoe manufacturer is trying to decide what price to charge for its new "Softshoe" model. A survey has found that the demand for shoes will be dependent on price. In particular, if price p is charged, the yearly demand will be approximately 15,000 - 100p.
  The total variable costs to manufacture the shoes are figured to be $30 and the cost of leasing the necessary shoe machines is $50,000 per year.

a) What price should be charged for the shoes to maximize yearly profits?

b) What would be the yearly demand at this price?

c) What is the expected yearly profit for the company for the Softshoe model?

SOLUTION 4

a) If p = the price charged, then demand is 15,000 - 100p.

Then, the revenue = (price)(demand) = p(15,000 - 100p) = $15,000p - 100p^2$. The variable costs are $30(demand) = 450,000 - 3000p and fixed costs are $50,000.

Thus if T = total yearly profit then,
$$T = (revenue) - (variable\ costs) - (fixed\ costs)$$
$$= (15,000p - 100p^2) - (450,000 - 3000p) - 50,000$$
$$= -100p^2 + 18,000p - 500,000$$

To maximize,

$$\frac{dT}{dp} = -200p + 18,000 = 0 \quad or \quad p = \$90.$$

To show this is a maximum:

$$\frac{d^2 f}{dx^2} = -200 < 0. \quad Thus\ this\ is\ a\ maximum.$$

b) Demand = 15,000 - 100(90) = 6000 per year.

c) Total Yearly Profit = $-100(90)^2 + 18,000(90) - 500,000 = 310,000$.

PROBLEM 5

A crude mathematical model for the return on two types of investments of under \$25,000 each is given by:

$$r(x_1,x_2) = -.00008x_1{}^2 - .00012x_2{}^2 + .00016x_1x_2 + .4x_1 + .8x_2$$

where x_1 and x_2 are the sums allocated to investment 1 and investment 2 respectively. How should an individual with \$10,000 to invest in these investments distribute his money? What would be the return on an extra investment dollar?

SOLUTION 5

The problem is:

$$\text{MAX } r(x_1,x_2) = -.00008x_1{}^2 - .00012x_2{}^2 + .00016x_1x_2 + .4x_1 + .8x_2$$

$$\text{s.t. } x_1 + x_2 = 10,000$$

Form the Lagrangian,

$$L(x_1,x_2,\lambda) = -.00008x_1{}^2 - .00012x_2{}^2 + .00016x_1x_2 + .4x_1 + .8x_2 + \lambda x_1 \\ + \lambda x_2 - 10000\lambda$$

$$\frac{dL}{dx_1} = -.00016x_1 + .00016x_2 + .4 + \lambda = 0$$

$$\frac{dL}{dx_2} = -.00024x_2 + .00016x_1 + .8 + \lambda = 0$$

$$\frac{dL}{d\lambda} = x_1 + x_2 - 10,000 = 0$$

Solving, from the first and second conditions,

$$\lambda = .00016x_1 - .00016x_2 - .4$$
$$\text{Also, } \lambda = -.00016x_1 + .00024x_2 - .8$$

Setting these two equal gives: $-.00032x_1 + .00040x_2 = .4$
Solving this equation in two unknowns with the third condition above, gives $x_1 = 5,000$, $x_2 = 5,000$ and $\lambda = -.4$

To show this is a maximum, consider the second partial derivatives when $\lambda = -.4$.

$$\frac{d^2 L}{dX_1^{\,2}} = -.00016 < 0$$

$$\left[\frac{d^2 L}{dx_1^{\,2}}\right] \left[\frac{d^2 L}{dx_2^{\,2}}\right] - \left[\frac{d^2 L}{dx_1 dx_2}\right]^2 = (-.00016)(-.00024) - (.00016)^2$$

$$= .0000000128 > 0.$$

Thus, this solution gives a maximum. The optimal solution is to invest $5,000 in investment 1 and $5,000 in investment 2. The return on an extra investment dollar is $-\lambda = \$.40$.

ANSWERED PROBLEMS

PROBLEM 6

Suppose a profit function is given by:

$$P(x) = x^4 - 8x^3 + 22x^2 - 24x + 15$$

a) Show that x = 1, x = 2, and x = 3 give the local maxima and minima for this problem. Identify which are local maxima and which are local minima.

b) What is the global minimum for this function with no constraints?

c) Find the global maximum for each of the following three intervals: (1) $0 \leq x \leq 5$; (2) $0 \leq x \leq 3.4$; (3) $.7 \leq x \leq 3.4$.

PROBLEM 7

As every business student knows, profit = revenue - cost. In economics, the derivative of a function (which gives the instantaneous rate of change of the function) defines what is called the <u>marginal</u> value of the function. Thus the derivative of the profit function is called the marginal profit, the derivative of the cost function is called the marginal cost.

a) Show that a necessary condition for a point to be optimal is that marginal revenue = marginal cost.

Given the following functions: Revenue: $r(x) = 100x$
                              Cost: $c(x) = x^2 + 10x + 100$

b) Determine the profit function.

c) Determine the optimal profit.

d) Verify by calculus arguments that this is a maximum, not a minimum.

e) Verify that at the optimal point, the marginal revenue equals the marginal cost.

PROBLEM 8

Columbia Mopeds has ascertained that monthly demand for its new moped will vary with the price charged. The best estimate is that it can sell x mopeds per month at a price of ($1,110-.10x).
   Fixed monthly costs are $100,000 and production costs are $110 per moped.

a) Determine Columbia's optimal production and pricing policy.

b) What is the maximum monthly profit?

c) Suppose a tax of $10 per moped is imposed on the manufacturer. How much of this tax should be passed along to the customer if Columbia wants to continue to maximize monthly profits?

PROBLEM 9

Solve the following problem:

$$\text{MAX } -5x_1^2 - x_2^2 - 2x_1x_2 + 80x_1 + 20x_2$$

$$\text{s.t.} \quad 2x_1 + x_2 = 10$$

PROBLEM 10

Halgreen, Inc. manufactures two styles of lawnmowers, the Z-model and the W-model. Halgreen had a study performed concerning price-sales ratios. The study shows that z model Z lawnmowers can be sold per week at a price of ($200 - .01z) and that w model W lawnmowers can be sold per week at a price of ($300 - .02w).
   Fixed costs are $40,000 per week. Manufacturing costs are $50 per unit for the model Z and $80 per unit for the model W. If both models are produced, there is an intermix cost of .025wz.

a) What is the optimal product mix, the optimal selling prices for each model, and the expected total weekly profit?

b) Suppose that manufacturing time for a unit of model W is 1 hour and for a unit of model Z is 1 hour. What would be the optimal production schedule if there were 5,000 man-hours available each week for production?

c) What would be the (marginal) value of an extra production hour?

PROBLEM 11

Togan Company manufactures two styles of toy wagons. The weekly profit (which takes into account all revenues and costs including changing production from one style to the other) is:

$$P(x_1, x_2) = -.01x_1^2 - .02x_2^2 - .01x_1x_2 + 30x_1 + 50x_2.$$

It takes .20 hours to make one unit of wagon 1 and .25 hours to make a unit of wagon 2.

a) Given no restriction on the number of production hours, determine the optimal weekly production mix. What is the optimal weekly profit?

b) Suppose Togan has 400 man-hours available weekly. What is the optimal product mix and the optimal profit if all 400 hours are to be used weekly?

c) What is the optimal product mix and weekly profit if no more than 400 hours are to be used weekly?

PROBLEM 12

Boxco is designing a new 32 cubic foot box requested by a customer. The base is to be rectangular with one side twice as long as the other. The base and four sides are to be made of wood costing $.20 per square foot and the top is to be made of wire costing $.10 per square foot. What is the best design to minimize total costs? What is the minimum cost of this box?

TRUE/FALSE

13. All n partial derivatives of an unconstrained function of n variables must equal 0 at any local minimum or local maximum.

14. For an unconstrained problem with one variable, if the first derivative at x* is 0 and the second derivative at x* is positive, then x* is a local maximum.

15. The first derivative of a continuous function evaluated at x = 4 is positive and first derivative at x = 9 is negative. This indicates there is at least one local maximum between x = 4 and x = 9.

16. For a continuous function in one variable, f(5) = 10 and f(9) = 20. At x = 7, the first derivative is 0 and the second derivative is negative. The maximum value of the function between x = 5 and x = 9 must be x = 9.

17. It is possible for the derivative of a function to equal 0 at points that are neither maximum or minimum points of the curve.

18. For (x_1^*, x_2^*) to be the optimal solution to an unconstrained function $f(x_1, x_2)$, the partial derivatives of $f(x_1, x_2)$ with respect to x_1 and x_2 must be zero.

19. For a function to be nonlinear, one of its variables must have an exponent value greater than one.

20. For (x_1^*, x_2^*) to be the optimal solution to a function $f(x_1, x_2)$ with one equality constraint, the partial derivatives of $f(x_1, x_2)$ with respect to x_1 and x_2 must be zero.

21. For (x_1^*, x_2^*) to be the optimal solution to a function $f(x_1, x_2)$ with one inequality constraint, the partial derivatives of $f(x_1, x_2)$ with respect to x_1 and x_2 must be zero.

22. The condition $dL/d\lambda = 0$, for a problem of the form: Max $f(x_1, x_2)$ subject to $g(x_1, x_2) = b$, simply says the constraint must be satisfied.

23. A saddle point is any local minimum (or maximum) that is not the global minimum (or maximum).

24. Both the first and second derivatives of an unconstrained function of one variable must equal zero at the global optimum.

25. At the optimum of a function of one variable constrained to a specific interval, the first derivative might not equal zero.

26. The optimal solution to a maximization problem with one constraint has an optimal Lagrange multiplier equal to -6. This means that if the right-hand side of the constraint was increased by one unit, the value of the objective function would decrease by 6.

27. We use differential calculus to identify the global optimum within the set of all possible local optima.

Answers to Problems and True/False

CHAPTER 1

PROBLEMS

5) a) Management science can provide a quantitative methodology for
deciding the job-machine pairings so that total job
processing time is minimized.
   b) How long it takes to process each job on each machine, and
any job-machine pairings that are unacceptable
   c) <u>Decision variables</u>: one for each job-machine pairing, taking
on a value of 1 if the pairing is used and 0 otherwise.
<u>Objective function</u>: minimize total job processing time.
<u>Constraints</u>: each job is assigned to exactly one machine, and
each machine be assigned no more than one job.
   d) Stochastic: job processing times vary due to varying machine
set-up times, variable operator performance, and more.
   e) Assume that processing times are deterministic (known/fixed).

6) a) The company because of its size and the newness of its
product should probably select the simplified model because
of the reduced costs and the time period for attaining
results. This first pass at the problem most likely will
give a "ballpark" figure. The model can then be refined
as more experience with production and demand is attained.
   b) Because of the large volume and the national distribution,
perhaps the more complete study should be done in this
case. Additionally, since the firm is a conglomerate, a
more complete justification of its policy to the
stockholders may be required.

7) a) MAX $10s_1 + 10s_2 + 25s_3$

$$
\begin{aligned}
\text{S.T.} \quad 25s_1 &\leq 5{,}000 \\
50s_2 &\leq 5{,}000 \\
100s_3 &\leq 5{,}000 \\
25s_1 &\geq 1{,}000 \\
50s_2 &\geq 1{,}000 \\
100s_3 &\geq 1{,}000 \\
25s_1 + 50s_2 + 100s_3 &\leq 10{,}000 \\
s_1, \ s_2, \ s_3 &\geq 0
\end{aligned}
$$

b) MAX $1.4x_1 + 1.2x_2 + 1.25x_3$

$$
\begin{aligned}
\text{S.T.} \quad x_1 &\leq 5{,}000 \\
x_2 &\leq 5{,}000 \\
x_3 &\leq 5{,}000 \\
x_1 &\geq 1{,}000 \\
x_2 &\geq 1{,}000 \\
x_3 &\geq 1{,}000 \\
x_1 + x_2 + x_3 &\leq 10{,}000 \\
x_1, \ x_2, \ x_3 &\geq 0
\end{aligned}
$$

c) Both give the same result.

CHAPTER 1

8) a) $N = L/25$; $C = 8C_gN$; $C = .32C_gL$

b) $TC = C_n + .32C_gL$; if $L = 50$, $TC = \$260$; if $L = 65$, $N = 2.6$ guards, so it must be decided whether to use 2 or 3 guards during the day.

9) a) X_1 = number of seats CPI manufactures in quarter 1
   X_2 = number of seats subcontracted in quarter 1
   X_3 = number of seats held in inventory from qtr.1 to qtr.2
   X_4 = number of seats CPI manufactures in quarter 2
   X_5 = number of seats subcontracted in quarter 2

b) Minimize $10.25X_1 + 12.50X_2 + 1.50X_3 + 10.25X_4 + 13.75X_5$

10) a)
$$X_1 \leq 3800 \qquad (1)$$
$$X_4 \leq 3800 \qquad (2)$$
$$X_1 + X_2 - X_3 = 3700 \qquad (3)$$
$$X_3 \leq 300 \qquad (4)$$
$$X_3 + X_4 + X_5 = 4200 \qquad (5)$$

b) The real problem is stochastic

c) Three decision variables must be introduced:
   X_6 = number of seats held in inventory from qtr.2 to qtr.3
   X_7 = number of seats CPI manufactures in quarter 3
   X_8 = number of seats subcontracted in quarter 3
   Addition to objective function: $+1.50X_6 + 10.25X_7 + 13.75X_8$
   Adjustment to constraint (5) above: $X_3 + X_4 + X_5 - X_6 = 4200$
   Three additional constraints:
   $$X_6 \leq 300$$
   $$X_7 \leq 3800$$
   $$X_6 + X_7 + X_8 = \text{3rd quarter demand}$$

11) a)
$$50s + 30c \leq 800$$
$$s \geq 5$$
$$c \geq 5$$

b) (1) Max $s + c$;   (2) Max $.03s + .05c$;   (3) Max $6s + 5c$

TRUE/FALSE

12. FALSE	13. TRUE	14. TRUE	15. TRUE	16. FALSE
17. TRUE	18. FALSE	19. FALSE	20. FALSE	21. FALSE
22. FALSE	23. FALSE	24. TRUE	25. TRUE	26. FALSE

```
CHAPTER 2
```

PROBLEMS

9) $X_1 = 0$, $X_2 = 4$; $Z = 48$

10) a) $X_1 = 4$, $X_2 = 3/2$; $Z = 19$
    b) All points on the line $2X_1 + X_2 = 6$ between $(3,0)$ and $(24/13, 30/13)$.

11) a-b) extreme points: $(0,4)$, $(1,2)$, $(3,1)$ -- feasible region is unbounded.
    c) (1) optimal solution $X_1 = 3$, $X_2 = 1$, $Z = 1$
       (2) alternate optimal solutions on $X_1 - 2X_2 = 1$ above $(3,1)$
       (3) unbounded linear program

12) a) $X_1 = 3$, $X_2 = 4$; $Z = 29$
    b) No change. If only a single point is feasible, the slope of the objective function is inconsequential.

13) a) $X_1 = 10$, $X_2 = 15$, $Z = 230$
    b) Any point satisfying all the other constraints will also satisfy constraint 1
    c) $X_1 = 20$, $X_2 = 15$, $Z = 310$

14) a) MAX $60X_1 + 43X_2$
       S.T. $X_1 + 3X_2 - S_1 \qquad\qquad = 9$
             $6X_1 - 2X_2 \qquad\qquad\qquad = 12$
              $X_1 + 2X_2 \qquad + S_3 = 10$
                   $X_1, X_2, S_1, S_3 \geq 0$
    b) The line segment of $6X_1 - 2X_2 = 12$ between $(22/7, 24/7)$ and $(27/10, 21/10)$.
    c) Extreme points: $(22/7, 24/7)$ and $(27/10, 21/10)$. The first one is optimal giving $Z = 336$.

15) a) $X_1 = 35$, $X_2 = 0$ $Z = \$630,000$
    b) $X_1 = 5$, $X_2 = 12$ $Z = \$630,000$
    c) $X_1 = 10$, $X_2 = 10$ $Z = \$630,000$

16) a) 100 dozen childs, 66 2/3 dozen professional, profit = $12,333.33; both slack variables equal 0.
    b) this point is an interior point in the original formulation

17) a) $X_1 = 2$, $X_2 = 4$, $Z = 32$
    b) $5 \leq C_1 \leq 10$; $3 \leq C_2 \leq 6$
    c) $X_1 = 0$, $X_2 = 6$
    d) 1; it is the improvement in the value of the objective function for an extra unit of iron
    e) The shadow price of zinc is 0 as long as this line does not determine the optimal point -- as long as its RHS ≤ 2.

CHAPTER 2

18) a) 120 containers of jade figurines, 60 containers of linen placemats; Profit = $13,200
   b) Between $30 and $120
   c) (1) $6.67; (2) $16.67; (3) $0

19) a) 105 minivans, 75 trailers; $673,500 profit
   b) $2812.50 $\leq$ minivan profit $\leq$ no upper limit, no lower limit $\leq$ trailer profit $\leq$ $5120.00
   c) Dual price for yardman hours is $1600. Thus, an increase of $1600 in monthly profit can be gained for each hour increase in the monthly availability of yardmen!

20) a) Put 10,000 miles on Harley; 35,000 miles on Hauler
   b) $15.00
   c) 7.5 cents

TRUE/FALSE

21. TRUE	22. TRUE	23. TRUE	24. FALSE	25. FALSE
26. FALSE	27. FALSE	28. FALSE	29. FALSE	30. TRUE
31. TRUE	32. TRUE	33. FALSE	34. TRUE	35. FALSE

CHAPTER 3

PROBLEMS

5) a) 1500 shares of airlines stock, 800 shares of insurance
     stock; the expected return is $5400
   b) Between $0 and $2.40

6) a) 6 product 1, 4 product 2, Profit = $540
   b) Between $50 and $75; at $70 the profit is $580
   c) No -- total % change is 83 1/3% < 100%
   d) Dual prices are the shadow prices for the resources;
      since there was unused copper (because $S_2 = 2$), extra copper
      is worth $0
   e) $30
   f) $10; this is the amount extra man-hours are worth
   g) The shadow price is the "premium" for aluminum -- would be
      willing to pay up to $10 + $30 = $40 for extra aluminum

7) a) Standard -- 33 1/3, Slim-Line -- 266 2/3, Z = $1100
   b) $5.60
   c) Standard -- 86 2/3, Slim-Line -- 213 1/3, Z = $1180

8) a) No
   b) No
   c) Yes -- Sum of % changes > 100%
   d) $10 -- Value of extra man-hours
   e) $1 -- this is the "premium" value for the boxes; hence
      extra boxes are worth $1.25
   f) They will stay the same -- Sum of % changes < 100%

9) a) 200 shares of James, 20 shares of QM, 40 shares of Delic.
      Total gain = $3200
   b) Each dollar increase in the allowed minimum investment
      in QM will result in a $.05 decrease in the total $ gain.
   c) Constraint #1 dual price (.25) X 1000 = $250
   d) No. It would be James Ind. (only stock with + dual price)
   e) Constraint #2 dual price (.15) X 1000 = $150
   f) Allowed max. investment could be raised to $8000
   g) No, cumulative change does not exceed 100%

TRUE/FALSE

10. TRUE	11. TRUE	12. TRUE	13. TRUE	14. FALSE
15. FALSE	16. TRUE	17. TRUE	18. TRUE	19. TRUE
20. TRUE	21. TRUE	22. TRUE	23. FALSE	24. TRUE

CHAPTER 4

PROBLEMS

10) a) MAX $1.5X_1 + X_2 + .75X_3 + .5X_4 + .75X_5 + X_6$
    S.T. $20X_1 + 18X_2 + 13X_3 + 7X_4 + 12X_5 + 15X_6 \leq 500$
    $X_1 + X_2 + X_3 + X_4 + X_5 + X_6 \geq 40$
    $X_1 + X_2 + X_3 - 2X_4 - 2X_5 - 2X_6 \geq 0$
    $X_1 + X_2 + X_5 + X_6 \geq 20$
    $X_j \geq 0 \; j = 1,\ldots,6$

   b) The variables must be integers.

11) P_i = the number of producers in month i (where i = 1,2,3)
    T_i = the number of trainers in month i (where i = 1,2)
    A_i = the number of apprentices in month i (where i = 2,3)
    R_i = the number of recruits in month i (where i = 1,2)

   MIN $3000P_1 + 3300T_1 + 2200R_1 + 3000P_2 + 3300T_2 + 2600A_2$
   $+2200R_2 + 3000P_3 + 2600A_3$
   s.t. $.6P_1 + .3T_1 + .05R_1 \geq 20$
   $.6P_1 + .3T_1 + .05R_1 + .6P_2 + .3T_2 + .4A_2 + .05R_2 \geq 44$
   $.6P_1 + .3T_1 + .05R_1 + .6P_2 + .3T_2 + .4A_2 + .05R_2 + .6P_3 + .4A_3 \geq 74$
   $P_1 - P_2 + T_1 - T_2 = 0$
   $P_2 - P_3 + T_2 + A_2 = 0$
   $A_2 - R_1 = 0$
   $A_3 - R_2 = 0$
   $2T_1 - R_1 \geq 0$
   $2T_2 - R_2 \geq 0$
   $P_1 + T_1 = 100$
   $P_3 + A_3 \geq 140$
   $P_j, T_j, A_j, R_j \geq 0$ for all j

12) X_j = the number of instrument j produced; where j = 1(deluxe
    trumpet); 2(prof. trumpet); 3(deluxe cornet);
    4(prof. cornet)
   MAX $80X_1 + 160X_2 + 60X_3 + 120X_4$
   S.T. $2X_1 + 1.5X_2 + 1.5X_3 + X_4 \leq 2000$
   $X_1 + 1.5X_2 + X_3 + 1.5X_4 \leq 1800$
   $X_1 \geq 500$
   $X_3 \geq 300$
   $X_2 \leq 150$
   $X_4 \leq 100$
   $X_1 + X_2 - 2X_3 - 2X_4 = 0$
   $X_j \geq 0 \; j = 1,\ldots,4$

CHAPTER 4

13) a) MAX $\quad 5X_1 + 12X_2 + 25X_3 + 4X_4 + 10X_5 + 18X_6 + 9X_7 + 16X_8$

S.T. $\quad 1.8X_1 + 2.2X_2 + 3X_3 + .74X_4 + 1.6X_5 + 2.2X_6 + X_7 + 1.5X_8 \leq 300$

$\quad\quad 1.8X_1 + 2.2X_2 + 3X_3 \quad\quad\quad\quad\quad\quad\quad\quad\quad\quad\quad \geq 75$

$\quad\quad 1.8X_1 + 2.2X_2 + 3X_3 \quad\quad\quad\quad\quad\quad\quad\quad\quad\quad\quad \leq 120$

$\quad\quad\quad\quad\quad\quad\quad\quad .74X_4 + 1.6X_5 + 2.2X_6 \quad\quad\quad\quad \geq 75$

$\quad\quad\quad\quad\quad\quad\quad\quad .74X_4 + 1.6X_5 + 2.2X_6 \quad\quad\quad\quad \leq 120$

$\quad\quad\quad\quad\quad\quad\quad\quad\quad\quad\quad\quad\quad\quad\quad X_7 + 1.5X_8 \geq 30$

$\quad\quad\quad\quad\quad\quad\quad\quad\quad\quad\quad\quad\quad\quad\quad X_7 + 1.5X_8 \leq 75$

$\quad .75X_1 - .25X_2 - .25X_3 + .75X_4 - .25X_5 - .25X_6 - .25X_7 - .25X_8 \geq 0$

$\quad\quad\quad\quad\quad\quad\quad\quad\quad\quad\quad\quad\quad X_j \geq 0 \quad j = 1,\ldots,8$

b) $X_1 = 0$, $X_2 = 0$, $X_3 = 40$, $X_4 = 41.28$,
$X_5 = 0$, $X_6 = 33.84$, $X_7 = 0$, $X_8 = 50$, $Z = 2,574.28$

c) The variables must be integers.

14) X_{11} = pounds of chocolate used in Chompers
X_{21} = pounds of chocolate used in Smerks
X_{31} = pounds of chocolate used in Delicious Chocolate
X_{12} = pounds of caramel used in Chompers
X_{22} = pounds of caramel used in Smerks
X_{23} = pounds of peanuts used in Smerks
Y_1 = number of one ounce Chompers bars produced daily
Y_2 = number of one ounce Smerks bars produced daily
Y_3 = number of one ounce Delicious Choc. bars produced daily
Y_4 = number of one pound Delicious Choc. bags produced daily

MAX $.128Y_1 + .148Y_2 + .138Y_3 + 2.261Y_4 - 1.60X_{11} - 1.60X_{21} - 1.60X_{31} - .95X_{12}$
$\quad\quad - .95X_{22} - 1.40X_{23}$

S.T. $\quad\quad (1/16)Y_3 + Y_4 \quad = \quad X_{31}$

$\quad\quad\quad (1/16)Y_1 \quad\quad = \quad X_{11} + X_{12}$

$\quad\quad\quad (1/16)Y_2 \quad\quad = \quad X_{21} + X_{22} + X_{23}$

$\quad\quad\quad\quad\quad X_{12} \quad \geq \quad .18(X_{11} + X_{12})$

$\quad\quad\quad\quad\quad X_{12} \quad \leq \quad .28(X_{11} + X_{12})$

$\quad\quad\quad\quad\quad X_{22} \quad = \quad X_{23}$

$\quad\quad\quad\quad\quad X_{21} \quad \geq \quad .20(X_{21} + X_{22} + X_{23})$

$\quad\quad\quad\quad\quad X_{21} \quad \leq \quad .40(X_{21} + X_{22} + X_{23})$

$\quad\quad Y_1 + Y_2 + Y_3 \quad \leq \quad 20,000$

$\quad\quad\quad\quad\quad Y_4 \quad \leq \quad 1,000$

$\quad\quad\quad\quad\quad Y_1 \quad \geq \quad 3,000$

$\quad\quad\quad\quad\quad Y_2 \quad \geq \quad 3,000$

$\quad\quad\quad\quad\quad Y_3 \quad \geq \quad 3,000$

$\quad\quad\quad Y_1 - Y_2 \quad \leq \quad .10(Y_1 + Y_2)$

$\quad\quad\quad Y_2 - Y_1 \quad \leq \quad .10(Y_1 + Y_2)$

$\quad X_{11} + X_{21} + X_{31} \quad \geq \quad 1,000$

$\quad\quad X_{12} + X_{22} \quad = \quad 350$

$\quad\quad\quad\quad X_{23} \quad \leq \quad 500$

$\quad\quad\quad X_{ij} \geq 0 \quad i = 1,2,3; \quad j = 1,2,3$

$\quad\quad\quad Y_j \geq 0 \quad j = 1,2,3,4$

CHAPTER 4

15) X_1 = number of bulldozers purchased for the year
X_2 = number of bulldozers leased for the year

Note: annual cost = (purchasing cost) + (leasing cost)
$\qquad$ - (salvage value) - (interest earned)
$\qquad$ = $(40,000X_1)$ + $(8000X_2)$ - $(20,000X_1)$
$\qquad$ - $0.08(1,000,000 - 40,000X_1 - 8,000X_2)$
$\qquad$ = $23,200X_1 + 8,640X_2 - 80,000$. Thus,

MIN $23,200X_1 + 8,640X_2$
S.T. $4,000X_1 + 8,000X_2 \leq 1,000,000$
$\qquad 8X_1 + 5X_2 \geq 240$
$\qquad X_1, X_2 \geq 0$

Answer: Buy 0 bulldozers, lease 48; Annual cost= \$334,720

16) X_j = \$ invested in investment j; where j = 1(Uni Eq.),
$\qquad$ 2(Col. Must.), 3(1st Gen REIT), 4(Met. Elec.),
$\qquad$ 5(Uni Debt), 6(Lem. Trans.), 7(Fair. Apt.),
$\qquad$ 8(T-Bill), 9(Money Market), 10(All Saver's)

MAX $.15X_1 + .17X_2 + .175X_3 + .118X_4 + .122X_5 + .12X_6 + .22X_7 +$
$\qquad .096X_8 + .105X_9 + .126X_{10}$
S.T. $X_1 + X_2 + X_3 + X_4 + X_5 + X_6 + X_7 + X_8 + X_9 + X_{10} = 400,000$
$100X_1 + 100X_2 + 100X_3 + 95X_4 + 92X_5 + 79X_6 + 80X_8 + 100X_9 \geq$
$\qquad 65(X_1 + X_2 + X_3 + X_4 + X_5 + X_6 + X_7 + X_8 + X_9 + X_{10})$
$60X_1 + 70X_2 + 75X_3 + 20X_4 + 30X_5 + 22X_6 + 50X_7 + 10X_9 \leq$
$\qquad 55(X_1 + X_2 + X_3 + X_4 + X_5 + X_6 + X_7 + X_8 + X_9 + X_{10})$
$X_1 \qquad\qquad + X_5 \qquad\qquad\qquad \leq 60,000$
$X_1 + X_2 + X_3 \qquad\qquad\qquad \leq 160,000$
$\qquad\qquad X_4 + X_5 + X_6 \qquad\qquad \leq 160,000$
$\qquad X_3 \qquad\qquad\qquad + X_7 \qquad \leq 160,000$
$X_1 \qquad\qquad\qquad\qquad \leq 80,000$
$\qquad X_2 \qquad\qquad\qquad\qquad \leq 80,000$
$\qquad\qquad X_3 \qquad\qquad\qquad \leq 80,000$
$\qquad\qquad\qquad X_4 \qquad\qquad \leq 80,000$
$\qquad\qquad\qquad\qquad X_5 \qquad \leq 80,000$
$\qquad\qquad\qquad\qquad\qquad X_6 \qquad \leq 80,000$
$\qquad\qquad\qquad\qquad\qquad\qquad X_7 \qquad \leq 80,000$
$\qquad\qquad\qquad\qquad\qquad\qquad\qquad X_8 \qquad \leq 80,000$
$\qquad\qquad\qquad\qquad\qquad\qquad\qquad\qquad X_9 \qquad \geq 1,000$
$\qquad\qquad\qquad\qquad\qquad\qquad\qquad\qquad\qquad X_{10} \leq 15,000$
$\qquad\qquad X_4 + X_5 + X_6 \qquad\qquad\qquad \geq 90,000$
$\qquad\qquad\qquad\qquad\qquad\qquad\qquad X_8 \qquad \geq 10,000$
$\qquad\qquad\qquad X_j \geq 0 \ j = 1,\ldots,10$

CHAPTER 4

17) X_1 = amount invested in new soda advertising
     X_2 = amount invested in traditional soda advertising

     MAX X_1 + $4X_2$ <==== 02($50X_1$) + .04($100X_2$)
     S.T. X_1 + X_2 ≤   10,000,000
             X_1 ≥   5,000,000
                        X_2 ≥   2,000,000
          $50X_1$ + $100X_2$ ≥ 750,000,000
             X_1, X_2 ≥ 0

Spend $5,000,000 on new soda advertising, $5,000,000 on
traditional soda advertising and see a profit of $25,000,000.

18) X_1-X_3 = number of students from NE to McHale,McCallum,McBride
    X_4-X_6 = number of students from SE to McHale,McCallum,McBride
    X_7-X_9 = number of students from SW to McHale,McCallum,McBride
    X_{10}-X_{12} = number of students from NW to McHale,McCallum,McBride
    X_{13}-X_{15} = number of students from Central to McHal,McCal,McBrid

MIN $1.5X_1$+$2.5X_2$+$.5X_3$+$4X_4$+$1.5X_5$+$3X_6$+$2.5X_7$+$3X_8$+$3.5X_9$+$.5X_{10}$+$4X_{11}$
     +$1.5X_{12}$+$1X_{13}$+$2X_{14}$+$1X_{15}$
S.T. X_1 + X_2 + X_3 =   700
        X_4 + X_5 + X_6 = 1100
        X_7 + X_8 + X_9 =   900
        X_{10} + X_{11} + X_{12} = 600
        X_{13} + X_{14} + X_{15} = 800
        X_1 + X_4 + X_{10} + X_{13} ≤ 1500
        X_2 + X_5 + X_{11} + X_{14} ≤ 1800
        X_3 + X_6 + X_{12} + X_{15} ≤ 1100
        X_j ≥ 0   j = 1,2,...,15

700 students from NE to McBride, 1100 from SE to McCallum,
500 from SW to McHale, 400 from SW to McCallum, 600 from NW
to McHale, 400 from Central to McHale, and 400 from Central
to McBride.

19) E = fraction of June Co.'s Alabama store's input resources
         required by the composite store
    W_1 = weight applied to the Georgia store's input/output
         resources by the composite store
    W_2 = weight applied to the Alabama store's input/output
         resources by the composite store
    W_3 = weight applied to the Mississippi store's input/output
         resources by the composite store

CHAPTER 4

19 con't) MIN   E

$$
\begin{array}{rl}
\text{S.T.} & W_1 + W_2 + W_3 = 1 \\
& 1.2W_1 + 0.8W_2 + 0.6W_3 \geq 0.8 \\
& 2.2W_1 + 1.4W_2 + 1.5W_3 \geq 1.4 \\
& 1.6W_1 + 1.5W_2 + 1.6W_3 \geq 1.5 \\
& 2.7W_1 + 2.0W_2 + 2.1W_3 \geq 2.0 \\
-24E + & 25W_1 + 24W_2 + 18W_3 \leq 0 \\
-210E + & 250W_1 + 210W_2 + 180W_3 \leq 0 \\
-750E + & 600W_1 + 750W_2 + 375W_3 \leq 0 \\
& E, W_1, W_2, W_3 \geq 0
\end{array}
$$

$E = .968$; The Alabama store appears moderately inefficient.

20) $X_1 - X_4$ = number of full-time clerks starting at 8,9,10,11 a.m.
    $X_5 - X_{11}$ = number of part-time clerks starting at 8,9,10,11 a.m.
    and 12,1,2 p.m.

$$
\text{MIN } 63X_1 + 63X_2 + 63X_3 + 63X_4 + 26X_5 + 26X_6 + 26X_7 + 26X_8 + 26X_9 + 26X_{10} + 26X_{11}
$$

$$
\begin{array}{rl}
\text{S.T.} & X_1 \geq 1 \\
& X_4 \geq 1 \\
& X_1 + X_2 + X_3 + X_4 \geq 4 \\
& X_1 + X_5 \geq 5 \\
& X_1 + X_2 + X_5 + X_6 \geq 4 \\
& X_1 + X_2 + X_3 + X_5 + X_6 + X_7 \geq 6 \\
& X_2 + X_3 + X_4 + X_5 + X_6 + X_7 + X_8 \geq 8 \\
& X_1 + X_3 + X_4 + X_6 + X_7 + X_8 + X_9 \geq 10 \\
& X_1 + X_2 + X_4 + X_7 + X_8 + X_9 + X_{10} \geq 9 \\
& X_1 + X_2 + X_3 + X_8 + X_9 + X_{10} + X_{11} \geq 7 \\
& X_2 + X_3 + X_4 + X_9 + X_{10} + X_{11} \geq 4 \\
& X_3 + X_4 + X_{10} + X_{11} \geq 7 \\
& X_4 + X_{11} \geq 5 \\
& X_j \geq 0 \quad j = 1,2,\ldots,11
\end{array}
$$

TRUE/FALSE

21. FALSE	22. FALSE	23. TRUE	24. FALSE	25. FALSE
26. TRUE	27. TRUE	28. TRUE	29. FALSE	30. FALSE
31. FALSE	32. FALSE	33. FALSE	34. FALSE	35. FALSE

```
┌─────────────────────┐
│                     │
│   CHAPTER  5        │
│                     │
└─────────────────────┘
```

PROBLEMS

8) a)   MIN Z = $2X_1 + 3X_2 + 8X_3$
        S.T. $4X_1 + 2X_2 + X_3 - S_1 = 15$
                $2X_1 + X_2 + 6X_3 - S_2 = 30$
                $X_j \geq 0$ j = 1,2,3
                $S_j \geq 0$ j = 1,2
   b) Cannot have negative numbers on RHS
   c) $X_1 = 15$, $X_2 = 0$, $X_3 = 0$, $S_1 = 45$, $S_2 = 0$, Z = 30

9) $X_1 = 5$, $X_2 = 3/2$, $X_3 = 0$, $S_1 = 0$, $S_2 = 19/2$, Z = 8

10) $X_1 = 3$, $X_2 = 0$, $X_3 = 4\ 2/3$, $S_1 = 0$, $S_2 = 2\ 1/3$, $S_3 = 2$;
    Z = $13\ 2/3$

11) a) Tableau infeasible at this stage, but cannot yet state
       whether or not the problem is feasible:

Basis	C_B	X_1	X_2	X_3	S_1	S_2	S_3	A_2	
		10	8	6	0	0	0	-M	
S_1	0	0	1	0	1	0	-2	0	4
A_2	-M	-1	0	0	0	-1	-1	1	6
X_3	6	1/2	1/2	1	0	0	1/2	0	5
Z_j		M+3	3	6	0	M	M+3	-M	-6M+30
$C_j - Z_j$		-M+7	5	0	0	-M	-M-3	0	

   b) Optimal: $X_1 = 0$, $X_2 = 14$, $X_3 = 0$, $S_1 = 18$, $S_2 = 0$, Z = 84
   c) Problem Unbounded: X_3 column is non-positive
   d) Problem Infeasible: A_2 positive in this "optimal" tableau
   e) Tableau is feasible, but not yet optimal

Basis	C_B	X_1	X_2	X_3	S_1	S_2	
		4	5	7	0	0	
X_3	7	0	0	1	0	0	12
S_2	0	0	0	0	-2/3	1	2
X_2	5	0	1	0	1/3	0	6
X_1	4	1	0	0	1/3	0	26
Z_j		4	5	7	3	0	218
$C_j - Z_j$		0	0	0	-3	0	
```
```

CHAPTER 5

12) a)

Basis	C_B	X_1	X_2	X_3	S_1	S_2	S_3	
		4	2	-1	0	0	0	
X_2	2	0	1	-1	6	0	1	10
S_2	0	0	0	4	2	1	1	20
X_1	4	1	0	0	-3	0	1	30
Z_j		4	2	-2	0	0	6	140
$C_j - Z_j$		0	0	1	0	0	-6	

b) $X_1 = 30$, $X_2 = 10$, $X_3 = 0$, $S_1 = 0$, $S_2 = 20$, $S_3 = 0$, $Z = 140$

c) (1) Z increases by 1; (2) Z increases by 3; (3) Z is unchanged; (4) Z decreases by 12

d) X_3 enters;   equations are:

$$X_2 - X_3 \qquad\qquad = 10 \qquad (1)$$
$$4X_3 + S_2 = 20 \qquad (2)$$
$$X_1 \qquad\qquad\qquad = 30 \qquad (3)$$

(1) shows X_2 increases as X_3 increases.   (2) shows S_2 decreases as X_3 increases, and (3) shows that X_1 is unchanged as X_3 increases.   Thus ratio test is applied only to positive numbers in the entering column.

e) S_2 would become -20.

f) 5

g) New values: $Z = 145$; $X_2 = 15$; $S_2 = 0$; X_1 unchanged.

h)

Basis	C_B	X_1	X_2	X_3	S_1	S_2	S_3	
		4	2	-1	0	0	0	
X_2	2	0	1	0	13/2	1/4	5/4	15
X_3	-1	0	0	1	1/2	1/4	1/4	5
X_1	4	1	0	0	-3	0	1	30
Z_j		4	2	-1	1/2	1/4	25/4	145
$C_j - Z_j$		0	0	0	-1/2	-1/4	-25/4	

13) a)

Basis	C_B	X_1	X_2	X_3	S_1	S_2	S_3	
		5	2	1	0	0	0	
X_1	5	1	0	1/2	-3	1/2	0	4
X_2	2	0	1	-1/2	7	-1/2	0	0
S_3	0	0	0	- 2	15	-5	1	4
Z_j		5	2	3/2	-1	3/2	0	20
$C_j - Z_j$		0	0	-1/2	1	-3/2	0	

Solution: $X_1 = 4$, $X_2 = 0$, $X_3 = 0$, $S_1 = 0$, $S_2 = 0$, $S_3 = 4$, $Z = 20$.   Not optimal (a positive number is in $C_j - Z_j$ row).

CHAPTER 5

13) b)

Basis	C_B	X_1	X_2	X_3	S_1	S_2	S_3	
		5	2	1	0	0	0	
X_3	1	0	-2	1	-14	1	0	0
X_1	5	1	1	0	4	0	0	4
S_3	0	0	-4	0	-13	-3	1	4
Z_j		5	3	1	6	1	0	20
$C_j - Z_j$		0	-1	0	-6	-1	0	

Solution: Same as (a). This time, the $C_j - Z_j$ row indicates that this is an optimal solution.

c) When degeneracy occurs, an optimal solution may have been attained even though some $C_j - Z_j > 0$. Thus, the condition that $C_j - Z_j \leq 0$, is sufficient for optimality, but not necessary.

14) a) Produce 250 deluxe doors
    b) There are many including the basic one of producing 200 standard doors and 100 deluxe doors

15) a) MAX Z = $2X_1 + 5X_2 + 5X_3 + 3X_4$
    S.T. $10X_1 + 12X_2 + 10X_3 + 9X_4 + S_1 = 150$
            $X_1 + X_2 + X_3 - S_2 = 12$
            $-X_1 + X_2 + X_3 - X_4 + S_3 = 0$
            $X_j \geq 0 \quad j = 1,2,3,4$
            $S_j \geq 0 \quad j = 1,2,3$

b)

Basis	C_B	X_1	X_2	X_3	X_1	S_1	S_2	A_2	S_3	
		2	5	5	3	0	0	-M	0	
S_1	0	10	12	10	9	1	0	0	0	150
A_2	-M	1	1	1	0	0	-1	1	0	12
X_3	0	-1	1	1	-1	0	0	0	1	0
Z_j		-M	-M	-M	0	0	M	-M	0	-12M
$C_j - Z_j$		2+M	5+M	5+M	3	0	-M	0	0	

c) $X_1 = 4\ 1/3$, $X_2 = 0$, $X_3 = 7\ 2/3$, $X_4 = 3\ 1/3$, $S_1 = 0$, $S_2 = 0$, $S_3 = 0$; $Z = 57$

TRUE/FALSE

16. TRUE	17. FALSE	18. TRUE	19. TRUE	20. TRUE
21. FALSE	22. FALSE	23. TRUE	24. TRUE	25. TRUE
26. FALSE	27. TRUE	28. FALSE	29. FALSE	30. FALSE

CHAPTER 6

PROBLEMS

7) a) shadow price is 4; $5 \leq b_1 \leq 8$
   b) $3 \leq C_2 \leq 6$;   when $C_2 = 4$, $Z = 28$

8) a) $X_1 = 10$, $X_2 = 0$, $X_3 = 0$, $S_1 = 0$, $S_2 = 4$; $Z = 50$; Ranges of
      optimality: $C_1 \geq 3$; $C_2 \leq 5$; $C_3 \leq 5$; $C_{S1} \leq 5$; $-1 \leq C_{S2} \leq 5/2$
   b) Yes since the shadow price is 5; Cannot tell as change falls
      outside the range of feasibility.

9) a) MAX $Z = 40X_1 + 60X_2 + 80X_3$
      S.T. $X_1 + X_2 + 2X_3 \leq 500$
              $2X_1 + 2X_2 + 2X_3 \leq 600$
                $X_1 + 2X_2 + 3X_3 \leq 900$
                    $X_j \geq 0$ $j = 1,2,3$

   Solution is: $X_1 = 0$, $X_2 = 100$, $X_3 = 200$, $Z = \$22,000$

   b) $40 \leq C_2 \leq 80$
   c) $23,000$
   d) Sunk cost -- No since the shadow price = $20
      Relevant cost -- Yes; Value = $20 + $16 = $36

10) a) It can be increased without limit.
    b) $500 \leq b_2 \leq 800$; $b_3 \geq 800$
    c) Relevant costs if one need only purchase the amount required
       and these costs are reflected in the objective function
       coefficients -- in this case the shadow price of $20 for
       aluminum would be the premium above its current value for
       extra pounds of aluminum. Sunk costs if these costs are not
       reflected in objective function coefficients because they
       were considered fixed costs. In this case the $20 would
       simply be the value of extra pounds of aluminum. In either
       case, the value of extra steel is 0.
    d) 400

11) a) 20 X12's, 0 T7's, 40 V8's; Daily Profit = $2,000
    b) Plastic package: (shadow price) x (quantity) is greatest.
    c) Yes; 33 1/3 X12's; 13 1/3 T7's; 0 V8's; Profit = $2066.67

12) a) MIN $Z = 15U_1 + 16U_2$
       S.T. $U_1 + 4U_2 \geq 10$
                 $3U_1 + U_2 \geq 8$
                    $U_1, U_2 \geq 0$
    b) Primal: $X_1 = 3$, $X_2 = 4$, $Z = 62$
       Dual: $U_1 = 2$, $U_2 = 2$, $Z = 62$
    c) The values for the dual variables are found in the Z_j row
       in the S_1 and S_2 columns

CHAPTER 6

13) a) MAX $Z = 3X_1 + 2X_2 - 3X_3$

S.T.

$$
\begin{aligned}
X_1 + 3X_2 + 8X_3 &\leq 56 \\
2X_1 - X_2 - X_3 &\leq 14 \\
-2X_1 + X_2 + X_3 &\leq -14 \\
- X_2 \qquad\quad &\leq -5 \\
X_1, X_2, X_3 &\geq 0
\end{aligned}
$$

b) MIN $Z = 56U_1 + 14U_2' - 14U_2'' - 5U_3$

S.T.

$$
\begin{aligned}
U_1 + 2U_2' - 2U_2'' &\geq 3 \\
3U_1 - U_2' + U_2'' - U_3 &\geq 2 \\
8U_1 - U_2' + U_2'' &\geq -3 \\
U_1, U_2', U_2'', U_3 &\geq 0
\end{aligned}
$$

c) The dual of the dual is the primal.

14) Dual is infeasible

TRUE/FALSE

15. FALSE	16. TRUE	17. TRUE	18. TRUE	19. FALSE
20. FALSE	21. TRUE	22. TRUE	23. TRUE	24. FALSE
25. TRUE	26. FALSE	27. FALSE	28. TRUE	29. FALSE

CHAPTER 7

PROBLEMS

8. a)

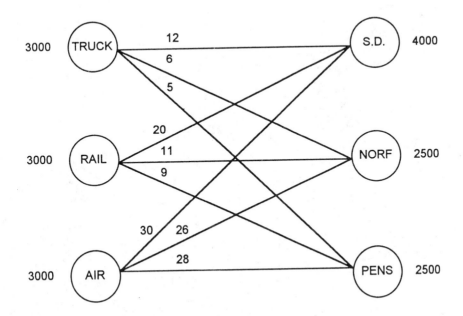

   b) Truck - Pensacola 2500; Truck - Norfolk 500;
      Railroad - Norfolk 2000; Railroad - San Diego 1000;
      Airplane - San Diego 3000
   c) Truck - San Diego 1000; Truck - Norfolk 2000;
      Railroad - Norfolk 500; Railroad - Pensacola 2500;
      Airplane - San Diego 3000

9) a) Newspaper - MR1 15; Newspaper - MR2 5; Newspaper - MR3 10;
      TV - MR2 15; Radio - MR2 5; Radio - MR4 20;
      Total Cost = $1,065,000
   b) Newspaper - MR2 20; Newspaper - MR3 10; TV - MR1 15;
      Radio - MR2 5; Radio - MR4 20;   Total cost = $1,065,000
   c) Many answers. One with TV-MR1 = 5 is: Newspaper - MR1 10;
      Newspaper - MR2 10; Newspaper - MR3 10; TV - MR1 5;
      TV - MR2 10; Radio - MR2 5; Radio - MR4 20;
      Total cost = $1,065,000

10) Ace: 25 Sanitation and 5 Police; Band: 25 Parks and 15
    Administration; QM: 20 Police and 10 Administration;
    Cost $1,035,000

11) LA-Denver 25; LA-NY 10; CHI-NY 30; NY-ATL 35; Profit $2,165,000

12) Abbey-Cabin3, Babbs-Cabin4, Carla-Cabin2, Diane-Cabin5,
    Ellsa-Cabin1; Performance rating total = 35

CHAPTER 7

13) a)

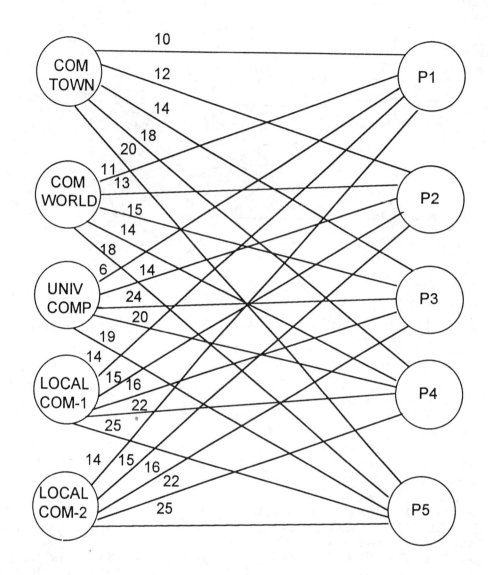

b) Computer Town - P5; Computer World - P4; Universal - P1;
   Local Computer - P2 and P3; Total Cost $71,000
c) +M placed in assignment matrix in row 2, column 5;
   no change in the optimal solution
d) +M's placed in assignment matrix row 2 column 4, and in
   row 2 column 5; Computer Town - P5; Computer World - P2;
   Universal - P1; Local Computer - P3 and P4;
   Total cost = $77,000

14) Division 1 - Bats; Division 2 - Golf Clubs; Division 3 -
    Racquetball Rackets; Division 4 - Tennis Rackets; Total 410

CHAPTER 7

15) a)

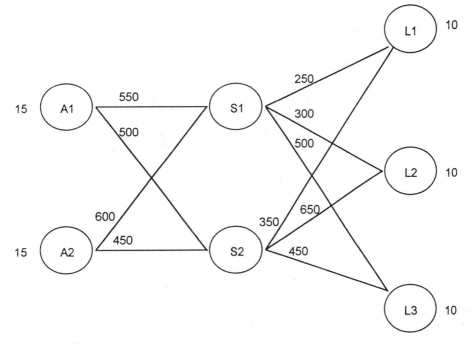

b) Denote A1 as node 1, A2 as node 2, S1 as node 3, S2 as node 4, L1 as node 5, L2 as node 6, and L3 as node 7

$$\text{MIN } 550X_{13} + 500X_{14} + 600X_{23} + 450X_{24} + 250X_{35} + 300X_{36}$$
$$+ 500X_{37} + 350X_{45} + 650X_{46} + 450X_{47}$$

S.T.
$$X_{13} + X_{14} \le 15$$
$$X_{23} + X_{24} \le 15$$
$$X_{13} + X_{23} - X_{35} - X_{36} - X_{37} = 0$$
$$X_{14} + X_{24} - X_{45} - X_{46} - X_{47} = 0$$
$$X_{35} + X_{45} = 10$$
$$X_{36} + X_{46} = 10$$
$$X_{37} + X_{47} = 10$$
$$X_{ij} \ge 0 \text{ for all } i,j$$

TRUE/FALSE

16. TRUE	17. TRUE	18. FALSE	19. TRUE	20. TRUE
21. FALSE	22. FALSE	23. FALSE	24. TRUE	25. TRUE
26. TRUE	27. FALSE	28. TRUE	29. FALSE	30. TRUE

CHAPTER 8

PROBLEMS

6) a) $X_1 = 2.8$, $X_2 = 3.4$, $Z = 48.8$
   b) $X_1 = 3$, $X_2 = 3$ -- infeasible
   c) $X_1 = 2$, $X_2 = 3$ -- feasible but not optimal
   d) Optimal $X_1 = 2$, $X_2 = 9$, $Z = 48 < 48.8$
   e) Additional integer constraints restrict the feasible region
      further; optimal solution values: ILP $\leq$ Mixed ILP $\leq$ LP.

7) a) $X_1 = 7/3$, $X_2 = 1/3$, $Z = 31/3$
   b) $X_1 = 2$, $X_2 = 0$, $Z = 6$
   c) L.P. -- optimal solution changes slightly; IP -- infeasible

8) a) $X_1 = 1$, $X_2 = 3$, $Z = 17$
   b) $X_1 = 1$, $X_2 = 3$, $Z = 14$

9) MAX $Y_1 + 1.8Y_2 + 2Y_3 + 1.5Y_4 + 3.6Y_5 + 2.2Y_6$
   S.T. $20Y_1 + 55Y_2 + 47Y_3 + 38Y_4 + 90Y_5 + 63Y_6 \leq 175$
        $15Y_1 + 45Y_2 + 50Y_3 + 40Y_4 + 70Y_5 + 70Y_6 \leq 150$
                                $Y_4 - Y_6 = 0$
        $Y_1 - Y_2 \geq 0$
                   $Y_3 + Y_5 \leq 1$
        $Y_1 + Y_2 + Y_3 + Y_4 + Y_5 + Y_6 \leq 3$
                        $Y_i = 0$ or 1

10) MAX $5.2X_1 + 3.6X_2 + 3.2X_3 + 2.8X_4$
    S.T. $.35X_1 + .50X_2 + .35X_3 + .50X_4 \leq 0.85$ (FIRST YEAR)
         $.55X_1 + .50X_2 + .40X_3 \leq 1.00$ (SECOND YEAR)
         $.75X_1 + .45X_3 \leq 1.20$ (THIRD YEAR)
         $X_1 + X_2 + X_3 + X_4 = 2$
         $- X_2 + X_3 \geq 0$
                    $X_i = 0$ or 1

11) a) $X_1 = 3$, $X_2 = 4\ 1/4$; $Z = 49$
    b) $X_1 = 1$, $X_2 = 5$; $Z = 45$

12) a) 4/5 container of Grain A, 2 containers of Grain B, $3960
    b) 2 containers of Grain A, 1 container of Grain B, $3900
    c) (1) (0,2) feasible, not optimal; (2-3) (1,2) infeasible

13) a) $X_1 = 3$, $X_2 = 3.2$, $Z = 34.4$
    b) $X_1 = 2$, $X_2 = 4$, $Z = 36$

TRUE/FALSE

14. FALSE	15. TRUE	16. FALSE	17. TRUE	18. FALSE
19. FALSE	20. TRUE	21. FALSE	22. FALSE	23. FALSE
24. FALSE	25. TRUE	26. FALSE	27. FALSE	28. TRUE

```
CHAPTER 9
```

PROBLEMS

5) Maximal flow is 4500 cubic feet. Routing shown below:

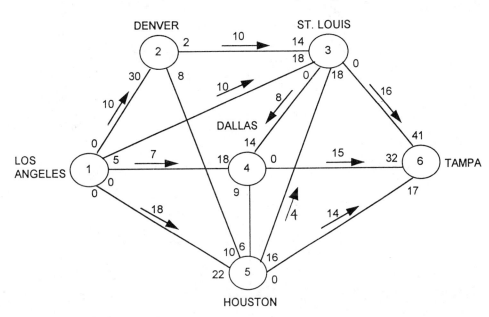

6) Total distance = 9,110 feet; Total cost = $455,500

7) Total cost $273; Philadelphia - Chicago - San Francisco -
   Los Angeles - Las Vegas

8) 180 megawatts

9) a) $3,750
   b) $175

10) At $6/hr. -- travel on C - J; Cost = $85
    At $60/hr. -- travel on B - L; Cost = $265

11) (River-1),(1-4),(4-6),(4-5),(6-7),(4-3),(3-8),(3-2); OR
    (River-1),(1-4),(4-6),(4-5),(6-7),(4-3),(3-8),(4-2); 2050 yards

12) Path: 1 - 4 - 6 - 7 - 8; Time = 53 minutes

13) 120,000 pounds of oranges

TRUE/FALSE

14. FALSE   15. TRUE   16. TRUE   17. FALSE   18. TRUE
19. TRUE   20. TRUE   21. TRUE   22. FALSE   23. TRUE
24. FALSE   25. TRUE   26. FALSE   27. FALSE   28. TRUE

CHAPTER 10

PROBLEMS

6) a)

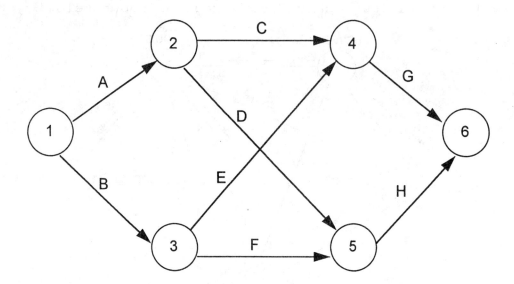

Expected Completion Time = 58;   Critical Path = A - D - K

b) Yes
c) Yes
d) Slack on G = 7 hours; Slack on L = 4 hours
e) 4 hours; the slack times are not independent as G and L are on the same path.

7) a)

Activity	ES	EF	LS	LF	Slack
A	0:00	4:00	0:00	4:00	0
B	0:00	3:00	6:00	9:00	6
C	4:00	9:00	17:00	22:00	13
D	4:00	7:00	8:00	11:00	4
E	4:00	9:00	4:00	9:00	0
F	9:00	11:00	9:00	11:00	0
G	9:00	10:00	15:00	16:00	6
H	11:00	13:00	20:00	22:00	9
I	11:00	14:00	20:00	23:00	9
J	11:00	16:00	11:00	16:00	0
K	13:00	14:00	22:00	23:00	9
L	16:00	23:00	16:00	23:00	0

b) A - E - F - J - L; 23 hours

CHAPTER 10

7) c) There are many; here is one. Note that for Man 2, activity D
       must precede activity C (D's LS is 8:00 and C's EF is 9:00).

	Intern 1				Intern 2	
A	0:00	-	4:00	B	0:00	-	3:00
E	4:00	-	9:00	D	4:00	-	7:00
F	9:00	-	11:00	C	7:00	-	12:00
J	11:00	-	16:00	G	12:00	-	13:00
L	16:00	-	23:00	H	13:00	-	15:00
				I	15:00	-	18:00
				K	18:00	-	19:00

8) a)

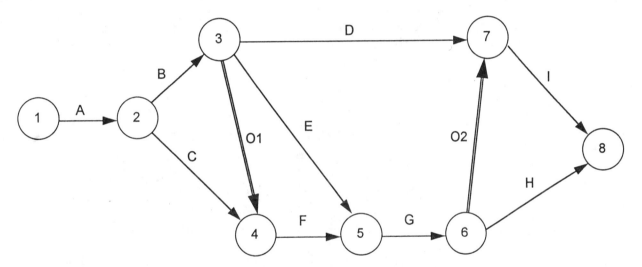

   b) 8 hrs.
   c) .8264

9) a)

Activity	ES	EF	LS	LF	Slack
A	0	6	1	7	1
B	0	8	0	8	0
C	6	7	7	8	1
D	6	9	9	12	3
E	8	11	9	12	1
F	8	12	9	13	1
G	8	18	8	18	0
H	8	13	10	15	2
I	11	14	12	15	1
J	12	13	14	15	2
K	12	17	13	18	1
L	14	17	15	18	1

   b) Critical Path: B - G; Expected completion time = 18 weeks
   c) Train its own employees

CHAPTER 10

10) a) 16 weeks = August 21
    b) About September 22 (20.66 weeks from May 1)
    c) Do not accept the offer

11) a) Expected Project Completion Time = 32;
       Standard deviation = 3.16
    b) Do not spend the money
    c) Activities off the critical path may vary enough so that a
       new critical path could be formed.

12) For this problem label the activities as follows:
    A = Feasibility Study   F = Manufacturing Staff Hired
    B = Building Purchased   G = Prototype Manufactured
    C = Project Leader Hired   H = Production Run of 100
    D = Advert. Staff Selected   I = Advertising Campaign
    E = Materials Purchased

   a)

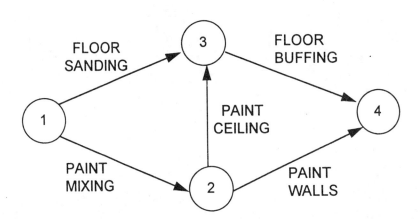

b) Define X_i = the time represented by node i
          Y_j = the amount of time activity j is crashed

   MIN $20Y_A + 50Y_C + 50Y_D + 70Y_E + 60Y_F + 350Y_H + 75Y_I$ (in \$000)

   S.T. $X_8 \leq 26$ $X_8 \geq X_7 + (8 - Y_I)$
         $Y_A \leq 1$ $X_8 \geq X_6 + (6 - Y_H)$
         $Y_C \leq 1$ $X_7 \geq X_6$
         $Y_D \leq 3$ $X_7 \geq X_3 + (6 - Y_D)$
         $Y_E \leq 1$ AND $X_6 \geq X_5 + 2$
         $Y_F \leq 3$ $X_5 \geq X_3 + (3 - Y_E)$
         $Y_H \leq 1$ $X_5 \geq X_4 + (10 - Y_F)$
         $Y_I \leq 4$ $X_4 \geq X_3$
                                    $X_4 \geq X_2 + (3 - Y_C)$
                                    $X_3 \geq X_2 + 4$
                                    $X_2 \geq X_1 + (6 - Y_A)$

              $X_i, Y_j \geq 0$ for all i,j

CHAPTER 10

12) c) The time reduction for each activity is proportional to the
       the crashing money that would be spent on that activity.
    d) Per-week reduction cost is shadow price for $X_8 \leq 26$.

13) The PERT network for this problem is:

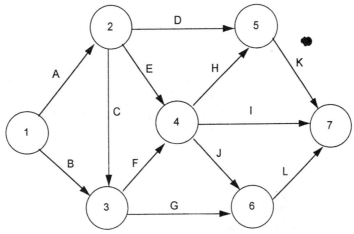

a) Define X_i = time represented by node i
   Y_j = the amount of time activity j is crashed

MIN $1250Y_A + 2000Y_C + 500Y_D + 500Y_E + 2000Y_F + 5000Y_G + 6000Y_H$
S.T.

$X_6 \leq 16$		$X_6 \geq X_5 + (7 - Y_H)$
$Y_A \leq 4$		$X_6 \geq X_4 + (5 - Y_G)$
$Y_C \leq 4$		$X_5 \geq X_3 + (3 - Y_F)$
$Y_D \leq 2$	AND	$X_5 \geq X_2 + (4 - Y_D)$
$Y_E \leq 1$		$X_4 \geq X_3 + (2 - Y_E)$
$Y_F \leq 2$		$X_4 \geq X_2 + (10 - Y_C)$
$Y_G \leq 1$		$X_3 \geq X_1 + 3$
$Y_H \leq 2$		$X_2 \geq X_1 + (6 - Y_A)$

$$X_i, Y_j \geq 0 \text{ for all } i \text{ and } j$$

b) Same formulation as (a) except that the objective function
   is now: MIN X_6, and the first constraint is now:
   $1250Y_A + 2000Y_C + 500Y_D + 500Y_E + 2000Y_F + 5000Y_G + 6000Y_H \leq 15,500$

14) a) No
    b) Cost Overrun
    c) Hopefully E could be sped up and costs reduced. Management
       should be told that a cost overrun is likely. The larger the
       cost overrun, the more likely the target date will be met.

TRUE/FALSE

15. TRUE	16. TRUE	17. FALSE	18. FALSE	19. TRUE
20. TRUE	21. FALSE	22. FALSE	23. FALSE	24. TRUE
25. TRUE	26. TRUE	27. FALSE	28. FALSE	29. TRUE

```
┌─────────────────────┐
│                     │
│   CHAPTER 11        │
│                     │
└─────────────────────┘
```

PROBLEMS

10) a) 75
    b) Q* = 273.861, order 274
    c) $164.32
    d) Order every 4 months based on forecasted demand

11) a) 1) Buy from Harrison: Q* = 800; Total Annual Variable
           Cost = $1200; Total Annual Cost = $76,200.
        2) Manufacture themselves: Q* = 5345;Total Annual Variable
           Cost = $5,986.65; Total Annual Cost = $75,986.65.
    b) Harrison should manufacture displays; total cost is cheaper.

12) a) Q* = 109,544.5 or 109,545
    b) 9.13
    c) 13.33
    d) 115 days = 365 - (9.13)(13.33 + 14)

13) Order 2000 every week

14) a) (1) Q* = 16
       (2) 20 or when inventory reaches 4 and one order is pending
       (3) $47,840
    b) No; Yearly net profit under this policy is only $45,774

15) Q^* = 233, Total annual cost = $64,695.54

16) a) Order 648 every 3.08 weeks when supply reaches 42
    b) 12 spark plugs
    c) $6.60

17) 196

18) Z = 1.43 ===> Pr(Stockout) = .0764

19)

Item	# Needed	Lead Time	
Barbecue	5000	2	x - 2
Broilers	5000	2	x - 4
Rack	2000	2	x - 6
Electrical	3000	2	x - 6
Shell	5000	5	x - 9
Element	0		
Plug	2100	3	x - 9
Rotisserie	2000	4	x - 6
Hardware	1000	4	x - 10 <-------
Motor	0		
Lava Briquettes	3000	6	x - 8

Answer: 10 weeks

CHAPTER 11

20) Yes; Annual manufacture = $38,600; annual purchase = $40,800

21) a) Annual profit for machine I = $40,000 (operating at full
       capacity with no inventory); profit for mach. II = $41,520.
    b) For machine II, Q* = 92,582. Thus the firm has 3.24 cycles
       per year each lasting approximately 112.6 days. As the
       production time of the 92,582 pounds of luncheon meat is
       33.8 days, some of the meat sold will be as old as 78 days.
          If Jim went to machine II, he would need more production
       runs per year thus incurring more setups and reducing his
       profit below the $40,000 he could earn from using machine I.

22) a) Order 32 when inventory reaches 7
    b) Total annual variable cost = $1,301

23) a) .0951
    b) 299

24) a) 71,600 loaves
    b) 61,280 loaves

25) a) 46 pumpkins
    b) .525

26) Order 1000 tubes each time

27)

Component	Net Req'mt.	Order Time	Component	Net Req'mt.	Order Time
Food Processor	15,000	12	Switch	9,000	5
Motor Assembly	10,000	10	Mixing Basket	10,000	11
Motor	8,000	5	Top Unit	8,000	2
Gear Unit	4,000	7	Pusher	7,000	0
Shaft	3,000	3	Bottom Unit	6,000	3
Gasket	0	-	Blades	8,000	2
Base Assembly	12,000	8			

28) Choose Option III

29) a) order 100 units when the supply on hand reaches 172 units
    b) Total Annual Variable Cost = $24,024
    c) Initially order 272 units

30) Order 555 bags; safety stock = 105 bags

TRUE/FALSE

31. TRUE	32. FALSE	33. FALSE	34. FALSE	35. TRUE
36. FALSE	37. FALSE	38. TRUE	39. FALSE	40. FALSE
41. FALSE	42. FALSE	43. FALSE	44. TRUE	45. TRUE

CHAPTER 12

PROBLEMS

10) a) $P(X = 0) = .1353$
    b) $P(T < 45 \text{ min.}) = .6321$
    c) $W_q = 2\ 1/4$ hours
    d) $P_3 = 27/256 = .105$

11) a) Yes; Total Cost = \$70 per day for computer vs. \$90 per
       day without computer
    b) Better off with computer; Total Cost for second employee
       is \$86.18 per day

12) 30 percent

13) a)   = 40 per hour
    b) $L_q = 4/3$
    c) $L = 2$
    d) $1 - P_0 = g/m = 2/3$
    e) $m = 97.2$ per hour

14) Purchase digital router; the total cost is \$204 per day vs.
    \$255 per day without the router.

15) a) $L_q = 1.04$ at each desk; Consolidated $L_q = .80$
    b) $P_0 = (3/8)(3/8) = .14$; Consolidated $P_0 = .23$
    c) $W = 1/3$ hour = 20 minutes; Consolidated $W = 12.31$ minutes
    d) $P(\text{both busy}) = (1-P_0)(1-P_0) = (5/8)(5/8) = .39$;
       Consolidated $P(\text{both busy}) = P_W = .48$
    e) Yes if it will not result in a substantial loss in business.
       Note that the average customer waiting time (part (c))
       decreases by more than 38% when the two servers are
       consolidated.

16) No system -- \$49.20; System A -- \$50.00; System B -- \$47.20
    Hence, install System B

17) a) George: W = 20 minutes; John: W = 3 1/3 minutes
    b) Total Cost: George -- \$46.00; John -- \$18.67. Hire John.

18) a) W = 6.22 minutes so total time in the store is 61.22 min.
    b) Yes; W = 6.01 minutes

19) a) .667
    b) .076 hours = 4.56 minutes
    c) 1.43 vehicles
    d) .9772

CHAPTER 12

20) a) No, 49.18 percent
    b) 18.03 percent

21) a) $k = 4$; $P_W = .021$
    b) $P_0 = .331$

22) a) $L_q = .15$
    b) $W_q = .028$ hr. $= 1.7$ minutes
    c) $P_W = .417$

23) a) $L_q = .7094$
    b) $W_q = 4.96$ days
    c) $1 - P_0 = .7151$

TRUE/FALSE

24. TRUE	25. FALSE	26. FALSE	27. FALSE	28. TRUE
29. TRUE	30. FALSE	31. FALSE	32. FALSE	33. FALSE
34. TRUE	35. TRUE	36. FALSE	37. FALSE	38. TRUE

```
┌─────────────────────┐
│    CHAPTER  13      │
└─────────────────────┘
```

PROBLEMS

FOR ALL PROBLEMS IN CHAPTER 13, IT IS ASSUMED THAT THE RANDOM
NUMBER MAPPINGS BEGIN WITH THE FIRST RANDOM NUMBER BEING 00. THE
COLUMN HEADINGS FOR THE EACH SIMULATION ARE GIVEN TOGETHER WITH THE
FIRST ROW IN THE SIMULATION. FINALLY, THE ANSWER BASED ON THE
SIMULATION IS GIVEN.

7)

	Routes 5 - 57				Routes 55 - 91		
RN	Time On 5	RN	Time On 57	RN	Time On 55	RN	Time On 91
63	7	59	6	71	8	51	4
	etc.				etc.		

Freeways 5 - 57 have a total of 62 minutes; Freeways 55 - 91
have a total of 61 minutes. Select freeways 55 - 91.

8)

Period	RN	Number of Arrivals	Service Free?	Number Waiting	RN	Service Time	Period When Service Completed
1	63	1	Yes	0	59	1	2
			etc.				

The average number of customers waiting in line for service is
the average of the entries in the Number Waiting column. This
average is 1.

9) a) There are three critical paths giving completion times of 17
      weeks: B-C-F-G-H; B-D-G-H; A-F-G-H.
   b) Five complete PERT analyses must be done. The first is as
      follows:

Job	RN	Change	Completion Time
A	14	-1	6
B	41	0	4
C	35	0	3
D	38	0	6
E	91	+1	6
F	78	+1	4
G	90	+1	4
H	18	-1	3

Its critical path is B-C-F-G-H with completion time = 18.
Repeating four more times gives:

CHAPTER 13

Trial	Critical Path	Completion Time
2	B-D-G-H	17
3	B-C-F-G-H	17
4	A-F-G-H or B-C-F-G-H	17
5	A-E-H	17

The average completion time of the five trials is 17.2 weeks.

10) a) Order 8 when inventory level reaches 2 units

b)

Day	Beg. Invent.	RN	Demand	End. Invent.	Order?	RN	Deliv. Time	Inv. Cost
1	6	59	2	4	No	--	--	$8

The average inventory cost per day is $13.00

11) a)

Week	Beg. Inv.	RN	Demand	End. Inv.	Avg. Inv.	Hold. Cost	Reord. Cost	RN	Lead Time	Stkout. Cost
1	5	51	3	2	3.5	$7	$40	80	2	--

The total cost for 8 weeks = $168.00

b)

Week	Beg. Inv.	RN	Demand	End. Inv.	Avg. Inv.	Hold. Cost	Service Charge	Stockout Cost
1	5	51	3	2	3.5	$7	$12	--

The total cost for 8 weeks = $194.00; Since this is more than $168.00, the company should keep its current policy.

12) a)

Per.	RN	# of Cust.	Cust.	RN	Here/ ToGo?	RN	Serv. Time	Compl. in Per.	# Cust. Pres.	Profit
1	63	0	--	--	--	--	--	--	0	--
2	88	1	1	59	ToGo	71	4	6	1	$.90

b) $3.04
c) 64%
d) .84

13)

Day	RN	# of Cust.	Cust. Number	RN	Type Purch.	In Stock?	RN	Switch?	Remain. Invent. A L T
1	58	2	1	93	T	Yes	--	--	3 2 3
			2	63	L	Yes	--	--	3 1 3

CHAPTER 13

13 con't) Archie will sell out in 8 days in this simulation.

14) a)

Day	RN	Number Rented	Car Rented	RN	Day Returned	Cost of Unused Cars	Shortage Cost
1	63	3	1	59	3		
			2	09	2		
			3	57	3	$5	--

The 10-day profit of this simulation is $885.

b)

Day	RN	Number Rented	Car Rented	RN	Day Returned	Cost of Unused Cars	Shortage Cost
1	63	3	1	59	3		
			2	09	2		
			3	57	3	$10	--

The 10-day profit of this simulation is $970.
Take the extra car.

15)

Per.	RN	# of Arr.	Serv. Area Free?	RN	Type Purch.	Serv. Time	# of Lost Cust.	# of Cust. Wait.	Serv. Compl. This Per.?	Prof.
1	63	1	Yes	59	Cone	30	0	0	Yes	$.12

a) Sum last column = $3.34
b) Divide total # lost customers by total # arrivals = 7/35
   = 20%.
c) Divide the total # of cust. waiting by 30 periods = 65/30
   = 2.17.

16) a)

A Last			B Last			C Last		
Next	A	00 - 49	Next	A	00 - 29	Next	A	00 - 09
	B	50 - 79		B	30 - 74		B	10 - 44
	C	80 - 99		C	75 - 99		C	45 - 99

b)

Flight	RN	Next Airline
1	71	C
2	95	C

20% of flights on Airline A
48% of flights on Airline B
32% of flights on Airline C

TRUE/FALSE

17. FALSE	18. TRUE	19. FALSE	20. FALSE	21. TRUE
22. TRUE	23. TRUE	24. FALSE	25. FALSE	26. TRUE
27. FALSE	28. FALSE	29. TRUE	30. FALSE	31. FALSE

CHAPTER 14

PROBLEMS

8) a) Stock C -- it dominates Stock B
   b) (1) Stock A; (2) Stock C; (3) Stock D
   c) Stock D

9) a)

| | | Rail Freight | |
		Bid $470,000	Doesn't Bid
Transrail	Bid $500,000	0	$100,000
	Bid $460,00	$60,000	$ 60,000

   b) Bid $460,000
   c) Bid $500,000
   d) $15,000

10) a)

| | Sales (in 1,000,000's) | | |
	100	50	1
Introduce	$1,000,000	$200,000	-$2,000,000
Do Not Introduce	-$400,000	-$400,000	-$400,000

   b)

| | Sales (in 1,000,000's) | | |
	100	50	1
Introduce	$0	$0	$1,600,000
Do Not Introduce	$1,400,000	$600,000	$0

   c) (1) do not introduce; (2) introduce; (3) do not introduce
   d) Yes
   e) No

11) a) Introduce the root beer; p ≤ .483
    b) EVPI = $112,000
    NOTE: The answers to (c)-(e) are very sensitive to roundoff
    error. Figures in parentheses are for two decimal places only.
    c) Stanton - EVSI = $13,200 ($11,862); Efficiency = .118 (.106)
       New World - EVSI = $6,400 ($6,424); Efficiency = .057 (.057)
    d) Hire Stanton (Stanton)
    e) Hire New World (Stanton); the expected gain is greater

CHAPTER 14

12) a)

Plan	\multicolumn{6}{c}{Number of Subscribers}
	10,000	20,000	30,000	40,000	50,000	60,000
I	-550	-400	-250	-100	50	200
II	-520	-340	-160	20	200	380
III	-500	-300	-100	100	300	500
IV	-460	-220	20	260	500	740

(Payoff table is in $1,000's)

b) (1) Plan IV; (2) Plan IV; (3) Plan IV
c) Plan II -- Expected Value = $11,000

13) a)

		\multicolumn{5}{c}{Number of Clients Purchasing a Computer}
		0	1	2	3	4
Number of	1	-40	50	30	10	-10
Computers	2	-70	20	110	90	70
Manufactured	3	-80	10	100	190	170
	4	-70	20	110	200	290

(Payoffs are in $1,000's)

b) Build 4 computers
c) Nothing

14) a) Yes, Dollar should sell the store
b) EVPI = $8,000
c) No; the cost of the survey exceeds the EVPI

15) a)

Plan	\multicolumn{6}{c}{Number of Copies (in 1,000's per month)}
	12.6	14.4	16.2	18.0	19.8	21.6
I	341.6	370.4	399.2	428.0	456.8	485.6
II	351.2	372.8	394.4	416.0	437.6	459.2
III	317.2	356.8	396.4	436.0	475.6	515.2
IV	363.0	372.0	381.0	390.0	399.0	408.0

b) (1) Plan III;   (2) Plan IV
c) Plan IV

CHAPTER 14

16)

		Demand For Ovens			
		0	1	2	3
	0	0	-25	-50	-75
Ovens	1	-70	80	55	30
Ordered	2	-140	10	160	135
	3	-210	-60	90	240

   a) Order one oven -- EV = $25.00
   b) EVPI = $63
   c) Favorable: order 2; Unfavorable: order 0; No opinion: order 1
   d) EVSI = $9.10

17) a) $1,075
    b) $5,000

18) Buy 3 leases

19) a) Risk averse
    b) Produce root beer as long as $p \geq 60/105 = .571$
    c) Choose Stanton

TRUE/FALSE

20. FALSE	21. TRUE	22. FALSE	23. FALSE	24. FALSE
25. FALSE	26. TRUE	27. FALSE	28. TRUE	29. FALSE
30. TRUE	31. TRUE	32. TRUE	33. FALSE	34. FALSE

```
┌─────────────────────┐
│    CHAPTER  15      │
└─────────────────────┘
```

<u>PROBLEMS</u>

8) a) Linear Programming constraints:

$$3X_1 + X_2 \leq 24 \text{ (total marketing employees)}$$
$$X_1 + X_2 \geq 6 \text{ (minimum required ads)}$$
$$50X_1 + 15X_2 \leq 250 \text{ (Goal 1: Budget in \$1000's)}$$
$$3X_1 + X_2 \leq 12 \text{ (Goal 2: 50\% of marketing employees)}$$
$$X_1 \geq 4 \text{ (Goal 3: TV ads)}$$
$$X_2 \geq 4 \text{ (Goal 4: Radio ads)}$$
$$X_1, X_2 \geq 0$$

There are no feasible points.

b) $\text{MIN } P_1(d_1^+) + P_2(d_2^+) + P_3(d_3^-) + P_4(d_4^-)$
S.T.
$$3X_1 + X_2 \leq 24$$
$$X_1 + X_2 \geq 6$$
$$50X_1 + 15X_2 + d_1^- - d_1^+ = 250$$
$$3X_1 + X_2 + d_2^- - d_2^+ = 12$$
$$X_1 + d_3^- - d_3^+ = 4$$
$$X_2 + d_4^- - d_4^+ = 4$$
$$X_1, X_2, d_j^-, d_j^+ \geq 0 \text{ for all } j$$

Optimal G.P. solution: 3 TV ads, 3 radio ads.
Priorities: $P_1(d_1^+) = 0$, $P_2(d_2^+) = 0$, $P_3(d_3^-) = 1$,
$P_4(d_4^-) = 1$

c) The new objective function is:
$\text{MIN } P_1(d_1^+) + P_2(d_2^+) + P_3(2d_3^-) + P_3(d_4^-)$

Optimal G.P. solution: Produce 2.67 TV ads, 4 radio ads.
Goal 3 is missed by 1.33 TV ads while the other goals are
achieved.

9) $\text{MIN } P_1(d_1^-) + P_2(d_2^+) + P_3(d_3^-) + P_3(3d_4^-) + P_3(d_5^-)$
S.T.
$$3X_1 + 2.5X_2 + 2X_3 \leq 200 \quad \text{(donation)}$$
$$X_1 \geq 20 \quad \text{(athletic sch.)}$$
$$X_1 + X_2 + X_3 + d_1^- - d_1^+ = 80 \quad \text{(P1, Goal 1: Total sch.)}$$
$$.75X_1 - .25X_2 - .25X_3 + d_2^- - d_2^+ = 0 \quad \text{(P2, Goal 2: 25\% ath. sch.)}$$
$$X_1 + d_3^- - d_3^+ = 25 \quad \text{(P3, Goal 3: desired ath. sch.)}$$
$$X_2 + d_4^- - d_4^+ = 40 \quad \text{(P3, Goal 4: desired min. sch.)}$$
$$X_3 + d_5^- - d_5^+ = 20 \quad \text{(P3, Goal 5: desired women sch.)}$$
$$X_j, d_j^-, d_j^+ \geq 0 \quad \text{for all } j$$
```
```

CHAPTER 15

9 con't) Optimal: Award 20 athletic, 40 minority, and 20 women's
         scholarships. Goals 1, 2, and 4 are met. Goal 3 is
         underachieved by 5 athletic scholarships and Goal 5 is
         underachieved by 10 women's scholarships.

10) X_1 = # new non-minority hires
     X_2 = # new minority hires
     X_3 = # non-minority management promotions
     X_4 = # minority management promotions

$$\text{MIN} \quad 3d_1^- + d_2^- + d_3^+ + d_4^+$$

$$
\begin{aligned}
\text{S.T.} \quad X_1 + X_2 & & & = 17,520 \\
X_3 + X_4 & & & = 598 \\
X_1 & - d_1^+ + d_1^- & & = 19,680 \\
X_3 & - d_2^+ + d_2^- & & = 472 \\
X_1 & - d_3^+ + d_3^- & & = 11,680 \\
X_3 & - d_4^+ + d_4^- & & = 399 \\
X_j, \, d_j^+, \, d_j^- & \geq 0 \quad j = 1,2,3,4
\end{aligned}
$$

11) Miss Northern State 18; Miss Central State 24; Miss Southern
     State 58.

12) a) Location: BG - .360; B - .512; H - .128
        Price: BG - .589; B - .252; H - .159
        Cleanliness: BG - .123; B - .320; H - .557
        Parking: BG - .102; B - .612; H - .286
        Selection: BG - .100; B - .713; H - .187

     b) GD - .255; B - .482; H - .264
     c)

	LOC	PRI	CLE	PAR	SEL
LOC	1	1/7	1/7	1	1/3
PRI	7	1	3	7	3
CLE	7	1/3	1	5	3
PAR	1	1/7	1/5	1	1/7
SEL	3	1/3	1/3	7	1

     d) CR = .073 -- good consistency
     e) GD - .340; B - .380; H - .280

CHAPTER 15

13) a) Goal: Choose the right candidate
       Criteria: Party, Issue
       Alternatives: Carter, Nixon, Anderson

b)

	Party		
	C	N	A
C	1	1/7	1/3
N	7	1	5
A	3	1/5	1

	Issues		
	C	N	A
C	1	6	5
N	1/6	1	1/3
A	1/5	3	1

c) Party: C - .083;   N - .723;   A - .193
   Issues: C - .707;   N - .092;   A - .201
d) .082 -- good consistency;
e) Party - .2;   Issues - .8
f) C - .582;   N - .218;   A - .199

14) a) Goal: Choose the best database program
       Criteria: Price; Ease of Use
       Alternatives: BASE 8; DATA RECORD

b)

	Price	
	B8	DR
B8	1	8
DR	1/8	1

	Ease Of Use	
	B8	DR
B8	1	1/6
DR	6	1

c) Price: B8 - 8/9;   DR - 1/9
   Ease of Use: B8 - 1/7;   DR - 6/7
d) (1)   B8 - .81;   DR - .19
   (2)   B8 - .22;   DR - .78
   (3)   B8 - .516; DR - .484
e) Ease of use is slightly preferred to price.

TRUE/FALSE

16. FALSE	17. FALSE	18. TRUE	19. FALSE	20. TRUE
21. FALSE	22. FALSE	23. TRUE	24. FALSE	25. FALSE
26. TRUE	27. FALSE	28. FALSE	29. FALSE	30. FALSE

CHAPTER 16

PROBLEMS

5) a) 4 period weighted moving average; MSE = 408
   b) exponential smoothing   -- $298.48
      weighted moving average -- $294.27

6) a) α = .6 is better MSE (9.12); α = .2 has MSE = 10.82
   b) For α = .6, F_9 = 22.86; for α = .2, F_9 = 21.72

7) Year 6: Quarter 1 -- 56; Quarter 2 -- 48; Quarter 3 -- 79;
           Quarter 4 -- 40

8) a) The 3 week moving average gives the better forecast (MSE =
      16,337 vs a MSE = 17,911 for the 4 week moving average)
   b) 3 week moving average forecast for week 11 = 1,200
      4 week moving average forecast for week 11 = 1,158

9) a) Yes
   b) Week 17 -- 29.0; Week 18 -- 30.0; Week 19 -- 31.0;
      Week 20 -- 32.0

10) b) 141.44, 144.18, 119.44, 157.72, 111.93

11) a) F_t = 34.80 - 1.329t
    b) 26 months
    c) After 27 months sales will be approximately -1 cars; this is
       clearly impossible; the assumption of a continued linear
       decline must be in error.

12) 42.15, 70.14, 52.17;   43.46, 72.30, 53.76

TRUE/FALSE

13. TRUE	14. TRUE	15. FALSE	16. TRUE	17. FALSE
18. TRUE	19. TRUE	20. FALSE	21. TRUE	22. TRUE
23. FALSE	24. TRUE	25. FALSE	26. FALSE	27. FALSE

CHAPTER 17

PROBLEMS

5) Pr(buy) = .357;   Pr(return) = .643

6) a) Network C
   b) $(\pi_A, \pi_C, \pi_N) = (.29, .41, .30)$
   c) Network A: $14,300;   Network C: $20,550;   Network N: $15,200

7) a)

		Next Day			
This Day		1	2	3	4
Route A not congested	1	.600	.200	.120	.080
Route A congested	2	.225	.075	.420	.280
Route B not congested	3	.075	.025	.540	.360
Route B congested	4	.450	.150	.240	.160

   b) .36 + .12 = .48

8) a) .16
   b) Austin: .199, San Antonio: .328, Houston: .473

9) B. Prince's and F. Fowl's shares will drop by .196 and .054.

10) a) .868
    b) .281
    c) .3 + .03 + .2 = .53

11) a) .6
    b) Making payments has higher probability (.4 versus .304)
    c) .06 + .03 + .10 = .19

12) a) $(\pi_A, \pi_B, \pi_C) = (.29, .37, .34)$
    b) (1) .15;   (2) .09;   (3) .14
    c) $42,333 per week

13) a)

	Fail-F	Fail-M	Fail-P	New	Est.
Failure - Finance	1	0	0	0	0
Failure - Management	0	1	0	0	0
Failure - Product	0	0	1	0	0
New	.15	.20	.05	0	.60
Established	.10	.06	.03	0	.81

    b) .394
    c) (1) .47;   (2) .39;   (3) .14

TRUE/FALSE

14. TRUE	15. FALSE	16. TRUE	17. FALSE	18. TRUE
19. TRUE	20. TRUE	21. FALSE	22. TRUE	23. FALSE
24. FALSE	25. FALSE	26. FALSE	27. TRUE	28. FALSE

CHAPTER 18

PROBLEMS

5) Produce one package of 16 ft. wire and one package of 12 ft. wire. (2 feet of wire will be sold for scrap). Total Profit = $1.66.

6) Produce 3 batches in Feb., 1 batch in March, 3 batches in April, and 2 batches in May. Total Cost = $125,000

7) a) 1-2-7-12-15; Distance = 36
   b) 1-4-9-13-14; Distance = 37

8) Total Profit = $245; Three solutions: (1) 2-A, 2-E, 1-B; (2) 1-A, 1-B, 3-D; (3) 1-A, 1-B, 1-C, 1-D, 1-E

9) Builder 1 -- 1 lot, Builder 3 -- 2 lots, Builder 5 -- 2 lots; Total revenue = $442,000

10) Give $4,000,000 to Bolivia Telephone, $6,000,000 to Camden Insurance, and sell Host Baking

11) There are four alternate optimal solutions giving a total of $45,000:

AUG	6		6		6	6
SEP	2	OR	3	OR	4	OR	5
OCT	4		4		4	4
NOV	3		2		1	0

12) Produce 4 boats in May, 3 boats in June, 0 boats in July, and 3 boats in August. Total Cost = $278,000

TRUE/FALSE

13. TRUE	14. TRUE	15. TRUE	16. FALSE	17. TRUE
18. FALSE	19. FALSE	20. TRUE	21. FALSE	22. FALSE
23. TRUE	24. TRUE	25. FALSE	26. FALSE	27. TRUE

CHAPTER 19

PROBLEMS

6) a) x = 1 -- local minimum;   x = 2 -- local maximum;
      x = 3 -- local minimum
   b) Both x = 1 and x = 3 are global minima
   c) (1) x = 5;   (2) x = 0;   (3) x = 2

7) a) $\dfrac{dp}{dx} = 0$. But $\dfrac{dp}{dx} = \dfrac{dr}{dx} - \dfrac{dc}{dx}$. Thus, $\dfrac{dr}{dx} = \dfrac{dc}{dx}$

   b) $p(x) = -x^2 + 90x - 100$
   c) Optimum profit occurs at x = 45 and is $1,925
   d) Second derivative = -2
   e) Marginal revenue = marginal cost = 100

8) a) Sell 5000 at $610 each
   b) $2,400,000
   c) Sell 4950 at $615 each; pass along $5.

9) $x_1 = 6$, $x_2 = -2$

10) a) Model Z -- 2857 1/7   price = $171.43
        Model W -- 3714 2/7   price = $225.71
        Total Weekly Profit = $591,845.33
    b) 500 Model Z's, 4500 Model W's
    c)   = $22.50

11) a) 1000 wagon 1's and 1000 wagon 2's; Weekly profit = $40,000
    b) 851 wagon 1's and 919 wagon 2's; Weekly profit = $39,526
    c) Same as part (b)

12) Base (top and bottom) are 2.52 in. x 5.04 in.;
    Height is 2.52 in.; Total cost = $11.43

TRUE/FALSE

13. TRUE	14. FALSE	15. TRUE	16. FALSE	17. TRUE
18. TRUE	19. FALSE	20. FALSE	21. FALSE	22. TRUE
23. FALSE	24. FALSE	25. TRUE	26. FALSE	27. FALSE

Appendices

APPENDIX A ▼ AREAS FOR THE STANDARD NORMAL DISTRIBUTION

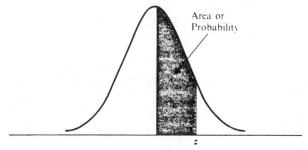

Entries in the table give the area under the curve between the mean and z standard deviations above the mean. For example, for $z = 1.25$ the area under the curve between the mean and z is 0.3944.

z	0.00	0.01	0.02	0.03	0.04	0.05	0.06	0.07	0.08	0.09
0.0	0.0000	0.0040	0.0080	0.0120	0.0160	0.0199	0.0239	0.0279	0.0319	0.0359
0.1	0.0398	0.0438	0.0478	0.0517	0.0557	0.0596	0.0636	0.0675	0.0714	0.0753
0.2	0.0793	0.0832	0.0871	0.0910	0.0948	0.0987	0.1026	0.1064	0.1103	0.1141
0.3	0.1179	0.1217	0.1255	0.1293	0.1331	0.1368	0.1406	0.1443	0.1480	0.1517
0.4	0.1554	0.1591	0.1628	0.1664	0.1700	0.1736	0.1772	0.1808	0.1844	0.1879
0.5	0.1915	0.1950	0.1985	0.2019	0.2054	0.2088	0.2123	0.2157	0.2190	0.2224
0.6	0.2257	0.2291	0.2324	0.2357	0.2389	0.2422	0.2454	0.2486	0.2518	0.2549
0.7	0.2580	0.2612	0.2642	0.2673	0.2704	0.2734	0.2764	0.2794	0.2823	0.2852
0.8	0.2881	0.2910	0.2939	0.2967	0.2995	0.3023	0.3051	0.3078	0.3106	0.3133
0.9	0.3159	0.3186	0.3212	0.3238	0.3264	0.3289	0.3315	0.3340	0.3365	0.3389
1.0	0.3413	0.3438	0.3461	0.3485	0.3508	0.3531	0.3554	0.3577	0.3599	0.3621
1.1	0.3643	0.3665	0.3686	0.3708	0.3729	0.3749	0.3770	0.3790	0.3810	0.3830
1.2	0.3849	0.3869	0.3888	0.3907	0.3925	0.3944	0.3962	0.3980	0.3997	0.4015
1.3	0.4032	0.4049	0.4066	0.4082	0.4099	0.4115	0.4131	0.4147	0.4162	0.4177
1.4	0.4192	0.4207	0.4222	0.4236	0.4251	0.4265	0.4279	0.4292	0.4306	0.4319
1.5	0.4332	0.4345	0.4357	0.4370	0.4382	0.4394	0.4406	0.4418	0.4429	0.4441
1.6	0.4452	0.4463	0.4474	0.4484	0.4495	0.4505	0.4515	0.4525	0.4535	0.4545
1.7	0.4554	0.4564	0.4573	0.4582	0.4591	0.4599	0.4608	0.4616	0.4625	0.4633
1.8	0.4641	0.4649	0.4656	0.4664	0.4671	0.4678	0.4686	0.4693	0.4699	0.4706
1.9	0.4713	0.4719	0.4726	0.4732	0.4738	0.4744	0.4750	0.4756	0.4761	0.4767
2.0	0.4772	0.4778	0.4783	0.4788	0.4793	0.4798	0.4803	0.4808	0.4812	0.4817
2.1	0.4821	0.4826	0.4830	0.4834	0.4838	0.4842	0.4846	0.4850	0.4854	0.4857
2.2	0.4861	0.4864	0.4868	0.4871	0.4875	0.4878	0.4881	0.4884	0.4887	0.4890
2.3	0.4893	0.4896	0.4898	0.4901	0.4904	0.4906	0.4909	0.4911	0.4913	0.4916
2.4	0.4918	0.4920	0.4922	0.4925	0.4927	0.4929	0.4931	0.4932	0.4934	0.4936
2.5	0.4938	0.4940	0.4941	0.4943	0.4945	0.4946	0.4948	0.4949	0.4951	0.4952
2.6	0.4953	0.4955	0.4956	0.4957	0.4959	0.4960	0.4961	0.4962	0.4963	0.4964
2.7	0.4965	0.4966	0.4967	0.4968	0.4969	0.4970	0.4971	0.4972	0.4973	0.4974
2.8	0.4974	0.4975	0.4976	0.4977	0.4977	0.4978	0.4979	0.4979	0.4980	0.4981
2.9	0.4981	0.4982	0.4982	0.4983	0.4984	0.4984	0.4985	0.4985	0.4986	0.4986
3.0	0.4986	0.4987	0.4987	0.4988	0.4988	0.4989	0.4989	0.4989	0.4990	0.4990

APPENDIX B ▼ RANDOM DIGITS

63271	59986	71744	51102	15141	80714	58683	93108	13554	79945
88547	09896	95436	79115	08303	01041	20030	63754	08459	28364
55957	57243	83865	09911	19761	66535	40102	26646	60147	15702
46276	87453	44790	67122	45573	84358	21625	16999	13385	22782
55363	07449	34835	15290	76616	67191	12777	21861	68689	03263
69393	92785	49902	58447	42048	30378	87618	26933	40640	16281
13186	29431	88190	04588	38733	81290	89541	70290	40113	08243
17726	28652	56836	78351	47327	18518	92222	55201	27340	10493
36520	64465	05550	30157	82242	29520	69753	72602	23756	54935
81628	36100	39254	56835	37636	02421	98063	89641	64953	99337
84649	38968	75215	75498	49539	74240	03466	49292	36401	45525
63291	11618	12613	75055	43915	26488	41116	64531	56827	30825
70502	53225	03655	05915	37140	57051	48393	91322	25653	06543
06426	24771	59935	49801	11082	66762	94477	02494	88215	27191
20711	55609	29430	70165	45406	78484	31639	52009	18873	96927
41990	70538	77191	25860	55204	73417	83920	69468	74972	38712
72452	36618	76298	26678	89334	33938	95567	29380	75906	91807
37042	40318	57099	10528	09925	89773	41335	96244	29002	46453
53766	52875	15987	46962	67342	77592	57651	95508	80033	69828
90585	58955	53122	16025	84299	53310	67380	84249	25348	04332
32001	96293	37203	64516	51530	37069	40261	61374	05815	06714
62606	64324	46354	72157	67248	20135	49804	09226	64419	29457
10078	28073	85389	50324	14500	15562	64165	06125	71353	77669
91561	46145	24177	15294	10061	98124	75732	00815	83452	97355
13091	98112	53959	79607	52244	63303	10413	63839	74762	50289
73864	83014	72457	22682	03033	61714	88173	90835	00634	85169
66668	25467	48894	51043	02365	91726	09365	63167	95264	45643
84745	41042	29493	01836	09044	51926	43630	63470	76508	14194
48068	26805	94595	47907	13357	38412	33318	26098	82782	42851
54310	96175	97594	88616	42035	38093	36745	56702	40644	83514
14877	33095	10924	58013	61439	21882	42059	24177	58739	60170
78295	23179	02771	43464	59061	71411	05697	67194	30495	21157
67524	02865	39593	54278	04237	92441	26602	63835	38032	94770
58268	57219	68124	73455	83236	08710	04284	55005	84171	42596
97158	28672	50685	01181	24262	19427	52106	34308	73685	74246
04230	16831	69085	30802	65559	09205	71829	06489	85650	38707
94879	56606	30401	02602	57658	70091	54986	41394	60437	03195
71446	15232	66715	26385	91518	70566	02888	79941	39684	54315
32886	05644	79316	09819	00813	88407	17461	73925	53037	91904
62048	33711	25290	21526	02223	75947	66466	06232	10913	75336

APPENDIX C ▼ VALUES OF $e^{-\lambda}$

λ	$e^{-\lambda}$	λ	$e^{-\lambda}$	λ	$e^{-\lambda}$
0.05	0.9512	2.05	0.1287	4.05	0.0174
0.10	0.9048	2.10	0.1225	4.10	0.0166
0.15	0.8607	2.15	0.1165	4.15	0.0158
0.20	0.8187	2.20	0.1108	4.20	0.0150
0.25	0.7788	2.25	0.1054	4.25	0.0143
0.30	0.7408	2.30	0.1003	4.30	0.0136
0.35	0.7047	2.35	0.0954	4.35	0.0129
0.40	0.6703	2.40	0.0907	4.40	0.0123
0.45	0.6376	2.45	0.0863	4.45	0.0117
0.50	0.6065	2.50	0.0821	4.50	0.0111
0.55	0.5769	2.55	0.0781	4.55	0.0106
0.60	0.5488	2.60	0.0743	4.60	0.0101
0.65	0.5220	2.65	0.0707	4.65	0.0096
0.70	0.4966	2.70	0.0672	4.70	0.0091
0.75	0.4724	2.75	0.0639	4.75	0.0087
0.80	0.4493	2.80	0.0608	4.80	0.0082
0.85	0.4274	2.85	0.0578	4.85	0.0078
0.90	0.4066	2.90	0.0550	4.90	0.0074
0.95	0.3867	2.95	0.0523	4.95	0.0071
1.00	0.3679	3.00	0.0498	5.00	0.0067
1.05	0.3499	3.05	0.0474	5.05	0.0064
1.10	0.3329	3.10	0.0450	5.10	0.0061
1.15	0.3166	3.15	0.0429	5.15	0.0058
1.20	0.3012	3.20	0.0408	5.20	0.0055
1.25	0.2865	3.25	0.0388	5.25	0.0052
1.30	0.2725	3.30	0.0369	5.30	0.0050
1.35	0.2592	3.35	0.0351	5.35	0.0047
1.40	0.2466	3.40	0.0334	5.40	0.0045
1.45	0.2346	3.45	0.0317	5.45	0.0043
1.50	0.2231	3.50	0.0302	5.50	0.0041
1.55	0.2122	3.55	0.0287	5.55	0.0039
1.60	0.2019	3.60	0.0273	5.60	0.0037
1.65	0.1920	3.65	0.0260	5.65	0.0035
1.70	0.1827	3.70	0.0247	5.70	0.0033
1.75	0.1738	3.75	0.0235	5.75	0.0032
1.80	0.1653	3.80	0.0224	5.80	0.0030
1.85	0.1572	3.85	0.0213	5.85	0.0029
1.90	0.1496	3.90	0.0202	5.90	0.0027
1.95	0.1423	3.95	0.0193	5.95	0.0026
2.00	0.1353	4.00	0.0183	6.00	0.0025
				7.00	0.0009
				8.00	0.000335
				9.00	0.000123
				10.00	0.000045

APPENDIX D ▼ A SHORT TABLE OF DERIVATIVES

1. $\dfrac{d(c)}{dx} = 0$ (where c is a constant)

2. $\dfrac{d(xn)}{dx} = nx^{n-1}$

3. $\dfrac{d(cu)}{dx} = c\,\dfrac{du}{dx}$

4. $\dfrac{d(u+v)}{dx} = \dfrac{du}{dx} + \dfrac{dv}{dx}$

5. $\dfrac{d(uv)}{dx} = u\,\dfrac{dv}{dx} + v\,\dfrac{du}{dx}$

6. $\dfrac{d(u^n)}{dx} = nu^{n-1}\,\dfrac{du}{dx}$

7. $\dfrac{d\left(\dfrac{u}{v}\right)}{dx} = \dfrac{v\,\dfrac{du}{dx} - u\,\dfrac{dv}{dx}}{v^2}$

8. $\dfrac{d(\ln x)}{dx} = \dfrac{1}{x}$

9. $\dfrac{d(e^x)}{dx} = e^x$

10. $\dfrac{d(\ln u)}{dx} = \left(\dfrac{1}{u}\right)\dfrac{du}{dx}$

11. $\dfrac{d(e^u)}{dx} = e^u\,\dfrac{du}{dx}$